JMTurner.
1998.

The Churches in England
from Elizabeth I to Elizabeth II

Kenneth Hylson-Smith

The Churches
in England
From Elizabeth I
to Elizabeth II

Volume III: 1833–1998

SCM PRESS LTD

1998.

(cased) 0 334 02726 8

(limp) 0 334 02727 6

First published in Britain 1998
by SCM Press Ltd
9–17 St Albans Place, London N1 0NX

Typeset by Regent Typesetting, London
and printed in Great Britain by
Biddles Ltd, Guildford and King's Lynn

Contents

Contents

Preface

Although this is the third of a three-volume history of the churches in England from Elizabeth I to Elizabeth II, like the previous two volumes it can be read either as part of the wider picture portrayed in the three works taken together, or as a separate history complete in itself. It picks up the story at that critical time for the churches in England following the repeal of the Test and Corporation Acts in 1828, the Catholic Emancipation Act of the following year, and the Reform Act of 1832, and with the Oxford Movement about to burst upon the scene; and it ends in 1998 at an equally climacteric time for all the churches. It is therefore concerned with all those factors which, in the cauldron of the modern era, have helped to create the character of late twentieth-century individual churches, and the English religious landscape as a whole.

In this book I try to provide an historical overview. I attempt to incorporate important recent research findings, scholarly conclusions reflections and insights from various disciplines. This means that I am deeply indebted to those who have contributed to our understanding of the religious history of England from 1833 to 1998, as will be seen from the notes and bibliography.

My use of many and varied secondary sources has been facilitated by the excellent service I have received from libraries, and I want in particular to express my appreciation to the Librarians and staff members concerned at the Bodleian Library, Oxford, the libraries of the Oxford Faculty of Modern History and the Oxford Faculty of Theology, Trinity Theological College, Bristol, Wesley Theological College, Bristol, and the University of Bristol.

Dr Mark Smith kindly commented most helpfully on the draft manuscript, and I greatly valued his advice. I have continued to receive unfailing encouragement and support from the Revd Dr John Bowden, the Managing Director of SCM Press, for which I am immensely grateful. Margaret Lydamore and Susan Molyneux of SCM Press have provided their usual thorough, efficient and yet good-humoured assistance, for which I thank them most sincerely.

Introduction

Nineteenth-century religion in England has attracted the attention of many historians in the last few decades and this has resulted in an unprecedented number of theses, articles and monographs, as will be evident from a glance at the bibliography for the present work. Twentieth-century English religious history has not been subjected to the same scrutiny and analysis, but there have been many notable studies of particular periods or topics. A much-acclaimed overall history of the Victorian religious scene has been provided by Owen Chadwick,[1] although this is now somewhat dated in view of the surge of historical work undertaken since its publication, and more recently Gerald Parsons has edited a magnificent collection of essays on religion in Victorian Britain.[2] Adrian Hastings has contributed an outstanding history of Christianity in England from 1920 to 1990.[3] What is needed is a comprehensive analytical narrative which bridges the Victorian age–twentieth-century divide, presents the one hundred and sixty-five years as a continuous period, embraces all the major Christian traditions, and takes into account the work of scholars in recent years. This is what the present volume attempts to do.[4]

As with the previous two volumes in my historical trilogy,[5] I am aiming at a wide readership, and I hope that in doing so I will not fall into the trap of pleasing nobody. By the careful use of notes and a full bibliography, and by adopting an appropriate style of presentation, I have attempted to make the work helpful to undergraduates, graduates, academics in general, and anyone who wants to use it as an aid to further study. I try to identify the most important features and trends in the life of the churches in the years reviewed, relate religious life to the constitutional, political, economic and social aspects of national and local life, and point out where more detailed and specific descriptions and analyses can be found. My purpose has been to provide a framework; to give a context for particular events, movements and personalities in the life of the churches in the period covered. I have also very much had in mind those who are not engaged in full-time academic work and who are simply seeking a greater understanding and

appreciation of the recent history of the English churches; that somewhat amorphous, ill-defined, collectivity most frequently designated
'the general public'. I have tried to make my account and analysis thoroughly readable, as well as being academically authentic, in order to
make it attractive to such 'general readers'.

In order to avoid being confused and submerged under a welter of
facts in what is a most eventful time of religious activity and change, I
have identified a number of themes. These should give coherence and
unity to the work and help the author as well as the reader not to loose
his way.

I will explain my first theme in some detail as it largely provides the
theoretical framework for my narrative. The subsequent themes, which
are then outlined very briefly, arise out of this first, overriding, theme,
and are related to it.

This dominant theme addresses the transition from the monopolistic
religious regime of the late fifteenth century, when one religious tradition, the Catholic Church, held sway despite challenges to its authority,
to the complex multi-faith pluralism of the late twentieth century.

With the English Reformation new forces were released and the
seeds were sown which in the course of the following four-and-a-half
centuries produced a society characterized as pluralistic. Churches,
denominations and sects were to abound, to be accompanied by a
variety of personal cosmologies and views, including agnosticism and
atheism. There was a severe fragmentation within the Protestant trad
ition as schism and secession multiplied. There developed, as it were,
a market situation in religious outlooks, so that Englishmen were
confronted with a seemingly infinite choice of religious options. Such a
society became noted for the high and increasing proportion of its
members who, in part as a result of the freedom to choose, opted for no
allegiance to any institutional form of religion, although they may have
continued to hold their own 'religious' opinions. In its more advanced
stage around the post-First World War period this resulted in a declining church membership. Fifty years later there was an almost limitless
range of 'religious' beliefs and practices. Sects and the more
emotionally free and unfettered expressions of religious belief tended to
prosper. In its even further advanced stage in the latter half of the twentieth century this religiously pluralistic society was in fact noted for the
vigour and health of the sects and the more charismatic or 'pentecostal-
type' groups, especially when compared with the Church of England
and the long-established mainline Free Church denominations.

The process of transition from a monopolistic to a religiously pluralistic society had been initiated by the early seventeenth century. In the dying years of the sixteenth century there appeared the first manifestations in England of organized dissent leading to long-lasting denominations.[6] This was well before the appearance of the type of society I have described as religiously pluralistic, but it was at a phase in the political, economic and social history of the country which allowed the seeds of future change to be sown. Subsequently, and especially since the second quarter of the nineteenth century, English religious life became increasingly variegated. It was a process which need not be regarded as a drift from religious belief and a move towards greater secularism. Looked at in an objective and dispassionate way it was simply a change from one social, and more especially religious, configuration to another. It does not pronounce the emergent society as more or less 'religious' than the former society from which it originated.

There reached a point where this pluralistic stage was complicated by the appearance on the scene of other 'world religions'. The country then entered the multi-faith pluralistic phase in its religious history. It was at that point in what was still a predominantly Christian country that the Christian faith itself, with its claims to exclusivity and uniqueness, was severely questioned, largely from within its own fold, and especially by 'radical' theologians and by a countless number of 'nominal' members. Thus began the 'post-Christian' society in which mankind was seen by many professional theologians and others to have 'come of age', in the sense that dogma relating to ultimates, and ethics based on unchangeable values or unalterable 'fixed points' was seen to have been replaced for most of the population by openness of mind and lack of commitment to any overriding, supernatural authority. For an increasing number of people reason was king, and faith was given little respect. Ethics and behaviour were almost universally accorded greater importance than beliefs and dogma. Such a change in the standing and status of supernaturalism, and of religion in general, was encouraged by the astounding advances in science and, perhaps most importantly, technology. The appearance and escalation of technical solutions and explanations, which attested to the human potential for control over the external world, produced an almost unconscious sense of the irrelevance of many concerns and concepts which are central to most religions. Thus, paradoxically, the multiplication of religious faiths and forms of individual and corporate religious expression in this multi-faith pluralistic society was accompanied by more prolific and stronger expressions of scepticism and atheism.

The religious history of England from 1558 to 1998 demonstrates two other features not so far highlighted. First, this major transformation in the religious scene was gradual. As we have already seen, there were signs of change as early as the seventeenth century, but the metamorphosis only accelerated from about 1828 onwards, and even then it was about a century and a half before the multi-faith pluralistic phase began in earnest. Secondly, there were always residual elements, especially as the monopolistic religious configuration had lasted for a great length of time, and had established deep and strong roots in society at every level. This helped to put a brake on the changes I have been describing.

My other themes can be summarized in a few words.

There is first the two-fold transformation of the Church of England in relation to the broader Christian environment. Within England the established church became increasingly but one of a number of alternative religious traditions. It became the established rather than the national church, and with that major shift of status came calls at various times, and with varying degrees of force and persistence, for its disestablishment. As we approach the late twentieth century we will see that such thinking infiltrated the Church of England itself; so that by the end of the twentieth century there was a real possibility that disestablishment might be recommended and implemented as a consequence of internal appraisal rather than external pressure. The second transformation was in the relationship of the Church of England to the ever-widening and powerful Anglican Communion; and this largely followed the changing fortunes of the British Commonwealth as it grew, achieved immense standing in the world, and then declined. The Anglican Communion persisted despite the achievement of political independence by many of the constituent countries. Quite remarkably, Canterbury and the Church of England remained at the centre of this worldwide fellowship. This is perhaps the more astonishing in view of the domestic transformation and loss of status to which I have just referred.

Within the Church of England itself there has, as a further theme in the present work, been the consolidation and ever more significant development of parties. This has been a complex process but it has fundamentally coalesced around the emergence and consolidation of Evangelicalism, High Churchmanship and Liberalism. The fortunes of these groupings have wavered throughout the period under review, but they have each contributed in an important way to the history and to the texture not only of the national church but of the churches in England as a whole.

The changing fortunes of Nonconformity will be described and analysed within the framework of an ever-more complicated religious pluralism. This will be the contextual setting for a consideration and interpretation of the history during the period of the mainline, long-established, denominations, and for a description and analysis of the astounding growth in the number and variety of Christian and non-Christian sects, together with the increasingly important presence of the great world religions as England developed as a multi-ethnic country.

The same frame of reference will be relevant when I come to review the metamorphosis of Roman Catholicism; although, in this case, it will be vital to take account of global changes in Roman Catholicism itself.

There are three final themes which impinge upon all the matters I have raised so far: the ecumenical movement, the place of women in the life of the churches, and the whole range of topics embraced by the term 'church and society'.

Part One

The Churches in England 1833 to 1901: An Overview

Religious yet restless

It is a strange paradox that England in the period from 1833 to 1901 was both highly religious and yet subject to unprecedented corporate and individual doubt and questioning about the faith which had been central to its life for over one thousand years.[1] The nation was as self-consciously orthodox in its Christianity, and as moral, upright and righteous, as it had ever been, and yet it gave birth to modern agnosticism and atheism, and to the unconventional moral behaviour which these and other secularist philosophies spawned. A prosperous country rapidly produced an expanded industrial, commercial, managerial and professional middle class; and it was in part to the credit of the churches that a great majority of this new breed of men were intent on pursuing a respectable, godly and morally acceptable pattern of life. 'The Church of England succeeded in capturing or maintaining the allegiance of new urban as well as old rural elites . . . Although failing to achieve their stated goal of attracting the entire nation to public worship, the churches succeeded in making public deference to religious values – and public acknowledgment of the importance of religion – almost universal among the upper and middle classes.'[2] And yet among these new men there were those who used a new-found liberty to question traditional beliefs and values; and they contributed to the 'crisis of faith' which we will consider later. Among the Nonconformists as well as within the Church of England there was at once vitality and yet insecurity and decline; there was confidence and yet crisis. There was massive institutional reorganization, and many signs of denominational revival, alongside deep, disturbing and prolonged theological turmoil. It was an odd and somewhat confusing mix, and we need to distil the brew in order to understand its constituent parts, and appreciate how they combined to produce the peculiar phenomenon of religion in the Victorian era.

'That Victorian Britain was, indeed, a society remarkable for the extent and intensity of its religious life is barely open to question.'[3] Victorian England (and I will use this term to cover the period 1833 to 1901) was characterized by religious confidence and vitality. Its churches and chapels were well attended. They multiplied impressively throughout the period, as did the number of clergy and ministers and the number of churchgoers and chapelgoers, even if such an increase did not keep pace with the phenomenal expansion of the population as a whole. The combination of church and chapel building and the remarkable effort and energy of clergy, ministers and people brought many of the expanded population within the orbit of church and chapel activities and provided facilities and pastoral oversight for them. As we will see later, the scope and the scale of activity in many churches and chapels was astonishing. This was an age of great, charismatic preachers, but it was also the period in which the Sunday School and the various church and chapel clubs flourished, and when the church or chapel quite frequently became a beacon and focal point in the local community.

> In retrospect what is remarkable in urban Britain in the nineteenth century is the extent to which a predominantly evangelical pietism managed to spread its values and preoccupations far beyond the doors of the churches it controlled. Its power lay not so much in its theology or dogma as in its energy and its ability to mobilise the middle-class laity – men, women and children – in an unremitting war against urban vice and irreligion.[4]

To augment the work of the churches and chapels there was an astonishing increase in the range of evangelistic, philanthropic and pastoral activities covered by a countless host of new societies. Temperance organizations such as the United Kingdom Alliance, the Band of Hope Movement and the Church of England Temperance Society mustered widespread and enthusiastic support; there were societies for the distribution of the Bible and religious literature, including the already established British and Foreign Bible Society, the Religious Tract Society and the Society for Promoting Christian Knowledge; and a vast array of other highly active bodies included the Lord's Day Observance Society, the Girls' Friendly Society, the Mothers Union, the Young Men's Christian Society and the Saint Vincent de Paul Society. And this does not include the innumerable organizations strictly outside the sphere of the churches, but very much linked to them, such as the YMCA and

ENORMOUS *Victorian*
energy of religion.

Dr Barnardo's Homes. All strove with unbounded energy to promote their particular aims. The English Church Union on behalf of High Churchmen and such bodies as the Church Association and the Protestant Truth Society on behalf of the more militant Protestants fought hard and long to further their causes. And there were the urban settlements and mission centres which laboured tirelessly to supplement local church and chapel ministries and to reach the unchurched masses. Even this merely indicates what was attempted, for the extent of such activities, and the agencies established to achieve multifarious ends, is measureless. It is all symptomatic of a vibrant, 'militant' church and chapel life, and of the power of Victorian Christianity to motivate so many to do so much.

It needs to be remembered that even if the 1851 Census caused alarm and despondency because it revealed that 30% of the population did not attend a place of worship, this did mean that a commendably high 70% were to be found in a place of worship. Questions have been raised about the statistical reliability of the Census and what it claimed to reveal, but its broad portrayal seems to have been reasonably accurate.[5] And those who did attend church or chapel were not all mere passive Sunday occupants of pews. The activist churches, chapels and organizations depended on an army of lay helpers. The Victorian churches cannot be dismissed as cosy fellowships of polite, perhaps hypocritical, respectable middle-class men and women who conformed to a socially conventional mode of religious behaviour which had little substance. This was no doubt accurate as a description of many Anglican and Nonconformist congregations, but it is far from the total, or even the typical, picture.

The Christian faith permeated the whole social and cultural life of the country, and in many spheres it was unchallenged. The great majority of authors,[7] painters, musicians, architects and academics accepted the fundamentals of the Christian faith, and allowed their thinking and their artistic and creative expressions to be governed by Christian norms and presuppositions. Men of business, legislators, and a host of citizens engaged in the daily life of a highly active and busy nation unquestioningly accepted the authenticity and relevance of Christian beliefs and values. Throughout most of society the core tenets of Christianity and the lifestyle it was supposed to inculcate were reckoned to be axiomatic. There was widespread apathy, and much of the nation's 'religion' was a blend of Christian orthodoxy, superstition and 'folk religion', but nevertheless Christianity set the 'tone' and provided the norm for most of the population. The Bible was still widely regarded as 'the good book', and religious literature was purchased in vast quantities.[6] A significant proportion of the population, especially among the 'working classes' never, or very seldom, attended public worship, except for the rights of passage. Nonetheless, there was a 'diffuse Christianity' which had its own beliefs and values, derived in part from orthodox Christianity but with its distinctive characteristics, including a strong emphasis on works and behaviour.[7] Also, as we will see, the extent of working-class alienation from institutional religion was not as great as it was once thought to be.

A further measure of the vigour of the churches, and of the concern of the population as a whole for the preservation and propagation of Christianity, was the response to the challenge of overseas mission. There was a distinct missionary zeal: a concern to spread the gospel to the uttermost parts of the world, and a concern to 'civilize' and 'improve' the 'heathen' by means of education and the teaching of the churches. Of course this was interspersed with commercial and nationalistic interests. The gospel and the flag frequently assumed equal importance; and, indeed, the gospel was sometimes seen as a useful aid to the furtherance of economic and political ends. But there was much unalloyed concern for the Christian message and way of life to be proclaimed. 'Endeavour to care for new people at home was paralleled by extraordinary and romantic endeavour to care for new people overseas. The expansion of English Christianity into Africa and Asia elicited rare heroism and devotion. Just as political expansion helped British self-confidence, so missionary expansion helped Christian self-confidence. If they disregarded the hidden needle which pricked them with a tiny pain, whether they carried nothing but truth, the Victorian churches had a message for the world and knew it.'[8]

What has been said so far relates almost entirely to the various Protestant traditions. Roman Catholicism will be considered in detail in another chapter, but a few comments at this stage will help to place it in the context of the churches as a whole.

The Roman Catholics certainly contributed to the making of Victorian England into a highly religious nation.[9] Their story up to the last quarter of the nineteenth century at least was one of remarkable growth and vigorous life. The Parliamentary 'Papist Returns' of 1767 had indicated a Catholic population in England and Wales of 69,376; whereas the religious census of 1851 showed about three-quarters of a million Catholics, representing approximately 3.5% of the total population. It is clear that Irish immigration largely accounts for this, although to what extent will be discussed in chapter 3 of the present work. Among the main landmarks and features in this expansion must also be mentioned the Catholic Emancipation Act of 1829; the increasing influence of Rome and of the Pope with the development of Ultramontanism;[10] the accession and influence of a number of distinguished Anglican converts of decidedly Ultramontane persuasion, headed by John Henry Newman; the introduction to Britain of a number of dedicated and active missionary orders, most notably the Rosminians, the Passionists, the Redemptionists and the Oratorians, served by some outstanding men of whom the two Italians Luigi Gentile and Dominic Barberi were the most charismatic; and the 1850 Papal Bull of Pope Pius IX which constituted England an ecclesiastical province of the Roman Catholic Church under the leadership of Cardinal Nicholas Wiseman. And all of this was underpinned by the steady, often heroic, work of the local clergy, the 'missionary priests' as they were known (because parishes as understood by canon law did not exist until 1918) which was crucial in the Roman Catholic expansion, for they not only provided the liturgy, priestly counsel and dedication to 'parochial' duties which was at the very centre of healthy growth, but inspired the laity to fund the places of worship, the schools and the clergy houses, which supplied the structural means for the revival which took place.

Anti-Catholicism was not far beneath the surface of English society. What is clear is that despite the Catholic Emancipation of 1829 and the astounding blossoming of Roman Catholicism both numerically and in terms of self-confidence, organizational effectiveness and integration into the social matrix, the religiosity of the country was essentially Protestant.[11]

The timetable and nature of decline

So, there was an awful lot of religion about in Victorian England. 'The nineteenth century was marked by a revival of religious activity unmatched since the days of the Puritans. This religious revival shaped that code of moral behaviour, or rather that infusion of all behaviour with moralism, which we still call, rightly or wrongly, "Victorianism". Above all, religion occupied a place in the public consciousness, a centrality in the intellectual life of the age, which it had not had a century before and did not retain in the twentieth century.'[12] Many historians assert that this did not last; indeed, that it did not even endure until the end of Victoria's long reign. That there was decline is clear. But it is difficult to identify when the decline began. I maintain that there were signs of a downward drift from about the 1880s, but that this deterioration became far more severe and evident after the First World War. I concur with the view of Hugh McLeod

> that in England during the period 1850 to 1914, a relatively high degree of religious consensus existed, which had diminished by the early twentieth century, but had not yet broken down. Features of this consensus included acceptance by most of the population of Protestant Christianity, including acceptance of the Bible as the highest religious authority, and of moral principles derived from Protestant Christianity, practice of the Christian rites of passage, and observance of Sunday.[13]

Such an interpretation is not incompatible with the view that the height of this religiosity was in the mid-century. There are those, and I count myself as one of them, who consider that the 'religious boom' belonged essentially to the first four-fifths of the century, when there was a spectacular growth in Nonconformity, and that a decline started in the last two decades of the century. The decline was to some extent masked by the continuing social importance of religion in a period of social upheavals associated with industrialization. But an inexorable process of secularization, largely fuelled by industrialization, urbanization and the growth of a concentrated working class, and increased Sunday leisure pursuits, spelt the ultimate transmutation of religion as a force in society. The 'increasing prosperity and sense of security resulting from economic, technological and medical progress meant that most people felt increasingly at home in the world and unwilling to seek other-worldly solutions to their problems'.[14] Jeffrey Cox and Callum Brown reject the implicit assumption that there is an integral connection between secularization and 'modernization', or that there was a link between the growth of cities and religious decline.[15] To this I would add the danger, discussed in the Introduction, of concluding that there was an inevitable, unrelenting and unstoppable process of secularization in the religious history of England during the nineteenth and twentieth centuries, rather than a process of change in the status and standing of religion.

It seems that most of the churches and denominations flourished more from the 1830s to the 1870s than they did in the succeeding fifty years, even if some of them did not keep pace numerically with the increase in the population, and some lost ground in comparison with other Christian traditions. In these decades the Nonconformists and the Roman Catholics in particular not only expanded numerically but, as we will see in chapter 3, they were transformed in their internal structures, their self-image, their self-confidence, and their status and standing in society. It was the decisive era when the shift of religious allegiance moved decisively away from the Church of England. These two features – overall prosperity and a new religious configuration – are seen in a number of local studies. In his investigation of Craven, Rycroft found that 'religion was a dominant feature in the lives of the people' in the period 1764 to 1851. 'The denominational orientation of the Deanery, however, shifted in this period, which began with the Church of England as the main provider of religious services in most parishes, and ended with the nonconformists attracting nearly three times as many worshippers as the Anglicans.'[16]

Likewise, R.B. Walker found that in Cheshire between 1821 and 1851, 'Roman Catholicism and Dissent had both expanded, the former notably concentrated in the industrial towns, the latter more evenly distributed. In particular Wesleyan Methodism had shown its adaptability.'[17] He also came to other important conclusions from the statistical tables of attendance he presented:

> Bearing in mind all that has been said about the alienation of the working-classes from the churches in the Victorian age the figures show surprisingly little difference between industrial and rural areas for non-attendance. Presumably, if remoteness was a greater disincentive in the latter, pew rents were more ubiquitous in the former. However, in respect of the Church of England taken alone, the table reveals the relative weakness of this church in the new towns. Altogether, judging from attendances, the non-Anglicans of 1851 in contrast to those of 1750 were playing as important a part in the religious life of the county as the members of the Established Church.[18]

In his important study of Oldham and Saddleworth in the period 1740 to 1865, Mark Smith came to conclusions which endorse the trends and patterns which I am suggesting were becoming evident in this period.

> The religious experience of the inhabitants of Oldham and Saddleworth, as well as its social meaning, would have varied considerably

with their age, gender, and the nature of the religious group to which they were linked. However, it is clear that the churches had succeeded in preventing the development of a culture in which they were marginalized. The proliferating industrial communities of the locality displayed resistance to regular weekly church-going, but not decisive indifference to the Gospel, especially when it came into their own homes and spoke to their own needs. The churches had sown and tended their crop with great diligence throughout the period . . .[19]

R.E. Chadwick, in a study of the churches in the Bradford area, found the late nineteenth century was not such a 'hey-day' as is sometimes portrayed.[20] Although the churches continued to be influential, and ministers made powerful utterances from their pulpits, laymen held important civic offices, and most Bradford citizens had been through Sunday school, there were clear signs of deterioration. Even the Nonconformists, who had experienced rapid expansion from relative obscurity, were losing members. There was a desperate and frequently unsuccessful attempt by individual churches to stem the tide of ever diminishing membership:

> Churchmen of all denominations, Nonconformists in particular, were proud of their relative progress, aware of their new social position and power. At the same time, membership was declining, they were struggling to keep hold of members moving to the suburbs, to keep young people brought up in the churches and to attract new recruits. Eager to recognize their place in the community they invested in new and imposing buildings which laboured under the weight of debt. Anxious to influence the wider society, to impose Christian ideals, they toiled to maintain an internal adhesion which was crumbling because of the new opportunities open to members and adherents. Desiring to meet working men on their own terms they continued to assume that working class culture was in need of elevation. Willing to do almost anything to attract working class congregations, the churches were more active and innovatory than ever before but they met with the smallest success.[21]

In his study of religion in industrial towns in the late nineteenth century and early twentieth century, with particular reference to the West Riding of Yorkshire, S.J.D. Green came to similar conclusions.[22]

GREEN shows how Halifax began t age :- population :- 1880 —
This came change :- the church.

The Churches in England 1833 to 1901: An Overview   11

It was, he asserts, not so much a matter of losing people, and even less a lamentable case of never having had them.

> Rather it was the case that, as the churches developed in the later-nineteenth-century town, by proliferation, extension and formalization, so they created, willingly and self-consciously, ecclesiastical institutions which were more open to public involvement and participation than they had ever been before, but which had evolved, often by self-conscious decision, into a form more like that of other voluntary organizations than ever before.[23]

Because of such changes, by the third decade of the twentieth century the 'threat' of the Labour Party, or the Sunday Lecture Society, or bicycle clubs, mattered so much more than their equivalents in 1870. 'It was not simply that an informed public could make, and did make, increasingly instrumental decisions about to which organizations it devoted its loyalty (and its time and money). It was also that, in making their individual decisions, each member of that public had less to choose between his or her affiliation with a religious or with an irreligious association. And for institutions committed to a comprehensive associational ideal, that was fatal.'[24] As Green points out, this does not deny the importance in the decline of religious organizations of general processes of social change. But it does focus attention on the fact that articulate spokesmen and women on behalf of voluntary organizations, in this case in the West Riding of Yorkshire, 'were so determined to tie the fate of what they believed in, and the fortunes of those institutions which expressed their faith, to a course of collective action which was doomed to so unsatisfactory a public fortune'.[25]

By the end of the nineteenth century the Church of England and the Nonconformists had more in common than they realized, despite their obvious differences and quite frequent conflicts. They all faced a situation of decline and associated internal problems regarding membership, finances and loss of self-confidence. In his study of Leicestershire in the late nineteenth century David M. Thompson concluded that in practice the tasks of all the Protestant churches were similar. 'After the state declined to give direct financial support to the established church in the early nineteenth century, the Church of England found that, like the non-established churches, it had to raise the money for further development itself. There was little difference in the pattern of organization between the archdeaconry church extension associations and the Leicestershire congregational union or the Leicestershire baptist association. Like other voluntary societies they had to be organized in such a way as to maximize contributions.'[26]

Other studies have drawn attention to various aspects of the mixed fortunes of the churches in their rural and urban ministries in the nineteenth century.[27] None of these invalidate the pattern of development I have outlined. Although too much reliance must not be placed on statistical evidence which is central to some of these studies,[28] the outlines of the picture seem to be emerging. I will have occasion to examine the process of religious institutional decline and changing religious affiliations when I look closely at the Church of England, the various Nonconformist denominations and Roman Catholicism throughout the period from 1833 to the present day. To some extent, as we will see, Roman Catholicism developed, or perhaps one should say declined at a greatly different pace, in accordance with a much different timetable, and in a far less dramatic way, than the various Protestant traditions. But the character of English Catholicism also undoubtedly altered in the last two decades of the nineteenth century. This was especially so with the advent of a new generation of 'liberals', who became part of a loose international network of Catholic thinkers known as Modernists, among whom were George Tyrrel, Fredrich von Hügel and George Jackson Mivart, but such a trend did not gain great momentum until the new century.

However interpretations of institutional 'religious decline' may differ, all concerned are agreed that it is to the nineteenth century that one must look for the origin of some of the components contributing to the eventual slide. This is not to suggest a single restricted span of time, such as the 1850s, when all such trends emerged or began to exercise their corrosive effect; far from it. Each can be traced back to a different starting point, and each was subject to a different timescale.

Although historians have frequently denounced the eighteenth-century churches for their sloth and ineffectiveness, this is far from universally true.[29] Whatever their shortcomings, the eighteenth-century churches were part of a society which retained its essentially Christian character. The Christian faith was almost universally accepted as authentic and as the yardstick for individual and national moral and ethical standards. The church and the state were inextricably intertwined and each recognized the value and need of the other. 'Within the eighteenth-century view, Divine Providence was a loyal subject of the Hanoverian monarch who through his Established Churches (Episcopalian in England and Wales, Presbyterian in Scotland) preserved godliness and good order. Assize sermons, parish homilies and the Prayer Book all commanded obedience and acceptance of the established order . . . The maintenance of orthodox religious beliefs through the "Church by Law Established" was therefore an essential feature of the old political order, and membership of the political elite was open only to those who subscribed also to the Established Church. Protestant Dissenters were tolerated but no more, and any who wished to progress in society were advised to discover the merits of Conformity.'[30] With the 1828 Repeal of the Test and Corporation Acts, the 1829 Catholic Emancipation Act and the 1832 Reform Act this consensus started to disintegrate, and religious pluralism, in the sense of a range of religious options, became increasingly a feature of society. Toleration and the opportunity to exercise choice were commendable qualities in an increasingly democratic society, but, in the long run, they introduced a sense of competition which had certain deleterious consequences. Then there were other very visible hallmarks of the transition to modernity.

Demographic, economic, social, and more especially class, changes, industrialization, urbanization, the development of railways and the new patterns of leisure were undoubtedly of importance to the history of the churches. An increase in population of the United Kingdom from 24.1 million in 1831 to 41.6 million in 1901 entailed immense stresses and strains and major social and religious adjustments, especially as it went hand in hand with a revolution in the quantity and concentration of industrial and agricultural production, and the methods used to achieve such economic growth. Every aspect of life was touched by such changes. Then, of course, there were the huge and life-transforming towns. The urban world of early industrial England was essentially one of small communities compared with what was to come. In 1801, at the time of the first census, only five provincial towns had populations in excess of 50,000, and no other town than London had a population exceeding 100,000. The next fifty years saw a rate of urban expansion twice that of any European country. The impact of such developments on religion and religious practice was bound to be profound.

There was first of all the much debated 'alienation' of the industrial working class from institutionally organized religion. It is almost futile to attempt to discern whether this major sector of the population was 'lost to the churches' or whether they never were actively involved in services of worship, and in the life of the churches and chapels, to any great extent. I argued in my previous volume, and continue to maintain, that the evidence points to the latter, but with qualifications. Although it seems that even the eighteenth-century revival did not make massive and permanent gains among the new urban classes the churches attracted working-class members to a greater extent in the period 1750 to 1833 than has generally been recognized.[31] The difference in the age of Victoria was that the numbers of those alienated from institutional church life were so much greater, and they were so much more visible as they lived for the most part in gigantic, sprawling industrial urban areas, made evident to the general public in a way not hitherto known because of the increasing cover provided by newspapers and broadsheets, by the railways which passed through some of the urban slums, and by the 1851 census. In his comments on the census findings Horace Mann raised the awareness of a shocked nation to what was going on in their midst.

But while the *labouring* myriads of our country have been multiplying with our multiplied material prosperity, it cannot, it is feared, be stated that a corresponding increase has occurred in the attendance of this class in our religious edifices. More especially in cities and large-towns it is observable how absolutely insignificant a portion of the congregations is composed of artisans. They fill, perhaps, in youth, our National, British, and Sunday Schools, and there receive the elements of a religious education; but, no sooner do they mingle in the active world of labour than, subject to the constant action of opposing influences, they soon become as utter strangers to religious ordinances as the people of a heathen country. From whatever cause, in them or in the manner of their treatment by religious bodies, it is sadly certain that this vast, intelligent, and increasingly important section of our countrymen is thoroughly estranged from our religious institutions in their present aspect. Probably, indeed, the prevalence of *infidelity* has been exaggerated, if the word be taken in its popular meaning, as implying some degree of intellectual effort and decision; but, no doubt, a great extent of negative, inert indifference prevails, the practical effects of which are much the same . . . They are unconscious Secularists – engrossed by the demands, the trials, or the pleasures of the passing hour, and ignorant or careless of a future. These are never or but seldom seen in our religious congregations; and the melancholy fact is thus impressed upon our notice that the classes which are most in need of the restraints and consolations of religion are the classes which are most without them . . .[32]

This heartfelt lament could, I believe, have been uttered a century before, or even two centuries before, but no census then revealed what was unearthed in 1851, and, in any case, the scale of alienation was far smaller, with a greatly reduced population and comparatively little industrialization or urbanization. But even so the greatest 'loss' sustained by the churches during the Victorian era (and even more especially during the Edwardian and post-Edwardian years) was arguably not from the working class but among the middle classes. These were the men and women who formed the nucleus and driving force of the churches, and the drift from organized religion of such stalwarts was devastating and depressing. This was the class in society whose virtues the churches most sanctified.

> The pressures the churches faced towards the expansion of their organizations and scale of activities in a society undergoing urban growth meant that they tended to become reliant for finance, active, voluntary, lay support and ultimately recruitment to ministry and membership on the middle and lower middle classes . . . Religion thus became moulded after the middle class fashion: religion itself became one vital facet of middle class culture in Victorian towns and cities, and although the churches constantly aimed to expand to embrace all social groups, methods by which they hoped to do so began to acquire specifically middle class forms.[33] (Morris

Not only did most of the Victorian churches and chapels assume in their membership and mode of corporate life and teaching a very middle-class aspect, but even such phenomena as revivalism was transmuted into a more restrained and acceptable form of evangelism. Traditional revivalism had been spontaneous and unstructured. Much of the evangelism of the Victorian years was planned, well ordered, and made conformable to middle-class values. Halls were booked, posters printed, the audience was seated, the preacher was restrained and invariably made an appeal and invited those concerned about their spiritual state to go forward to 'the anxious seat' before the whole congregation. Charles Grandison Finney in his *Lectures on Revivals of Religion*, and in his teaching generally, described a revival as 'the right use of the appropriate means'; and many took heed as he encouraged 'planned revival'. The climax was reached with the evangelistic visits of Dwight L. Moody and Ira D. Sankey. They 'represented the triumph of the new professional version of revivalism'.[34] And such 'professionalism' was encouraged by the new brand of clergy and ministers who were

We need to stop
using "middle class"
as a pejorative as ? define it

largely based in the cities. This meant that the former, mainly rural, revivalism was to a great extent superseded by the great evangelistic ministries and campaigns of the late nineteenth century, such as Charles Haddon Spurgeon's, which were urban-based.[35] Revivalism was further institutionalized with the founding of the Salvation Army and the Church Army.[36] The High Church and Nonconformist equivalent was the Settlement Movement which in many cases was dominated by middle-class concepts and conduct; and the same may be said of Christian Socialism, which we will be considering in some detail.

This was all part of the overall middle-class image which was assumed by a high proportion of the churches locally, and many of the religious organizations. It was therefore traumatic, and nothing less than a crisis, when the members of that class started to desert the ship. The first signs of such a shift of allegiance and commitment came in the middle of the century; and it was to do with intellectual matters. This was the period when, for the first time 'those special segments of the middle class which served as culture-bearers to their age and shapers of the next, the intellectual and professional classes, had their faith eroded in a distinctive and decisive manner'.[37] It was the beginning of a process, which was reinforced by the attractions of new and luring leisure-time activities, such as seaside resorts and spa towns, greater ease of transport, and a more 'secular' attitude in society as a whole. The declension was gradual, and it was not until the early part of the twentieth century that it became unmistakable. That perspicacious observer of his own generation Charles Masterman was unequivocal in his verdict:

> It is the middle class which is losing its religion; which is slowly or suddenly discovering that it no longer believes in the existence of the God of its fathers . . . Among the middle classes – the centre and historical support of England's Protestant creed – the drift away is acknowledged by all to be conspicuous.[38]

It was a supreme tragedy for the churches as a whole. And yet there is a positive way of viewing what took place, for at least the churches had managed to attract a great number of the middle classes; the active church-going members of that class had achieved much; and a considerable if diminishing number remained, so that the churches continued to be strengthened by them up to the nineteen-nineties. Perhaps too much attention has been directed to the 'loss of the working classes', so that a too pessimistic view has been taken of the evangelistic and pastoral effectiveness of the Victorian churches. More emphasis should be given to the outstanding achievements of the Victorian churches, first of all in attracting so many of the middle class, and then for what they accomplished. It was to a large extent because of the ability, energy and dedication of a host of unremembered middle class men, women and children that so much was successfully undertaken.

What gave Victorian Britain its religious temper by comparison with some other western European states was the sheer strength of its middle-class religiosity together with a much greater acceptance of religious values among the working classes than social historians, in the main, have been prepared to acknowledge. Thus, industrialization and urbanization, far from being the nemesis of British religion, possibly stimulated greater religiosity in the short term while eroding its popularity in the long term. In the light of these suggestions secularization theory is not only in need of fresh analysis, but also requires a considerably revised time scale.[39] *Hempton)*

Lastly, in considering the 'decline' of institutional religion and of religion more generally, it is most important to probe a little deeper into the inner life of popular culture in order to gauge something of what 'religion' meant for the late nineteenth-century and early twentieth-century working classes; and to assess if such 'religion' was also subject to decline. Jeffrey Cox discovered a very distinctive and sincere popular religion in Lambeth: 'The people of Lambeth thought of themselves as Christians but insisted upon defining their own religious beliefs rather than taking them from clergymen.'[40] Such 'religion' is difficult to tap, describe and analyse. As William James wrote, during these years:

We are dealing with a field of experience where there is not a single conception that can be sharply drawn. The pretention under such conditions to be rigorously 'scientific' or 'exact' in our terms would only stamp us as lacking in understanding of our task. Things are more or less divine, states of mind are more or less religious, reactions are more or less total, but the boundaries are always misty and it is everywhere a question of amount and degree.[41]

Certainly the type of religion Cox was adumbrating was not expressed in regular weekly church attendance. Occasional church appearances for rites of passage, and periodic conformity to church practice because it seemed the right thing to do might form part of the cluster of 'beliefs' and conduct which was regarded as 'religious' but such conformity was not at the heart of what was conceived as 'religious'. In her important study of religious belief and popular culture in Southwark in the period from about 1880 to 1939 S.C. Williams makes a similar point:

> There existed within popular culture an agreed code of moral conduct which embraced certain dimensions of church-based religious practices in a manner that was distinctly conditional in its conformity to church-based practices. Individuals fitted themselves into a religious demarcation, by which believers and unbelievers, Christians and non-Christians were identified, but this demarcation, whilst drawing on church-based religious language, denied the need for an absolute association with the church . . . It was a dynamic and vibrant system of belief which retained its own autonomous existence. It drew on elements, images and ideals of church-based religion, but these were appropriated, reinterpreted and internalized in a distinctly popular manner in combination with a folk idiom.[42]

Williams emphasizes that 'there existed a personal, familial and corporate familiarity with a series of religious images and symbols which were passed down from one generation to the next as part of the fabric of family and community life'.[43] The popular religion of Southwark 'consisted of a general belief in God, a belief that this God was just and benevolent, a confidence that good people would be judged favourably by Him with regard to the life to come and a belief that the Bible was a special book to which children in particular should be exposed'.[44] Such beliefs incorporated survivals of semi-pagan magic but were essentially Christian. Changes in the character and content of this popular religion took place at the end of the nineteenth century and later, especially during the period 1914 to 1945 but 'they were complex and amorphous and they cannot simply be classified as "decline"'.[45]

Whatever the timetable of decline may have been, there is no doubt that intellectual turmoil, to which I have alluded, was of central importance to all the Victorian churches, including, to a lesser extent than any of the rest, the Roman Catholic Church, which I will treat separately towards the end of this chapter.

The Victorian 'crisis of faith'

The so-called Victorian 'crisis of faith' may be reckoned as having its major focus in the 1850s, although it had a long gestation period and it continued, in some of its aspects with accelerating effect, until and beyond the end of the Victorian era. It was, in fact, a number of 'crises' which came together in a particularly potent way in the mid-century period, and set in train movements of thought which have persisted until the present day.[46] The strands that can be identified, and which I will briefly describe and analyse, are the development of the geological, biological and related sciences, and the various attempts to relate these to 'what the Bible says'; a theological ferment, which included changing theological perceptions and perspectives, biblical criticism, and a changing attitude towards the authority and teaching of the Bible; and the study of 'religion' and other religions, with the impact this had on the perception of Christianity by friend and foe alike. There was also a conflict of views within the churches themselves about how best to respond to these possibly hostile new developments.

The first area of debate in time as well, it may be said, in importance, was between science and Christianity. I deliberately avoid the use of the word 'conflict' as this prejudges the nature of the relationship between these two areas of intellectual activity. There had, of course, been such 'conflicts' in the past, perhaps most notoriously in the case of Galileo, although that particular confrontation may be regarded as owing much to the exceptional personality, situation and theories of the eminent scientist involved, and the state of the church at the time, rather than being indicative of a conflict between science and religion. But, whatever the interpretation of such pre-nineteenth-century incidents, the nineteenth century was to witness the first prolonged debate on a fairly wide front which was to become a permanent item on the intellectual agenda of Western society.

From time immemorial the Bible had been generally accepted in England as the divine revelation not only on 'religious' issues but also on matters of historical and scientific fact. Such confident reliance on scripture was first seriously challenged with the advances made in geological study; and the initial focus was upon the timing and method of creation. In the seventeenth century James Ussher, Archbishop of Armagh, had used the chronological lists and other data from the Old Testament to calculate the date of creation as 40004 BC; and, although his precision was not universally accepted as sacrosanct, an age of some six thousand years for the world appeared about right.[47] It was therefore quite traumatic when scientists, mostly with no anti-religious axe to grind, started to question both the date of creation and its 'catastrophic' method as depicted in the Bible. In the 1820s the influential Professor of Geology at Oxford, William Buckland, later Dean of

Westminster, who at first argued for 'catastrophism', came to question the widely accepted chronology for the creation and Noah's flood in the light of the growing knowledge of rock strata. He tried to harmonize the first phrase of the Bible, 'In the beginning', with a massively different time scale from that previously assumed by suggesting that the biblical term covered a very long period, and that the six 'days' of the Bible should not be taken as literal twenty-four hour periods but immense epochs. Nonetheless, despite such efforts he was roundly criticized by some commentators.

The new orthodoxy of 'uniformitarianism' was taken up by Charles Lyell in his *Principles of Geology*, which appeared between 1830 and 1833. 'If Buckland feared that without cataclysm there was no God, Lyell was as fundamentally apprehensive lest, without uniformity, there be no science.'[48] But both of them, and others at the time, were essentially in the tradition of natural theology, and argued from the evidence of design to a designer. The Scottish divine Thomas Chalmers stressed the limitations of natural theology, and the need for revelation in order to arrive at a true knowledge of God, and most contemporay scientists would probably have concurred with this.

Then there was the science of biology. The challenge for the catastrophists was 'how to explain the progression of organic forms in view of the uniformitarian requirement of an unvarying natural law'.[49] Another Scotsman, the eccentric publisher Robert Chambers, tried to face the issue in 1844 in an anonymous publication *The Vestiges of the Natural History of Creation*. It was immensely popular, and provoked widespread excitement with its theory that man should be included in the evolutionary process. But, especially in its first few editions, it was full of nonsense and was savagely criticized by the scientific fraternity, so that what it propounded was made to appear ridiculous.

Despite these various examples of animated interchange of views, there was no general conflict over the new scientific pronouncements as between the scientists and the men of faith; indeed they were often not even different people. 'Science was not generally seen as in opposition to religion before the publication of the *Origin of Species*, but as part of a widely accepted natural theology.'[50]

Nonetheless, the stage had been set for the entrance of Charles Darwin. After his voyage of scientific discovery in the *Beagle*, in which a visit to the Galapagos archipelago was of particular importance, he published his epoch-making work in 1859 with a title which succinctly encapsulated his main theses; *On the Origin of Species by Means of*

Natural Selection; or, The Preservation of Favoured Races in the Struggle for Life. It was a unique work on evolution in that it came from an established and recognized scientist whose great strength was his capacity for observation and classification; and it amassed such a wealth of data that the theory which emerged had to be taken seriously. Darwin tried to make scientific sense of the observable survival of plants and animals with structural features which made them clearly adaptable to their particular environment. He noticed that there were random variations among individual members of the same species, and these were transmitted from one generation to another. He also knew that only some of the young produced by animals and plants survived to continue the species; that there was a struggle for food and living space; and that some variations gave advantages in this struggle. Over a long time span the individuals which had the advantage become the majority within the species. Those which were fittest, or best adapted, to survive were in fact the ones which did survive. The variations occur by chance, but chance does not mean chaos. Darwin was at pains to hold both random selection, or chance, and law together. He did not explicitly apply his theory to man in *The Origin of Species*, but what he said was in the context of earlier work by evolutionists in which man had been included, and the whole debate triggered by the book was based on the assumption that man was part of the evolutionary process. In 1871, in *The Descent of Man*, he discussed human origins and explained how man could have descended by natural selection from ape-like creatures, and before that from even lower forms of life. But by that time the theory of evolution had gained scientific respectability, the religious world had largely come to terms with it, and the second book caused far less furore than the first.

The excitement and discussion aroused by *The Origin of Species* was extensive and intensive. It provoked the passions of theologians as well as fellow scientists. Those most indignant considered that the theory, and especially its application to human beings, undermined the authority and authenticity of scripture and the Christian doctrine of man. Theologians and others were also incensed by what they regarded as an assault on human dignity and human worth; and the response on that score was emotional rather than rational. It was epitomized in the celebrated exchange between Thomas Henry Huxley, an ardent supporter of Darwin and the evolutionary theory, including its application to man, and Bishop Samuel Wilberforce at the Oxford meeting of the British Association in 1860, as reported long after the event.

There are several versions of this!

Wilberforce opposed the notion of evolution and argued in favour of fixity of species. Although there are no contemporary reports, he is said to have sarcastically asked Huxley whether he was descended from an ape through his grandfather or his grandmother, with all the implications for the highly sensitive Victorian view of womanhood which this evoked. Huxley's own version of his reply was: 'If . . . the question is put to me, would I rather have a miserable ape for a grandfather or a man highly endowed by nature and possessed of great means of influence and yet who employs these faculties and that influence for the purpose of introducing ridicule into a grave scientific discussion – I unhesitatingly affirm my preference for the ape.' The implication of Wilberforce's remark that descent from an ape is degrading also lies behind the reported comment of a Christian critic to a supporter of evolution: 'If you will leave me my forefathers in heaven, I will leave you yours in the Zoological Gardens.'[51]

But the picture can so easily be distorted. On closer examination there is little evidence that Wilberforce actually used the words attributed to him in the debate with Huxley, and in earlier comments he was at pains to warn critics of the contemporary science against obscurantism. Thus, in a review, he wrote:

> Our readers will not have failed to notice that we have objected to the views with which we are dealing solely on scientific grounds. We have done so from our fixed conviction that it is thus that the truth or falsehood of such arguments should be tried. We have no sympathy with those who object to any facts or alleged facts in nature, or to any inference logically deduced from them, because they believe them to contradict what it appears to them is taught by Revelation. We think that all such objections savour of a timidity which is really inconsistent with a firm and well-intrusted faith.[52]

On the strength of the review 'it would be quite impossible to make out Wilberforce as the prelatical apostle of ecclesiastical authority trying to down the honest observations of simple science'.[53]

At the popular level there was considerable disturbance, but this was to a large extent due to the vulgarizing of what was being asserted. A substantial number of the scientific and theological leaders at the time and subsequently had little difficulty in reconciling their traditional and conservative theological views with Darwin's theories.[54] Scholars have recently 'pointed out that Darwinian evolution was rooted in the Christian culture of the day, that science and belief were not inevitably antagonistic, and that advocates of science were not necessarily hostile to religion'.[55]

One recent commentator has provided a useful summary of the specifically religious responses to *The Origins of Species*. He writes:

That some found Darwinism religiously offensive has, I think, been amply demonstrated. What should also be clear is the fact that religious opposition to Darwinism was not uniform, that indeed some believers found that they could go part or practically all of the way with Darwin, and that these varied religious reactions are just what we would expect after studying the science-religion relationship in the thirty years prior to the Origin. We must therefore be careful in thinking of the Origin as a watershed. In the purely scientific sense it clearly was, but from the viewpoint of the science-religion quarrel it was much less of one. Darwin's work certainly seems to have occasioned a general shift toward the view that evolutionism was compatible with science, and there is no doubt that by offering a naturalistic explanation of organic adaptation he made far more plausible the position of scientists like Huxley, who wanted to have no truck at all with religion. However, . . . religious men, even religious Englishmen, had been dealing sympathetically with science long before the *Origin*, and in many respects the various attitudes taken towards the science-religion relationship were the same both before and after the *Origin*. [56]

There was a lively debate, but it was not a simple confrontation between science and religion, and where there was disagreement 'the forces of religion were remarkably skilful in parrying the threat from naturalism'.[57] It might well be true that where antagonism did occur, and this was not infrequent, 'religious tensions were part of a greater struggle between the forces of conservatism and the forces of change, indeed between an old and a new theodicy'.[58] As one commentator has said, the 'Victorian crisis was a crisis of legitimation'.[59] And, as another historian has observed, there was 'a clash between established and emerging intellectual and social elites for popular cultural preeminence in a modern industrial society'.[60]

At the very least it needs to be acknowledged that a 'crisis of faith' is 'less easy to detect, define, and date' than has been asserted by many in the past, 'and the hunt for it is much obfuscated by characteristic perceptions of both the mid-nineteenth and the late-twentieth centuries'. [61] It was, perhaps, both less serious and more for the Christian faith than has often been perceived or acknowledged. Less, in the sense that there was an animated debate at the time and subsequently, but less explicit clash than has frequently been depicted. More, in the sense that the 'crisis' contributed to what was a long-term major and fundamental shift in the intellectual presuppositions, and the general cast of mind, not only of academics but of the public as a whole. But even this can be interpreted either as essentially hostile to religion or complementary to it. Some leading churchmen at the time were not unduly alarmed. The Tractarians, including E.B. Pusey and H.P. Liddon, took a moderate line. F.J.A. Hort welcomed *The Origin of Species* and encouraged others to read it. And when Darwin died it was proposed by the Broad Churchman Canon F.W. Farrar that he should be buried in Westminster Abbey. Many church leaders and Christian academics almost a century and a half later were also still able to recognize the intellectual shift which took place, but to accept it as not incompatible with distinctive Christian perceptions and interpretations.

Perhaps those who were most disturbed at the time by the whole debate were at opposite poles, for it was noticeable not only at the popular level, as already mentioned, but among some of those most sensitive to undercurrents in society. This unsettling effect was most poignantly expressed by the poet Alfred Tennyson, and most especially in his fantastically popular and widely read poem *In Memoriam*.

> From his earliest manhood Tennyson breathed the atmosphere of scientific theory and discovery, and throughout his life his meditations were governed by the conceptions of law, process, development and evolution – the characteristic and ruling ideas of his century.[62]

In *In Memoriam* he confronted personal problems, and problems generated by the spirit of his age; but he also faced up to problems which were neither local nor ephemeral, but universal:

> Has man an immortal soul? Is there any meaning in life? Any purpose or design in the world-process? Any evidence in Nature, in philosophy or in the human heart, for a beneficent Providence? These issues are dealt with by Tennyson, not in the manner of a thinker – whether philosopher, theologian or scientist – but in the manner of one who, though not ignorant of what the specialists are saying, cares for their results only insofar as they are felt in the blood, and felt along the heart, affecting there the inmost quality of living.[63]

A subtle by-product of the developments in geology and biology in particular, but in science as a whole, was the status assumed by scientists. This had an ethical and moral dimension, for in the eyes of some people the scientists appeared as morally superior to some Christians. They were seen as seeking after truth; honestly searching after truth in science wherever that might lead them. This gave them an aura of altruism. They were regarded by many people as commanding the moral high ground, especially if the alternative was what appeared as a crude religious dogmatism, in which the propounders of religious doctrine were bent on asserting certain beliefs even if such dogma seemed to fly in the face of what was being discovered by the scientists.

The Christian doctrine relating to hell was an especially poignant example of such a comparison. It could so readily be viewed as morally inferior to the attitude of the tolerant, non-judgmental non-Christian who rejected any such idea as unethical. 'How could a benevolent and sensitive conscience accept the morality of a Jehovah who behaved, as the young Darwin put it, like a "revengeful tyrant" and who condemned the majority of his human creatures to an eternity of torment disproportionate to their wickedness or based on no personal fault at all?'[64] It was this issue which resulted in Frederick Denison Maurice being dismissed from his professorial chair at King's College, London, in 1853; an event which was one of the theological *causes célèbres* of the nineteenth century. Although it was not clear exactly what he believed about eternal life and eternal death, most people at the time thought that in his *Theological Essays* he had denied the popular view of hell, and that he was adopting an unacceptable universalist eschatology. His protestation that he was not a universalist was couched in his typically cloudy phraseology, although it seems that whilst he hoped for a universal salvation, he never actually affirmed that this would in fact be the case. He insisted 'that the end for which God had made the world and man, was not the apportionment of rewards and punishments, but the knowledge of himself, which was eternal life, a real knowledge with sanctifying power. Those who rejected God would indeed suffer punishment, but the heaviest punishment the wicked man could expect was "that he should be alienated from goodness and truth", for to be in such a state was "to be in the deepest pit of hell".'[65]

Most importantly from the point of view of the comparison between the morality and ethics of the scientists, and the champions of the scientific method, compared with Christian dogmatists, was the perception of some observers that Maurice was being more loving, and presenting a more morally acceptable case than his detractors. 'His vision, if not the details of the philosophical position adumbrated in his writings, was enduring. That this was so, was perhaps mainly the consequence of his clearly existential concern, his appeal to experience rather than to authority, and his endeavour to hold together the truths of the heart and of the head.'[66] Some leading theologians were prepared to identify in part with what he declared. F.J.A. Hort regretted his 'unequivocal rejection of purgatory, but agreed with Maurice on the three points at the heart of the controversy: that eternity was independent of duration; that the power of repentance is not limited to this life; and that it is not revealed whether or not all will ultimately be saved".[67]

In many cases the 'spokesmen of orthodox faith narrowed the ground on which Christianity was to be defended and allowed their scientific opponents to appear more honest than themselves. In these conflicts, the position of orthodox doctrine was, as presented by its upholders, not only less valid but less moral than that of irreligious science. As events unfolded, not merely the intellect but the moral sense, particularly the sense of truthfulness, revolted against orthodoxy.'[68] It was a process which Josef L. Altholz has designated 'the warfare of conscience with theology'.[69]

This leads on to a core feature in the nineteenth-century 'crisis of faith', the shaking of the theological foundations. It took various forms throughout the period I am at present reviewing, but it amounted to a disturbance of theological presuppositions and an undermining of received beliefs on a scale unknown since the sixteenth century, and in a form which was so varied and complex that it caused confusion and bewilderment. In the limited space available in the present work I can but indicate some of its most salient features which had the greatest impact at the time, and which have had the most powerful long-term consequences.

A reasonable starting point is Samuel Taylor Coleridge (1772–1834). He was 'a poet as well as a critic and philosopher', and he 'proclaimed the ideals of a new age of visionary romanticism'.[70] Many contemporary and later poets, philosophers, theologians and others freely admitted their indebtedness to his inspirational originality. He did not develop any coherent system, for he was erratic and disorganized in his thinking and in the form in which he expressed it. Perhaps his most important and lasting emphasis was on the part played in any form of belief by feeling. He postulated that the basis of faith was not argument but experience. Deep thinking was attainable only by people of deep feeling.

'All truth is a species of revelation; it cannot be possessed unless the heart has "fed" upon it.'[71] The authority of Christianity rests not upon logical demonstration, but in its power to meet the needs of humanity. Spiritual truth is apprehended only in the fullness of the personal being of the seeker after truth. The 'most trustworthy guide in matters of faith was the spirit of God working in the Church and in the soul of the individual Christian'.[72] Dean Farrar boldly asserted that 'If in later days the Church of England has made an immense advance (in theology) the progress is perhaps more due to Samuel Taylor Coleridge than to any ordained or professed theologian.'[73]

The other 'lay' person of enormous importance was Thomas Carlyle (1795–1881) who, like a prophet of old, and some of his contemporaries hailed him as such, denounced sin and evil and, above all, anything which he saw as pretence and humbug. His teaching contained a great amount of unorthodoxy, for he denied miracles and the divine personality and tended to exalt strength, and might of intellect and character, rather than poverty of spirit as the divine ideal. But he did continually emphasize divine power behind all matter, man as the offspring of such a divine power or being, and the centrality in the affairs of men of moral law and the eternal distinction between right and wrong. And he expressed a belief, vague though it may have been, in immortality.[74] Carlyle represents that stress on morality, combined with a serious questioning of some of the basic tenets of the Christian faith, which was a hallmark of much of the Christianity of the Victorian age.

The new geological and biological teaching of the first half of the nineteenth century relating to the early chapters of Genesis contributed to a surge of radical Old Testament criticism. The first major indication in England of such criticism came with the publication in 1829 of Dean H.H. Milman's *History of the Jews*, in which Abraham was depicted as an Arab Sheikh, and there was a tendency to rationalize some of the miracles. Meanwhile, the Tübingen School in Germany was developing its revolutionary reconstruction of the received version of early Christian history. Its distinctive teaching was confined to a select academic circle in England until the appearance of *Das Leben Jesu* by Friedrich Strauss in 1835, translated into English by George Eliot in 1846. Strauss accepted the Tübingen critical conclusions without question and tried to explain exactly how the Gospel narratives had evolved. He portrayed Jesus as a Galilean teacher of pure and holy life who had inevitably come into collision with the ecclesiastical authorities, had been put to death, and had been surrounded by an ever increasing aura of mystery and miracle. The miraculous was not introduced with any intention to deceive, but because the early Christians viewed Christ with messianic expectations. For Strauss miracles did not happen.

A final strand in this complex interlocking of various intellectual developments some of which, at least superficially, appear to have been hostile to the Christian faith, and were regarded in that light by a number of contemporary churchmen, was the development of what may be termed 'the science of religion'. It can be traced back to debates in the early seventeenth century when academics were beginning to consider and explain new data from various parts of the world which appeared to place a question mark over biblical accounts of origins. But it was not until the late seventeenth century and early eighteenth century that 'religion' and 'religions' appeared to some scholars to be legitimate subjects for an objective academic study which was uncluttered by theological or philosophical assumptions.[75] By the second quarter of the nineteenth century such a 'science' appeared more feasible and, some said, desirable, in the light of works like those of Milman.

Many of the issues I have been discussing which relate to 'science and faith' and the understanding of the Bible, but especially the latter, were articulated with the publication in February 1860 of a composite volume entitled *Essays and Reviews*. It represented 'a crisis of faith contemporary with that provoked by Darwin's *Origin of Species* but more central to the religious mind'.[76] The book appeared only two months after the publication of *The Origin of Species*. The debates engendered by both overlapped, but it is clear that biblical criticism and not evolution was the main concern of the *Essays*.

Although the book is part of the specific history of the Church of England, which I will be narrating and analysing in the next chapter, it caused such widespread consternation, and had such extensive and lasting effects on Christianity as a whole in England, that I will at this stage indicate something of its character, contents and consequences. In its preface *Essays and Reviews* is described as 'an attempt to illustrate the advantage derived to the cause of moral and religious truth, from a free handling, in a becoming spirit, of subjects peculiarly liable to suffer by the repetition of conventional language, and from traditional methods of treatment.'

The volume comprised seven essays, six by clergymen and one by a layman. The essay by Frederick Temple was orthodox and theologically uncontentious. The one by Rowland Williams introduced a formidable array of critical results and conjectures: the Pentateuch was a gradual growth, the 'child' of Isaiah 7 was to be born in the reign of Ahaz and did not refer to Jesus, chapters 40 to 66 of Isaiah were not by the prophet Isaiah, the book of Daniel was written in the second century, and the Epistle to the Hebrews was not Pauline. He argued for the idea of progressive revelation, and appeared to be scornful of a number of traditional doctrines, such as atonement through the substitutionary sacrifice of Jesus. Baden Powell was a wholehearted evolutionist, and in his essay he enthusiastically welcomed *The Origin of Species*, evidently had no place for miracles and distinguished two separate spheres, the natural and the spiritual, which he placed in separate compartments. A.B. Wilson called for a drastic amendment of the terms of subscription for the Church of England, and caused considerable offence by referring to passion and error in the Bible. C.W. Goodwin declared that theologians should accept the discoveries and conclusions of modern science. The essay by Mark Pattison was purely historical. The most provocative contribution was by Benjamin Jowett, who asked that the Bible should be approached like any other book; and it was forgotten that he qualified this by saying that there were many respects in which scripture was unlike any other book. It was supposed that when he pleaded for open enquiry he was casting Christianity away. His essay gave the impression of antagonism to the prevailing orthodox inter-pretation of scripture, with little offered in its place. It was marked by a clear tendency to resolve Christianity into a set of ideas and a moral way of life. He seemed to be convinced that modern scholarship had 'made the exclusive claims of the Hebrew Christian tradition untenable, religion is historically conditioned and the final court of appeal is the moral consciousness of modern man'.[77]

The reactions to the book were immediate and vehement. One message was clear in the response of the critics: the essayists were not entitled to be heard. Biblical criticism was dangerous in the way it questioned the accuracy and reliability of the Bible, and this was unacceptable in itself to these critics: such new approaches to the Bible might lead to a weakening of faith, to doubt, to Socinianism, and finally to unbelief. The orthodox opponents of *Essays and Reviews* may appear from a comfortable distance, and after the intervening period of adjustment to biblical criticism and the emergence of much more radical theology, to have been obscurantist in their reaction to the higher criticism of their day. But their response was consistent with theological developments over the previous century and more, especially within the Church of England. There was 'an ultimate reliance on a rigidly rational line of argument, resting on eighteenth-century evidential apologetics. An Anglican scholasticism (as we may call it) had produced a consistent rationalistic case for the acceptance of the Christian revelation. It was only after this rationalism had laid the intellectual foundations for belief that Anglican orthodoxy invoked the distinctively Victorian demand for certainty of faith.'[78] And therein was a cause of immediate, medium, and long-term tension and difficulty for some Christians, for it was fundamentally an either–or argument which, in its more extreme forms, did not allow for any compromise between what was regarded by some Christians as the inalienable, unalterable Christian view and any other conclusion.

> It represented a willingness to stake all of Christian faith on the text of the Bible and ultimately on a particular scholastic argument which justified that reliance. In one sense this may have been a sign of insecurity, in that it obviated analysis of specific biblical difficulties by an overriding appeal to faith, in another sense it was a supreme act of self-confidence, in that it was prepared to rest the case for Christianity on its most vulnerable point. In any case it was an act of hubris, a tremendous raising of the stakes. The either-or argument, argued so forcefully as to impress itself even on doubters, was responsible more than anything else for the peculiar dimensions and intensity of the Victorian crisis of faith.[79]

It was a double-edged argument to state unequivocally that it was necessary either to accept all of revelation and of orthodox theology, without denial of any of its elements, or the whole edifice would fall. In its extreme form this confronted individuals with no option. The doubter was not given the alternative, previously open to him, to be a heretic, holding the wrong faith, but faith nevertheless. The new approach gave the alternative of orthodoxy and total 'infidelity'.[80] *Essays and Reviews* encouraged this fateful dogmatism because it was in its own way dogmatic. The authors largely followed in the steps of Schleiermacher who had emphasized that religion was based on intuition and feeling; that it was independent of dogma; and that its highest experience was a sensation of union with the infinite. 'There was nothing else quite like *Essays and Reviews* in its fearless solution of the problem of authority, and its authors were before their time in accepting Schleiermacher. This argues for a degree of theological awareness and sensitivity on the part of, at least, Jowett and Wilson which entitles them to more recognition as religious thinkers than they have been usually given. The achievement was also to the credit of the Latitudinarian tradition which had never died out in Oxford and which grew to a quite astonishing confidence in the post-Newman reaction that produced the radical Broad Churchmen.'[81]

In the short-term *Essays and Reviews* sharpened the distinction between true believers and non-believers; in the long-run it contributed to the development of that 'market' situation, with competing claimants as the bearers of the true gospel, which we will see as a particular characteristic of the late twentieth century.

Three further stones were cast into the theological pool in the thirty years after the appearance of *Essays and Reviews*. The first was hurled by the Cornish mathematician and Bishop of Natal, J.W. Colenso, in 1862 when he published the first of a number of books under the title *The Pentateuch and the Book of Joshua critically examined*. He relied heavily on critical German works in what amounted to a frontal attack on the traditional acceptance of the historical authenticity of the accounts and the authorship of the biblical books he examined. He drew attention to duplications and inconsistencies. He questioned certain stories and suggested redating of some parts. It was all done in what seemed to be a rather negative manner, with an apparent greater concern for historical accuracy than spiritual truth; an approach which was seen by many as particularly inappropriate in a bishop.

Next, chronologically, was the anonymous *Ecce Homo* (1865), later found to have been written by Sir J.R.Seeley. It attracted considerable attention with its portrayal of Jesus as the founder of a morality which changed history. It was not an assault upon orthodox Christianity, but its emphasis on the manhood of Christ was regarded in some quarters as very dangerous. Lord Shaftesbury promptly castigated it as 'the most pestilential book . . . ever vomited from the jaws of Hell'.[82]

The third theological disturbance was in 1889, when *Lux Mundi* appeared. It was a series of essays edited by the prominent High Churchman Charles Gore. Because it was even more than *Essays and Reviews* an internal Church of England event, without the same widespread ramifications and reactions as the earlier book, I will not dwell on it, but leave a full consideration of its subject matter and significance to the next chapter. I mention it here as it was yet another landmark in the advance of those 'liberal' views which were becoming more widespread among all Protestant denominations, and which were even beginning to infiltrate Roman Catholicism, as we will see when we consider that church towards the end of this chapter.

Among Protestants as a whole there were those who were not satisfied with the restated orthodoxy of either *Essays and Reviews* or *Lux Mundi*, and who looked for a more extreme 'liberal' theology. With the great advances in science and biblical criticism they wanted something more radical. By his emphasis on subjectivity F.D.E. Schleiermacher, in the early years of the century, helped to lessen the importance attached to the doctrinal elements in Christianity. He taught that there is a radical discontinuity between science and religion; religion is not concerned with ideas about the world and man which are to do with the intellect, that is the realm of science; neither is it concerned with what in conduct is 'right', for that is the province of morality. The right area of religion is beyond science and morality. Albrecht Ritschl was critical of traditional orthodoxy and the concept of an infallible Bible, and he concurred with Schleiermacher in not reducing Christianity to science, philosophy or anything else, but he did not agree that we should begin with subjective experience. What was crucial, he asserted, was the objective facts which gave rise to subjective Christian experiences: and supremely this meant the person of the historic Jesus. Christianity for him was basically a personal and moral response to the person of Jesus, in which the believer makes a 'value judgment' about Jesus.

These two strands of thought gave the Liberal Protestants of the latter half of the century their essential 'mood', for it was a mood rather than the rigidity of a 'school' which distinguished them.[83] Characteristically they were rationalists, not bowing with unquestioning acceptance to the inherited dogmas of the church; optimists about the progress of humanity, as they saw the potential future for evolving man, and as they contemplated the idealism of Hegel; enthusiasts about the high status of man as the pinnacle of creation, with immense potential for moral perfectibility, and with a low regard for the concept of sin; champions of a Christianity which was fundamentally the religion *of* Jesus and what he practised, rather than a religion *about* Jesus, with the emphasis on Jesus as a person to be worshipped; and earnest seekers after the 'Jesus of history'.

It was in this spirit that Frederick William Farrar published his *Life of Christ* in 1874, although he was much more conservative than most of the other 'liberals'. The two previous greatest lives of Jesus in the nineteenth century, *Das Leben Jesu* by Strauss and *Vie de Jesus* by

Renan, were written by unbelievers who were convinced that no practising Christian could summon up the necessary detachment to engage in the task. Farrar did not agree. He 'was convinced that a recognizable human figure emerged from the Gospels when they were treated as historical sources, and he supplemented this information with what Renan had called the "fifth Gospel"; the evidence of archaeology, numismatics, Jewish sources contemporary with Christ and, above all, the local colour and psychological atmosphere derived from seeing the geography of the Holy Land at first hand'.[84] An important component in this whole 'quest for the historical Jesus', of which Farrar's work was an example, was the claim of some of its purest exponents that 'Jesus did not need the spurious authentication provided by miracle and supernatural intervention: he could stand alone'.[85] But, although the freedom of Farrar's rendering, both in respect of biblical language and traditional exegesis, shocked many, others found it convincing. And Farrar did retain most of the supernatural structure of the Gospels, accepting the miracles as they were depicted. He did not treat the fourth Gospel as different from the rest, and he did not raise any really critical problem about the nature of the Gospel history.

The works and theology of the 'liberals' as a whole, however, amounted to a Christianity which demoted, disregarded or dismissed dogma. Such an orientation thus had its origins in the nineteenth century, and ultimately, of course, much further back than that, but it was not to surface very explicitly, or in its more extreme forms, in England until the twentieth century.

The churches and society

All this reflection and debate on scientific, biblical and theological matters meant little to the average 'man in the street', and certainly not to the manual labourer in the still extensive rural areas of the country, or in one of the rapidly growing industrial towns.[86] In many ways the real battle for the minds and hearts of the nation was to be fought at a much lower intellectual level, and in an environment which was dominated by family concerns, by ambitions which were frustrated or fulfilled, by the financial and employment demands of daily life, and by personal considerations of birth, marriage, health and death. And in such spheres, in a rapidly changing nation, the churches had patchy success.

Although it is generally accepted that throughout the nineteenth century working-class church and chapel attendance was low, there was a wide-ranging Anglican, Nonconformist and Roman Catholic presence in working-class communities which had an important influence in the lives of many people who seldom attended a church or a chapel. This took the form of the parish church, a countless number of Nonconformist chapels and Roman Catholic churches, Protestant and Roman Catholic mission 'stations' of all sorts, settlements, a numberless host of specialist centres provided and organized by numerous charities and voluntary bodies, and, later in the century, the enthusiastic and effective ministry of the Salvation Army and Church Army. Then there was that 'popular religion' which we have already encountered, and which has been so usefully described and analysed by Cox and others.[87] 'Revisionist' historians have stressed that the nineteenth-century working classes were no less 'religious' than the middle classes, but religious in different ways. They had beliefs which were just as firmly held as those of clergy and churchgoers, and which were important in shaping their view of the world and the way they related to other people. Some of these 'revisionists', such as Sarah Williams, have focussed their attention on trying to interpret the alternative forms of religious belief prevalent among non-churchgoers.[88]

There is the further question of the degree to which the churches fulfilled a creative social role, or were conservative and essentially instruments of social control. Generalizations are difficult; for they were more active, innovative and creative at certain times and in certain areas than at others. Patrick Joyce, in his study of the 'factory culture' of Lancashire industrial towns, stresses the paternalism of medium-size family firms, which were often run in close conjunction with one of the local churches or chapels, and the emphasis this gave to the importance of the *status quo*.[89] However, Robert Moore, in his study of a coal-mining district in County Durham, discovered considerable variation from one pit to another, and a pattern of church or chapel role and status which differed according to local employer-union relations, and the extent to which the Methodists were involved in local unionism and socialism.[90]

The 'social gospel' of the late nineteenth century and early twentieth century was a response to the problems of the city. It showed that some church people were alert to this area of responsibility for the churches. And there were many initiatives by Nonconformists, High Churchmen and Evangelical Anglicans to meet what they felt deeply as their social responsibilities, as we will see in the next two chapters. The yearning and concern of the few was well expressed by a Baptist lay social investigator: 'That gospel which does not concern itself with man's body, mind, and environment, as well as his soul, is a contradiction in terms . . . If we cannot make our politics part of our religion, we have no right to cast even a vote . . . If cleaner streets, better housing, sweeter homes, do not come within the scope of our aim, neither will those who are convinced that they have a right to these things come within the shadow of our places of worship.'[91] As D.W. Bebbington commented: 'A Christian appeal to city-dwellers must embrace their aspirations. So the social gospel was born.'[92]

Of great importance in the matter of 'church and society' in the nineteenth century was the changing attitude to women, and the changing function and role accorded to women in the churches. In general it may be said that the churches, and perhaps especially the Church of England, managed to combine a strong belief in the notion of women's subordination with an increasing involvement of women in their life, work and witness.

> The development of an Anglican theology of gender relations in the nineteenth century was intimately connected with the economic and social changes that had begun in the previous century, but whose full impact was only felt in the Victorian period. The Church of England was part of an increasingly powerful and self-confident middle-class world, whose definition of respectability was based upon a clear separation between the spheres of work and domesticity, and upon its ability to sustain a lifestyle in which women were above the necessity of undertaking paid employment – a crucial distinction between 'ladies', and the 'women' upon whom they often depended for domestic labour.[93]

And what is said there about the Church of England can, in varying degrees, be applied to the other, at least Protestant, churches. But such a protective attitude to women, and more especially to 'ladies' was gradually eroded, or at least subject to many and increasing exceptions, as a result of a rapidly increased need for extra helpers at all levels in the churches. There were mounting demands upon the limited human resources of the churches as a whole as they confronted unprecedented evangelistic, pastoral and intellectual challenges; and there was the tempting possibility of drawing upon a hitherto virtually untapped female resource to help meet these demands. The resulting employment of women to undertake a range of duties, albeit mostly of a fairly routine nature, undoubtedly entailed ambiguity, if not blatant double-standards. 'On the one hand, public religious activities allowed an increasing number of women to satisfy to some extent their frustration and desire for status and occupation; on the other, the same religious attitudes which fostered this independent female activity within the Church also taught female subordination outside it.'[94] It was a dilemma which was to disappear, not without trace, during the ensuing century and a half.

We will encounter these various manifestations of the churches' struggle to achieve a full, satisfying and acceptable role in society when we consider the Church of England, the Nonconformists and the Roman Catholics in detail. But there is one movement in the area of 'the churches and society' which needs to be considered quite extensively and intensively at this point, because it had such widespread ramifications for all churches, and that is Christian Socialism.

Christian Socialism

Christian Socialism was inextricably bound up with the life and teaching of John Frederick Denison Maurice.[95] He was born in 1805 into a highly gifted family whose members were ardently interested in the religious, political, social and cultural questions of the day, with a father who was a Unitarian. His childhood was blighted by severe religious divisions within the family as first his sister and then his mother came under evangelical influence and broke with his father's beliefs. The moral confusion and religious tension caused the brilliant and precocious Maurice much agony. It was therefore with relief that during this time of religious uncertainty he made the acquaintance of Coleridge and other 'romantic' thinkers. He was thereby led into a new conception of Christianity which took him away from Unitarianism but not into the evangelical fold. He combined this with the political traditions of the Unitarians and the Philosophic Radicals. He was not only opposed to the Tories, but critical of the Whigs. He believed that the spiritual and political life of the nation should embrace all the people. He therefore declared that all classes must be endowed with political power.

Maurice had a far wider concept of Christianity than was common in his day. To him it went way beyond institutions and dogma: as it sprang from the inner nature of man and consisted of experiencing God as the cosmic harmony it could not be so confined and restricted. But then, in

1828, largely as a consequence of death-bed talks with his sister, he came to an evangelical consciousness of sin and personal redemption. He was baptized into the Church of England in 1831 and ordained in 1834. He thus brought to the established church a unique intellectual and religious development. He had an intense awareness of the brotherhood created by Christ, and that man could only live a truly human life when he spent it in self-sacrifice and love towards his fellow-men.

> To Maurice the Divine Order, or synonymous with it 'the kingdom of God', was an existing reality in which man was already living. Therefore it was not the task of man to create forms of organization in which true brotherhood of love and fellowship could be expressed, God Himself had already placed man in a 'Human Order' with 'human relationships'. Every individual had here been given a distinct vocation by which he must consider himself a minister of God under the guidance of the Holy Spirit.[96]

The Church was the manifestation and expression of this Divine Order. It was the witness to the eternal truth that Christ was, always had been, and would ever be the 'Head of every man'; 'the Church existed in order to tell the world the truth about its own existence'.[97] Maurice believed that the church parties of his generation had denied such principles, and such a divine calling, by setting up their own religious opinions and systems; and he was fiercely critical of the contemporary Church of England. At the same time he asserted that the Church of England contained the whole truth in contrast to the Nonconformists who had only caught glimpses of the truth. In 1838 he published *The Kingdom of Christ*, in which he gave the first elaborate exposition of his thoughts. It was a seminal work for the forthcoming Christian Socialists.

The other important contributor to the foundation and early life of Christian Socialism was John Malcolm Ludlow. He was born in India in 1821. A highly-gifted child, he was educated in France, and nurtured in a family of church goers, who were keenly interested in politics and social issues. While he was still young he had a broad religious outlook. Rigid orthodoxy did not appeal to him, and he found no difficulty in embracing biblical criticism and the findings of modern science into his Liberal Protestantism. He was also very sympathetic to the form of Liberal Catholicism proclaimed by Lamennais and others.[98] In politics, he abhorred all forms of political and social privilege but his social outlook remained definitely middle class. When he came to England he was horrified at the extent of class differences, and disgusted with the Church of England. He was critical of its liturgy and found the preaching of the clergy devoid of life and ardour. He thought it was corrupt and stood far beneath any other church in Christendom; and he fully understood why people left it in great numbers. He was most incensed that it was a political institution which was dominated by the aristocracy who oppressed the people. It had no roots in the ordinary people of the land.

Ludlow experienced a turning point in his own life in 1839, from which time he dated 'his personal surrender to the will of God and the feeling of an inward peace, based on the conviction that he could trust to the mercy of God'.[99] He did not become a wholehearted evangelical. He retained his passionate cultural interests and his preoccupation with politics. He was deeply affected in 1844 by A.P. Stanley's *Life and Correspondence of Thomas Arnold*, and Arnold became a model for him. What attracted him was the strong and independent character of Arnold, and his resolute political principles in which he resisted conservatism, championed political and social reform, and in effect sided with the radicals.

It was in 1848 that he started to work among the poor in the slums of London, and was thereby faced with the actual problems of poverty and misery. This was the beginning of the activities of the Christian Socialists, a term which was only applied to them some years later. The experience evoked in Ludlow a growing dissatisfaction with contemporary English forms of religious-philanthropic enterprise. 'It seemed to me', he wrote, ' that no serious effort was made in any single instance to help a person out of his or her misery, but only to help him or her in it.'[100]

The movement soon achieved considerable publicity, largely because of the work of Charles Kingsley. He created a stir with his *Cheap Clothes and Nasty*, in which he passionately attacked the slop-system; but it was with the publication in 1850 of *Alton Locke: An Autobiography* that he really made Christian Socialism known in wide circles, while at the same time laying the foundation of his literary fame.

But despite the concern of the early brotherhood to rescue their distressed and disadvantaged fellow-men and women, and their burning desire to apply Christian principles to alleviate the pressing problems of the slum dwellers, the early Christian Socialists had but vague ideas about where and how to set to work. What distinguished them, and justifies the appellation Christian Socialism to a group of what would otherwise be a rather disparate collection of individuals, is the fact that to a large extent they expressed the same fundamental views in their approach to the problems of the day. It was only in Kingsley that there was a tendency to dream romantically about the possibility of bringing back pre-industrial England. As a whole the Christian Socialists accepted the industrial revolution and unhesitatingly recognized the benefits it had the potential of conferring on mankind, provided that it was not dominated by the accumulation of wealth for individuals. The new machinery should be seen as a gift from God, to be held in trust for the good of one's fellow men. They therefore went into battle against the Political Economists, who in their opinion advocated the principles of individualism and selfishness.

The movement appeared to be quite healthy and prosperous in the first four years of its life; but not far beneath the surface there were serious differences of opinion among its leaders, and especially between Maurice and Ludlow, which quickly tore it apart. Ludlow was far more willing than Maurice to declare a Christian Socialist view. Maurice thought they ought to be silent as they had no clear message to proclaim. He thought that their ideas were so divergent that only confusion ensued when they spoke up. Both Ludlow and Maurice were desperately anxious to conquer the new industrial world for the kingdom of Christ, so it was a personal tragedy, as well perhaps as a major blow for the churches as a whole, when Maurice finally dissolved Christian Socialism as an organized force in 1854. The first generation Christian Socialists

> had sown the seeds, which, together with other influences, in due course bore fruit. It would be misrepresentation, however, to maintain that their influence had been of decisive importance. The short span of time allotted to them quite simply made it impossible for them, in any appreciable way, to put their mark on, or to change, the beliefs of contemporary Christianity.[101]

What they had done was to provide an inspiration, and to some extent a pattern, from which future generations could draw, and which did spur others on to new and vigorous efforts. They were the fore-fathers of that band of High Church and Broad Church Anglicans, Quaker socialists, Swedenborgian socialists and other Christian socialists in other denominations who, towards the end of the century, felt 'that it was impossible to be what they deemed "Christian" without being simultaneously what they deemed "socialist"'. For to such men and women, as to the early Christian Socialists we have just considered, 'Christian socialism was not conceived as merely one particular reading of the Christian message, but as its only possible ultimate meaning.'[102]

Secularism

The nineteenth-century secularist movement had its roots in a very different form of socialism: that of Robert Owen.[103] He formed the British and Foreign Consolidated Association of Industry, Humanity and Knowledge in 1834 after he had left the declining Grand National Consolidated Trade Union. The following year this became the Association of All Classes of All Nations, with the objective of preparing public opinion for the coming of the 'new moral world'. At a Congress in 1837 a second society was formed, the National Community Friendly Society, to raise funds for a socialist experiment, and the Owenites officially described themselves as 'Socialists'. They appointed two 'social missionaries' to help Owen in the propagation of his gospel. In 1839 the two bodies were amalgamated to form the Universal Community Society of Rational Religionists (or Rational Society, for short).

In 1845 George Jacob Holyoake wrote a short but influential work, *Rationalism, a Treatise for the Times*, in which he tried to resurrect the basic doctrines of Owenism. The City Road Hall of Science became the centre of London Secularism; and in the provinces some Socialists, as at Stockport and Sheffield, kept their Halls of Science open so that when Holyoake started the Secularist movement they simply transferred their allegiance. Many of the leaders of the new movement were lifelong Socialists.

Secularism reached a peak around 1854, with Holyoake as its undoubted leader. The committed membership probably did not exceed four thousand, although there were many more adherents, but the circulation of the movements periodical, the *Reasoner*, reached five thousand, and nearly forty local societies were reported in its pages. 'Secularism became a topic of conversation. It was denounced from the pulpits, discussed in the press, and declaimed against from the platform.'[104]

Although mass meetings flourished in the 1850s, the influence of Holyoake had begun to wane. He became what was later known as an 'agnostic', and the movement turned to Robert Cooper as the continuing herald of its traditional atheism.

It was at that stage that Charles Bradlaugh came to the fore. He was intelligent, alert, and a naturally brilliant orator. He could not tolerate Holyoake's cautious moderation and avoidance of the word 'atheist', and he launched out on a vigorous and successful campaign to reinvigorate organized secularism and atheism. The Secularists created a new body, the National Secular Society; and its story between 1866 and 1890 is in large measure the story of Bradlaugh's career.

It was in 1874 that he met Mrs Annie Besant, the wife of a clergyman, who had begun to lose her Christian faith about two years before. A very ambitious and able woman, she made a major contribution to the more militant wing of the secularist movement. But Bradlaugh remained dominant, especially with his elevated public reputation, resulting in part from his attempt to enter Parliament. In 1880 the membership of the National Secular Society reached a new peak of six thousand; and five years later there were over one hundred branches throughout the country. Then decline set in. Bradlaugh managed to enter Parliament and was able to give less attention to Secularism. There was increasing competition from the new Socialist movement. By 1890 only sixty-two branches of the National Secular Society remained. Bradlaugh died in 1891; his journal, the *National Reformer*, came to an end in 1893; and in the same year Mrs Besant left the Secularists and the Socialists to join the Theosophists. By the end of the century it was clear that there was no immediate prospect that the movement would revive.

The Secularists had achievements to their credit, even if some of their causes were denounced by orthodox Christians. They had involved themselves in a large number and variety of reform movements, including those for temperance or total abstinence; women's rights; the spreading of knowledge about birth control; and, above all, national secular education, the total abolition of church rates and tithes, and the repeal of Sabbatarian legislation. They had been enthusiastic and active advocates of full civil rights for all members of society, and for freedom of speech. For a small group they certainly had considerable impact.

A separate but associated development was the growth and formalization of agnosticism in the latter part of the century. By 1885 there was an agnostic publication, the *Agnostic Annual*, which was reporting that a movement was afoot to found the first agnostic temple, to be located in South London. The agnostics were not inherently anti-religious. 'The basis of their criticism of the rigid dogmatism of the churches was their belief that Victorian Christianity was a perversion of the original, pure religion as founded by Christ.'[105] They regarded the

Bible as a book of great wisdom and beauty which, if read without prejudice, 'contains within itself the refutation of nine-tenths of the mixture of sophistical metaphysics and old-world superstition which has been piled around it by the so-called Christians of later times'.[106]

The agnostics of the latter half of the century appear to have been a distinct and peculiar collection of individuals. 'The conclusions that can be drawn as to why this group of men lost faith in Christianity cannot be extended to the general decline of religious influence during the period, which was partly a decline of belief but mainly the removal of general support and respect from religious institutions.'[107] They had sufficient in common as a group to allow a measure of generalization about their social composition and motivations:

> As can be seen from contemporary analyses of unbelief, there were far more working-class Agnostics and Atheists than middle class, and a large number of these passed through or were casually associated with the Secular movement. The loss of faith for these men was associated with extreme individualism; an often anomic social situation; radical or Socialist involvement; and a strong moral sense. These causes were not sufficient nor perhaps even always necessary; but the revolution in scientific and theological thinking seems largely irrelevant. The loss of faith for Freethinkers was not an intellectual but a moral matter.[108]

Huxley and others thought that the new reformation which they preached could involve the founding of new, pure institutions to replace the corrupt churches of the day. But by the 1890s the movement was in a state of atrophy, and it did not long survive into the twentieth century.

The churches at the end of the Victorian era

As the churches entered the twentieth century they stood in stark contrast to their counterparts in 1833; and trends were afoot which would separate them even further in almost every way from what they had been less than seventy years before. We can now appreciate that a further fourteen years were to inaugurate a new world in which so much of the nineteenth-century assumptions, values, modes of behaviour and living, as well as institutions and structures, were to be cast into the melting pot. The new century was to witness not only the trauma of two World Wars, but quite unprecedented and revolutionary changes in every sphere of life. In many ways the Victorian era came to an end in 1914. But I am concluding this first part of the present book in 1901, not only because that saw the actual end of Victoria's reign, but because the treating of 1901 to 1945 as one period helps in the appreciation of just what changes were introduced by those cataclysmic four years of the First World War, as well as by scientific, medical and technological innovations.

The transformations wrought in the churches in the last seven decades of the nineteenth century were astounding; the more so when we see how they were but a prelude to even greater and more rapid transmutations in the following one hundred years. But this can only be fully understood if we readjust our focus and look in some detail and depth at the nineteenth-century Church of England, the Nonconformists and the Roman Catholics; and we will begin with the established church.

Further reading

The following are selected works from the bibliography at the end of the book which may be found especially helpful as further reading on the topics covered in this chapter. A similar list is appended to each of the chapters.

Bebbington, D.W., *Evangelicalism in Modern Britain. A history from the 1730s to the 1980s*, London 1989

Chadwick, Owen, *The Victorian Church*, 2 vols, London 1966, 1970; reissued London 1987

Christensen, T., *Origins and History of Christian Socialism 1848–54*, London 1962

Cowherd, Raymond G., *The Politics of English Dissent. The Religious Aspects of Liberal and Humanitarian Reform Movements from 1815 to 1848*, New York 1956

Cox, J., *The English Churches in a Secular Society: Lambeth 1870–1930*, Oxford 1982

Currie, R., Gilbert, A., and Horsley, L., *Churches and Churchgoers: Patterns of Church Growth in the British Isles Since 1700*, Oxford 1977

Davies, Horton, *Worship and Theology in England: From Watts and Wesley to Maurice, 1690–1850*, Princeton 1961

Davies, Horton, *Worship and Theology in England: From Newman to Martineau, 1850–1900*, Oxford 1962

Elliott-Binns, L.E., *Religion in the Victorian Era*, London 1936

Elliott-Binns, L.E., *English Thought 1860–1900. The Theological Aspect*, London 1956

Evans, Eric J., *The Forging of the Modern State. Early Industrial Britain 1783–1870*, London 1983

Gay, John D., *The Geography of Religion in England*, London 1971

Gilbert, A.D., *Religion and Society in Industrial England: Church, Chapel and Social Change 1740–1914*, London 1976

Gill, Sean, *Women and the Church of England From the Eighteenth Century to the Present*, London 1994

Hempton, David, *Religion and Political Culture in Britain and Ireland From the Glorious Revolution to the Decline of Empire*, Cambridge 1996

Hylson-Smith, Kenneth, *Evangelicals in the Church of England 1734–1984*, Edinburgh 1989

Hylson-Smith, Kenneth, *High Churchmanship in the Church of England From the Sixteenth Century to the Late Twentieth Century*, Edinburgh 1993

Hylson-Smith, Kenneth, *The Churches in England from Elizabeth I to Elizabeth II*, 3 vols, London 1996–98

Jones, P.d'A., *The Christian Socialist Revival, 1877–1914. Religion, Class, and Social Conscience in Late Victorian England*, Princeton 1968

Knight, Frances, *The Nineteenth-Century Church and English Society*, Cambridge 1995

Laqueur, T.W., *Religion and Respectability: Sunday Schools and English Working-Class Culture, 1780–1850*, Yale 1976

Machin, G.I.T., *Politics and the Churches in Great Britain 1832 to 1868*, Oxford 1977

Machin, G.I.T., *Politics and the Churches in Great Britain 1869 to 1921*, Oxford 1987

McCord, Norman, *British History 1815–1906*, Oxford 1991

McLeod, Hugh, *Religion and Society in England, 1850–1914*, Basingstoke 1996

Morris, Jeremy, *Religion and Urban Change. Croydon, 1840–1914*, Woodbridge 1992

Norman, E.R., *Anti-Catholicism in Victorian England*, London 1968

Norman, E.R., *Church and Society in England 1770–1970. A Historical Study*, Oxford 1976

Norman, E.R., *The English Catholic Church in the Nineteenth Century*, Oxford 1984

Norman, E.R., *The Victorian Christian Socialists*, Cambridge 1987

Obelkevich, J., *Religion and Rural Society: South Lindsey 1825–75*, Oxford 1976

Parsons, Gerald (ed), *Religion in Victorian Britain*, 4 vols, Manchester 1988

Ramsey, Arthur Michael, *From Gore to Temple. The Development of Anglican Theology between Lux Mundi and the Second World War, 1889–1939*, London 1960

Reckitt, Maurice B., *Maurice to Temple. A Century of the Social Movement in* the Church of England, London 1947

Rowell, Geoffrey (ed), *Tradition Renewed. The Oxford Movement Conference Papers*, London 1986

Royle, E., *Radical Politics, 1709–1900: Religion and Unbelief*, London 1971

Royle, E., *Victorian Infidels: The Origins of the British Secularist Movement, 1791–1866*, Manchester 1974

Royle, E., *Radicals, Secularists, and Republicans: Popular Freethought in Britain, 1866–1915*, Manchester 1980

Royle, Edward, *Modern Britain. A Social History 1750–1985*, London 1987

Rycroft, P., 'Church, Chapel, and Community in Craven 1764–1851', Oxford D Phil. 1988

Smith, M.A., *Religion in Industrial Society: Oldham and Saddleworth 1740–1865*, Oxford 1994

Stephenson, Alan M.G., *The Rise and Decline of English Modernism*, London 1984

Tulloch, John, *Movements of Religious Thought in Britain during the nineteenth century*, Leicester 1971

Ward, W.R., *Religion and Society in England 1780–1850*, London 1972

Wickham, E.R., *Church and People in an Industrial City*, London 1957

Williams, S.C., 'Religious Belief and Popular Culture: A Study of the South London Borough of Southwark (*c.*1880–1939)', Oxford D Phil. 1993

Wilson, Bryan R., *Religion in Secular Society. A Sociological Comment*, Harmondsworth 1969

Wolffe, John, *The Protestant Crusade in Great Britain 1829–1860*, Oxford 1991

Wolffe, John (ed), *Evangelical Faith and Public Zeal. Evangelicals and Society in Britain 1780–1980*, London 1995

Worrall, B.G., *The Making of the Modern Church. Christianity in England since 1800*, London 1988

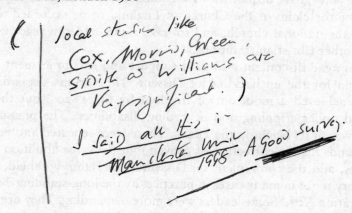

2

The Church of England 1833 to 1901

'The Church in Danger'

On many occasions in the seventeenth and eighteenth centuries the cry had gone up that the Church of England was in danger; but at no time since it was established in the sixteenth century was the danger to its status and authority, if not to its very existence, greater than in 1833. The 1820s had been a bad decade for the national church. It had always had critics, but the whole tide of increased radicalism, and the widespread demand for change in various aspects of national life, gave the more extreme detractors a larger and more sympathetic audience than they might have had in almost any previous age. Radical writers such as Richard Carlile, William Sherwin and the ex-Anglican London clergyman Robert Taylor were severe in their condemnations of the established church, and characterized it as 'the corrupt and bloated lackey of the unreformed system'.[1] And this anti-Anglican vituperation was given statistical support when, in 1820, John Wade published his extensively read and digested *Black Book: or Corruption Unmasked*. He provided a comprehensive catalogue of church plural livings,[2] absenteeism[3] and gross disparities of income. All such attacks helped to undermine the claim of the Church of England to be accorded the standing of the national church, and to have rights and privileges not enjoyed by other Christian traditions.

The widespread discontent also gave support and encouragement to the campaign for the unshackling of Dissent. The various dissenting bodies had achieved a modicum of freedom by the 1820s, but they still suffered under crippling and degrading disabilities. The pressure for change was at its height in the 1820s. There were repeated and persistent demands for the correction of proven injustices, the abolition of church rates, and the conferment on Dissenters of rights withheld, at least in theory if not in many cases in practice, by the long-standing Test and Corporation Acts.[4] Some leaders were more demanding. They urged disestablishment and acceptance of the voluntarist principle, whereby all churches would be supported entirely by the voluntary contributions of the faithful. In political terms the sympathies of Dissenters as a whole were overwhelmingly Whig, as contrasted with the dominant Tory support among Anglicans; and in towns like Birmingham, Leeds and Hull, with a substantial middle-class dissenting presence, a consistent Whig return in national elections was very largely a consequence of dissenting support.

The Dissenters won a major, if only partial victory, with the 1828 Repeal of the Test and Corporation Acts. As significant as the details of the restrictions removed was the breaching of the principle of monopoly of religious status and standing by the Church of England. The Act was a milestone in the emergence of a religiously pluralistic society; and this trend was reinforced the following year with the Catholic Emancipation Act.

The tide was flowing strongly against Church of England traditionalists, and indeed any who wished to maintain the security of the Church of England within a confessional state; and this erosion of status and standing continued into the 1830s. The unpopularity of the established church, and more particularly the fierceness of anti-clerical hostility, was clearly demonstrated during the Swing Riots of 1830-31,[5] and was intensified by the strong, and very public, way the Church of England ranged itself unhesitatingly against political reform. The climax was reached when the bishops stopped the Reform Bill in its tracks in 1831 by voting twenty-one to two against its passage into law. Never had the bench of bishops been more unpopular or subject to such open and heartfelt venom and abuse. The Whig government of 1830, and the post-1832 Reform Act Parliaments, filled parochial clergy and other Anglicans with fear and apprehension for the future. The expansion of the electorate as a consequence of the 1832 Reform Act was sufficient to raise in the minds of affrighted churchmen the spectre of a radical and reforming Parliament in which Nonconformists (for, from then onwards, this term better describes the non-Anglican Protestant denominationalists than Dissenters) would have a major voice, and the prevailing spirit would be highly Utilitarian. When the Whigs were returned with a massive majority in December 1832 there were genuine fears that they might undermine or even destroy the church establishment. 'Were the Whig leaders even Christians? Some doubted it. Lord Dudley thought that Charles Grant, ex-Tory and evangelical, was the only member of the Government who believed in a soul. Charles Lloyd, bishop of Oxford, had fearfully imagined these men in office:

"Lord Holland, his wife an atheist, and himself not far from it. Lord Landsdowne, a confessed Unitarian, Brougham a Deist, and others whom I could easily enumerate, of the same principles." [6]

So, when we reach 1833 we are confronted with a Church of England in disarray and in quite serious distress. The signs were ominous; the outlook seemed gloomy. The *ancien régime* was visibly crumbling; the authenticity of the established church as the spiritual and theological basis for the ordering of society was being seriously questioned; the previously inextricable union of throne and altar was being undermined; the Church of England appeared to be under threat as the bulwark of the Reformation, as the repository of Protestant virtue, and as the guarantor of order and morality; the possibility was openly debated that its administrative, financial and pastoral standing and arrangements might be subjected to far-reaching reform by a Parliament in which political and religious radicals held a commanding position; and there were even whispers that disestablishment was not wholly implausible. The demand that 'all Churches should be supported by voluntary means alone without State aid',[7] was to be adopted as a central tenet in the philosophy of an increasing number of those most hostile to the Church of England. It was all rather discouraging for loyal and committed Anglicans. Thomas Arnold, the theologically 'liberal' headmaster of Rugby School, morbidly asserted that 'the church as it now stands no human power can save'.[8]

But the next seventy years were to witness reform and renewal as well as onslaughts, massive problems and set-backs. The Victorian era was a peculiar mixture for the Church of England. It included changes in the relationship with a vibrant Nonconformity; internal administrative, financial and structural reforms; episcopal and diocesan reform; parochial regeneration; theological and spiritual renewal; evangelistic and pastoral innovations; the advance of 'liberal' theology and ideas; and the emergence in new and more public and explicit forms of agnosticism and atheism. There was also a remarkable expansion in the scope, content and character of Church of England involvement in worldwide Anglicanism, and more generally in the task of global mission, which I will review in chapter 10.

Administrative, financial and structural reforms

During the period from about 1800 to 1870, the Church of England underwent a transformation more rapid, dramatic and enduring than any which it had experienced since the Reformation. The process of change was complex and in certain respects ambiguous, but the most significant adjustment was that which took place in the relationship between Church and State. The Church moved from a uniquely privileged relationship with the State, in which it was closely bound up with the political and legal system, to being one denomination, albeit still the most powerful one and still formally and legally Established, among several in a society in which it appeared that half of those who professed any form of religious allegiance expressed a preference for a non-Anglican variety. This modification in Church-state relations was accompanied by the de-Anglicanization of English institutions.[9]

The admission of Nonconformists to Parliament on equal terms with Anglicans in 1828 was but the first major step, followed by the partial emancipation of the Catholics from the shackles which had bound them for so long, and then the spreading outwards of Nonconformist rights and privileges in the municipal corporations, the universities and the grammar schools. After 1832, however, the process slowed down.

'By 1840 it was already clear that the more apocalyptic visions of 1832 were unfounded. The reformed Parliament had not swept away the religious establishment and a steady process of reform had changed the Church of England from within.'[10] A House of Commons which consisted exclusively of Christians was determined that the Christian faith should continue as the faith of the nation; and because it was still largely composed of members of the Church of England it made sure that the main channel for mediating that faith should remain the established church. As a sign of good intentions towards other Christian traditions, as an indication of a resolve to remedy some of the disabilities which hampered the Nonconformists, and in order to facilitate the putting in order of its own house, a few concessions were granted to the rival Nonconformists or Roman Catholics, but these were not extensive. Notwithstanding the numerical gains of the previous fifty years Nonconformity was not a very formidable force in the 1830s, and a predominantly Anglican Parliament refused to abolish church rates, which remained a festering sore until 1868, being content with an act in 1836 which eliminated the troublesome business of the payment of tithes in kind; and, in addition, only somewhat reluctantly conceded the right of Nonconformists to marry in their own chapels. 'In the first half of Queen Victoria's reign, until Gladstone's electoral victory of 1868, the

Church of England enjoyed its last comparatively secure period of national strength.'[11]

The most far reaching attempt at internal reform was the Commission of 1835, which was set up to 'consider the state of the Established Church'. The following year an Act of Parliament renamed it the Ecclesiastical Commission, and made it permanent. The initiative was conceived and generated by Sir Robert Peel. It has been said that it bore the marks of his personality: 'bureaucratic, capable and cold'.[12] But this is to undervalue the unsensational, more mundane but nonetheless vital aspects of a total pattern of reform and renewal, which included, but was not confined to, the more obviously 'spiritual' elements to be considered later in this chapter. The process did not save the Church of England, as claimed by the rather complacent Bishop Blomfield of London, but it did accomplish much at a structural and administrative level. It 'set the Church of England decisively on the road to reform'.[13] It addressed the problems of plurality and non-residence and, although it could only inaugurate measures to tackle these long-standing issues which mainly arose out of widespread clerical poverty, it tried to reduce disparities in beneficed income. It also took action to create an ecclesiastical structure which was more relevant to a greatly changed industrial and social situation by redrawing the map of episcopal boundaries. It was bold in the measures it introduced to achieve these ends, and for instance weathered a High Church storm when in 1840, by means of the Dean and Chapter Act, it abolished a number of cathedral offices and redistributed the money so saved either in order to augment the revenues of very poor parishes or in order to create completely new parishes. It faced the need to improve the church's presence in the mushrooming towns and, for instance, ensured that sufficient revenue was available to provide adequate stipends for the incumbents required for the many churches constructed under the ambitious programme of the Church Building Commission.

Quite remarkably, between 1835 and 1851 the Ecclesiastical Commission and the Church Building Commission in concert supervised a programme of church building which more than matched the rate of population growth in the major industrial areas. In the period 1831 to 1851 the number of Anglican churches in Lancashire rose from 292 to 521, and in the West Riding of Yorkshire the increase was from 287 to 556. For the country as a whole 2,029 new churches were constructed, in the vast majority of cases with Church of England rather than with government money. Much publicity has been given to the building of

churches after the Church Building Act of 1818, but the rate of construction of churches after 1831 was three times that of the proceeding
twelve years.[14]

Episcopal and diocesan reforms

Together with the measures just outlined a transformation took place
at diocesan level in both the role and function of bishops and in the
organization of dioceses. As with the activities of the Ecclesiastical
Commission, there was no sudden, radical, and entirely self-imposed
revolution. It was a steady process, in which change was introduced as
a combined consequence of external pressures and local efforts to adapt
to changing circumstances. Although the changes in diocesan administration and life generally consisted of a series of piecemeal practical
initiatives together with reforms and developments which were
frequently overlapping and sometimes conflicting, the totality of what
was accomplished did in fact amount to a minor revolution. 'By 1865
dioceses were equipped with an array of organizations in most fields of
Church activity, involving many of the diocesan clergy and laity in
projects to improve the spiritual condition of the diocese. All these
developments transformed the diocese into an active community with a
sense of purpose and identity, which was a constant presence in the life
of both clergy and church-going laity.'[15]

A good start was made to this process of limited diocesan revival in
1836 with the Established Church Act which adjusted episcopal salaries
and thereby removed the glaring inequalities which hitherto had
encouraged unseemly scrambles for translation to wealthier sees. The
same Act created new dioceses to serve new centres of population,
and so re-ordered diocesan boundaries that it alleviated the problems
previously caused by absurdly large dioceses.

Leading the way in the new concern to put diocesan houses in order,
and to adapt the life and operation of dioceses so that they were more
geared to the new industrial, urban, political, social and economic
situation of the mid-nineteenth century era, was Bishop Charles James
Blomfield of London (1828–56). He was in many ways a strange
character, who combined in his personality a peculiar blend of sometimes contradictory elements. 'Endowed with high practical talents he
was all his life remote from practical men, never invited familiarity or
possessed the common touch. Something of the eighteenth century hung
about him.'[16] He was probably the most unpopular bishop on the bench

in the 1830s, with a reputation for high-handedness, sarcasm, meddle-someness, undue hastiness, an over-bearing nature, and an over-developed sense of his own ecclesiastical and episcopal dignity. In his conduct over the Reform Bill he managed to alienate both the Tories and the Whigs, and in his strong sabbatarian leadership of the move-ment to legislate for Sunday observance he became a target for all the Sunday newspapers. He was austere, severely clerical, insisting on correct clerical dress, and was possessed of neither charm nor tact. Although he was not rigidly conservative and, for example, was the first bishop not to wear a wig, and although in company he exhibited an agreeable streak of caustic humour and anecdotal skill, he was not a winsome or generally endearing man, and yet he was resolute, forthright and highly effective as bishop of arguably the most difficult and most important diocese in the country. In the administration of his diocese Blomfield was thoroughly pragmatic. He demonstrated how the measures and means offered by the Ecclesiastical Commissioners could be most readily implemented; and by doing so he offered a model for future development. He had little patience with the abstract and theoretical arguments of High Churchmen, which we will consider in a moment, but was a dedicated practitioner of the art of the possible. His concern was to achieve effective and creative reform for the good of his beloved Church of England. 'The route to effective pastoral reform, Blomfield held, was the moderate and pragmatic co-operation of church and state. In this political pragmatism Blomfield was undoubtedly correct: he established a mode of operations and approach for the Ecclesiastical Commission which continued after his own retirement from its work and enabled it to consolidate its achievements in the second half of the century.'[17] He was the most noteworthy exponent of the new policy of the Ecclesiastical Commissioners, and their most distinguished episcopal partner in what was a moderate, non-revolutionary, series of reforms which paved the way for a thorough-going reform of the church's pastoral administration. The creation of new dioceses and the augmentation and endowment of 5,300 parishes between 1840 and 1855 testifies to the importance of this reforming effort.

Blomfield was not alone in what was a surge of diocesan reform. Other bishops, of varying churchmanship, introduced a variety of reforms throughout the country. Samuel Wilberforce, a son of the leading Evangelical William Wilberforce, was in many ways similar to Blomfield, 'eager for work, impulsive, darting here and hurrying there, restoring or building churches, diligent in business and zealous in pastorate, no wide reader nor profound thinker but a man of strong character and practical energy'.[18] He was also a keen manager, and effective as an administrator except when he was led astray by impulse. Unlike Blomfield, he united these qualities with missionary enthusiasm, derived from his evangelical parents, eloquence, and a profound combination of sympathy for the needs of others, fervent devotion and a charm which was conveyed to most people he met. He seemed to have all the qualities necessary for a great ecclesiastic; but his openly declared ambition to be Bishop of London, Archbishop of York, or even Archbishop of Canterbury, gave the appearance to his critics of worldliness. There were also those who thought that his outward, exuberant gestures were kinder than his heart; that he was often guilty of insincerity. Nevertheless, despite any such failings he was greatly and almost universally admired, and he achieved much as Bishop of Oxford (1845–69) and Bishop of Winchester (1869–73). In each of his dioceses he tirelessly travelled about exercising an evangelistic and pastoral ministry and imposing a new discipline on the life of the church. He was assiduous in securing the building, rebuilding or restoration of churches; and he massively increased the number of livings. While at Oxford he founded a teachers' college at Culham and a theological college at Cuddesdon. He was a promoter, a prime mid-Victorian exemplar, and the epitome of the new reformed episcopal ideal which was pioneered by Blomfield; and he showed what a conscientious and pastoral bishop might achieve.

Although Wilberforce was from an evangelical home he did not retain the type of evangelicalism which characterized his parents. But the Victorian era was a golden age for bishops who were unambiguously evangelical. Charles Richard Sumner has been described as the 'first of the modern type of Bishop'.[19] In his short, one-year, tenure of the Bishopric of Lllandaff (1826-1827) he demonstrated his pastoral concern by renting a house in order to live in his diocese because no episcopal palace was provided and he was opposed to clerical non-residence; by immediately undertaking a visitation of his diocese; and by his strenuous efforts to rouse the clergy of the diocese from a state of lethargy and indifference. As Bishop of Winchester (1827-69) he adopted a similar pattern of visitation. He initiated the division of the diocese into rural deaneries. He waged a vigorous war against absentee incumbents, and he set before the clergy a new standard of work and efficiency. In one hundred and sixty-one parishes a second Sunday service was instituted. Neglect of existing churches was not tolerated, and he gave an impetus to a church-building programme. Many extra churches were constructed, and in 1837 he founded a Church-building Society in an effort to raise the additional subscriptions required. The Society received warm support, and the awakened zeal for church extension continued for many decades so that by 1875 over £2,000,000 had been spent on building projects in the diocese. Education was promoted, and a Diocesan Board of Education was established.

In the meantime Charles' older brother John was engaged in vigorous pastoral and evangelistic work, first as Bishop of Chester (1828–48), the largest and most populous diocese in England at the time, and then as Archbishop of Canterbury (1848–62).[20] His Chester diocese embraced the whole of Cheshire and Lancashire, and much of Cumberland and Westmorland, as well as parts of the West Riding of Yorkshire; a region which had experienced unprecedented industrial expansion. In attempting to meet his daunting responsibilities he laid great stress on preaching and individual instruction, and he urged his clergy to arrange house meetings and cottage lectures by means of which the exposition of the Bible could be thoroughly undertaken. He established District Visiting Societies in which suitable lay people were prepared and served as visitors under the direction and supervision of the incumbent in an effort to explain the Christian faith to neighbours who might not otherwise hear the Christian message. The visitors also offered sympathy and help as required. The scheme was not original, but Sumner adopted it to great effect. In an attempt to make church attendance more attractive and amenable he fought against the reservation of paid pews which then remained unused, and encouraged flexibility in the times of Sunday services. Like his brother he promoted the building of new churches, and in nineteen years he consecrated two hundred and thirty-two. He supported an extension of the activities of the Church Pastoral-Aid Society in the north of England, and he tried by various means to further the influence of the church in various spheres of community life, most notably in education. He was convinced that religion should be the basis of all education; and he encouraged the establishment of evening classes for the youth of the diocese as well as provision for infant schooling for the poor.

It is not too much to say that, during the term of his tenure of the see, a revolution was effected in the episcopal office. Prelates with wigs, great state and corresponding haughtiness of manner gave place to real overseers of the clergy, sympathizing in the pastors' struggles, cheering them in their disappointments, counselling them in their difficulties. Bishops Blomfield, Kaye, and the two Sumners were in the van of the movement. The perfunctory discharge of customary duties was felt no longer the ideal of perfection to be aimed at. Real hard work was the order of the day.[21]

When he was elevated to the Archbishopric of Canterbury he maintained his accustomed simple lifestyle. By his teaching and conduct he was instrumental in bringing to an end the old prelatical arrogance of some church dignitaries, and he was a prime mover in adopting the new concept of a bishop or archbishop as a person who was in touch with the aspirations, ways of life, sorrows and joys of ordinary people, and who acted as a father in God to those committed to his charge.

As Bishop of Liverpool from 1880 until his death in 1900 J.C Ryle was able to put into practice the teaching which he had for many years expressed in sermons, speeches, and in his many and widely-read books, which had helped to make him the most trusted of all the Evangelical clergy, and perhaps the first undisputed leader among the Evangelicals since the days of Charles Simeon.[22] The diocese to which he came had no diocesan machinery. He 'had to lay essential foundations and build for the future from ground level'.[23] He appointed archdeacons and canons, both Evangelical and non-Evangelical, and substantially increased the number of incumbents and curates. Even allowing for a massive growth in the population, there were clear indications of the greatly extended outreach of the church during his bishopric, as in the increase from 4,500 to 8,300 in the number of young people presented to him for confirmation in the period from his first year as bishop to 1896. He unhesitatingly used lay people as paid workers to complement the ministry of the clergy. He expanded the work of the Scripture Readers Society in the diocese by employing their members, who were licensed to take services in mission-rooms, to conduct Sunday schools and to visit the sick. He employed members of the Bible Women's Society to help in the poorest and most needy districts.

The extension of the clerical and lay ministry throughout the diocese made additional churches and mission halls imperative. Ryle was concerned that the churches were frequently only used for about four or five hours on Sundays and the same amount of time during the rest of the week. He encouraged their greater use, and he licensed mission halls and school rooms for worship in order to attract those who shrank from entering a large parish church, and who found the Prayer Book service daunting and incomprehensible. He wanted to make simple, elementary services available in more intimate, less threatening, rooms or halls; and during his episcopate forty-eight mission halls were built or licensed.

When he resigned in 1900 Ryle left a diocese with a firm and wisely constructed foundation upon which his successors could build. His initiatives, and the energetic and dedicated way he approached his responsibilities, vividly illustrate the transformation which had taken place in the role and function of bishops in the course of Victoria's reign.

As a final example of such episcopal transmutation I will turn to that most worthy representative of the Anglican High Church tradition, Bishop Edward King of Lincoln. He was a ritualist, and he was chosen as the target for the final nineteenth-century legal action by the militant Protestant Association in their protracted campaign against ritualists, but this was sadly ironic as he was most cautious and restrained in his ceremonial practices, was possibly the most respected ritualist in England, and combined this with being arguably the saintliest bishop on the bench, loved and admired even by some Evangelicals. He was the most pastorally minded of bishops. He was 'rightly revered as an outstanding example of pastoral care and holiness of life rooted in a deeply sacramental faith'.[24] A contemporary, Henry Scott Holland, vividly said of him that 'he could draw love out of a stone', and his surpassing pastoral sympathy was his outstanding quality. King himself said of his time at Cuddesdon theological college, where he was chaplain from 1857 to 1863 and Principal from then until 1873, that 'we were brought to love God, and one another in God, in a real and special way, not understood by people unless they themselves knew what it was to be thus free',[25] and he was a key figure in establishing such a fellowship. He applied this experience to his episcopal duties when Gladstone made him Bishop of Lincoln in 1885. 'I shall try', he wrote, 'to be the Bishop of the Poor. If I can feel that, I think I shall be happy.'[26] He was assiduous in visiting the scattered village parishes of his diocese, and he strove to make provision for new churches in growing towns like Grimsby. 'His concern to be the bishop of the poor took him into places where Victorian England considered bishops should not go, such as the death-cells of Lincoln prison.'[27] In his episcopate he showed himself to be 'the most saintly of men and the most human of saints',[28] and he provided another example of a new model and standard of episcopal life and responsibility.

The bishops I have briefly considered graphically demonstrate a process of nineteenth-century episcopal metamorphosis. The shift was from an overall pattern in which the tone was set by prince-bishops and aristocratic lifestyles, with attendance at court and political obligations to the fore, with widespread resistance to reform, to a new ideal in which there was openness to change, and in which the emphasis was upon local evangelistic and pastoral obligations. Clearly there were many bishops who broke through the dominant mould in the previous centuries, but the nineteenth century witnessed a massive change in priorities, and in what was considered the most important duties of a diocesan bishop. The hallmarks of the change included such things as 'frequent and locally held confirmation services, the public institution of new incumbents, personal care of ordinands, greater solemnity at ordinations, public leadership of the diocese, and the development of a knowledge of and pastoral relationship with the clergy. The Victorian bishops progressively worked harder and were closer to their clergy and laity than their predecessors had been: a fact reflected in the growth of the call for more bishops – both in the form of new dioceses and through the creation of suffragan bishops and the use of ex-colonial bishops as assistants.'[29] Episcopal control and oversight of a diocese was also extended as a result of the bishops, as a group, managing to increase their influence over the patronage of the benefices under their jurisdiction.

In all of this expanded responsibility and increased 'professionalism' the bishops were also helped by developments in the office of archdeacon. In the diocesan hierarchy the archdeacon ranked immediately below the bishop and was the bishop's lawful representative at the local level. In 1836 there were just fifty-eight of them for the whole of England and Wales, and even by 1865 they had only increased to sixty-nine. But, although a small group they became more disciplined and influential.

There was also the added help of rural deans. 'From being almost totally dormant at the turn of the century, this office was revived in every diocese of the Church of England. By 1865 the Church had at its disposal over six hundred additional disciplinary and investigative officers who played a crucial role in supporting their superiors' efforts to improve their jurisdictions.'[30] The ruridecanal system was further developed in the 1830s and 1840s by the creation of annual diocesan conferences of deans and ruridecanal chapters, so that the decanal clergy had an opportunity to convey their collective views to the bishop. 'The revival of rural deaneries afforded an unparalleled opportunity for making use of those incumbents who were known to be conscientious and reliable, whose services were secured without the necessity of additional expenditure.'[31] They had a flexible role, not defined by law, and they commonly had first-hand knowledge of people and places in their area and could adopt an informal approach which was complementary to the more formal, legally defined, role and function of the bishop and the archdeacon.

Parochial renewal

Concurrent, analogous changes took place at the parochial level. And what was happening was apparent to all with eyes to see. 'No one doubted in 1860, and few will doubt now, that the clergy of 1860 were more zealous than the clergy of 1830, conducted worship more reverently, knew their people better, understood a little more theology, said more prayers, celebrated sacraments more frequently, studied more Bible.'[32] When G.A. Selwyn, the colonial Bishop of New Zealand, returned to England in 1854 after an absence of thirteen years, he spake of 'a great and visible change' in the Church of England since he departed in 1841. 'It is now a very rare thing to see a careless clergyman, a neglected parish or a desecrated church.'[33]

Underlying the changes in parochial ministry in the Victorian period was a process, comparable to that among the bishops, of what may legitimately be called 'professionalization'. This does not mean that clergy before 1837 were untrained, undisciplined, 'amateurs', with no recognized 'professional' standards. A large number could be so described, but many did achieve a certain measure of 'professionalism'. Nonetheless, the attaining of any such standards was more by accident than design, it was accomplished in an unsystematic and haphazard way, and without any national framework to provide uniformity and basic minimums. The movement for the professionalization of various ministries, for the process touched the Nonconformists as well as the Church of England, was part of a general development of 'the professions'.

Perhaps the single most important element in the nineteenth-century professionalization of ministers was the conviction, increasingly shared by the public at large, that they required formal academic instruction and training in order properly to fulfil their vocation. There was considerable variation from one Nonconformist denomination to another as to the degree to which ministerial training of a specific type qualified a recruit for ministry; but within the Church of England there was an increasing conviction that in addition to a direct call from God, the knowledge of God's will and of the scriptures, which was independent of human learning, there was a need for that kind of knowledge which colleges or universities could impart. The demand <u>for more</u> <u>educated, theologically equipped clergy</u> accelerated as the population as a whole became better educated. In particular, a much expanded, more academic, or at least more intellectually aware, middle class considered it necessary that incumbents should be able to offer a reasoned and intelligent ministry. The Church of England, in common with all the Nonconformist denominations, was feeling considerable and increasing pressure during the nineteenth century to try to win over minds and souls in an ever more hostile or indifferent environment. The new or developing sciences with their explicit or implicit questioning of certain Christian dogmas, and the new biblical criticism, put great strains upon the ministry, and called for intellectual ability among the clergy of a higher order than in the past. Then there were the unprecedented problems of population growth, urban development, secular counter-attractions and the spread of democratic ideals. A new style of ministry was imperative in order to meet these challenges.

The need to educate and train a large body of young clergy was heightened by the increase in the number of Anglican clergy in post. In 1834 there were about 13,000; by 1841 this had grown to 14,613; and by 1851 the number had expanded to 17,463.[34] It should be borne in mind that a substantial majority of these ordinands had graduated at one of the ancient universities, and this came closest to providing the clergy as a group with a common background and intellectual baggage.[35] The peak was reached in the 1830s and 1840s when over 80% of new ordinands had attended Oxford or Cambridge; and, although the contribution of the universities subsequently declined, the proportion of Oxbridge men remained high. Anglicans continued to regard a graduate clergy as the norm and the ideal. But the demand rapidly outmatched the supply. 'The universities continued to pour graduates into the Church of England throughout the Victorian period but these graduate ordinands formed a smaller proportion of the clergy than the hierarchy would have wished. Moreover, the church which had attracted graduates of high intellectual quality before 1850 signally failed to do so after that date. The calibre of graduate ordinands plunged particularly dramatically in the 1870s.'[36] Nonetheless, 'three quarters of all ordinands in the late nineteenth century were graduates; a majority of vacant benefices were still filled with graduates'.[37] And the situation remained favourable by comparison with the eighteenth century when Oxbridge had been too small to supply the church with a largely graduate ministry.

But there was a growing crisis. The need for many more well-educated clergy was to a great extent met by additional graduates from Trinity College, Dublin, Durham University, King's College, London and Queen's College, Birmingham, and by the emergence towards the end of the century of new 'civic' universities.

The growing demand within the church for more clergy, and for ordinands to possess specific expertise before acceptance led also to the foundation of theological colleges. Among these St Bees was pre-eminent. It was founded in 1816 particularly for non-graduates. By 1870 nearly three-quarters of all theological college students came from this one college, and even as late as 1890 it had admitted over half of the 5,300 students known to have attended Anglican theological colleges during the century.[38] Among other such colleges were St David's College, Lampeter (1822), St Aidan's, Birkenhead (1846) and St John's, Highbury (1863). The oldest colleges specifically for graduates were Chichester, which was founded by Bishop Otter in 1839, Wells (1840), Cuddesdon (1854), Lichfield (1857) and Salisbury (1860). Lincoln was started in 1874, and two years later Ely, Leeds, and St Stephen's House, Oxford were founded. Towards the end of the century came the Evangelical colleges, Wycliffe Hall, Oxford, and Ridley Hall, Cambridge (1881), and the seminary High Church college Kelham (1891).

Although specific, specialized training was becoming more necessary even as early as the first half of the Victorian era, there was still a place for the outstanding ministry which a not-well-educated clergyman could, and often did, provide, and such ministries were of great importance. There was great scope for local charismatic clergy to dominate local communities, especially in small towns, in a way which was far less possible towards the end of the century when urban areas were larger, and when there was a noticeably greater and more wide-spread 'secularism' and indifference in the population as a whole. 'By 1870 it was becoming clear that the cities needed a new type of parson, theologically and pastorally trained to work in the new urban culture.'[39] This was expressed in the mid-century by J.C. Miller of Birmingham. 'We have a morbid horror of being *vulgar*,' he wrote. 'Our ministers have not been trained for a work among "the common people"; and "the common people" have soon discerned their want of adaptation to their wants and tastes.'[40]

There was also a change in the character of parishes, especially in urban areas. In the late Victorian towns there was not the same merging as in most rural parishes of civil and ecclesiastical government. The new urban parishes were usually just ecclesiastical.

> The parochial system remained in principle, but in practice the parish church was regarded more and more as a private association with its own property, dependent upon its own members and supporters for its continuing life. The 'congregational principle', so long denounced, had made increasing inroads upon parochial life, and the partisan policies of ritualists and evangelicals were to encourage it still further. The urban parish might well have its little commonwealth, as well ordered as a private family, but it achieved it only at the expense of being separate from the general life of the community around it.[41]

This changing character of the Church of England parish churches gave a different role to lay people in general. It is an exaggeration to say that 'lay membership of the Church of England during the mid and late nineteenth century largely ceased to be an involuntary act and became, instead, a voluntary one',[42] for the process of transforming the parish congregation into a 'gathered' people was protracted, and was still not completed in the 1990s, but there was a marked re-definition of 'laymen' in those years. As late as the 1840s there was a general acceptance that every person in a parish, and the parishes covered every portion of land and every person in the country, was, at least for some purposes, a layman or laywoman of a national church, even if some wished to be Nonconformists. By the 1880s that view was severely dented, and it was much less likely that a man would regard himself as a churchman merely because he was born in England, or merely because he had been baptized in the parish church. Although not by then pronounced, such a change of outlook was becoming far more common.

There was also a noticeable change in attitude to women and their place in the life of the church. There was an increasing involvement of women in church life across the whole spectrum of churchmanship. As we have seen in the previous chapter, the greater engagement of women in church work was held to be compatible with a continued stress upon their essentially subordinate role in society as a whole. They were perceived as peculiarly endowed with qualities of devotion and self-sacrifice which found a natural outlet in homemaking and motherhood. The prevailing somewhat paternalistic and condescending male attitude to women ensured that even when given tasks in the church at home and abroad they were normally assigned rather menial and inferior duties. But changes were taking place, and many women broke through such a mould and carved out for themselves more independent and distinctive careers. As pioneers in social work, as deaconesses, as leaders in the Salvation Army, the Church Army and other bodies where they had scope for advancement and outstanding service, and in notable service as missionaries, they made a contribution to the home and overseas work of the Church of England which was remarkable and distinguished.

But to return to the ordained ministry. It will make the changes in the scope, role and function of clergymen clearer if I take a few examples. I will therefore briefly consider the ministries of the High Churchman William Farquhar Hook; the Evangelicals Francis Close and Hugh McNeile in the earlier period and William Pennefather, whose ministry was a few years later; and some of the High Church 'slum priests' who ministered in some of the most notorious ecclesiastical urban 'black spots' during the third quarter of the century. They well illuminate the changing character and the frequent high quality of Victorian parochial work. *Walter*

William Farquhar Hook (1798–1875) became Vicar of Leeds in 1837. His responsibilities were onerous. His parish embraced the whole of Leeds, with a population variously estimated as between 125,000 and 150,000. All the other seventeen churches in the city were chapels of ease of the parish church; and they were poorly attended and without endowment. Hook was devoted to the evangelization and pastoral oversight of the urban poor of Leeds. He laboured day and night in order to achieve these ends, and he sacrificed a third of his income in order to help create new parishes and endow them. He made the parish church itself 'a focus for the style of choral and sacramental worship which became characteristic of Victorian Anglicanism'.[43]

Francis Close (1797–1882) was appointed curate of Holy Trinity, Cheltenham, in 1824, and his ministry in the town continued for thirty-two years. During that time, while the population increased from about 14,000 to over 35,000, almost all the changes in the town were in some way identified with his life and labours. It has been said that throughout this period 'the history of the town . . . was the history of a single clergyman'.[44] He ruled Cheltenham from his pulpit throne to such an extent that the wits described it as 'a Close borough'.[45] *The Times* portrayed him as the 'Pope of Cheltenham, with pontifical prerogatives from which the temporal had not been severed. In the bosom of hundreds and thousands of households his social decrees were accepted without a thought of the possibility of opposition.'[46] This status was achieved as a consequence of the comprehensive discharge of his parochial duties, and as a result of his extensive and intensive involvement in the affairs of the community. He exercised a remarkable influence on all sectors of the population as he fearlessly declared and applied his principles. He undertook a vigorous campaign for scriptural-centred education in the face of considerable opposition; he fought the local magnates and stopped the local races; he was largely responsible for shops being closed on Sundays, and for Sunday trains not running between 1840 and 1846; few meetings if any were held in the town without his permission; he was active in generating charitable relief for the poor; and he enlisted the support of many local people for overseas and home mission work.

In Liverpool Hugh McNeile (1795–1879) exercised a similar influence. This 'big, impetuous, eloquent Irishman'[47] was regarded by Eugene Stock, the historian of the Church Missionary Society, as 'unquestionably the greatest Evangelical preacher and speaker in the Church of England'[48] during the nineteenth century. From the moment he went as curate-in-charge of St Jude's in 1834 he plunged into the government and life of Liverpool. Within a short time his power and authority in municipal life were prodigious. In the debates of the powerful town council and in the appointment of mayors his will was sought and seldom thwarted. Through the force and persuasiveness of his oratory and the magnetism of his character he was listened to, trusted and followed. Although he was frequently unwise in his decisions, and was capable at times of blatant indiscretions, this did not detract from his undoubted and unrivalled influence in the city between 1834 and 1868, when he departed to be Dean of Ripon. He left behind him a city which owed much of its strong Evangelicalism and the shape of its civic institutions to his energetic, and in certain respects brilliant, ministry.

William Pennefather (1816–73) represents the type of comprehensive, vigorous and effective urban parochial life which flourished in various parts of the country in the middle and latter years of the Victorian era, but which was to disappear almost without trace by the second quarter of the following century. His most significant parochial work was undertaken at St Jude's, Mildmay Park, in London from 1864 to 1873. Confronted with an inadequate provision for the education of the very poor and neglected children who abounded on every side, he strenuously sought and found the necessary funds for the erection of a school where elementary instruction was given at a low cost. In the meantime he supervised a soup kitchen for the poor, another kitchen where meals were cooked for the sick, and clubs of various kinds. He also provided facilities for the infirm and aged in a specially constructed building. He ran a wide range of activities for all ages of people, operated a Sunday school which on occasions numbered in excess of one thousand, and organized a very popular annual conference 'to promote personal holiness, brotherly love, and increased interest in the work of the Lord'.[49] Together with his wife he began a work for the training of women. He enlarged the church to accommodate all these varied forms of ministry, and he opened a conference hall in 1870 which could seat 2,500 people, with ancillary classrooms, offices and other amenities. Such was the magnitude of the work that three, and later four, curates were needed. With his eyes on evangelism beyond the confines of his parish he, in conjunction with Cuthbert Bainbridge, invited D.L. Moody to conduct a series of evangelistic meetings in England which, as we will later see, were to be a highlight in nineteenth-century evangelism. But by the time of the visit Pennefather was dead.

A common feature of all these active parish churches was a lively and flourishing Sunday school. The extent to which such an organization contributed to the growth of the adult church has been a matter of debate.[50] It appears that Sunday schools were most effective in producing conversions from among the many young church members whose parents were active in the church, or at least in retaining such youngsters in the church so that they continued to be committed to the church when they became adults; and that they were less effective in reaching out to those who were completely outside the orbit of the church, and whose parents were not churchgoers. There was also the socializing function they performed, either intentionally or as an unintended consequence of what they taught and inculcated. Sunday schools tended to promote conservatism and conformity to the prevailing middle-class norms. They were middle-class organizations helping to train middle-class children in middle-class ways, or, in parallel with this, they 'were the bastion of the respectable working class from which the leadership of popular politics was drawn'.[51] The period 1780–1850 'witnessed the birth of a working-class culture that was deeply rooted in that ethic of education, religion and respectability which was embodied in the Sunday school'.[52]

Another, much neglected and little studied, sphere of activity which was central to the evangelistic work of the Church of England in the 1830s and 1840s was the development of district visitation societies. By the end of the 1820s they were probably quite common features in well-run, mainly Evangelical, parishes alongside cottage meetings, schools and provident societies. They were possibly 'the most characteristic device during the second quarter of the century for extending religious influences to adults outside the Church'.[53] They were more typical in an urban rather than a rural setting, and sometimes grew into large scale enterprises. They acted as a supplement to the traditional piecemeal visiting by conscientious clergy as a result of their attempts totally to cover poor areas. They divided such territories into small and manageable units. For each they provided one or more agents who were most frequently laymen. These would be committed to regular and systematic visitation, recording their results and reporting them to the clergy or a committee. By such means they tried to carry the church to the homes of the uncommitted. They also attempted to relieve or mitigate poverty on the basis of reliable knowledge of individual circumstances; and, most notably, 'to attack poverty at its assumed roots by recreating a capacity for self-help in the poor; and to improve social relationships and reduce class-tension'.[54] It was an ambitious programme and the extent to which it was achieved, albeit on a quite small scale, was impressive.

Examples of lively, innovative, flexible and effective parochial ministry in the period being reviewed could be multiplied. In addition to those I have already considered there were the ministries of Hugh Stowell in Manchester, William Champneys in Whitechapel, London, William Cadman in Southwark, Anthony Thorold in St Giles and St Pancras in London, Edward Bickersteth in Hampstead, and a host of others. In his study of Oldham and Saddleworth up to 1865 Mark Smith comes to the conclusion that far 'from being ineffectual or marginalized, the local churches were extremely vigorous institutions, growing steadily in absolute size, commanding the active support of a substantial minority of the population, and exercising a considerable influence over most of the remainder.'[55] A similar picture of the healthy evangelistic and pastoral life of local churches in various circumstances, including predominantly working-class urban areas, is given by K.D.M.

Snell,[56] Jeffrey Cox,[57] Donald Lewis[58] and Hugh McLeod.[59] Although I think that there was substantial working-class alienation from institutional life I would agree with the conclusion of Mark Smith:

> The cumulative effect of these various studies has been to pose a challenge to the 'pessimistic view' that presented nineteenth-century industrial society as an arena in which struggling churches fought a loosing battle to impose an essentially middle-class religiosity on a working-class culture characterized by mass indifference. Instead, they have drawn attention to the vitality of church life in an urban environment where the predominantly voluntaristic nature of church affiliation seems to have produced a particularly dynamic form of religious culture.[60]

Even in urban areas where there was not a particularly dynamic ministry, or where the local congregations had little impact on the non-churchgoing public, the church exercised a powerful influence simply because it was there. It was certainly the case in thousands of English villages and hamlets in which the dominance of the parish church as a building accurately reflected the central place the church still held in the life of most rural communities. Reforms, and a general climate of opinion, meant that the country clergyman had by the middle of the century become a working parson who was expected to do a job thoroughly and conscientiously. In addition, pluralism and absenteeism were restricted by law. As a consequence of all these factors during the latter half of the nineteenth century the majority of the inhabitants of most villages would attend a Sunday service. As in former days, the rectory was the centre of village life around which everything else revolved. The rector himself, who was the landlord of the glebe farm and the recipient of tithes, usually acquired the status of a country gentleman. In his large and comfortable rectory, with his ample domestic staff, he, along with the squire, ruled the village like a benevolent autocrat. It was a golden age, even if there were signs that the peak had been reached by the end of the century, and certainly by 1918.[61] It is even possible that in the 1880s 'more communicants attended services, more priests were ordained and more churches were built than in any previous decade'.[62]

The pre-eminence of the church as a building and as an institution, and the rector as a social figure of note, was not so apparent in towns and cities, where the church had competitors in the form of Nonconformist chapels and Catholic churches, town halls, museums, factories and warehouses, and the rector did not exercise the same central role as his fellow clergy in the countryside. But the church still held its own. 'Not only in small market towns, such as Ludlow, Warwick or Oakham, or in places like Norwich or Bristol with a great mediaeval past, but in modern industrial cities, such as Birmingham or Leeds, the parish church was a formidable presence. Similarly with the position of the clergy in the social landscape: in most villages the vicar was the most powerful individual, or the most powerful individual next to the squire; in the town the vicar was part of a much larger and more variegated elite, but he still enjoyed a great deal of prestige and influence.'[63]

The 1851 census had revealed the power of Nonconformity, but the Church of England parishes were in many respects retaining their status, standing and influence. 'There remained something about the Church of England that the mushrooming meeting-houses could not rival. In the minds of Methodists, the Church was associated with citizenship and loyalty to the Crown and Englishness – and it gave a reassuring sense of being legal – 'by law established' – which lingered even after full civil rights had been granted to Dissenters. It had a clear appeal to the temperamentally conservative.'[64] And then there were persistent signs that religious practices were widespread among parishioners; such as the reading of the Bible at home, which was not of course confined to Anglicans; the continuing popularity of cottage meetings which extended the influence of Anglican piety in the domestic realm; the unwavering love of the Prayer Book which was remarkably pervasive; the unrivalled popularity of the occasional offices;[65] the undiminished desire of women to be churched after childbirth;[66] the broad appeal of confirmation; the perceived ability of Anglicanism to confer respectability on those associated with it; and the attraction which the church had for women.

In the 'optimist' v. 'pessimist' debate a balance needs to be struck. Recent studies seem to show that an undue pessimism among many historians has created a somewhat distorted picture. Parish ministry was in general in quite a healthy state throughout the whole of the Victorian era, and in many places was flourishing. But the picture was patchy. The Church of England remained distinctly stronger in the south than in the north, and in rural areas compared with urban areas. There were some cities and large towns where Anglicanism was relatively well supported in 1851. These included places such as Bristol or York which had a long history and where nineteenth-century growth had been relatively gradual, or the new resort towns like Brighton and Bath. But in

Liverpool, Manchester, Birmingham, Leeds and Sheffield, and many smaller industrial centres, Anglican attendance was well below the national average. Also, within the cities Anglican attendance patterns were socially highly skewed. In this respect the best figures are provided by the religious censuses of London in 1886–67 and 1902–3. The 1902–3 census showed that the percentage of adults attending an Anglican service on the day of the census rose with each step up the social hierarchy, from 4% in the poorest districts to 22% in the aristocratic West End.[67]

Then, of course, there was that ill-defined and difficult to detect and analyse phenomenon of 'popular religion' which did not manifest itself in any statistics about institutional church life. As I have already indicated, it represented one aspect of English nineteenth-century, and indeed twentieth century, religion which cannot be ignored if a full and true picture is to be drawn. It is therefore a topic which I will be exploring later.

But to return to my illustrations of nineteenth-century parochial life and ministry, I conclude this section by focussing on the High Church 'slum priests' of the mid-Victorian years. I will take three clergymen who exemplify in their characters and ministry the core characteristics, qualities, and perhaps shortcomings of this noble band of High Church clergy.

Charles Lowder (1820–80) was a pioneer, and one of the great figures, in the mid-Victorian High Church attempt to penetrate working-class urban areas both with the message of the gospel as he interpreted it, and the associated activities which accompanied, and were an essential part of, that proclamation.[68] Frustrated in his desire to undertake overseas missionary work, in 1851 he joined the staff of St Barnabas, Pimlico, just as it was rapidly becoming the most notorious of London's ritualistic churches, and when it was experiencing some of the worst and most brutal mob demonstrations. His time there intensified his appreciation of both the possibilities and the difficulties of a ministry among the very poor. In 1855 he was inspired by reading Abelly's life of St Vincent de Paul, the seventeenth-century initiator of French town and country missions. Lowder was the principle founder of a small fraternity of priests called The Society of the Holy Cross, which in its early days consisted of all the staff members of St Barnabas. Its objects, as he wrote later, were:

. . . to deepen and strengthen the spiritual life of the clergy, to defend the faith of the Church, and then, among others, to carry on and aid mission work both at home and abroad. The members of the Society, meeting together as they did for prayer and conference, were deeply impressed with the evils existing in the Church, and saw also, in the remedies adopted by St Vincent de Paul, the hope of lessening them. They all felt that the ordinary parochial equipment of a rector and curate, or perhaps a solitary incumbent, provided for thousands of perishing souls, was most sadly inadequate; that in the presence of such utter destitution, it was simply childish to act as if the Church were recognized as the Mother of the people. She must assume a missionary character.[69]

For the Society mission was not, as in the later and widely-held concept, a few days of special preaching in the parish targeted at non-church people, but the establishment of a permanent Christian missionary presence in areas where there was a mass alienation from the church of the resident population. The members of the Society started a mission-house in an area with 6,000 grossly deprived and poor people in the parish of St George's-in-the-East. They organized daily prayer and frequent preaching, and they gradually attracted a small congregation. A boys' choir was formed and classes were conducted for instruction in the Bible and as preparation for confirmation. In 1856 a temporary 'iron church' was erected in the garden of the mission-house, and in the services eucharistic vestments were used. Opposition to such 'ritualism' was fierce and embittered. From the summer of 1859 there began what became known as the St George's Riots. The disturbances were even more violent, and attracted even greater publicity, than those of St Barnabas, Pimlico, which had occurred nine years earlier. News of what was happening was spread by a full press coverage. More and more people came from far and near to reinforce the attacking mob, to join in the fun, or just to watch the spectacle. Many of those who participated in the protests were sponsored by such bodies as the National Protestant Society and a kindred organization the Anti-Puseyite League. Services were interrupted, with the uproar so great on occasions that it prevented the saying of the Litany or the conduct of worship.

In addition to this harassment, the Mission had been gravely compromised by the defection of two of its priests, and it had survived other serious troubles. Nonetheless, Lowder and his fellow-workers persisted in their labours, and the work progressed. Public interest and sympathy were aroused by the evident dedication of the fraternity, and in particular by the devoted service of Lowder and his staff during the East London cholera epidemic of 1856.

By the time of his death in 1880 Lowder had won the affection and respect of the East End population whom he had lovingly served for almost forty years. He had gained the honourable title of Father Lowder, and he had been the means of bringing a large number of East Londoners to the Christian faith. His funeral in Wapping, as described by Alexander Mackonochie afterwards, was a testimony to the mutual love and high regard which had grown over the years between priest and people:

> It was most striking when compared with twenty-five years since, to see the patient crowd on each side lining the way, many in tears, some audibly praying for the rest of his soul, while a long, slow procession of surpliced clergy and weeping parishioners first met the body at Old Gravel Bridge, conducted it to the church, after service again escorted it to the bridge, and returned at the same slow processional pace to the church. Traffic, of course, was stopped, but all was most reverent and respectable. The scene at Chislehurst [where the internment took place] was equally striking, as we walked across the great common amid throngs of people and stood in the crowded churchyard. Clergy of all schools of thought came to show their respect for the man whom they were obliged to look up to, though they differed from him.[70]

A man of equal calibre to Lowder was Alexander Heriot Mackonochie (1825-87) who became known, affectionately, as Father Mackonochie of St Alban's, Holborn. In 1852 he joined the staff of one of the most dynamic and innovative Anglican Catholic parish priests of the day, W.J. Butler, the Vicar of Wantage. As a fellow-curate he had the brilliant protégé and disciple of Dr E.B. Pusey, Henry Parry Liddon; it was a formidable team. But he hankered after more arduous service under harsher conditions; and he found this in his move to join Lowder at the St George's Mission. It was in 1862 that he was placed in charge of the newly-built church of St Alban's. To the condescending wonder of many observers, it was open to and attracted the poor. 'The bonnetless and the shoeless were in sufficient numbers, and as there were no pew-rents and no appropriations, they were enabled to feel that they had as good a right to their own church as anyone else.'[71]

Mackonochie led a closely-knit clergy team. It was a hand picked, compact body of assault troops whose commitment to service had 'something of the proud, carefree quality of laughter under fire'.[72] Foremost among the young warriors was an early recruit, Arthur Stanton, 'the personification of the St Alban's tradition, with its élan, buoyancy, self-abandonment and devotion'.[73] Stanton remained at St Alban's for more than fifty years, until his death. By then he was one of the most famous priests and preachers in the country, and yet he was still an assistant curate, but content. And he could well have afforded a life of far greater ease, for his father in his lifetime kept him well supplied, and on his death in 1863 left him not a great fortune but enough to make him independent. He was also offered the congenial living of Tetbury in Gloucestershire. But he resolved to give his service to St Alban's, and from the start it was, by agreement, without pay.

St Alban's developed a powerful and elaborate parochial organization which included guilds and associations for men and boys, women and girls; an infant nursery; a choir-school; parochial schools; night-schools for boys and girls; and various other agencies ranging from a blanket-loan fund to a cricket club. From the time of its consecration until 1867 there was steady progress, with large and increasing congregations. The annual total number of communicants rose from about 3,000 to more than 18,000. A significant reinforcement was the arrival in 1869 of a group of Sisters from the Clewer Community who began work under Mackonochie's direction.

For these 'slum priests' ritualism was an authentic expression of their beliefs, and gave visible form to their passion to worship God 'in the beauty of holiness'. They were part of a new generation who rejoiced under the name of Anglo-Catholics. They 'saw themselves as missionaries within the church to bring the implicit catholicity of the church into full light. The means would be the explicit teaching of ritual demonstrably catholic.'[74] The ceremonial at St Alban's was no more elaborate than in several other London churches but it acquired greater notoriety, and this was accompanied by what had become familiar, violent demonstrations, augmented in this case by prolonged, vicious and persistent personal attacks on Mackonochie himself, who became the victim of extended and highly publicized litigation.

The more pronounced forms of High Church ritualism had, by the late 1860s, resulted in animated debate in the Convocation of Canterbury and in Parliament; and the battle lines became more stark and clearly defined with the involvement of the English Church Union and the Church Association, as well as some lesser bodies. Both organizations were predominantly lay. The English Church Union was the High Church body. The Church Association, which championed a quite extreme brand of Protestantism, spent £40,000 between 1868 and 1880 in legal actions against ritualists, which included the prosecution of scores of priests. And Mackonochie was at the top of the list. The concern of the Church Association was not ritualism *per se*, but the whole sacramental system which it represented, and especially the doctrine of the Real Presence. Particular exception was taken to the elevation of the sacrament in the Holy Communion, excessive kneeling during the prayer of consecration, ceremonial use of incense, the mixed chalice and altar lights.

The Church Association hounded Mackonochie for year after year, but in the end the ritualism was not stopped, little was achieved, and Mackonochie himself was a broken man. He died on holiday, in the snow at night on a bare mountain in Scotland, guarded only by his two dogs. His funeral, like that of Charles Lowder, was a testimony to what he had accomplished. The great number who came out of deep respect as he lay in the chapel preparatory to the day of the funeral; the hundreds of bare headed and silent people who lined the way as his hearse passed through Holborn; the packed church for the Requiem and the crowd which was unable to gain admittance; the massive funeral procession, with hundreds of clergy and scores of mourners; and the presence of some who had shown scant sympathy for him during his lifetime, was all a fitting tribute to such a servant of God and friend of the people.

Space does not permit a full account of the dedication, fortitude and service of that company of self-giving Anglican 'slum priests' of whom I have taken but a small sample. They included J. Bell Cox, George Body, C.C. Crafton, Robert Dolling, R.W. Enraught, George Rundle, Arthur Tooth and R.J. Wilson, and others of equal distinction. All of them were High Churchmen, and the underlying impulse behind such sacrificial lives may, in part, be traced to the Oxford Movement.

The Oxford Movement and its aftermath

The Oxford Movement needs to be placed in its historical context.[75] The constitutional revolution between 1828 and 1833 undoubtedly undermined the *ancien régime* in which religion and politics were, to quite a large extent, but two aspects of the same thing.[76] There may have been a drift in this direction in the previous centuries, but the events of these critical years were of crucial importance. A glance across the channel heightened fears at the time that more was to come. It only needed a modicum of appreciation of what was happening on the home front to make it clear that the Church of England needed to change if it was to prosper, or even to survive, but there was a deep-seated conservatism among the Anglican hierarchy which hindered such awareness or willingness to adapt to new circumstances. Confronted with a society which was undergoing radical transformation as a consequence of industrialization and urbanization, and with the pressure from a growing proletariate and a much enlarged middle class for increased religious tolerance, extended franchise, social justice and the abolition of certain long-held and cherished privileges within the establishment, the Church of England, with the exception of a few notable individuals, remained almost totally inflexible and clung tenaciously to its long established rights and entrenched prerogatives. Clerical sympathies were with the Tories, and a long Tory rule had created a bench of bishops of the same hue. When conservative statesmen at the end of the 1820s and in the 1830s were obliged to implement some of the most vociferously demanded reforms their motives and actions were seen by almost all Christian leaders as antipathetic to the established church, and to the cause of Christianity in the country in general.

The Oxford Movement triumvirate of John Keble, Richard Hurrel Froude and John Henry Newman, and the Tractarians as a whole, were foremost in their opposition to what they regarded as the pernicious prevailing spirit of rationalism, liberalism, erastianism and Utilitarianism. 'They portrayed the Bethamite school of philosophers as unfeeling and rational, the Whig aristocracy as insensitive and mercenary. This was the atomised society built on self-interest, laissez-faire and Utilitarianism.'77

Keble's understanding of society was diametrically opposed to that of the political economists. His 'Anglicanism in its social manifestations accorded well with the poetic, pre-industrial, anti-commercialist spirit about which he wrote, spoke, preached and prayed with such intensity, vehemence and commitment. Within its confines, the rich and the poor had their appointed destinies, and destinations. Keble's concern was that Tradition was being replaced by Utilitarianism.'78 He placed great value on order and decency in all spheres of life, political, social and commercial as well as religious. 'The vision which Keble had of the ideal society was hierarchical, authoritatively structured and scrupulously ordered along traditional lines.'79 Order in society made it imperative that men and women should be content with their position and status. He regarded insubordination and rebellion as wicked, and indeed blasphemous. Individual striving should be subordinated to the peace of society and the church. 'In Keble's society the corporateness, homogeneity and totality of things took precedence over all that was individualistic, personal and subjective.'[80] Keble found the contentment of his church congregation far sounder than the discontent encouraged by the social philosophers of the age. He greatly valued a Christian society nurtured by tradition, 'which encouraged that perfect resignation, that humility of character which was conducive to sanctification'.[81] This was in accord with the commonplace assertion of pre-Tractarian Churchmen that there was an inseparable connection between political insubordination or disloyalty and theological heterodoxy.

For Froude the emphasis was similar. But in his case he sought resolutely for the restoration of the church to its perceived mediaeval splendour at the centre of society. He shared with Keble and Newman a hatred of the Whigs and every appearance of liberalism.

Newman regarded Benthamite philosophy as solely concerned with expedients. It was preoccupied with facts which made an instant appeal to the intellect and attempted to turn man into a person of calculus only. The pursuit of truth was seen merely as a syllogistic process. Imagination and feeling were at a discount: logic ruled. Newman made clear his detestation of the way society was inebriated with the attractions of the Utilitarian spirit, and he strenuously opposed liberalism in its various semblances. He was particularly concerned about the liberal Anglicans and all that they represented. Whigs, with their adulation of progress, knowledge, civilization and the march of the mind, wished to rid Christianity of its supernatural element. To Newman there was an unequivocal choice between the liberal way and the dogmatic principle, which alone had strength. In Newman's estimate the liberal Anglicans believed that statements about Christian truth could and should be modified to suit the spirit of the age in which they were made, whereas he believed that the revealed message was given once and for all by God, to be ever more fully comprehended as time went on. For Newman the task of the church was to 'sanctify individuals, spiritualize society and redeem the times. Let her be associated with movements which have mere political ends, the result is always the same. Her life is imperilled.'[82]

Before I briefly chart the course of events of the Oxford Movement in its first phase, and its sequel during the remainder of the century, the whole phenomenon needs also to be placed within a specifically Church of England historical setting. It is important to appreciate that Tractarians were not the sole inheritors of the High Church tradition.[83] By 1833 there were a number of strands of High Churchmanship. In addition to the Hackney Phalanx[84] these included representatives of the eighteenth-century 'High and Drys' such as Godfrey Faussett, and moderate or orthodox churchmen such as C.S. Bird. Then there were the High Churchmen especially identified and labelled as Zs by the Tractarians themselves, prominent among whom were Hugh James Rose, Edward Churton, W.F. Hook, William Palmer of Worcester College, William Sewell, Benjamin Harrison, William Cresley, George Ayliffe Poole and Richard Jelf. All these groups and individuals in propagating their own notions of 'church principles' and 'reformed catholicism' regarded themselves as true heirs of the Catholic tradition. The non-Tractarian High Churchmen were not united in any clearly recognized school or movement, but they tended to be concentrated in London, and their common support or membership of organizations such as the Society for Promoting Christian Knowledge (SPCK), the Society for the Propagation of the Gospel (SPG) and the National Society gave them a sense of identity and relatedness. Of special importance in this respect was the Club of Nobody's Friends, founded in 1800. The elected membership of the Club between 1800 and 1850 fully represented the leadership of the old High Churchmanship, as distinct from those who came to be tagged Tractarians. Indeed, after 1841 the Club became something of a focal point for those Zs who were opposed to what they considered were the excesses of the Oxford Movement. In contrast to the more innovative, progressive nature of the Oxford Movement, the Club had an essentially establishment character, with many of its High Church members being archdeacons, deans and bishops, or, among the laity, lawyers. It strove to retain and enhance the independence, authority and influence of the Church of England.

There is some debate over whether Keble's Assize Sermon on 14 July 1833 signalled the beginning of the Oxford Movement. But it certainly appears to have been a clarion call which was heeded by at least some of the central figures in the succeeding movement, and it encapsulated and made public thoughts which had been agitating many High Churchmen and others for years past. In it Keble expressed the fear that England was wilfully, and to a large extent consciously, rejecting her ancient belief that 'as a Christian nation she is also a part of the Christian Church, and in all her legislation and policy bound by the fundamental rules of that Church'.[85] Keble saw evidence of a British 'apostate mind', in which the nation wished to free itself from religious restraints. Although this was most unfortunately demonstrated in the 1833 church temporalities (Ireland) bill,[86] of more importance was the widespread spirit of religious indifference, a notable increase in perjury and disregard for the sanctity of an oath, and a growing disrespect towards 'the successors of the Apostles', that is, the bishops. It was lamentable that the bishops themselves had little belief in the sacred nature of their own authority. The sermon articulated Keble's alarm at the Erastian principles of subjection to the state. It was intolerable that the state legislature, whose members were not even bound to express their belief in the atonement, had virtually usurped the commission of the Church of England to make ecclesiastical laws in matters wholly or partly spiritual. It was likewise an affront that the Apostolic Church should be regarded and treated as one denomination or sect among many, dependent for any pre-eminence she might still appear to retain merely upon the accident of having at the time a strong party to champion its interests.[87]

Keble had an exalted view of the Anglican Church, seeing it as the representative in England of the whole Church Catholic and Apostolic. The Church of England was in grave danger of being betrayed into the hands of libertines. But even if it succumbed and disappeared, as other churches had done in the past, still the Church Catholic and Apostolic would live on. The gates of hell could not prevail against it. The Churchman has an unfailing, certain hope that victory will finally be complete, universal and eternal.

This magnificent vision of the church, which was shared by the other early Tractarians, 'burst upon the stagnant waters of contemporary Anglicanism with all the dynamic force of something new and surprising'.[88] Eleven days after the sermon the Revd Hugh James Rose met with Richard Hurrell Froude, William Palmer and Arthur Perceval at his rectory at Hadleigh, in an intensive debate on the issues raised by Keble. Although the only apparent results from this gathering were an abortive project to form an association for the defence of the church, an address presented to the Archbishop of Canterbury, signed by 7,000 clergymen, and a Lay Address from 230,000 heads of families, which some would consider no mean achievements, it was important as a prelude to the Oxford Movement.

On 9 September 1833 the first of the Tracts was issued. It made a wider audience aware of the movement and gave it a name. The author

was Newman, and it was entitled *Thoughts on the Ministerial Commission, respectfully addressed to the Clergy.* In a four-page leaflet cost-
ing 1d, in a clear, excellent style which arrested attention at once, he
expressed strongly-held opinions in a mood of intense exuberance and
joyous energy which he never experienced before or afterwards. With
his fellow Tractarians he was on a crusade. They were, he said, 'upholding that primitive Christianity which was delivered for all time by the
early teachers of the Church and which was registered and attested in
the Anglican formularies and by the Anglican divines'.[89] He was concerned to restore an ancient unchanging and unchangeable religion
which he was convinced had well-nigh faded out of the land during the
previous one hundred and fifty years. What he was calling for would, he
asserted, be a second Reformation, but better than the first, for it would
return not to the sixteenth but to the seventeenth century; to the time
and to the teaching of the Caroline Divines. The Whigs had come to do
their worse, bishoprics were being suppressed, church property confis-
cated, and sees would soon receive unsuitable occupants. The church
was in danger. There was no time to be lost.

Other tracts followed. The first few were uncomplicated and brief,
and all were stern appeals to conscience and to reason, challenging and
calculated to startle and even offend or annoy, and with an earnestness
of purpose which was evident to every reader. They taught people to
give less regard to preaching than to the sacraments and services of the
church. They discouraged all that was showy and ostentatious, and
stressed the value of inner and unseen self-discipline, the cultivation of
industry, humility, self-distrust, obedience and, above all else, holiness.
'These, then, were the first public utterances of the Movement as a
whole, and they rang out like pistol shots.'[90]

A campaign had been launched. Newman and his friends proceeded
to promote it. In the summer of 1833 they visited country vicarages dis-
tributing parcels of Tracts; Newman advocated the Tractarian views in
a series of letters to the *Record* newspaper, and by means of his peerless
sermons in the University Church of St Mary of which he was vicar.
Recruits began to be gained, including William Gladstone and Dr
E.B.Pusey. Pusey introduced changes, not merely in that he wrote a tract
which was initialled rather than anonymous, as previously had been the
case, longer, more erudite, weighty and elaborate than the earlier Tracts,
but because of who he was. 'He gave us a position and a name . . . Dr
Pusey was a Professor and a Canon of Christ Church; he had vast
influence in consequence of his deep religious seriousness, the munifi-

cence of his charities, his professorship, his family connections, and his easy relations with the University authorities . . . Dr Pusey was, to use a common expression, a host in himself; he was able to give a name, a form, and a personality to what was without him a sort of mob.'[91]

The first pitched battle with the Liberals was over the election of Dr Renn Dickson Hampden for the Oxford Regius Professorship of Divinity. Dr Hampden was orthodox in that he accepted the doctrines of the Church of England and the Creeds, but he considered that there were 'formularies which may be only the interpretations of doctrine and inferences from scripture of a particular time or set of men; and he was desirous of putting into their proper place the authority of such formularies'.[92] His views may have been misinterpreted and misrepresented, but they outraged not only many Tractarians, but also Evangelicals and 'High and Dry' Churchmen as being an assault on subscription. Dr Hampden was appointed, although convocation resolved that he should be deprived of his vote in the choice of university preachers. The strength of the Tractarians, as shown by this campaign and the votes they managed to command, aroused the indignation of Dr Thomas Arnold, who forthrightly condemned them and all they stood for in an article entitled 'Dr Hampden and the Oxford Malignants', denouncing them as 'formalist, judaizing fanatics who have ever been the peculiar disgrace of the Church of England'.[93]

Opposition soon came from the Evangelicals as well. At first they had been muted in their reaction. There was no serious controversy between the two groups for about three years, and they found common cause in opposition to the removal of subscription to the Thirty-Nine Articles at matriculation, and in the campaign against the appointment of Dr Hampden. More generally, and more fundamentally, the two traditions shared a conviction that the passion for political, social and ecclesiastical reform could be viewed as an assault on the church, that it signalled a battle between the church and the state, and that Christians as a whole needed to meet the challenge in institutional terms. Evangelicals appreciated the zeal of the Tractarians, and it was not clear in the early formative years of the movement that sacramentalism, and all that flowed from high sacramental teaching, might cause division, especially as the Evangelicals had been instrumental in re-awakening Churchmen to the importance of frequent communion. But it was the common pursuit of holiness which most strongly bound Evangelicals and Tractarians. Even when Evangelicals had developed a profound distaste for Tractarian principles and teaching they retained a deep appreciation of the religious poetry of Keble, and they continued to greatly admire the sermons of Newman.

So much has been written on the Oxford Movement, and such great attention has been paid to an analysis of it that I will confine myself to a mere sketch of the main events.[94] A stir was caused in 1838 with the publication of Tract 80 on *Reserve in Religious Teaching*, and more especially by the appearance of the first two volumes of Froude's *Remains*. Not only Evangelicals but a wide spectrum of Churchmen were gravely shocked by the latter work. The issuing of the book for general circulation was a major and disastrous indiscretion, not only because it revealed much of the private reflections and self-examination of a devout man who expressed himself with utter frankness, but because it set forth Froude's slashing and devastating criticisms of the leaders of the English sixteenth-century Reformation. It was traumatic in an age in which faithfulness to the Reformation was a widely held norm in society to learn that an English clergyman, a Fellow and Tutor of an Oxford college, could declare – 'I am becoming less and less a loyal son of the Reformation',[95] and, 'Really, I hate the Reformation and the Reformers more and more',[96] or again, and perhaps most vehemently of all, 'The Reformation was a limb badly set; it must be broken again to be righted.'[97] In Oxford the Martyrs Memorial was erected as a declaration of loyalty to the Reformation and in order to embarrass the Tractarians.

Within the movement there was a visible bifurcation, with one part looking to antiquity and to the Caroline Divines, and the other to Rome. It was accompanied by a perceptible erosion of Newman's confidence and belief in the Church of England, first in 1839 as a result of his study of the Monophysite controversy,[98] and then as a consequence of an examination of the Donatists.[99] Both made him wonder if Rome had been right after all. But he persisted in his belief that the Church of England was part of the Catholic Church, with its roots in antiquity, and in 1841 he set out to prove this in the fateful Tract 90. This was made the more necessary by the very marked Romeward tendencies of such able men within the movement as Frederick Faber, J.D. Dalgairns, Frederick Oakeley, J.R. Bloxam and W.G. Ward. Tract 90 was written to assure the Romanisers, and incidently Newman himself, that it was possible to hold all Catholic doctrine while assenting to the Articles. Its effect was immediate, widespread, violent and decisive. It set the whole university and much of the country ablaze with heated debate and forthright condemnation.

Events were moving towards a climax. In September 1843 Newman took leave as it were of the Church of England with his Littlemore sermon on the Parting of Friends. In 1844 fuel was added to an already raging fire with the publication of W.G. Ward's *The Ideal of a Christian Church*, with its sting in the claim by the author that he could keep his place in the English Church while holding and teaching Roman doctrine. Then on a wet and windy evening on 8 October 1845, a remarkable-looking man, Father Dominic Barberi, shabbily dressed in black, made his way to Littlemore, and the following day received Newman into the Roman Catholic Church.

The blow had fallen and Newman was gone. But the movement did not end. Under the leadership of Pusey, Keble, R.W. Church, Charles Marriott and J.B. Mozley it continued and widened its geographical spread. Some even seemed to regard the departure of Newman as a liberation as it helped to free the movement of its Romish influences and allowed it to spread beyond the confines of Oxford. Between 1845 and the end of the Victorian era it was to manifest itself in various ways. There was the revival of religious communities, with such foundations as the Sisterhood of Mercy at Albany Street in London, established in 1844; the Sisterhood of Mercy in Devonport and Plymouth, started in 1848; the Community of St Thomas the Martyr in Oxford, begun in 1847; and, the following year, the Sisterhood of St Mary the Virgin, Wantage, under the guidance of the vicar of the town, W.J. Butler. During the last half of the century the number of communities multiplied, with a total perhaps in excess of thirty within seventy years of the start of the Oxford Movement. Although communities for men emerged more slowly they included such distinguished bodies as the Society of St John the Evangelist in Oxford, the Society of the Sacred Mission begun by Father H.H. Kelly, which moved to Kelham in 1903, and the Community of the Resurrection founded by Charles Gore in 1892, which moved to Mirfield in Yorkshire in 1898. Such a number and range of societies, and all they achieved over the years, is a remarkable indication of the Oxford Movement's prolonged vitality and ability to evoke a response of dedication and commitment.[100] Then there was the development of a distinctive form of architecture and ceremonial. Of particular note in this sphere was the pioneer work of John Mason Neale. By means of a magazine, *The Ecclesiologist*, founded in 1841 in his undergraduate days, he 'succeeded in stimulating an avid, informed and deepening interest in church architecture as the setting for traditional Catholic worship and thus stimulated the liturgical and ceremonial revival of the Anglican church of the later nineteenth century'. [101] He founded the Ecclesiological Society, and almost all the neo-Gothic churches of the latter half of the century were built under its impetus and inspiration. Neale was also a hymnologist and liturgiologist of some distinction, and an historian of the Eastern and Western churches. He maintained the Tractarian tradition in his outpouring of hymns, which included 'Jerusalem the Golden', 'For thee, O dear, dear country', and two more, 'Art thou weary, art thou languid?' and 'O happy band of pilgrims' which, although based on Greek originals, were in effect his own original compositions.

Although the work of the slum priests owed much to the Oxford Movement the associated ritualism was not an obvious child of the Tractarians. Ceremonial had been of little concern to them, and despite their sacramentalism they were not ritualists. Pusey deprecated any attempt to restore the richer style of vestments used in Edward VI's reign as likely to minister to vanity. Newman also attached minor importance to 'externals'.

Lastly, in tracing elements of continuity and change in the post-Oxford Movement High Churchmanship, I must introduce the most dominant High Churchman since the Tractarians were at the centre of the stage, Charles Gore, and the development of Liberal Catholicism of which he was the main architect. A man of superlative intellect he played a leading part in the Church of England in general as well as within the High Church fold as the first Principal of Pusey House in Oxford, as Bishop of Worcester from 1901 to 1904, then Bishop of Birmingham from 1904 to 1911, and finally as Bishop of Oxford from 1911 to 1919. [102] In his life and ministry up to 1901, the end of the period at present under review, two particularly momentous initiatives attract our attention. There was first of all his editorship of that epoch-making publication *Lux Mundi*, in 1889. It encapsulated the new 'liberal' teaching which the writers, and in particular Gore, thought was demanded in order to be true heirs of the Tractarians. They felt 'compelled for their own sake, no less than that of others, to attempt to put the Catholic faith into its right relation to modern intellectual and moral problems.' They wrote not as 'guessers at truth', but 'as servants of the Catholic Creed and Church'. But they were also convinced that they lived in an epoch of 'profound transformation, intellectual and social, abounding in new needs, new points of view, new questions; and certain therefore to involve great changes in the outlying departments of theology, where it linked on to other sciences, and to necessitate some general restatement of its claim and meaning'.[103]

The most controversial of the essays in *Lux Mundi* was the one by Gore himself; and within that the particularly contentious part was where he expounded his kenotic view of the 'self-emptying' of God. Gore insisted that Christ revealed God 'but through, and under conditions of, a true human nature. Thus He used human nature, its relation to God, its conditions of experience, its growth in knowledge, its limitation of knowledge . . . He shows no signs at all of transcending the science of His age. Equally He shows no signs of transcending the history of His age. He does not reveal His eternity by statements as to what happened in the past, or was to happen in the future, outside the ken of existing history.' Such a view was typical of the Liberal Catholicism championed by Gore, which he considered was precisely embodied in the Anglican appeal to scripture, antiquity and reason, but which to his detractors was anathema.

The second outstanding initiative in the latter part of the century was the founding by Gore, Henry Scott Holland and Brooke Foss Westcott of the Christian Social Union in the same year as *Lux Mundi*, 1889. It was a demonstration of Gore's concern to apply his Liberal Catholicism to the world of the needy, the poor and the deprived. The same impulse led other latter day High Church Christian Socialists to found similar bodies such as the Guild of St Matthew, established by Stewart Headlam in 1877.[104]

The Evangelicals

Turning to the Evangelicals, I will consider their activities and impact on society in the areas of revivalism, evangelism, renewal movements, social action, and controversy.[105]

Revivalism may be distinguished from evangelism, although it is sometimes difficult to determine when the one merges into the other. With revivalism there is a sudden, spontaneous, dramatic and sustained increase in the extent and intensity of the commitment of a number of individuals in a particular area to the beliefs and practices of their faith, with an accompanying renewed sense of fellowship with fellow believers and a corporate awareness of new energy and vibrancy, an increased concern for the conversion of outsiders and 'nominal' members of the religious tradition, and a marked increase in the number of such conversions. In the Christian tradition there may also be associated phenomena such as glossolalia (speaking in tongues) and bodily manifestations of intense mental, emotional and religious experience. Somewhat in contrast, evangelistic campaigns, however successful they may be, are usually pre-planned, and consist of organized activities. There is less of the spontaneous upsurge of religious renewal, revitalization, and the sudden increase in conversions, which are the central features of revivalism.

In the period 1833 to 1901 the Church of England experienced both revivalism and effective evangelism. The foremost revival was in the period 1857 to 1860. During those years there were revivals in Hamilton, Ontario, Canada, in New York and then in various parts of North America, in Ulster, Scotland and Wales.[106]

Although it has been argued that the revival at this time in England was of such major proportions that it can with justification be called a second evangelical awakening,[107] it is difficult to sustain such a case. There were a great number of prayer meetings for revival, and a spate of evangelistic activity, but it is difficult to find even isolated instances, let alone a general movement, which can compare with what was happening in other countries at the time, or with the revival in England in the eighteenth century.

When it comes to evangelism, there is more to tell. As we have already noted, High Churchmen in various ways, but especially with their parish missions, were concerned about, and actively involved in evangelism: evangelism was not a monopoly of the Evangelicals, but it was central to their outlook and activities. But even in that sphere they, like the High Churchmen, showed a decided preference for parish-based activity. The three American revivalists and evangelists who made the greatest impression in visits to England between 1800 and 1860, Lorenzo Dow, James Caughey and Charles Grandison Finney, received their greatest support from Nonconformists. The Evangelicals were fearful that revivalism and inter-denominational or non-denominational evangelism might be used in an effort to subvert the Anglican establishment. Finney's first preaching tour in Britain in 1849 was totally ignored by the *Christian Observer* and the *Record* in spite of a protracted campaign in London; and the *Record* was once more noticeably silent about Finney's second tour in 1858-60. The *Record* commended the prayer meetings organised by the Evangelical Alliance during the time of the 1858-60 revivals, but it was not wholehearted in its advocacy of the revival. The *Christian Observer* was more consistently in favour, but it only reached a certain segment of Evangelicalism.

The link between mid-nineteenth century revivalism and such later developments as the Keswick movement is a matter of debate.[108] From the 1820s onwards 'a small but important Holiness Movement developed on the outskirts of nineteenth-century Protestantism'.[109] It emanated from North America and was associated with James Caughey, Phoebe Palmer (and her husband), Robert Pearsall Smith (and his wife) and Asa Mahan. At the core of the holiness teaching was a 'second conversion' theory. There was a repudiation of the common notion that holiness resulted only from a process of gradual change. A post-conversion experience was advocated, with a sudden and instantaneous granting by God of complete victory over all consciousness of sin. Pearsall Smith undertook a tour of southern England and continental Europe in 1873 in which he proclaimed the holiness teaching at conferences and consecration meetings. He attracted considerable support, most notably from Evan Hopkins, the Revd E.W. Moore and Sholto Douglas. Evangelicals were divided. The doctrine of immediate holiness was not acceptable to many of them. The annual Keswick convention in the Lake District was started in 1874. It not only promoted the holiness teaching but also resulted in many people offering themselves for Christian service at home and abroad. As we will see in chapter 10 its foundation coincided with a remarkable missionary advance in Africa and Asia in particular, and the Church Missionary Society was especially indebted to the challenge to Christian service offered by the convention.

At the same time that the Keswick convention was profoundly assisting the work of the church, a movement was taking place in the student world which made its own incalculable contribution.[110] It started in 1827 when five student members of Holy Trinity, Cambridge, established a Sunday school in a hall in Jesus Lane. This not only served the children and families of the area, but it proved to be an influential training-ground for many ordinands, schoolmasters and lay leaders. The Sunday school helpers in effect formed a small Christian union in the University. Out of this in 1862 arose the Daily Prayer Meeting; and in 1878 the Cambridge Inter-Collegiate Christian Union was founded. An Oxford Prayer Union was started in 1850, and a Daily Prayer Meeting in 1867. The Oxford Inter-Collegiate Christian Union was inaugurated in 1879. In 1892 Robert Wilder, one of the leaders of the American Student Volunteer Missionary Union which had been formed as a consequence of the D.L. Moody campaigns, came to England and initiated a Cambridge Student Volunteer Missionary Union. Later in the same year representatives from Oxford, Cambridge, London, Belfast and the Scottish universities met in Edinburgh to inaugurate the Student Volunteer Missionary Union of Great Britain and Ireland, with its primary aim of inspiring students to offer themselves for missionary service. By the following year it had 491 members, of whom 25 had sailed, 13 had been accepted for missionary service abroad and 46 belonged to missionary institutions. The first student conference was held at Keswick in 1893, during the week before the main convention began, and there the title Inter-University Christian Union was adopted. The following year, again at Keswick, the American watchword 'the evangelization of the world in this generation' was taken as a rallying call to service. It was a buoyant time of high hopes and ideals; and the whole movement was invigorated, led and supported largely by Anglican Evangelicals.

A major contribution to this whole late nineteenth-century evangelistic and missionary climate of opinion was made by the campaign of Dwight L. Moody in the years 1873 to 1875.[111] It was the most remarkable example of mass evangelism in England in the nineteenth century. But it began haphazardly, with little initial support from Anglicans, except for the invitation originally offered by William Pennefather. After campaigns in York, Newcastle, Edinburgh, Dundee, Glasgow, Belfast, Dublin, Manchester, Sheffield, Birmingham and Liverpool, after which he had become extremely well known, he arrived in London in March 1875 and commenced a series of meetings in the Agricultural Hall. In addition he preached at evangelistic services at Bow Common and at the Queen's Opera House in the Haymarket. The attendance figures were unprecedented for nightly evangelistic meetings in Victorian England, and were regarded at the time as fantastic. Moody was probably seen and heard by at least a million and a half people in London in 1875. Although he returned to the United Kingdom in 1881, the meetings in Scotland, Wales and certain English provincial towns were less spectacular than in the former visit; but it was those held in Cambridge which produced the most sensational and lasting results for the church worldwide. At first he was mocked and derided by the students, but he soon won their attention and deep respect, and at the conclusion a host of undergraduates responded to the appeal, which was customarily given at these events, and they included some of the finest Christian missionaries and church leaders of the nineteenth century.

One feature of evangelistic campaigns such as those of Moody was the use of secular buildings for evangelistic purposes; and the nineteenth century witnessed a small-scale adoption of this practice by the Church of England. This was especially so after the 1855 Religious Worship Act, the passing of which was largely due to the efforts of Lord Shaftesbury. It allowed the holding of services in unconsecrated buildings; and two years later twelve evening services were held in Exeter Hall, London, arranged by a committee under the chairmanship of Lord Shaftesbury. He wrote in ecstatic terms about the new venture:

> Last Sunday (May 24th) a glorious triumph for religion and the Church of England. Blessed be God! a splendid proof of the use and value of the Religious Worship Act passed two years ago! Under the powers of this Act, in Exeter Hall, an evening service was conducted by the Bishop of Carlisle in full canonicals, for the benefit of all-comers who were 'not habitual church or chapel goers' – such was the advertisement. An attendance of more than three thousand – order, decency, attention, and even devotion. They sang well and lustily and repeated the responses with regularity and earnestness. Villiers preached the sermon on 'What saith the Scripture?' practical, pious, affectionate, true; delivered with dignity and power, and deeply impressive.[112]

After great effort and difficulty arrangements were made for St Paul's and Westminster Abbey to be opened for evening services. It was an innovation to use cathedral naves for such services. The first one was on Advent Sunday 1856, and the overflowing congregations persuaded the Dean and Chapter to continue them indefinitely. Of particular note was the preaching of the High Churchman Henry Parry Liddon.

In 1860 a further evangelistic effort was made when theatre services were started. These attracted a different stratum of the population from either St Paul's or Exeter Hall. Men and boys came to them in their shirt-sleeves, women without bonnets and with babies. The outcry was loud and impassioned against what many regarded as a travesty of religious worship; and even some Evangelicals disliked the novelty.

Despite such imaginative attempts at evangelistic outreach, Anglican Evangelical evangelistic energy was largely focussed in the parishes. I have already illustrated this with brief accounts of various Evangelical ministries, and they have touched on a range of parochial activities; but there is one extra Evangelical initiative which deserves a mention: the employment of women as full-time evangelists. The churches as a whole, with some notable exceptions, for instance the Methodists, tended to discourage preaching by women, but this did not restrain some of those who were determined to pursue what they considered their God-given ministry. 'In the mid-nineteenth century there were on both sides of the Atlantic some women . . . who did not lose their faith in the face of criticism, but worked even more actively either within their own regular churches . . . or within the expanding framework of non-denominational evangelical piety.'[113] The popularity of women preachers in the 1860s was a result in part of the impact of the 1859 revival and the Holiness Movement, but it appears that some Evangelicals were moving towards supporting broader ministry roles for women well before that. [114] The Church Pastoral-Aid Society had pioneered the employment of lay men and women as early as the 1830s as part of its total aim to provide funding and support for parochial clergy. Women helpers were also enlisted in many of the parochial organizations and activities and in the bewildering array of phil- anthropic societies which were a feature of Victorian Anglicanism.[115]

The Church Army was an important auxiliary to the ordinary parochial ministry. It was the Church of England counterpart to the non-denominational Salvation Army.[116] William and Catherine Booth were originally Methodists, but William left that denomination when the Methodist Conference of 1861 refused to sanction certain of his schemes, and he forged ahead on his own. In establishing the Salvation Army he was concerned to weld together a band of Christians who would be devoted to evangelism and the service of the poor and needy in urban areas of deprivation. He asked of his followers that they should believe in the possibility of instantaneous conversion, even for the most degraded; that they should have courage; and that they should, like the members of the military army, accept absolute obedience. In all their activities they were to display that simplicity, directness and commit- ment which were the hallmarks of their founder and leader. The Army met with much abuse, verbal and physical attacks, misunderstanding and discouragement, but its members persisted in their efforts and service, and in many poverty stricken and degenerate environments they achieved countless remarkable 'victories'. Although there have been trenchant criticisms of Booth and of the Salvation Army, and it has been said that there was 'tension between its revivalist and social missions',[117] its achievements in the first forty years of its life, and indeed sub- sequently, were staggering in their extent, range and quality.

In 1881 Evan Hopkins began a similar work in his own parish of Holy Trinity, Richmond, with a band which he termed the Church

Gospel Army. It had military rules and membership cards, the men wore a red cord in their button-holes, Sunday began with a drill at seven, and on Sunday evenings a band and army banner would lead a procession to the mission hall for a mission-type service with testimony, prayer and choruses, followed by the increasingly familiar after-meeting. Similar organizations were started independently in other parishes. It was Wilson Carlile who, in 1882, began to bring together these various local parish armies into one large Church Army.[118] Despite critics from within the Church of England, including Evangelicals, who were especially anxious about some of its methods, by 1891 there were 166 officer-evangelists and 44 mission nurses, and about 40,000 meetings were held each year. Towards the end of the century both the Salvation Army and the Church Army introduced similar schemes for relieving social distress. These included Labour Homes, which were communities providing food, shelter and employment for the very poor. Church Army sisters were recruited in 1887 to work mainly with destitute girls. Other enterprises included market gardens and coffee houses, sales-rooms for the sale of clothing to poor families at minimal prices on the presentation of chits from their vicar, and help to discharged prisoners.

These two Armies were illustrative of not insignificant social action by Evangelicals throughout the Victorian age. And in this Lord Shaftesbury was by far the most prominent, active and distinguished Evangelical involved. Many of the nationwide campaigns were linked with him. It was in 1833 that he became engaged in factory reform, and entered upon a crusade which was to last a lifetime. He took on the mantle of Michael Sadler as the representative in Parliament of the Ten Hours Movement. He had to face relentless, fierce and yet subtle opposition, especially from factory owners, but he and the other campaigners were finally rewarded with legislation in 1874 and 1878 which consolidated the previous measures. He also strove hard and long in an effort to improve the lot of those who were labelled as lunatics, and more generally in an attempt to promote better public health. He successfully introduced a Bill in 1845 which established a Lunacy Commission responsible to the Lord Chancellor, and he concurrently steered a Bill through Parliament which made it obligatory for Justices of the Peace of a county or borough to make provision for asylums if they had not already done so. Throughout the rest of his life he tried to ensure that the measures were effectively implemented, and for many years acted as the Chairman of the Commission. He also vigorously took up the cause of ragged schools for poor and destitute children. He chaired the London Ragged School Union, gained first-hand knowledge of the situation by personal visits to slum areas, and helped to found ragged schools. In addition, he took a lively interest in such associated activities as refuges and dormitories for needy children, and an emigration scheme for children. All of this only hints at the range of his involvement in causes for the well-being of others, for there were many more to which he devoted countless time and effort.

'Most of the great philanthropic movements of the century have sprung from the Evangelicals.'[119] he declared almost at the end of his life, in 1884, and he was right. What they attempted and what they achieved was massive and significant, and much of it went unsung in the active social programmes of countless Evangelical churches. Evangelicals have been accused of lacking any social policy, and of accepting the prevailing class structure; for being concerned with palliatives rather than with radical social change.[120] There is some truth in this. The essential conservatism of Shaftesbury and other Evangelicals is undeniable. They largely accepted the *status quo* and performed their good works with little questioning of the social framework which, arguably, helped to produce the very problems requiring attention. They were pragmatists rather than theorists. Where they did theorize it was in order to defend the existing order in its essentials; and they deprecated any radical change. But it is perhaps harsh to condemn them for being children of their time. In many ways, as we have seen, they were in the van of change, and they advocated reforms which flew in the face of the real conservatives in society.

The Church of England Evangelicals were also conservative in their reluctance to co-operate with Nonconformists in social action; and in adopting such a stance they reflected the attitude of the Church of England in general for there was considerable tension between the Church of England and Nonconformity throughout the post-1832 nineteenth century. There were longstanding issues on which they disagreed, such as church government, the relationship of the churches, and of the Church of England in particular, with the state, and various theological matters; they had differential privileges, different class structures and different attitudes on social matters. In addition, they were by then in greater competition because the legislation of 1828 to 1832 had raised the status and standing of Nonconformity and thus made it a much more viable and forceful alternative to Anglicanism. Co-operation between Evangelicals and Nonconformists was not entirely prevented. There was, for example, in the twenty years after the Reform Act of

1832, what might be termed negative Evangelical co-operation when they joined forces with evangelical Nonconformists in common opposition to Tractarianism, the Government grant to the Roman Catholic Maynooth College and the mid-century Papal Aggression (the last two of which I will describe and discuss in the next chapter). There was also some positive co-operation, most notably in urban evangelism. 'The catholicity of the lay and clerical supporters of the London City Mission represents an aspect of Victorian evangelicalism that is often ignored by historians and demonstrates a liberality of spirit rare to that age.'[121]

But despite this measure of co-operation there was a reluctance to join with Nonconformists in pan-evangelical activity. This was demonstrated in the attitude of Church of England Evangelicals to the foremost nineteenth-century attempt at evangelical unity and co-operation, the Evangelical Alliance.[122] Founded in 1846, this body gave expression to the strong currents flowing in favour of pan-evangelicalism, but it also helped to reveal the extent of Anglican Evangelical resistance to such a trend. The majority of Evangelicals stood stiffly aloof.[123] Very severe things were said in the *Christian Observer* about those who were willing 'to fraternize with Anabaptists'.

And it was on this matter of baptism that one Evangelical in particular was drawn into a controversy which shook the Church of England. Although the Evangelicals were paedobaptists, supporting the baptism of children rather than restricting baptism to adults who were able to profess belief for themselves, they were not prepared to place the same emphasis on the operational significance of the rite which some other churchmen did. The issue came to a head when George Cornelius Gorham found himself in conflict with his bishop on this point in one of the most highly publicized church events of the century, while other Evangelicals, and High Churchmen as well, watched from the wings with bated breath.

Gorham was the Evangelical vicar of St Just with Penwith in Cornwall. He was determined to resist Tractarianism, and in 1846 incurred the displeasure of his bishop, Phillpotts, by advertising for a curate who should be 'free from Tractarian error'. When Gorham applied for transfer to another living two years later Phillpotts took the opportunity to examine him intensely and at very considerable length on his beliefs regarding baptismal regeneration, and declared his doctrine to be unsound. He declined to institute him to his new living.

Gorham asked the Court of Arches to compel the bishop to institute him. Over a year later the Court pronounced that though the meaning of regeneration was imprecise the infant was regenerated at baptism. Gorham, the Court concluded, had maintained a doctrine contrary to that taught by the Church of England, the bishop had shown sufficient reason for his refusal, and the case must be dismissed with costs to the bishop. To many Evangelicals the decision, if upheld, was catastrophic. Gorham appealed to the judicial committee of the Privy Council, and on 9 March 1850 it delivered judgment. Not satisfied that he had contradicted the formularies of the Church of England, Gorham was allowed to continue as an Anglican priest.

For many churchmen the primary question in this whole affair was not whether Gorham was a heretic, or whether the Evangelical repudiation of baptismal regeneration excluded them from the Church of England; it was what authority possessed the right to determine whether Gorham was a heretic or not. Had the patron, whoever he be, the right to present whomsoever he liked without regard to objections from the relevant authority of the church? To what extent should ecclesiastical affairs be influenced or determined by a secular power? What were the limits of the power and authority of individual bishops? The Gorham case raised, but did not answer, these and other major questions about Anglican belief and practice.

The Liberals

To Newman and a host of others liberalism consisted essentially of the anti-dogmatic principle. He and others of the same cast of mind particularly denounced and abjured the following principles, which they asserted lay at the heart of the liberal approach to matters of dogma and faith:

1. No religious tenet is important, unless reason shows it to be so.
2. No one can believe what he does not understand.
3. No theological doctrine is any thing more than an opinion which happens to be held by bodies of men.
4. It is dishonest in a man to make an act of faith in what he has not had brought home to him by actual proof.
5. It is immoral in a man to believe more than he can spontaneously receive as being congenial to his moral and mental nature.
6. No revealed doctrines or precepts may reasonably stand in the way of scientific conclusions.

7. Christianity is necessarily modified by the growth of civilization, and the exigencies of times.
8. There is a system of religion more simply true than Christianity as it has ever been received.
9. There is a right of Private Judgment: that is, there is no existing authority on earth competent to interfere with the liberty of individuals in reasoning and judging for themselves about the Bible and its contents, as they severally please.
10. There are rights of conscience such, that every one may lawfully advance a claim to profess and teach what is false and wrong in matters, religious, social, and moral, provided that to his private conscience it seems absolutely true and right.
11. There is no such thing as a national or state conscience.
12. The civil power has no positive duty, in a normal state of things, to maintain religious truth.
13. Utility and experience are the measure of political duty.
14. The Civil Power may dispose of church property without sacrilege.
15. The Civil Power has the right of ecclesiastical jurisdiction and administration.
16. It is lawful to rise in arms against legitimate princes.
17. The people are the legitimate source of power.
18. Virtue is the child of knowledge, and vice of ignorance.[124]

This of course embraces political and social as well as theological liberalism, and any one individual or group at the time or throughout the rest of the nineteenth century may have identified themselves with some of these tenets and not others, and even in the case of the specifically religious ones religious liberals may have at least qualified what Newman attributed to them; and indeed some may have repudiated much of what he enumerated as their salient convictions. But Newman was an intelligent, well informed, observant person, deeply involved in the religious affairs of his day, and his list of characteristics is most illuminating. It captures the essential qualities of Victorian religious liberalism as perceived by its often hostile critics.

Liberalism attained prominence in the public arena of the Church of England at four nodal points: with the publication of Thomas Arnold's *Principles of Church Reform*, in 1833; with the appearance in quick succession of Charles Darwin's *The Origin of Species* in 1859, *Essays and Reviews* in 1860, and William Colenso's *Commentary on the*

Epistle to the Romans and Part 1 of his *Pentateuch and Book of Joshua Critically Examined*, both in 1862; and, finally, with the publication of *Lux Mundi*, edited by Charles Gore, in 1889. I have already considered the last three, so I will confine myself to a brief comment on the first.

Arnold's was not a major or particularly erudite work, but it had considerable impact partly because of the character and reputation of its author, partly because of its timing, and partly because of its teaching. Arnold was widely respected, and his status and standing in educational matters was outstanding. His pamphlet was also issued in the wake of the 1828 to 1832 reforms which had so shaken the Church of England, and which had raised fundamental questions about the privileges and place in society of the established church. Arnold attempted to address the new situation in which religious pluralism was an evident fact of life, and he set forth a vision of an inclusive national church which would embrace the widest possible range of Christian people, and even non-Christians. In his new order Erastianism seemed to rule supreme, for he advocated the use of church property for such public purposes as the provision of schools, hospitals and almshouses, and such an integration of church and state that the distinctive independence and role of the church would be severely undermined and compromised.

What Arnold declared contained elements of what was typical of the varied manifestations of religious liberalism during the remainder of the century. Common to all the forms which it took was a concern to be free from bigotry and to welcome new ideas. Many of the liberals added a determination not to be bound by any dogma or presupposition, and in its more extreme forms some strands of liberalism adopted a humanitarian, anthropocentric reconstruction of the Christian faith which almost eliminated all distinctive Christian doctrinal elements. Other liberals, such as Charles Gore, managed to be open to new intellectual developments and to engage in dialogue while retaining thoroughly orthodox Christian dogmatic convictions.

The Church of England at the beginning of the twentieth century

The religious scene in England at the beginning of the twentieth century was a cause of great concern for Protestants and Roman Catholics alike. For a combination of reasons, and we have indicated some in this and the former chapter, England was far less formally and overtly religious than in 1833, whatever yardstick is taken. It was alarming for the churches to be confronted by unfamiliar blatant and openly declared agnosticism and atheism. But indifference to them as Christian institutions was perhaps more concerning and hurtful, and certainly more widespread. There had developed 'a widespread "diffusive Christianity", a vague religiousness, clearly derived from orthodox Christianity but lukewarm towards, and but loosely attached to, *any* regular religious practice or institution'.[125] Perhaps the Church of England was least affected by this marginal, nominal, religious allegiance and lack of religious involvement, as it was the religious tradition more than any other in which participation and commitment could most easily be minimal, and in which anonymity could most readily be preserved: it was an inclusive, territorial church rather than an exclusive, congregational church. But the crisis was nonetheless severe.

The last twenty years of the dying century witnessed the first clear signs of the collapse of the Victorian middle-class religious consensus. No longer was the denial of hell or the espousal of heterodox theological opinions almost bound to prove controversial. It was a time when secular recreational and leisure activity mushroomed and assumed such importance that it became a major, if not the most significant, challenge to religious practice. Quite rapidly previously emotive ecclesiological matters, such as the confrontation of church and chapel, establishment and dissent, ceased to have their former relevance in helping to shape local and national politics:

> the 1880s do, indeed, take on the appearance of a significant watershed in the history of religion in modern Britain. Where once they had been central to the life of Victorian Britain, religious issues and controversies were, by the last two decades of the nineteenth century, well on their way towards a new location somewhere nearer to the periphery of national life. It was a new location in which for the most part – odd flurries of atypical twentieth century interest apart – they have continued to reside.[126]

The death of Archbishop Tait in 1882 seemed to symbolize and coincide with the end of an era.

Tait's death marked the end of a generation in Church and State. Dean Stanley, Disraeli and Edward Miall died in 1881, Pusey before Tait in 1882; Shaftesbury who died in 1885 knew that he had lived beyond his age; Gladstone was revered as a figure from the past before he died in 1898. Their generation had not been just one in a continuing story. It was the last age in which bishops and the leaders of schools of thought within the Church were figures of national importance. It marked the last serious attempt to make the Church of England the Church of the English. The heights of the Church of England's mid-Victorian strength and security sloped away to inconsequential lowlands.[127] *(pT Marsh*

The diminishing passion to stand up for the rights and privileges of the Church of England is echoed in the establishment, rise and decline of the Church Defence Institution. Founded in 1859, this was 'the most important independent pressure group acting on behalf of the Established Church in English politics'.[128] It was 'the first nationally co-ordinated extra-parliamentary organization specifically devoted to Church defence'.[129] There were four main impulses which drove early and mid-Victorian churchmen into such organized political activity. There was the anxiety that governments and Members of Parliament might use their traditional powers in ecclesiastical matters to disrupt or obstruct the Church of England in the regulation and conduct of its affairs. This was seen in the bitter debates over the Irish Church in the 1830s and in the Gorham case as well as in a number of other affairs. There was, secondly, concern that unsympathetic politicians might provide official assistance to the Church's rivals. This was highlighted in the Protestant backlash against Peel's proposal in 1845 to make a grant to the Roman Catholic Maynooth College. Then there was the fear that antagonistic politicians might be persuaded to use the Parliamentary authority over the Church 'in order openly to dismantle it by depriving it of its civil privileges and property'.[130] Finally there was resistance to the activities of the Nonconformist Liberation Society with its demand for disestablishment.

The membership of the Church Institution was largely lay. This itself was potently indicative of the commitment of people at all levels of society, although chiefly from the middle classes, to work with energy and enthusiasm in order to defend the Church of England. The demise of the Institution in 1896 was one more piece of evidence that such fervour, dedication and support was waning. An age of passionate commitment to the Church of England was passing away.

In such a dire situation, the Church of England had the inestimable advantage of being the established church, even if it had ceased to be the national church. It was to cling on to that advantage for the whole of the new century.

Further reading

Bebbington, D.W., *Evangelicalism in Modern Britain. A history from the 1730s to the 1980s*, London 1989

Bell, G.K.A., *Randall Davidson Archbishop of Canterbury*, 2 vols, Oxford 1935

Chadwick, Owen, *The Victorian Church*, 2 vols, London 1966, 1970; reissued London 1987

Chadwick, R.E., 'Church and People in Bradford and District, 1880–1914; the Protestant Churches in an Urban Industrial Environment', Oxford D Phil., 1986

Cox, J., *The English Churches in Secular Society: Lambeth, 1870–1930*, Oxford 1982

Davies, Horton, *Worship and Theology in England: From Watts and Wesley to Maurice, 1690–1850*, Princeton 1961

Davies, Horton, *Worship and Theology in England: From Newman to Martineau, 1850–1900*, Oxford 1962

Elliott-Binns, L. E., *Religion in the Victorian Era*, London 1936

Gilbert, A.D., *Religion and Society in Industrial England: Church, Chapel and Social Change 1740–1914*, London 1976

Hylson-Smith, Kenneth, *Evangelicals in the Church of England 1734–1984*, Edinburgh 1989

Hylson-Smith, Kenneth, *High Churchmanship in the Church of England From the Sixteenth Century to the Late Twentieth Century*, Edinburgh 1993

Knight, Frances, *The Nineteenth-Century Church and English Society*, Cambridge 1995

Newman, *Apologia Pro Vita Sua*, London 1846; Everyman edition London 1912

Nockles, Peter B., *The Oxford Movement in Context. Anglican High Churchmanship 1760–1857*, Cambridge 1994

Parsons, Gerald (ed), *Religion in Victorian Britain*, 4 vols, Manchester 1988

Pickering, W.S.F., *Anglo-Catholicism*, London 1989

Prestige, G.L., *The Life of Charles Gore. A Great Englishman*, London 1935

Rowell, Geoffrey (ed), *Tradition Renewed. The Oxford Movement Conference Papers*, London 1986

Rowlands, John Henry Lewis, *Church, State and Society. The Attitudes of John Keble, Richard Hurrell Froude and John Henry Newman 1827–1845*, Worthing 1989

Rycroft, P., 'Church, Chapel, and Community in Craven, 1764–1851', Oxford D Phil. 1988

Smith, M.A., *Religion in Industrial Society: Oldham and Saddleworth 1740–1865*, Oxford 1994

Stephenson, Alan M.G., *The Rise and Decline of English Modernism*, London 1984

Thompson, K.A., *Bureaucracy and Church Reform: The Organizational Response of the Church of England to Social Change, 1800–1965*, Oxford 1970

3

The Nonconformists and Roman Catholics
1833 to 1901

The Nonconformists – a general survey

Throughout the period 1833 to 1901 the Nonconformists played a prominent role in English public life. The legislation of 1828, 1829, 1832 and 1835 established them more securely in the political and social, as well as the religious, life of England than ever before. The Municipal Reform Bill of 1835 reinforced the rights conferred on Nonconformists in 1828 and 1832. It gave to them a larger share in local government, and expanded the representation which had been granted to them by the 1832 Reform Act. They were no longer Dissenters, mainly treated with derision or disregard, but accepted as a significant and irremovable feature in the political and social scene of the nation and a major element in the new and acknowledged religious pluralism. 'At the end of the Victorian period, after a fifty-year sequence of reform which removed the majority of the remaining Nonconformist disabilities, and a parallel series of developments within the theological life of Nonconformity which made it, as a whole, more churchly, the notion of the main Nonconformist denominations being "Free Churchmen" – *Free* as opposed to *Established*, but *churchmen* nonetheless – had taken root.'[1] They were still divided into various denominations and sects, but in total they continued to constitute an acknowledged interest group. They also continued to possess a certain cohesiveness of social composition, culture and political orientation. As a proportion of the total population the Nonconformists appear to have reached a peak in mid-century; although neither they nor the Church of England managed to keep pace with the increase in the population as a whole in the second half of the century.[2] As a proportion of the church going public they more than held their own: about half according to the 1851 census, but rather more than this by the turn of the century as suggested by numerous local evidences.

Politically there was a progressive association of Nonconformity with the Liberal party. This was so with Congregationalists, the Baptists and the various schismatical Methodist bodies during the whole of the period, and increasingly so with the Wesleyans from the middle of the century onwards. 'An overwhelmingly Anglican Liberal party was increasingly persuaded to promote objectives favoured by rank-and-file Liberalism in which dissent was a powerful force.'[3] The most important issues from the Nonconformist point of view were church rates and, by the late 1860s, Irish Church disestablishment. The Nonconformist association with the Liberals started to assume particular importance from the General Election of 1847 onwards; and Edward Miall, the leading Nonconformist protagonist for many years, was a Member of Parliament for Rochdale from 1852 to 1857. The impact of the Nonconformist vote, which was given as a reward for supporting agreed reforms, was especially evident in the counties.

The Reform Acts of 1867 and 1884 extended the franchise to social groups outside the range of the churches, but this was to some extent countered by the greater Nonconformist identity with a powerful political party. Also, there was improved central organization in most of the denominations, and greater co-operation among the denominations towards the end of the century with several national free church congresses in the 1890s, and eventually, in 1896, the National Council of Evangelical Free Churches, so that Nonconformity could more readily speak with a united voice. Religious journalism made its contribution, with periodicals and newspapers of high quality, such as the *Eclectic Review*, the *British Quarterly Review*, the *Methodist Magazine*, and the *British Weekly*, which was the principal voice of moderate free church opinion.

Of course the Nonconformists still suffered under serious disabilities after 1832 which even their increasing influence was not entirely able to remedy for a considerable time. The institution of civil marriages in 1837 allowed marriages to be performed by the civil registrar of births, deaths and marriages, or by Nonconformist ministers in chapels licensed for marriages so long as the registrar was present, and this was an improvement on the previous situation when Dissenters could not be married in their own chapels by their own ministers, but only in the established church by an Anglican priest. The new provision solved the basic problem, although it left lingering minor irritants. The introduction of civil registration of births, deaths and marriages as an attempt to improve record keeping met another Nonconformist complaint, as the only previous official records were in parish registers kept by the parish priest. Also, births were actually a record of baptisms, so that in order to be so registered Nonconformists had to have their children baptized in an Anglican ceremony. Civil registration not only avoided this, but it was one more step in the separation of the church and the state, which, however obnoxious to Anglicans, was highly approved by Nonconformists. Other issues remained which entailed prolonged struggles, including full access for Nonconformists to the universities of Oxford and Cambridge, the placing of Nonconformist education on an equal footing with that of the Church of England, and the full availability of burial grounds for Nonconformists, with Nonconformist ministers administering the burial service.

But among all the persisting grievances the matter of church rates was most prominent, and hugely symptomatic as well as being a practical grievance. It represented the main focus for Nonconformist campaigning. Church rates were annual levies which helped towards the upkeep of Anglican churches. Once approved by a vestry meeting which was open to all, they were a legal obligation on all property owners, Nonconformists as well as Anglicans. The refusal of a church rate by a meeting in Birmingham in 1832, presumably packed with Nonconformist and other opponents, was but the best known of a series of *causes célébres* during the 1830s and 1840s, which involved imprisonment of Nonconformist leaders and many well-publicized expressions of anti-Anglican sentiment through such organs as the *Leicester Mercury* and the *Leeds Mercury*, as well as Nonconformist magazines and newspapers.

A significant number of Nonconformists found it a natural progression to move from particular causes of grievance to a more general campaign against the Church of England itself. In 1844 about 700 Nonconformist delegates gathered in London to establish an organization to promote 'the extinction of the union between Church and State'. The resulting Anti-State Church Association, which changed its name in 1853 to the Society for the Liberation of Religion from State Patronage and Control (known colloquially as the Liberation Society), was the brainchild of Edward Miall, who at the time was editor of the journal *Nonconformist*. Although there were always Nonconformists who shied away from political agitation, the new society attracted much support and was a most effective pressure group. The case for those dissident Nonconformists who did not support the society is clearly stated by the *Congregational Magazine* in 1844: 'Its design is to employ worldly influence for the advancement of Christian objects, and to use Christian Churches for the promotion of political objects. We think that Christian societies should be used only for Christian ends.'[4]

The main phase of 'liberationism' was from the 1840s to the 1870s. 1871 saw the passing of a bill whereby degrees and offices still subject to restriction at Oxford, Cambridge and Durham universities were opened to non-Anglicans, with the exception of divinity degrees. In 1880, the Burials Act made burial in parochial churchyards a right for any Christian, and permitted any orderly form of burial service. In 1882 compulsory clerical headships in most colleges were abolished, and likewise compulsory clerical fellowships except in the case of college chaplains. These measures remedied some of the last of the Nonconformist disabilities which had inflamed the Nonconformists for so long.

Great progress had been made, but elementary education remained a vexed topic which was particularly potent in keeping the church-chapel confrontation alive. 'The Church of England's control over education was regarded as an important symbol of establishment status; hence the education quarrel became largely integrated with the conflict over establishment.'[5] By 1870 the majority of Nonconformists had abandoned their commitment to the voluntary principle in education. The task of educating the nation's children was too great to be undertaken by even the Church of England, the Nonconformists and the Roman Catholics together. Only the resources of the state could provide an adequate elementary education for all children. Nonconformists therefore welcomed the overall principle of the 1870 Education Act. But they fought successfully to ensure the exclusion of specifically Anglican teaching from the newly-founded schools. There remained the possibility of poor children being sent to church schools at the expense of ratepayers. Although this was not a very significant matter numerically, it continued to provide a cause of conflict in the early twentieth century. But this was to be a short-lived issue; largely restricted to contention over the 1902 Education Act. 'The education crisis had administered a powerful dose of *sal volatile* to the decaying strength and drooping spirits of Nonconformity. From the encouragement which it gave to disestablishment, few would have predicted in 1902 that the education conflict was 'the last great battle in the war of the English sects'.[6]

Mackn)

The 'Nonconformist conscience'

Ever since the term 'Nonconformist conscience' was used towards the end of the nineteenth century, perhaps initially in the correspondence columns of *The Times* in 1890, it has been applied to the influence exercised by the collective Nonconformist morality over political and other decisions in the last few decades of the nineteenth century and the opening years of the twentieth century. In the latter part of the twentieth century there was a debate among historians as to the existence, strength and nature of such a 'Nonconformist conscience'; whether there was a coherent theology behind Nonconformist thought and action in those years; and, if such a theology existed, whether it was important.[7] In 1966 John Kent argued that there were increasing political strains upon any late Victorian claim to a Christian conscience in public affairs, and that the Nonconformists did not enjoy a monopoly of moral concern in politics. In common with other political Liberals they 'found themselves trying to reconcile the older Cobden-type ideals of liberty, peace, arbitration and anti-militarism with a new belief in the positive values of an allegedly Christian British Empire'.[8] Although David Bebbington acknowledged that there was a theological element in the 'Nonconformist conscience', of overriding importance were the 'political issues that concerned Nonconformists *en masse*, so that 'the theological views of their leaders, and even their versions of the social gospel, do not loom large'.[9] Richard J. Helmstadter criticized the Nonconformists of the time for failing to provide a theology which gave specific political guidance. He claimed that 'their vague theology encouraged vague humanitarianism'.[10] David Thompson made a good case for a more solid theological basis for late nineteenth-century Nonconformist social thought than these or other historians had recognized. This was manifested in the teaching not only of Hugh Price Hughes and John Clifford, but also the Congregationalists J.B. Paton, R.W. Dale and A.M. Fairbairn.[11] Nonetheless, I think that the reinterpretation of Helmstadter, in which he seriously questions the extent of any 'Nonconformist conscience' in that late Victorian and early Edwardian era, is substantially correct.[12] It has the additional merit that it provides a useful, and I think fundamentally accurate, explanatory framework for interpreting the nineteenth-century history of Nonconformity. I will therefore summarize his main assertions.

Helmstadter notes that although Nonconformity was still enjoying considerable strength in the last decade of the nineteenth century, it was beset by troubles and confusion from which it never recovered. It had been much more unified in its culture and clear in its political orientation earlier in the century. His main argument is 'that Nonconformist culture began to disintegrate in the late nineteenth century, and that the "Nonconformist conscience", when compared with the synthesis achieved earlier, sheds some light on the nature of that collapse.'[13] Although the Nonconformists constituted a smaller proportion of the population than they had done in the middle of the century, and the extension of the electorate had given the vote to sections of the public who were not so committed to chapel (or church) going as the existing electorate, and had thus reduced the relative size and importance of the Nonconformist proportion of the electorate, Nonconformity could still hope to wield considerable political power. It continued to have links with the Liberal party, it had improved its machinery for organizing opinion and it had efficient and effective journals. Nonetheless it did not exercise the same influence upon the collective moral conscience of the nation after 1880 as it had done in the previous fifty years. 'Ironically, the late Victorian improvements in the organization of Nonconformity, and the appearance in general usage of the expression "Nonconformist conscience," occurred when the heroic days of politics and conscience were over for religious dissenters. Their leaders at the turn of the century seemed frequently concerned with problems too petty to warrant energy and grand language expended on them, and the Nonconformist conscience seemed too often to draw on what was narrow than on what was heroic in the Nonconformist tradition.'[14] There was no rootedness in a coherent view or philosophy of society and politics. The emphasis was on personal problems; on drink, impurity and gambling. The Nonconformist conscience was weak, and there was a tendency to concentrate on the trivial.

All of this was in marked contrast to the synthesis Nonconformists had achieved in the period from the 1830s to the 1880s. In spite of less organizational machinery and a less well-developed journalism 'their community was probably more solidly united by widely held social and religious attitudes that interlocked and therefore reinforced each other. Central to these interrelated attitudes and ideas was the theology of evangelicalism'.[15] In this the emphasis was upon individuals and individual responsibility rather than upon corporate entities such as the church or the state. The voluntary principle, a version of *laissez faire*, underlay the Nonconformist attitude to such matters as education, and it was couched in the language of political liberty. There were many

de Helmstadt thesis has been coloured heavily by Jebbinston's model. It ignores Wesleyan opinion as distinct.

working-class Nonconformists, but Victorian Nonconformity was dominated by urban middle-class families who epitomized this liberal philosophy. Nonconformists shared with other liberals a vision of society in which privilege and patronage were to be replaced with equality and individual independence; and they most typically expressed this in the support they gave to the movement for free trade. Because the Corn Laws artificially maintained the price of corn with tariffs, and thereby benefitted the landowning aristocracy, the anti-Corn Law campaign of the 1830s and 1840s attracted very strong Nonconformist support. Because drink was an obstacle to individual improvement and social progress, inhibited work, demolished ambition and ruined health, and because it interrupted the orderly rhythm of effort required by modern industrial life, diminished self-control and anaesthetized the conscience, it flew in the face of the sturdy independence, thrift, self-motivated effort, and success which Nonconformists held dear. They consequently regarded it as a device of the devil, and they provided most of the temperance movement leaders from the start of the movement from the 1830s onwards.

The mid-Victorian Nonconformist synthesis, which was suffused with individualism, began to crumble in the 1880s. Although no single cause can be assigned, there were three primary changes. First there was a major reorientation in theology, in which the previous evangelical individualism was discarded as old-fashioned and outworn, and with it there came a softening of views on damnation, an emphasis on the mercy of God, a stress on the incarnation rather than the atonement, and a fuller acceptance of biblical criticism. Secondly, there were important developments in the social situation of Nonconformists, with a greater assimilation to the norms of society, especially as Non-conformists increased in prosperity and education. This was reflected ecclesiastically in the calls for reunion and the distinctly reduced calls for disestablishment. And, lastly, the robust individualism, so highly valued by Nonconformists a short time ago, was rapidly castigated as a social vice as Nonconformists softened their attitudes towards privileged groups in society, and looked to the state to remedy social evils.

This interpretation of nineteenth-century, and more particularly Victorian, Nonconformity, is endorsed by the conclusions of other historians. Thus, Raymond G. Cowherd draws attention to the disintegration of the traditional Whig and Tory parties, and the search for new alignments in the 1830s, which eventually resulted in the Liberal and Conservative parties, in which the Nonconformists emerged as leaders of liberal reform.[16] Even in the decade before the passing of the Reform Bill Dissenting preachers had proudly identified themselves with the middle-class reformers of the industrial cities of Manchester, Birmingham and Leeds. It was a continuation of the eighteenth and early nineteenth-century association of the Dissenters with the Whigs. And it persisted as the nineteenth century progressed. During the 1847 election Cowherd concluded 'that voluntaryism was an essential part of the new liberalism. Free traders and voluntaryists were the same people and their object was one – to abolish exclusive aristocratic privileges in church and state. To achieve this end they desired a thorough reform of Parliament. The Liberal party consisted of free traders, Benthamite Radicals, and Dissenters; and their faith in religious liberty, *laissez faire*, and democracy were the ingredients of the new liberalism.'[17]

The strength and influence of mid-nineteenth century urban Nonconformity is attested by John D. Gay;[18] and K.S. Inglis found that of the twenty-nine towns designated in the 1851 Census report as 'chief manufacturing districts' Nonconformists accounted for 50% of the total church and chapel attenders in fifteen, with the Anglicans only exceeding 50% in three cases.[19] The Nonconformists continued to have a firm grip upon the life and politics of the cities until at least the 1880s, but this was largely in the spheres of middle-class entrepreneurial and local government activity. The dimming of the Nonconformist vision for outreach to the urban working classes is perhaps indicated by the foundation of the Salvation Army to fulfil the tasks which the Booths and others thought the Methodists, and the churches in general, were neglecting.[20]

The extent and rate of Nonconformist decline in the thirty years or so before the outbreak of the First World War must not be overstated. I concur with Helmstadter in locating the peak of Nonconformist consensus and political and social influence in the period from the 1830s to the 1870s, but I think the subsequent deterioration of that influence and standing can be exaggerated. The most alarming slide came at and after the First World War. It is a misreading of history to assert that the period 1890 to 1914 'was the hey-day of Nonconformist power' and that 'English Nonconformity was as powerful and influential a force in national life as any organized religious minority has ever been.'[21] As I Munson) have already indicated, it was still arguably the greatest single power behind the Liberal Party, and in the 1900 election of the 186 Liberal Members of Parliament returned 129 were Nonconformists, including H. H. Asquith, David Lloyd George and R. B. Haldane.[22] It was also remained a force to be reckoned with in municipal life. But it was not as vibrant and self-assured as it has sometimes been portrayed. Its halcyon days were fifty years in the past. The shift was towards more institutional organization and influence and, as we will see, Nonconformists in the twentieth century did produce leaders of national stature, and were taken seriously in ecumenical and other affairs.

Changes in Nonconformist worship and ministry

The adoption of new patterns of worship was one of the most important features of nineteenth-century Nonconformity taken as a whole. Three characteristics were foremost; a radical revaluation of free prayers, an increase in the number of full-time, trained, ministers, and the power of charismatic preaching.

Ever since the late sixteenth century free prayer had been one of the distinguishing marks of Dissent. It was an expression of the determination to break away from the perceived rigidity of the Church of England and Roman Catholicism, and to allow the Spirit of God to direct the one praying. However, with the growth of Nonconformity, and with its greater acceptance by the establishment and by society in general, Nonconformist denominations started to assume some of the sociological characteristics of a church,[23] and there was a greater emphasis on order and uniformity in services. Various specific contributory causes favouring this development included the abuses to which free prayers were subject, most notoriously their rambling repetitiveness, which often contrasted so poorly with the well-prepared sermon; the influence of Romanticism which found beauty and spiritual value in worship, devotions and a sensitively used liturgy; a new awareness, after the disruptions and excesses of the French Revolution, of the value of time-tested tradition, institutions and customs; and the influence of the Tractarian movement, despite opposition to its teaching. All of this lead 'first to the supplementation of free prayers with read prayers, then to the provision of printed prayers in which both minister and people might join in various congregations, and, finally, at the end of the century and the beginning of the next, to the provision of formularies of prayer by the denominations themselves'.[24] (Davies

Part of the transmutation of Nonconformist denominations into more church-type bodies was their changing attitude to full-time trained ministers. It is one of the characteristics of the sociological 'church-type' structure, as compared with the 'denominational' or 'sect-type' body

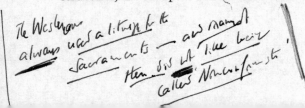

The Wesleyan always used a liturgy for the Sacraments — and named them, did not like being called Nonconformist.

that there is a charisma of office rather than a charisma of person. The sect is entirely the latter, and most typically there is no full-time, paid and specially trained ministry, setting a category of people apart from the generality of believers. The denomination is a half-way house in this as in other respects. In the nineteenth century there was a distinct move towards a greater number of ministers who were increasingly recognized as 'professionals'. It has been calculated that the number of full-time Congregational ministers went up from 1,400 in 1847 to 3,000 in 1900, Wesleyans from 1,125 in 1851 to 2,202 in 1900, Primitive Methodists from 518 in 1851 to 955 in 1900, and Baptists from 1,577 in 1870 to 1,963 in 1900.[25] They were, inevitably, mostly non-graduates, but efforts were made to remedy this. Early in the nineteenth century the Congregationalists and the Wesleyan Methodists made efforts to provide specific training for ministers, and the Baptists did so towards the end of the century with the increasingly urban and middle -class focus of the denomination.[26]

Despite the liturgical and ministerial changes just outlined, preaching remained as a top priority for many Nonconformist chapels. Joseph Parker, John Clifford, Robert William Dale, Hugh Price Hughes and Charles Haddon Spurgeon are but a sample of how much preaching loomed large in the Nonconformist scale of values. These were the kind of men who commanded immense respect and were of pivotal importance in their denominations. They were the ones who attracted public attention, and who helped to keep the Nonconformists prominent in the national public consciousness. *How typical were the?*

The distribution and social structure of Nonconformity

The 1851 census not only showed the strength of Nonconformity in urban areas, and more especially in the new manufacturing towns; it also revealed a marked rural pattern. The chapel was dominant in Cornwall, in a thin belt running through Bedfordshire, Huntingdonshire and the Isle of Ely to the Wash, in large areas of the north midlands, in east Lancashire, Yorkshire and most of the north-east. It was a close run thing between church and chapel in East Anglia and the east Midlands, in parts of the north Midlands and in the industrialized areas of north Somerset, north Wiltshire and south Gloucestershire. The Church of England was well ahead in most of southern England from east Devon to Kent, in most of the south and west Midlands, in west Lancashire and Cumbria.[27]

During the whole of the reign of Victoria Nonconformity embraced a wide range of social classes. Every town of any size had at least one prestigious Nonconformist congregation which could number citizens of high social status among its members, and some cities had several such chapels. There were other chapels where the working class was predominant or, more commonly, where the prevailing tone was lower middle class, with small tradesmen and artisans well represented. A high proportion of the chapels had a working-class element, mostly, as shown in local studies, skilled workers and working-class women, rather than unskilled and semi-skilled men. Rosemary Chadwick found this to be so in her study of Nonconformist congregations in Bradford in the latter part of the nineteenth century.[28] Clive Field in his study of the social composition of Methodism concluded that there was a pre-dominantly working-class membership in the nineteenth century.[29] K.D.M. Snell, in a comparative study of denominations in the north Midlands, discovered that the Wesleyans and the Primitive Methodists both had a largely working-class membership. The Primitives had fewer middle-class members and a higher proportion of unskilled workers. [30] In his work on Oldham and Saddleworth, Mark Smith found that around the middle of the century most congregations were predominantly working class, and many included a considerable proportion of factory workers.[31] At the other extreme, J.C.G.Binfield in his close examination of East Anglia has shown that Nonconformity included not only the old-established 'urban aristocracies' and the new rich industrialists, but also, at least in that region, an element of country gentry.[32] 'This was not to survive the social pressures of the later Victorian period, when the upper strata of both town and country Nonconformity began to filter through the public schools towards Oxbridge and the Church of England'.[33] All of this points to diversity of social composition, and is a warning against a too facile assumption of a Victorian middle-class Nonconformity as the norm.

Moves towards intra-denominational union

Throughout the nineteenth century the Congregationalists, Baptists and Presbyterians moved towards greater internal coherence and organic union, whereas the Unitarians and Quakers made little progress in that direction.'Between 1830 and 1860 the chapels of Congregational dissenters turned from a loose federation into something like a modern denomination.'[34] In common with all the other Nonconformist denominations we are about to consider, the Congregationalists had a sense of new-found liberty and status as a result of the repeal of the Test and Corporation Acts in 1828, and they sought to be more united as they moved into a future with more scope for recognition and influence. But there was disquiet in their midst about the chosen way to proceed. Some Congregationalists thought that all those congregations that accepted the principle of the supremacy of the local congregation to run its own affairs without interference in any way from another body, who were collectively known as Independents, and that included Baptists as well as Congregationalists, should join in union. But there were doctrinal differences dividing the two traditions, and the 1830s were years when doctrinal disagreement loomed large, so each formed their own union.

The Congregational union of 1831 narrowly survived its first decade, with financial and leadership problems and a lack of widespread enthusiastic support. This was understandable in view of what some regarded as a self-contradictory arrangement, it being an agreement to unite among men who, in principle, agreed not to unite but base their denomination on the independent local chapel.[35] Nevertheless, the union survived and was reinforced in 1833 with the adoption of a declaration of the faith, church order and discipline of the denomination. This was again extraordinary for a body in which many believed that they should subscribe to no human creed or formulary. Regardless of these apparently anomalous developments the union carried on, and the loose bond successfully endured the tensions of biblical criticism in the fifties and a series of internal problems. In 1877 J. Allanson Picton, a Unitarian who regarded dogma and even the historicity of Christianity as of little moment, tried to persuade the denomination to dispense with any theological agreement. But the Conference of 1878 rejected the proposal and re-affirmed the need for a common doctrinal basis.

The growth in influence and power of the Union was perhaps the greatest institutional change in the life of Congregationalism in the second half of the century. The immensity of the change can be gauged by contrasting the view of the Chairman for 1855, Robert Halley, with that of his successor in 1901, Joseph Parker. The former expressed the hope that the Union would never become a meeting of delegates appointed by the churches, for such a body 'whatever precaution was taken, would soon overrule the free and independent action of our own people'.[36] The latter called for the formation of the 'United Congregational Church' which would comprise everything Congregational throughout the land.[37]

The Congregational Union allowed Congregationalism to have a more united and powerful voice on political and social issues. During the whole of the period 1833 to 1901 the Congregationalists were to the fore in the wider Nonconformist involvement in politics to which I have alluded. They, like other Nonconformists, were dismayed at the failure of the Whigs in the 1830s to introduce more wide-ranging measures to relieve them and Nonconformists in general of persisting disabilities, and they tended to turn from the Whigs to the Radicals. They co-operated in the creation of a new radical Liberal party. They were active in the Anti-Corn Law League, formed in 1839, but they gave little support to the Chartists who were bitter critics of the repeal campaign. In many matters, including education, Congregationalists tended to support a policy of *laissez faire*, and in 1843 the Congregational Union committed itself officially to Voluntaryism. But the Congregationalists were far from unanimous or enthusiastic about disestablishment, and they did not give wholehearted endorsement to the Anti-State-Church Association.

In 1833 the Baptists were theologically divided in a way that was unknown to the Congregationalists who were mostly moderate Calvinists, or the Methodists, most of whom, with the exception of the Calvinistic Methodists of Wales, were Arminians. They were divided into three groups; the Arminian General Baptists, the Particular Baptists who were moderate Calvinists, and the Strict and Particular Baptists who were Calvinists but not moderate. Although the General Baptists had declined severely in the eighteenth century, with many becoming Unitarians, the Arminian tradition was revived by the General Baptists of the New Connexion established in 1770. Because of the acute theological awareness of these various Baptist denominations within a denomination the attempt to form a union similar to that of the Congregationalists was all the harder.

In 1813 a 'Society' had been formed, which was described rather optimistically as a 'General Union'.[38] It consisted of Baptist ministers and churches maintaining Calvinistic doctrines and the church-polity known as congregational. It achieved relatively little in the next nineteen years. In 1832 a revised constitution for the Union was adopted which widened its declared theological basis to encompass all 'Baptist ministers and churches who agree in the sentiments usually denominated evangelical.' It thus opened the way for closer association between the New Connexion and the Particular Baptists on a formal basis; and they eventually fused in 1891. The Union helped to promote the Baptist denomination as a total entity and contributed to a healthy growth in Baptist numbers. The Union also raised afresh the question of a possible amalgamation of the two parts of the Congregational family, Baptist and paedobaptist. Spurgeon writing about the meetings of the Union was able to say that the 'numbers attending, and the harmony exhibited, appear to increase every year'. But trouble was just ahead. It took the form of the Down Grade Controversy in 1887-88.

The crisis surrounded Charles Haddon Spurgeon, the most prominent of Baptist preachers in the nineteenth century, and arguably the most important and influential of all Victorian preachers. By the 1880s he had been ministering in London for thirty years. He was at the height of his astounding fame. He had established the Metropolitan Tabernacle with seating for over five thousand as his base and his sway extended throughout the country. He had shown himself friendly to the Union and had frequently preached one of its special sermons. But he was gravely troubled at its growing departure from the traditional doctrines of Calvinism. In 1864 he had spoken strongly against the Evangelicals in the Church of England for remaining in a church which taught baptismal regeneration; and he had never been happy at the change in the constitution of the Union in 1873, when the phrase regarding 'the sentiments usually denominated evangelical' was dropped. He favoured an elaborate doctrinal statement similar to that of the Evangelical Alliance.

Public controversy was ignited by two unsigned articles under the title 'The Down Grade' which abhorred what was seen as widespread contemporary apostasy from evangelical truth. It does not appear that Spurgeon inspired them, but he was impressed by what they declared, and he seized upon the opportunity to express his similar views in three further articles which were widely circulated. There was animated debate about the issues raised. Spurgeon denounced the Union as not being Christian and withdrew his membership. The resulting shock waves went far beyond the Baptist denomination. The Union emerged from the controversy shaken but not shattered.

The story of the Presbyterians was very different, although they also attained a greater measure of unity.

During much of the eighteenth century and into the early nineteenth century there had been a devastating defection of Presbyterians to Unitarianism, Socinianism and also to Independency in some cases. By the 1830s the residue of English Presbyterianism that had survived this haemorrhage clung to its Presbyterian identity largely through looking to Scotland for inspiration and occasional moral support. Some new

Presbyterian congregations were formed by Scottish immigrants, and in 1876 these joined with the surviving English Presbyterianism to form the Presbyterian Church of England. Whether the Scottish factor was the main cause or not, the 1851 census showed that half the total number of attendances on Census Sunday were in Northumberland, Durham and Cumberland, and these three counties also had the highest proportions of Presbyterians to the total population. Lancashire, Metropolitan London, and isolated congregations in Westmorland, Yorkshire, Cheshire, Staffordshire, Warwickshire and Worcestershire accounted for most of the other English Presbyterians. The pattern was almost identical in 1876, the year of Union, although the Presbyterians had spread over large tracts of central and southern England. It has been estimated that well over two-thirds of the congregations in existence at the end of the twentieth century were founded after 1851. For the entire Victorian era, and then for the whole of the next century, they retained a high quality of ministerial education, and they tended to be a high prestige denomination with more middle-class congregations than in other Nonconformist denominations.

During the nineteenth century union and unity eluded the Unitarians. Their apogee was the late eighteenth century and the early nineteenth century; after that they experienced great difficulties as a body. In an attempt to forge themselves into a more cohesive and co-ordinated entity they founded The British and Foreign Unitarian Association in 1825. But it failed to establish itself as an effective focus of denominational life. It was particularly rent by legal battles over the legitimacy of their possession of property and endowments previously held by the Presbyterian churches which had seceded to Unitarianism. The cases caused much tension and ill-feeling, and in 1836 a majority of London Unitarian congregations separated themselves from the Dissenting pressure group of the eighteenth and early nineteenth centuries known as the Protestant Dissenting Deputies. The separation was not complete. In great centres of urban Nonconformity such as Birmingham and Manchester, and in Liverpool, Unitarians played a leading role in establishing Nonconformism as a dominant force, and 'in the evolution of a provincial urban culture dominated by Nonconformist wealth and values and, especially, in the evolution and implementation of the concept of the civic gospel'.[39] These were, however, exceptions, and for the most part the other Nonconformists were content to see Unitarianism, and its heterodox, liberal, theology pushed towards the periphery of the Nonconformist community.

The Unitarians themselves were divided into those who shared a biblical-based orthodoxy with other Protestants, except for their conviction that the doctrine of the Trinity was unscriptural, and those who were heirs of the rationalism and deism of the Enlightenment. In this latter form especially it was cerebral, and essentially middle class in its appeal. Throughout the nineteenth century and beyond it was attractive to a small group of quite intellectual individuals who rejected orthodox Christianity and sought a spiritual home broadly within the Christian fold, but in a milieu which was characterized by calm and reason rather than faith and fervour. 'For most of the nineteenth century Unitarianism served as a kind of halfway house for those who found themselves no longer able to accept orthodox Christian belief and who did not as yet wish to pass entirely into agnosticism.'[40]

Two particular marks were left on the nineteenth century by the more rational, unorthodox brand of Unitarianism. It 'nurtured and sustained a tradition of provincial politicians, mayors and leaders of provincial civic life whose socially reforming contributions to Victorian society gave Unitarianism an importance out of all proportion to its actual size'; and in James Martineau it produced a theologian 'whose liberal divinity, inspired by both a deep devotionalism and a critical intellect aware of the challenges of philosophical, historical and scientific thought, was well able to confront the Victorian intellectual crisis of faith and present a viable theological alternative to orthodoxy or disbelief'.[41] The kind of Unitarianism represented by Martineau had a considerable impact on other denominations, and it exercised a powerful influence on the thinking of F.D.Maurice who, as we have already seen, consciously allowed his Unitarian background to mould his ideas.

Martineau and others of a similar Unitarian intellectual and spiritual disposition drew upon and added to a radical tradition and theological liberalism which had already debated many of the questions which were to agitate churchmen and Nonconformists in the course of the century. But this very strength proved their greatest weakness. 'Towards the end of the century Unitarianism was waning. The liberalism of its theology, if not the detail of its arguments, had become the property of almost all the major denominations, and its distinctive witness had consequently become less striking.'[42]

Nonetheless, although the Unitarians did not exhibit the signs of purposeful corporate life which had typified them in earlier years, they were far from moribund. They were depleted in numbers, and did not make much of a mark on society. 'Yet it must be noted not only that nineteenth-century Unitarians had strong social and humanitarian impulses but also that in some areas they possessed a significant home missionary tradition and something of a "working-class following".[43] They entered the twentieth century still very much a part of the religious scene.

The Quakers did not follow the Congregationalists, Baptists and Presbyterians in establishing a new structure for unity. For much of the century they were somewhat weak and suffered from divisions, but in view of these shortcomings and deficiencies they exercised a considerable influence.

Their halcyon days had been from the late 1640s to the end of the seventeenth century. That was the period when they were founded and when the heroic pioneer figures of Quakerism made such an impression on society at large. It had also been the time of their greatest and most rapid expansion. The eighteenth century and the first three decades of the nineteenth century were comparatively uneventful years of decline. By 1833 they were numerically weak, and they were divided into two sectors. There were the conventional Quakers who stressed the 'Inner Light', were undogmatic, and adopted the traditional and distinctive Quaker style of dress, speech, custom and behaviour, and by doing so cemented their separateness from all the other Nonconformists. Then there were the evangelical Quakers who were a strong force in many Quaker Meetings, where they emphasized the supremacy of the Bible rather than the Inner Light as the source of authority and tended to undermine some of the stricter Quaker conventions. A leading representative of this strand of Quakerism was Joseph John Gurney, the rich Norwich banker, who ministered to his local Meeting from 1818 to 1847, and who had close connections with local Church of England Evangelicals. Only once, with the Beaconite Movement and schism of the 1830s, did the two groups seriously confront each other.[44] 'Very real differences existed and controversies were often intense, but they were always kept within limits and restraints, and the unity and integrity of the Society were maintained.'[45] But the internal division may have weakened the Quakers and contributed to their slide downwards. Another factor was their marriage rule enshrined in the Marriage Act of 1836 which required both partners to be Friends; and to marry outside the denomination meant disownment. It was amended in 1860 to permit one or even both partners merely to be in sympathy with the Friends; but much damage had been done in the intervening years.

The Quakers as a whole were markedly middle class, with particular strength among the commercial and business fraternity. They in fact constituted a social elite among the Nonconformists. Their social impact was reinforced by 'their close family networks and powerful social sanctions against bankruptcy', and by the fact that they 'provided more than their share of entrepreneurs for the early industrial revolution, as well as country bankers whose firms are now household names'.[46] They did not develop a fully centralized denominational structure but, most noticeably, and rather like the Unitarians, they exerted a remarkable provincial social and political influence. This was 'out of all proportion to their numbers as they provided civic leadership through Literary and Philosophical Societies and as members of reformed corporations after 1835 in towns such as Manchester, Birmingham and Liverpool'.[47] In Birmingham alone they provided seven mayors before 1892. 'Gradually but steadily the public interests and sympathies of Friends throughout the nation widened. They turned their thought and attention to the elevation of the public press, to city planning and to many other ways of raising the scale and value of life in city and country.'[48]

The internal life of the Quakers in the nineteenth century was somewhat disturbed by three schisms. But it needs to be borne in mind that as they occurred within a denomination which itself may not have numbered more than 14,000, they were minuscule. The so-called Beaconite schism in the 1830s, mentioned earlier in this section, was a result of concern for a greater evangelical emphasis; the Fritchley schism was an expression of quietist conservatism, and evolved gradually in the late 1860s; and the third was engendered by the activities of some Manchester free-thinkers in the early 1870s who accepted the findings of liberal theology and contemporary biblical criticism, and who tended to be unitarian. In the Beaconite schism about 300 Friends were involved, and the others were confined to a few dozen Friends. All three were localized to a single place.[49]

Local chapel life and ministry

The nineteenth century also witnessed a new attitude among Nonconformist denominations to ministry and ministers.

Despite the ramifications of union development and activities and involvement in politics, the focus of Congregationalism remained the local chapel. Congregational services for much of the century were built around extemporare prayers, which not uncommonly lasted up to half an hour, and more particularly the sermon, which might be an hour or more. Some congregations were large and thriving; and in most cases this depended largely on the preacher. In London in the late 1830s Surrey Chapel attracted about 3,000 to a Sunday service when James Sherman was at the height of his powers. John Leifchild filled Bridge Street Chapel, Bristol, with a congregation of 900 people, and when he moved to the well-nigh derelict Craven Chapel in London, he promptly filled it with a congregation of 2,000 people. Angell James packed Carr's Lane Chapel in Birmingham, and in Liverpool Thomas Raffles had a congregation of 2,000. The chapel goers revelled in attending packed services, and in hearing good preachers.[50]

The second half of the century was a time of extensive chapel-restoring and chapel-building for Congregationalists as well as for other Nonconformists. This was made possible largely because the Congregational system appealed particularly to the new class of traders and industrialists. Unfortunately enthusiasm somewhat outpaced moderation and financial prudency in a number of cases, for many of the new chapels were erected without sufficient proof that they were needed and the debt was sufficient to stifle any effective spiritual work within their walls. There was also a tendency to over-elaboration. Congregational church building was inclined to copy the Anglican styles, moving from Greek to Gothic. 'The late Victorian Congregationalists were successful and this spirit of achievement had to be expressed visually. The older humble meeting places were pulled down and replaced by 800–1,200-seater Gothic cathedrals. Some of these were filled Sunday by Sunday; others were built on the pious hope that some day a large congregation might be developed; and yet others were simply colossal monuments to Victorian prosperity with no chance of them ever being filled. Especially in the north of England these cathedrals have now become a constant source of embarrassment to their dwindling congregations.'[51]

But where they were viable success was measured by busyness. A great variety of social activity took place. A pioneer of this approach was Urijah Rees Thomas who became minister of Redland Park Chapel in Bristol in 1862. Here he gave a lead in the provision of a multiplicity of societies. 'The most important of them were; the Young Men's Mutual Improvement Society, The Book Society, The Recreation Club for Young Men, Penny Readings Society, The Redland Field Club, The YMCA, The YWCA, The Sunday School Teachers' Preparation Class, The Evening Classes Association, The Young Men's Missionary Society,

The Youth's Bible Class, The Young Men's Literary Society, The Young Men's Liberal Association, The Society for Giving Prizes for Clean and Tidy Homes and the Durdham Down Musical Band.'[52] A widespread and extremely popular activity was the Pleasant Sunday Afternoons. They were inaugurated in 1875 by John Blackham, an Independent deacon in West Bromwich. The core of most of them was a very informal, friendly, often largely lay-led, service with congregational hymns and choruses, short readings and a short address. Alongside the religious services there was help given through such means as a benevolent and sick provident fund, a savings bank, a poor man's lawyer and a temperance society. Most of the Pleasant Sunday Afternoon Societies were Nonconformist. They were frequently well supported, the one at Christ Church, Westminster Bridge Road, recording attendances around 800 in the last decade of the century. All of this shows that despite the overall signs of Nonconformist decline in the thirty years prior to the First World War, there was still much life left in Congregationalism as it entered the new century.

Among the Baptists there was by 1833 an awareness of the need to supplement calling with training in the provision of a pastoral ministry. 'Yet nineteenth-century Baptists could never wholly forget the story of Arian and Socinian decline in the eighteenth century, and that memory served to foster a suspicion of the intellectual world.'[53] So it took some time before initiatives were taken. The number of formally trained Baptist ministers in contrast to those who conformed to the older pattern of 'learning on the job' rose markedly after 1850; but as late as 1871 only 58% had training at an academy or college. By 1911 this figure had risen to 84.5%. This is not meant to imply that the Baptist ministry in the first half of the century was fustian and dominated by 'very obscure men' as has frequently been depicted. It was not, and it included a number who were sons of the manse together with perhaps 5% from the professional classes.[54] Small craftsmen represented the typical social origin for Baptist ministers at that time, whereas, from 1860 onward white-collar workers, including teachers, were increasingly the source of recruitment; and after 1880 they outnumbered artisans.[55]

The main Baptist colleges for the education of ministers were Regent's Park College and Spurgeon's College. Regent's Park was founded in 1810, affiliated with the University of London in 1841 and became a constituent college after 1900. It was academically respected. Spurgeon's (originally Pastors') College, was founded in 1856. It attempted to train 'a class of ministers who will not aim at lofty scholarship, but at the winning of souls – men of the people'. It played a major role in the late nineteenth century surge of Baptist training; and it has been calculated that it provided about 10% of the total Baptist ministry in 1871, approximately 20% in 1891, and 24% in 1911.[56]

Throughout the century Baptist chapels were concentrated largely in a block of counties stretching from the east Midlands to the coast of East Anglia, in Gloucestershire and Wiltshire, and with some gains in all the southern counties of England.[57] As the century advanced the places of worship multiplied. In 1801 there were only 652 buildings and 176,692 sittings in England, whereas in 1851 they had 2,789 buildings and 752,343 sittings. This expansion continued during the second half of the century; and it was especially marked in the new industrial districts. It has been said that 'the largest number of "converted working men" was probably to be found among the Baptists who had a large lower middle-class membership and a few distinctly wealthy chapels, but also a considerable working-class element in most of their chapels.'[58] So the local chapels, at least in some of the urban areas, looked for expansion and tried to attract the outsiders to their fellowship. It was but one sign of concern for evangelism, and there were other indications of an outward-looking attitude. The Baptist Home Mission Society was increasingly active. The Baptists co-operated in the 1859–60 revival, with the Home Mission Society reporting that 'not a single church had been without additions'. Baptists took an active part in the Moody campaigns of the 1870s and the Torrey-Alexander campaigns at the turn of the century, and urban evangelism was pursued with vigour.

This stress on evangelism cut across the range of theology and outlook represented by nineteenth-century chapels. Such diversity is illustrated by the three leading Victorian Baptist ministers: the conservative Calvinist, fiery preacher and teacher, Spurgeon; the pastor with a burning concern for social justice, John Clifford; and the expository preacher Alexander Maclaren. It is arguable that as the century came towards its end the 'future lay with Clifford, liberalism, the social gospel and the Free Church movement which he helped lead in the 1890s'.[59]

The Methodists

At a national level, and in terms of its policy, strategy and direction, 1833 dawned for the Wesleyan Methodists with one man pre-eminent and exercising a rule which was to last to the middle of the century. Jabez Bunting was unquestionably the most prominent and authoritative Methodist since John Wesley. He drew his strength from his administrative ability. 'He rationalized the administrative procedures and finances of Wesleyanism. He was "the grateful servant of the Conference" as he put it, ubiquitous, indispensable. By 1837 the Conference could not proceed if Bunting was absent from its sessions.'[60] He had mastered its working, and the operation of its Connexional committees, and had established a body of supporters around him. In 1844 ten leading Buntingites held eighty-nine committee seats between them; while six other leading ministers who were more or less opposed to him held seven. By his control over major committees he could determine Conference decisions. The Conference was the only venue for constitutional opposition to him, and he so dominated it that there was no threat to his iron grip. And the Conference itself was thoroughly authoritarian, with only a minute twenty-seven out of the 1,216 speaking at its annual meeting in 1844.

The power of Bunting was also enhanced by the assertion of the priestly power inherent in the 'pastoral office' of the Wesleyan minister. 'Never have the clergy claimed a more ample authority in virtue of the pastoral office than amongst the descendants of those primitive preachers whom the Wesley's summoned to their assistance,' a critic wrote.[61] Bunting had such an exalted view of the ministry that he demanded for the Conference an authority which was not dissimilar to that of papal sovereignty. 'Bunting believed that God himself placed the local Methodist congregation in the charge of the pastor, who would have to answer for the souls of his people at the last day.'[62] Such a view could not, and did not, go unchallenged. It tended in some situations, and overall as a policy and strategy, to set ministers not only over the laity but in opposition to them, especially if an individual or corporate, local, district or national lay opinion arose which was counter to the ministerial line. There was no room for any manoeuvre in Bunting's theology of ministry. 'METHODISM was as much opposed to DEMOCRACY as to SIN', he declared.[63]

The main gain as a consequence of the Bunting regime, although some would see it as a loss, was its ability to accelerate the transition from a sect to a denomination. Late eighteenth-century Methodism still had many of the sociological characteristics of a sect. It was not well structured; it depended upon charismatic leadership; and it throve most among alienated groups including those on the fringe of eighteenth-century society. In the first half of the nineteenth century it developed a charisma of office, with ministers or Superintendents who owed their authority mainly to the office they held; and the organization, theology and official ethical stance was widened to embrace a more comprehensive range of social strata. A sound administrative framework assumed greater importance as Wesleyan Methodism membership went up from about 89,000 in 1801 to about 328,000 in 1841. This was accompanied by the first great Methodist chapel-building period. In such a situation Bunting helped 'to give structure and depth to the idea of Wesleyanism as a national Connexion'.[64] His forceful character, and his dogmatic and uncompromising authoritarianism were highly relevant, but there was more to what was going on than that. 'The many problems and bitter controversies he encountered were not so much the result of heavy handed ecclesiastical management as the inevitable consequence of coping with the inner contradictions of Methodism which he inherited but did not create.'[65] It may be argued, as David Hempton does, that the continued growth of Methodism throughout the nineteenth century was a vindication of Bunting's strategy, and that those critics of his who looked for a more unstructured Methodism, with its former reliance on charismatic leaders and direct appeal to the working class, were guilty of holding a romanticized view of early Methodism. But critics there were in abundance, and in some cases they led a mass of fellow-critics out of the Wesleyan Methodist fold.

The first secession in our period which was attributed at least in part to the authoritarianism of Bunting and the Conference was ostensibly over a proposal to install an organ in Brunswick Chapel, Leeds. The majority of the local leaders, members and local preachers in the circuit were against the scheme, and they were supported by the District Meeting. A number of trustees who wanted the installation appealed to the Conference which overrode local opinion and granted the desired permission. The blame was laid upon Bunting. There was local agitation with disciplinary action taken against the dissidents. The outcome was the loss, either by expulsion or secession of a thousand members, and they formed the beginnings of the Protestant Methodists. The issue went far deeper than permission to install an organ, and so the movement attracted support elsewhere than Leeds; most notably Burnley, Barnsley, Keighley, Preston, Sheffield and London.

The second controversy had much more serious consequences. It originated when Dr Samuel Warren had the temerity to oppose Bunting on a scheme for a Theological Institution and was suspended from his superintendency for writing a pamphlet expressing his views. He sought restitution by legal action. Opposition to the scheme had become widely organized, and laymen had been expelled in many circuits. A meeting was held in Manchester in November 1834 and the 'Grand Central Association' was constituted. The first assembly of the Wesleyan Association was held in Manchester the following year. The Association grew by accretion as almost 8,000 members in all seceded or were expelled from the Methodist societies. By 1838 the membership of the Association had risen to 26,521, and there were 67 travelling preachers and 946 local preachers, with 663 chapels and preaching places. *(By Her Warren was Recta of Ancoats)*

The most serious of these secessions of the second quarter of the nineteenth century was in the 1840s and arose out of pressure within Wesleyan Methodism for constitutional reform in which the central spokesman was a minister of long-standing, James Everett. For many years he had been critical of the Bunting regime when there appeared a series of anonymous *Fly Sheets* of which he was the suspected author. The first was published in 1844, a second in 1846, one more in 1847 and a fourth in 1848. They very skilfully analysed the Buntingite system, and presented well-authenticated but scandalous accusations against Bunting and his followers. The writing was caustic and even abusive. Some of Bunting's supporters inflamed the situation by issuing a venomous and scurrilous counterblast in 1849 called 'Papers on Weslyan Matters'. The *Fly Sheets* were promptly bound in one volume and issued to the public, whereas they had initially been sent only to ministers. Although the case against Everett was not proved, the Conference was sufficiently convinced to order his expulsion, and also pronounced the same fate for Samuel Dunn and William Griffith. Intense passions were aroused on both sides of the argument, and in five years expulsions or secessions from societies reached more than one hundred thousand, almost one-third of the Wesleyan membership. Most of these banded together to constitute the Wesleyan Reform movement.

In 1857 the Protestant Methodists, the Wesleyan Methodist Association and the Wesleyan Reform movement combined to form the Methodist Free Churches. *He was known out :- 1/46*

The Methodist New Connexion had originated in 1797 when Alexander Kilham had seceded from the existing Methodist body because of discontent with the pace of Methodist separation from the Church of England, and its perceived failure to establish itself as a new denomination with a high degree of lay participation. The New Connexion remained a phenomenon of the Midlands and the north, with its main strength in the complex of counties formed by

Worcestershire, Staffordshire, Cheshire, Nottinghamshire and the West Riding, and in the north-east.

The Primitive Methodists arose as a consequence of frustration with what was regarded by the seceders as the increasing formality and rigidity of Methodism in the early years of the nineteenth century, in which it was felt that there was an undue stifling of enthusiasm and restriction on evangelistic initiatives. Hugh Bourne and William Clowes were the leaders of the new body which emerged in 1810 and grew steadily in numbers and geographical coverage during the first half of the century. By 1851 they appeared to account for over 20% of the total Methodist attendances on Census Sunday, and this made them the second largest Methodist group. They were particularly strong in rural areas other than Durham and the Potteries. Their numbers and their influence both as a force within Methodism and as a champion of the underprivileged agricultural workers seems to have diminished considerably by the end of the century.

The Bible Christians were not a breakaway group, but under the powerful leadership of William O'Bryan they coalesced as a localized cluster of chapels in Devon and Cornwall area. Their expansion was very limited and they persisted as a small and not especially powerful fellowship for the rest of the century.

All of what has so far been described is important in any account of the public face of Methodism, but it should not be at the expense of examining what was taking place in local congregations on a day-to-day basis. And first of all it is clear and needs to be recognized that whatever the official formulations of Methodism might have been there was, as is usually the case, an abundance of what the sociologist David Martin calls 'subterranean theology'. In most of the Methodist congregations throughout the century there was to be found a mixture of 'superstitions', belief in luck and fate, and a whole range of inherited attitudes and assumptions which can be labelled 'folk religion' or even 'magic'. As the century progressed it appears that years of preaching, the spread of education, and the adoption by ever more people in society of a middle-class way of life with all its associated values resulted in a kind of progression from 'visionary and magical aspects of Methodism' to 'restrained Biblicism and a middle-class ethic of individual attainment'. [66] But 'the theology of the average Methodist and adherent' remained 'intellectually unsophisticated, confused, unclear, and at times totally unformulated'.[67] In common with many other Nonconformists, the main significance and consequence of being converted for the ordinary Methodist was the resulting pattern of ethical behaviour. This is what defined a man's religion to his neighbour. And in this lifestyle the pivotal ethical issues were drink, gambling, thrift and sabbatarianism. 'Methodism was an evangelistic religion offering the simple alternatives of eternal life or eternal death. These were plainly represented in this life in the distinction between the upright man and the indebted drunkard.' [68] Methodism was ultimately and in essence both intensely individualistic and profoundly communitarian.

Another main characteristic of Methodism at the local level was its flexibility in catering for a wide range of needs, from those associated with the fervid convert to the hanger-on with little theological or spiritual awareness. In a study of Methodism in Cornwall, David Lucker concludes that such accommodation was one of the attractions of Methodism. 'Fluctuations in membership, recurrent conversion and widespread superficial adherence suggests that, for many, Methodism provided religious and social fellowship – often, in Cornwall, for the release of joyous exultation – rather than a stifling model for disciplined living; and that Methodism for the 'part-time' majority had the fluidity and flexibility to be utilized for a wide range of objectives: as entertainment, for company, social protest or support in times of particular communal or personal crisis, as well as satisfying basic needs of "primary religion". In this sense, Cornish revivals were only the most dramatic and obvious indications of Methodism functioning truly as a "popular religion".' [69]

But before leaving the Methodists I want to stand back and see what can be discerned of the broader, less obvious, historical process which Methodism underwent in the period 1833 to 1901. Was there one or more 'unintended consequence of intended human action' which can only be understood from a distance of time ?

Were there economic and social factors which help to explain the rapid yet chronologically and geographically uneven growth of Methodism ? Various attempts have been made in recent decades to establish such a link, most notably by E.P. Thompson, who identified a coincidence between economic decline and Methodist growth, and the reverse, [70] and E. Hobsbawm who, in contrast, suggested that economic and Methodist prosperity went hand in hand. [71] Other important contributors to the debate on such matters have included W.R. Ward, [72] A.D. Gilbert [73] and David Hempton. [74] 'What does seem to be the case', says Hempton, 'is that whereas short sharp bursts of economic hardship or epidemics of contagious diseases could temporarily stimulate religious enthusiasm, long-term economic decline was a disaster for religious connexions dependent upon voluntary subscription. Similarly, the relationship between the growth of Methodism and political radicalism is more complicated than either Thompson's oscillation theory or Hobsbawm's concurrent expansion ideas would permit.'[75]

Hempton asserts that a 'more constructive approach to understanding the expansion of Methodism, without in any way diminishing its distinctive theology, organization and evangelical zeal, is to see it as part of much wider structural changes in English society in the generation overshadowed by the French Revolution'.[76] With this I would agree, but I would ask for an even wider frame of reference. The growth of Methodism should be seen within the context of the total political, economic and social changes which characterized the nineteenth-century phase of the transformation from the monopolistic to the pluralistic pattern of religion in English society.

Other denominations and sects

The foundations for the modern phenomenon of religious pluralism had been laid with the emergence and growth of the Presbyterians, Congregationalists, Baptists, Quakers, Unitarians and Methodists in the sixteenth, seventeenth and eighteenth centuries. The nineteenth century was the time when these existing Protestant denominations were consolidated and new sects and denominations emerged in greater profusion than ever before. There had been a variety of Christian sects in the past, most notably during the mid-seventeenth century period of the Interregnum, but most of them had been of short duration. They were like meteors passing across the sky, perhaps startling and impressive for a few months or years but then only a matter of historical interest. They had not persisted and become one of many stars in the religious firmament. But in the nineteenth century many came and lasted. There was an acceleration in the process of religious diversity. The modern confusing array of religious options was made infinitely more complex in the nineteenth century and early twentieth century. A brief survey of some of the smaller denominations and new sects which managed to survive, will reinforce this point.

The Catholic Apostolic Church owed its foundation to the remarkable events surrounding the person and activities of Edward Irving.[77] In brief, he was a licensed preacher of the Church of Scotland who in 1822 was appointed minister of the Caledonian chapel in

Hatton Garden, where he quickly and sensationally attracted an overflowing congregation which included some of the leading political, social and literary figures of the day. His teaching contained a strong eschatological element, a feature which was greatly encouraged by Henry Drummond, a rich banker and Member of Parliament. In 1830 he was excommunicated by the London presbytery for a tract which declared Christ's human nature to be sinful. But he rejected the decision and continued to minister. In the following year there were such 'charismatic' manifestations as glossolalia (speaking in tongues), prophecy and spiritual healing. Irving was finally removed in 1832, and his followers constituted themselves the Catholic Apostolic Church. They emphasized the imminent second coming of Christ, in preparation for which they appointed apostles, prophets, evangelists, pastors and teachers, to which they later added others such as 'angels', or bishops and deacons. They grew quite substantially and the 1851 census revealed 3,077 members. In 1853 they built a large church in Gordon Square, London.

The other millennial sect to emerge in the 1830s was the Plymouth Brethren. It originated with a small group of evangelicals in Dublin in 1827 who held that anyone might celebrate the Lord's Supper or preach. They received their name when their foremost leader, the somewhat strange yet powerful Irish ex-Anglican clergyman J.N. Darby, moved to Plymouth in 1830. He was very rigid in his theology and separatist in his attitude to those who would not conform to what he regarded as essential, and in the years 1847 to 1849 the new sect divided into Open Brethren and Exclusive Brethren, the latter refusing to have communion with anyone outside their tight-knit circle. By 1851 the total membership of the Brethren in England and Wales was 7,272.

Of the other sects I will first consider the Mormons, or the Church of Jesus Christ of Latter-Day Saints as they should more correctly be designated, because they were early on the scene, were one of the first Christian or quasi-Christian groups to originate outside Great Britain and to become a long-term part of the English religious scene, and because they grew so rapidly.[78] The first Mormon missionaries arrived in 1837. Within ten years the new sect outnumbered the Quakers in membership, and they continued to spread with surprising speed. They were remarkably active in promoting their beliefs. They sent missions round the country, and they took every opportunity to preach in the streets or parks when they could not gain access to chapels. Their preachers proclaimed an apocalyptic gospel of atonement and baptism by immersion and used a hymnbook which drew upon Methodist hymnody. But they also added heterodox beliefs, chief among which was the declaration that the word of God was not only in the Bible but in the sacred *Book of Mormon*, which their founder Joseph Smith dug out of a hill. The kingdom of Christ would, they preached, shortly appear at Nauvoo in the state of Illinois. They prophesied, claimed to perform miracles of healing, and instituted an elaborate hierarchy of elders, bishops, priests and deacons. Many English men, women and children who suffered from the poverty and squalor of the hungry 1840s took advantage of the Mormon offer to flee to the promised city of Nauvoo. Brigham Young, a Mormon missionary, was particularly active in organizing this exodus. By 1850 there were, according to their own statistics, 30,747 Mormons in the United Kingdom, and almost 17,000 who had emigrated. But the 1850s marked the end of the first flowering of this foreign sect in England. The numbers sank slowly to 2,000 by the end of the century. Nonetheless, they had come to stay.

A yet further example of an apocalyptic sect was the Seventh-Day Adventist Church whose members originally expected the Second Coming of Christ in 1844. Later in that same year they began to observe the seventh day of the week (Saturday) as the Sabbath, in keeping with the creation ordinance of the book of Genesis, rather than observing Sunday in commemoration of the resurrection of Christ. They were otherwise orthodox Protestants, although they laid special stress upon the human body as the temple of the Holy Spirit, and from this applied a rigid embargo on alcohol and tobacco, with a recommended abstinence from tea, coffee and meat.

Christian Science remained an American phenomenon until 1897 when Mrs Julia King brought the movement to England. From the time of their arrival they were not a proselytizing group, unlike their American counterparts, but relied upon their reading rooms, their Sunday services and their occasional advertisements to propagate their views.

Spiritualists of various kinds had in common a belief that the spirits of those who have died are able to communicate with the living. Spiritualism came to Britain from America in the 1850s. It soon had converts from the middle class, who tended to accept it as complementing Christianity, but also from lower middle class and working class groups. By the mid-1860s it had established itself in working-class areas, and especially in the industrial towns of Lancashire and Yorkshire, where it was able to attract a number of adherents from

Nonconformity, and Methodism in particular. It is mentioned not because it held any distinctively Christian beliefs but because it contributed to a sort of non-institutionalized, quasi-religious environment which harmonized well with some forms of late-nineteenth century socialism, and with contemporary agnosticism or atheism. The foundation of the Society for Psychical Research in 1882 marked the point when the study of psychic phenomena was finally established in a serious way.

Of the small 'fringe' groups I will only mention the Swedenborgians and the Theosophists. Emanuel Swedenborg was a Swedish scientist and mystical thinker who, in the years 1743 to 1745, became conscious of what he interpreted as direct personal contact with the angels and the spiritual world. He was convinced that the Lord wanted him to establish a New Church in order to make known his elaborate combination of pantheistic and theosophic doctrines, which do not admit of any brief summary. By the end of the nineteenth century there were still a few scattered upholders of his beliefs.

The Theosophical Society was founded in 1975 in New York by the Russian adventuress H.P. Blavatsky and Colonel H.S. Olcott. After Mme Blavatsky's death in 1891 Mrs A. Besant was made its leader, and it was at about that time that it appeared in England. It was a mixture of pantheism, magic and rationalism, which purported to derive its teaching on the transmigration of souls, the brotherhood of men irrespective of creed and colour, and complicated systems of psychology and cosmology, from Indian sacred books. The Theosophists denied both a personal God and personal immortality and regarded Christ as purely human. They advocated universal toleration of all religions and of atheism. They were small in numbers, but they attracted people who sought some cosmic belief but could not accept the Christian faith.

Such a variety of beliefs and practices was to be but the beginning of an astounding escalation in the number and range of Christian, quasi-Christian and, increasingly as the twentieth century advanced, non-Christian religious options. For reasons still to be fully fathomed such a multiplication of religious expressions, each with its band of devotees, was accompanied by ever more widespread religious indifference in society as a whole, and the growth of a 'secular' spirit. It was to be one of the enigmas of the late twentieth-century religious scene.

The Roman Catholics

Edward Norman rightly emphasizes that the nineteenth-century English Roman Catholic Church was poor, but that her greatest resource and richness lay in the local clergy, or 'missionary priests' as they were correctly known in view of the fact that parishes as understood by canon law did not exist until 1918.[79] It was largely their efforts and their inspiration of the laity which resulted in the provision of the places of worship, the schools, the clergy houses, the Catholic orphanages and conventual institutions which became some of the greatest external manifestations of the impressive revival and expansion of Roman Catholicism in England during the nineteenth century.[80] The national events, such as the mid-century establishment of the English Roman Catholic hierarchy and the development of a confident and buoyant Ultramontanism, were important, but the foundations were laid, and the Roman Catholic building mainly constructed, by local ordained workers, with able lay assistance in a number of cases, scattered throughout the country who applied themselves with diligence and persistence to their tasks. They were the almost unsung heroes of what was achieved.

On the surface, taking the national public face of English Catholicism, the nineteenth century can appear as a period of accumulated disputes. At the centre of most of these was the clash between the Ulramontanes, the 'Roman' party which looked to Rome in all matters, and often partook of the triumphalism which sometimes characterized the post-French Revolution Roman approach to church affairs, and 'the "Old Catholics", conscious of their quiet English spirituality, their rootedness in the virtues of common English notions of liberty, and their antipathy to centralized authority'.[81] Ultramontanism was associated with the previous rise of clerical authority in England.

English Catholicism grew and developed in various ways. There was first of all the increase in numbers. The Parliamentary 'Papist Returns' of 1767 revealed a Catholic population of 69,376 for England and Wales; although this figure should probably be inflated to 80,000 to allow for all the rural communities. But whatever the precise number it dramatically contrasted with the estimated three-quarters of a million by the time of the 1851 census. This expansion far outstripped the increase in the population of the country as a whole. By the mid-nineteenth century Catholics accounted for about 3.5% of England's population. Evidence of revival was apparent to everyone. In Cardinal

Nicholas Wiseman's first two years in London, in 1850 and 1851, seven new religious communities for women were established and three for men; two Catholic orphanages were opened, a secondary school for boys, and eleven new missions. During the second half of the century there was a steady but not spectacular Catholic increase, although it is not at present possible to determine the rate of this modest growth.

The Irish immigrants, who were the single most significant contributors to the numerical expansion, introduced a working-class membership which gave the Catholic community a unique social structure, especially as they represented about 80% of the entire Irish congregations.[82] The overwhelming majority of the new immigrants came from rural Ireland, although they included an artisan and small middle-class element.[83] They came from Ulster and North Connacht to Scotland; from Connacht and most of Leinster via Dublin to the north of England and the Midlands; and from South Leinster and the Munster counties to London, often via Bristol. There was much family migration, and with few exceptions they converged on the main cities and towns of industrial Britain, such as London, Liverpool (where in 1861 a quarter of the population was Irish born), Glasgow, Tyneside, Cardiff and Bradford. This radically changed the distribution pattern of Roman Catholicism. They were heavily concentrated in socially disadvantaged areas in which living conditions were appalling. There was some improvement in their status towards the end of the century in terms of job mobility and living conditions, but a remarkably large proportion of them remained tied to the old pattern of employment and localities. This tended to reinforce a stereotype image of the Irish which was far from flattering. It was extremely difficult for the Catholic Church to minister to such a great number of people, dispersed throughout different regions of the country in areas which were noted for their low level of institutional church attendance; and human and financial resources were intolerably over-strained, especially during the time of the famine influx.

The task was not made easier for the Catholic Church in England because of the resentment shown by the host society to the new immigrants. 'Anglo-Irish tensions in urban society, coloured by a variety of local social, economic and cultural factors, sometimes erupted in open violence and popular disorders, although these tensions were progressively diminished towards the end of the nineteenth century as the Irish adapted to their new environment and the English increasingly tolerated their presence.'[84]

In view of all the internal and external problems confronting it in its urban ministry, the English Catholic Church made an impressive effort, and achieved a remarkable amount. The roots of its urban work went back into the previous century. In the late eighteenth century the Catholic Church, unencumbered by an ancient and outmoded parochial and diocesan structure, had adapted well to the social dislocation of the new industrial concentrations. In the first decade of the nineteenth century this continued to be so. Despite a generally hostile climate of anti-Catholic feeling and so soon after the era of the penal laws which had severely inhibited its public activities, it built thirty new chapels in the Northern District. In 1840 four districts under four vicars-apostolic were increased to eight. In 1824 there had been 357 chapels. By 1835 this was 423; and by 1839 453. The figure had soared to 587 by 1850, and to about 660 by 1870, the year of the Vatican Council. The traditional post-Reformation Catholic centres in Lancashire, the west Midlands and parts of the north-east continued to provide the basis of Catholic organization. The Irish did not greatly change the leadership of English Catholicism which remained in the hands of traditional Catholic families with the addition of some of the more distinguished converts, mainly, but not exclusively, from the High Church wing of the Church of England. The persisting aristocratic strain is shown by the *Catholic Year Book* of 1900 which included a list of forty-one Catholic peers in Great Britain and Ireland, fifty-four Catholic baronets, and twenty-eight knights. They were a distinct, largely Tory-voting, interest group who were influential at key points in the central and local decision-making processes, and as such were to a great extent separate from the mass of Liberal-voting urban Irish Catholics and others. It may be, as John Bossy has asserted, that developments within English Catholicism presaged expansion, and that modifications are needed to the widely-accepted view that nineteenth-century English Catholicism grew in a form largely dictated by the Irish influx.[85]

The escalating confidence of Catholics after the emancipation of 1829 and with the increase in numbers is reflected in their buildings and worship. Up to the 1830s chapels were generally undistinguished and avoided any external sign of their religious use in order to avoid giving offence to the Protestants. Also, as the Irish immigrants needed churches quickly and cheaply, this meant 'tin roofs, deal altars, tawdry ornaments, paper pots with artificial flowers, dingy discarded vestments'. [86] All this changed around the middle of the century with new churches constructed in the neo-classical Italianate style so enamoured of the Ultramontanes, or in the Gothic tradition designed by Augustus Pugin and others. Pugin was astonishingly energetic and was responsible for an astounding number of churches, the rebuilding of St Chad's Cathedral in Birmingham, and the design of many secular buildings. Difference of architecture was not just a matter of aesthetics; it was regarded by the supporters of one or the other school as having a theological and ideological dimension. The opponents of the Gothic style regarded it as symptomizing a sort of Gallicanism. Pugin's position was simple. 'It was that good architecture and design resulted from sound faith and morals, and conversely, that wrong interior beliefs produce corrupt styles. The middle ages, the age of true Catholic faith, inspired Gothic: Gothic was the only authentic "Christian" art.'[87]

And the worship within the new chapels also underwent a transformation. In the early part of the century the services of the 'Old Catholics' were extremely plain and subdued in tone, with a low overall standard of preaching. There were exceptions where, for instance, under the influence of Bishop Richard Challoner of London and the traditional Catholic works translated by him, the services of some chapels displayed a commendable vitality and beauty; but the general standard was poor. The mid-nineteenth-century revival of worship introduced more ornateness, with the revived use of some 'continental' practices, encouraged by some of the charismatic members of Roman Catholic orders working in England, such as Father Gentili. It was part of an integrated cluster of new or renewed styles of life for clergy and laity alike:

> Devotions before the crucifix, public processions, wearing of habits by monks in the street, affection for the Sacred Heart, kneeling before statues, votive candles, gentleness of the Lady Virgin and the saints, fostering of miracle and dislike of rational thinking, sermons of harrowing enthusiasm, familiarity instead of fear, cradle of Bethlehem instead of thunders of Sinai, soft penance instead of rigour, frequent communion and frequent confession, mass daily.[88]

The number of clergy increased throughout the century, as did their professional self-consciousness. This was a consequence of general developments within the secular professions, an expansion of Catholic education, and the example and encouragement given to schoolboys in Catholic schools to regard the priesthood as the highest calling. Most of the clergy were required for the mushrooming churches, although some of them still acted as chaplains to the gentry. They certainly played their part in what has been described somewhat tendenciously as the 'appearance in nineteenth-century England of an aggressive and exclusive Roman Catholic Church with an appetite for contentious dogma, authoritarian rubric, clerical omnicompetence and often tasteless obsequiousness towards the papacy'.[89]

Then there was the establishment of a missionary-apostolate in 1841. It was born as a consequence of the passionate concern of Monsignor Nicholas Wiseman for the rapid growth of Catholicism in England. He had fire in his bones, and he longed for a scheme whereby places would be visited in which the Catholic religion was entirely, or to a great degree, unknown; missions would be held in places where there were Catholics, in order to arouse them to a greater zeal and fervour; preaching courses would be held during Lent and Advent in cities where the secular clergy were too overburdened with their normal daily work to be able to undertake such extraordinary forms of ministry; and spiritual exercises would be provided in colleges and convents. Something of his vision, which was so magnificently executed by the Passionists in the following years, is contained in words of his in 1841:

> . . . send forth men of mortified looks and placid demeanour . . . bearing on their breasts the seal of Christ's passion, as on their countenances the marks of its mortification (like the followers of Venerable Paul of the Cross), whose garb allows no comparison of superior fineness or affected poverty, with that of the poorest that surround them, but whose attire is at once majestic and coarse, and with bare heads and feet, holding the emblem of redemption, let them preach judgment, and death and future punishment, and penance, and justice, and charity. And they will be heard by thousands with awe and reverence; and we shall see wonders of reformation, pure faith revive with better lives, and the head converted by the converted heart.[90]

A reinvigorated, expanding and self-confident English Catholicism was also marked by the rebirth of monasticism on English soil, and the growth and consolidation of certain Catholic orders. The revival of monasticism was heralded by the foundation in 1835 of Mount St Bernard on the initiative of Ambrose Phillipps de Lisle: the first Cistercian house to be built in England since the reformation. It provides additional evidence of the confidence of the Catholic Church in the re-establishment of historic institutions which were reminiscent of a former, more glorious, age for the Catholics. The same is true of the religious orders. The Jesuits were strong in the first half of the century, but even more influential in the second half. The most numerous of the orders were the Benedictines. The Cistercians returned in 1837, the Oratorians were established by Newman in Birmingham in 1848, and in 1850 the Dominicans and the Franciscans re-established themselves. Missioners of the new orders became important, and in the case of Father Luigi Gentili well known. He was responsible for hundreds of conversions, and he immensely enhanced the morale of English Catholics. The other great missioner was Father Dominic Barberi, who received Newman into the Roman Catholic Church. His ministry from 1841 until his death eight years later was based on the Passionist houses at Aston and Stone in Staffordshire, although his influence extended far afield.

The growing Catholic community was reinforced by converts from other Christian traditions, most notably from the Church of England in the middle years of the century. The latter in particular were placed in a position of special prominence, their secession being seen by Catholic leaders as an important comment on trends within the Church of England, and their acquisition as of great consequence for the Church of Rome. The numbers were not great but the expectations were high. There was talk of the imminent conversion of England. But there was also hostility from hereditary Catholics towards the new proselytes which may be 'a measure of their transforming effect on a deeply conservative body'.[91]

In all these ways English Catholicism in the two decades after 1829 showed clear evidence of gaining in confidence, numbers and the mobilization of its resources. And with this came a perceptible refocussing of loyalty in the direction of Rome. 'For Catholics, the religious revival in England in the 1840s was a repudiation of the liberal and national strains of cisalpine old Catholicism.'[92] In its place came a self-confident renascent Ultramontane Roman Church. 'The mood of regenerate English Catholicism was one of sanguine hope for the conversion of England, and of a boundless faith in the new wisdom of the ultramontanes.'[93]

The greatest public declaration of a rejuvenated English Catholicism was the restoration of the Roman Catholic hierarchy in 1850, and the trumpeting of this by Cardinal Wiseman. The Pope sanctioned thirteen new bishoprics, mostly in the densely populated industrial urban areas which had expanded so dramatically during the previous century, such as Birmingham, Liverpool and Salford. In an injudicious pastoral letter

Nicholas Wiseman announced the hierarchy, and his elevation as Archbishop of Westminster and England's first cardinal since the reign of Mary I. He publicly and with immense satisfaction celebrated the fact that 'Catholic England has been restored to its orbit in the ecclesiastical firmament from which its light had long vanished.'[94] He must have overlooked or seriously underestimated the prevailing anti-Catholicism in England.[95] Lord John Russell reflected much of the current reaction in a letter to the Bishop of Durham. 'I agree with you', Russell wrote, 'in considering "the late aggression of the Pope upon our Protestantism" as "insolent and insidious", and I therefore feel as indignant as you can do upon the subject . . . There is an assumption of power in all the documents which have come from Rome; a pretension of supremacy over the realm of England, and a claim to sole and undivided sway, which is inconsistent with the Queen's supremacy, with the rights of our bishops and clergy, and with the spiritual independence of the nation, as asserted even in the Roman Catholic Times.'[96] As Russell pointed out in the same letter, there was the even greater danger that Popish practices which were clearly evident in the High Church wing of the Church of England would spread.

Heat and not much light was injected into the situation by the rhetoric adopted. 'The papal brief, Wiseman's pastoral, Russell's Durham Letter, the press and the pulpit all elevated the issue to a level of principalities and powers unmatched by anything here below.' Such unbridled language aroused the element of anti-Catholicism which undoubtedly still persisted in English society as a whole. It 'touched all the deepest feelings of the Protestant majority, and for a brief season they were able to luxuriate in the ancient battle with popery'. But it is a measure of the by then quite low level of intensity and extent of that feeling that within a few months 'the language of alarm and outrage had become threadbare, and nothing is clearer than the embarrassment of Russell and his government when stuck in the parliament of 1851 with an issue from which all sensible minds had turned away'.[97]

By the time the next Roman Catholic stone was cast into the English religious pool, with the 1854 formal declaration on the Immaculate Conception as part of the dogmatic teaching of the Roman Catholic Church, a more restrained and tolerant attitude prevailed, and leading politicians were not prepared to exhibit Russell-like passions in public. And the storm had subsided even more by 1870, when the Vatican Council was held, with its pronouncement of Papal Infallibility. This is not to say that both these pronouncements were received without protest. Voices were raised, but Roman Catholicism as a permanent feature in the English religious landscape was more widely, if reluctantly accepted. The new Roman Catholic vitality was viewed as a threat, but the reactions among the public as a whole gradually became more muted. This was partly because of the fact, already discussed, that religious matters as a whole were beginning to be treated with more indifference. The onslaught by militant Protestants on the ritualists in the Church of England as an incursion of Roman Catholic practices into the establishment, which took place in the last decades of the nineteenth century and on into the first few years of the twentieth century, may be seen in retrospect as the last major attempt to capitalize on anti-Catholic sentiments; and they failed.

Within English Catholicism itself what agitated many of the traditionalists, both 'Old Catholic' and Ultramontanist, and what they found repellent, was not this unfamiliar forthrightness and dogmatism, but the so-called Catholic Modernism.[98] Such leading figures as Alfred F. Loisy, George Jackson Mivart, Baron J.E.E.D. Acton, the Revd George Tyrrell, Baron Friedrich von Hügel and Maurice Blondel spear-headed a movement which, although as difficult to define as Liberal Catholicism and, like it, subject to internal changes, was in essence the attempt 'to apply historical and scientific knowledge to Biblical criticism, and to seek to claim for intellectual enquiry, and the methods by which it is conducted, a measure of autonomy from ecclesiastical authority'.[99] It was at its zenith from about 1890, during the time of the liberalizing pontificate of Leo XIII, until it was condemned in a number of papal enactments beginning in 1907 and culminating in 1910 in Pope Pius X's imposition on the clergy of a stringently anti-Modernist oath.

Throughout the Protestant 'crisis of faith' and in the face of the Modernist movement, mainstream English Catholicism in the last six decades of the century was largely dominated at the national level by five very different types of men: John Henry Newman, Bishop William Bernard Ullathorne, Cardinal Nicholas Wiseman, Cardinal Henry Edward Manning and Cardinal Herbert Vaughan. I will therefore conclude this summary of English Catholicism by a brief consideration of these Catholic leaders.

John Henry Newman had a varied and in some ways rather sad and unfulfilled life as a Roman Catholic. His very public and dramatic reception into the Catholic Church in 1845 heralded a long period of significant actions and events interspersed with unsuccessful under-takings and tension. After establishing the Oratorians in Birmingham in

1849 he was rector of the short-lived Roman Catholic university in Dublin from 1854 to 1858. On his return to England he became involved with the *Rambler,* a periodical which, by publishing a disparaging review of a book by Henry Manning for which Newman was held responsible, caused a rupture between the two men and a prolonged period of strained relations with Rome.[100] But there were fruitful publications, including his *Apologia pro vita sua* (1864), *The Dream of Gerontius* (1865) and *A Grammar of Assent* (1870). It was long after his death, and even as late as the Second Vatican Council (1962-65), before his contribution to the restoration of English Catholicism and the advance of Catholic ideas was fully appreciated.

William Bernard Ullathorne[101] was Bishop of Birmingham from the time of the restoration of the hierarchy in 1850 until 1888. He was a firm Ultramontane, but he occupied an independent position at the Vatican Council. He was the embodiment of what was conceived as a pastor. For forty years he was 'the standard of reference for the Catholic tradition in England. Few men have filled the pastoral office with such success, unalterable devotion and common sense. Surrounded by the meteors men felt at home with him.'[102]

We have already met Cardinal Wiseman.[103] His Ultramontanism was made evident at the time of the 'Papal Aggression' in 1850, and the influence of Henry Manning helped to make him even more rigid in his attitude to the acceptance of Roman authority and Roman methods of devotion. This in turn aroused the opposition of the older school of English Catholics. He sought to establish a religious culture on a Catholic basis.

Henry Manning[104] went from being an Evangelical in his youth, to being a Tractarian, and finally became a Roman Catholic, stating that the Gorham judgment of 1851 finally destroyed his faith in Anglicanism. It was an event which precipitated the secession to Rome of not only Manning but also Robert Isaac Wilberforce and a number of other Anglicans. Like so many converts, he was more dogmatic and unbending in his Catholicism than some lifelong Catholics. He was a staunch advocate of a declaration of Papal Infallibility, and he was bitterly hostile to the admission of Catholics to the universities. He was made Archbishop of Westminster in 1865, in succession to Wiseman, and cardinal in 1875. In the last years of his life he was active in social work of all kinds, most prominently in 1889 when he mediated successfully in the London Dock Strike.

Finally, there was Cardinal Archbishop Herbert Vaughan,[105] another

Ultramontane, who took the English Catholic Church into the twentieth century. His archiepiscopacy was marked by his eliciting of permission from Rome for Roman Catholics to attend the ancient English universities; the construction of Westminster Cathedral; discussions on the validity from a Roman Catholic viewpoint of Anglican ordinations which ended in the condemnation of Leo XIII in 1896; and his involvement in the debate over the 1902 Education Bill in which he managed to gain the acceptance of the principle that all schools, whether denominational or state, were the concern of the state.

The Catholic Church in England made more progress, almost however measured, than any other church or denomination in the country in the nineteenth century. It not only gained numerically. It was less battered than other churches. It withstood more successfully than them the potentially detrimental and destructive effects of urbanization, industrialization and political and social changes. It was less vulnerable to the corrosive effects of the growth and change in the character of leisure, the advances in science and the impact of biblical criticism. It was harmed less than other churches by the debilitating effect of the general drift of society away from institutionalized religion. By the end of the century it was probably more robust, better led, more united and more buoyant, optimistic and confident than any other church or denomination. It clearly had its internal problems and it suffered from pressures and problems from without, as I have shown, but it was quite well prepared for the varied, unpredictable and devastating manifestations of 'secularization'.[106]

Further reading

Bebbington, D.W., *The Nonconformist Conscience: Chapel and Politics 1870–1914*, London 1982

Bebbington, D.W., *Evangelicalism in Modern Britain. A history from the 1730s to the 1980s*, London 1989

Bossy, J., *The English Catholic Community 1750–1850*, London 1975

Briggs, J.H.Y., *The English Baptists in the Nineteenth Century*, Didcot 1994

Chadwick, Owen., *The Victorian Church*, 2 vols, London 1966, 1970; reissued London 1987

Chadwick, R.E., 'Church and People in Bradford and District, 1880–1914; the Protestant Churches in an Urban Industrial Environment', Oxford D Phil. 1986

Cowherd, Raymond G., *The Politics of English Dissent. The Religious Aspects of Liberal and Humanitarian Reform Movements from 1815 to 1848*, New York 1956

Cox, J., *The English Churches in a Secular Society: Lambeth, 1870–1930*, Oxford 1982

Currie, R., *Methodism Divided*, London 1968

Davies, Horton, *Worship and Theology in England: From Watts and Wesley to Maurice, 1690–1850*, Princeton 1961

Davies, Horton, *Worship and Theology in England: From Newman to Martineau, 1850–1900*, Oxford 1962

Davies, Rupert E., George, A.Raymond and Rupp, Gordon (eds), *A History of the Methodist Church in Great Britain*, 4 vols, London 1965–88

Drysdale, A.H., *History of the Presbyterians in England. Their Rise, Decline and Revival*, London 1889

Elliott-Binns, L.E., *Religion in the Victorian Era*, London 1936

Field, C.D., 'The Social Structure of English Methodism, Eighteenth-Twentieth Centuries', *BJS*, 28, 1977, pp. 199–225

Gilbert, A.D., *Religion and Society in Industrial England: Church, Chapel and Social Change 1740–1914*, London 1976

Hempton, D., *Methodism and Politics in British Society 1750-1850*, London 1984

Hempton, David, *The Religion of the People. Methodism and popular religion c.1750–1900*, London and New York 1996

Jones, Rufus M., *The Later Periods of Quakerism*, 2 vols, London 1921

Jones, R. Tudur, *Congregationalism in England 1662–1962*, London 1962

Norman, E.R., *Anti-Catholicism in Victorian England*, London 1968

Norman, E.R., *The English Catholic Church in the Nineteenth Century*, Oxford 1984

Nuttall, Geoffrey and Chadwick, Owen (eds), *From Uniformity to Unity 1662–1962*, London 1962

Parsons, Gerald (ed), *Religion in Victorian Britain*, 4 vols, Manchester 1988

Ralls, W., 'The Papal Aggression of 1850: a study in Victorian anti-Catholicism', *CH*, 43, 1974, pp. 242–56

Royle, E., *Radical Politics, 1790–1900; Religion and Unbelief*, London 1971

Royle, E., *Victorian Infidels: The Origins of the British Secularist Movement, 1791–1866*, Manchester 1974

Royle, E., *Radicals, Secularists, and Republicans; Popular Freethought in Britain, 1866–1915*, Manchester 1980

Rycroft, P., 'Church, Chapel, and Community in Craven, 1764–1851', Oxford D Phil. 1988

Smith, M.A., *Religion in Industrial Society: Oldham and Saddleworth 1740–1865*, Oxford 1994

Turner, J.M., *Conflict and Reconciliation: Studies in Methodism and Ecumenism in England 1740–1982*, London 1985

Ward, W.R. (ed), *The Early Correspondence of Jabez Bunting*, London 1972

Watts, Michael R., *The Dissenters*. Vol II: *The Expansion of Evangelical Nonconformity*, Oxford 1995

alas! out April 2003.

A good survey but not very exciting / and I do not agree with the whole of the Helmstadter thesis as it bundles together "Nonconformity" in a slightly misleading way — as David Jebbinston and Gerald Parsons have clearly shown.

Part Two

Part Two

4

1901 to 1945: General Decline for All the Churches

'At least until the 1880s, and (despite early symptoms of organizational decline) with little apparent diminution before the First World War, British religion retained an historical importance among the central institutions of society.'[1] Although the society and culture of late Victorian and Edwardian England was in many ways growing more 'secular', however such a concept is defined, religion continued to play an important part in society, and figures relating to religious practice were, at least superficially, not too depressing. They certainly compared unfavourably with what had been revealed by the 1851 census, which as we have noted caused alarm at the time, but they were not bad enough to cause widespread despondency. Membership, attendance and other related statistics indicated 'that in all the major Churches organizational expansion continued to the eve of the First World War'.[2] From then onwards organizational decline, although uneven, became definite and ever more pronounced. There was considerable loss during the 1914-18 war for all churches. Throughout the 1920s most of the churches virtually held their own even taking into account the increase in the total population of the country. There was then further deterioration as measured by absolute membership figures and membership as a proportion of the population as a whole. The Second World War exacerbated the trend downwards. I think that this is a true picture of the approximate timetable and the general pattern of decline although other interpretations, or at least modifications, of what I have indicated have been offered. These include the suggestion that major decline did not occur until the 1960s.[3]

From the death of Victoria to the end of the Second World War was not a happy period for religion in general in England, and certainly for none of the mainline Protestant churches in particular. I will review this fraught time under four sub-divisions: 1901 to 1914; the First World War; 1918 to 1939; and the Second World War.

The Victorian twilight

The Victorian era ended at 11.00 p.m. on 4 August 1914. At that moment England declared war on Germany. From then onwards the former political, economic, social and religious world rapidly began to disintegrate. Christianity, which so recently had been the backbone of English life and the determinant of the country's moral and ethical standards, was still at the very centre of the nation's corporate life.[4] Right up to 1914 one is 'struck by the degree to which Christianity was at least passively accepted by the great majority of the population, and to which it helped to shape people's world-picture, provided a basis for widely accepted moral principles, and provided rites which were used by the great majority of the population'.[5] The content of Edwardian legislation was still largely determined by Christian values, and social attitudes and behaviour were to a great extent still governed by Christian precepts. The Church of England was still the established church of the land, with its chief bishops exercising influence as a major element in the House of Lords and its leaders in general regarded as guardians of the nation's religious and moral life. Christianity was very much part of the established order in a country which was enjoying its security and its sense of worth and well-being as one of the great powers of the world with an Empire on which the sun never set, oblivious of the precipice towards which it was rapidly advancing. Clerical educational standards and levels of efficiency were advancing, fed by the newly-established theological colleges. Church of England attendances at services remained high in comparison with what was to come, with the number of Easter Day communicants at 1,110,000 in 1871, 1,225,000 in 1881, 1,490,000 in 1891, 1,945,000 in 1901, 2,293,000 in 1911, and 2,226,000 in 1914. This is impressive when measured against the 1,899,000 for 1966. Such a conclusion is reinforced when the density figure is considered, which registers such attendance as a percentage of the total population. In this case 1871 showed 8.2, 1881 7.9, 1891 8.4, 1901 9.4, 1911 9.8, 1914 9.2 and 1966 5.4.[6] In addition Sunday schools continued to attract large numbers, and they did not lose ground until after 1918.

These signs of continuing health and effectiveness were also apparent among the Nonconformists. In numerical terms membership remained strong as compared with the latter half of the twentieth century. Thus, among the Methodists taken as a whole, including the Wesleyans, the New Connexion, the Primitive Methodists, the Bible Christians and the

United Free Churches, the membership in 1871 was 570,936; in 1881 630,575, in 1891 690,022, in 1901 732,668, and in 1906 800,234. [7] The density figures were 4.1 in 1871, 4.0 in 1881, 3.8 in 1891, 3.6 in 1901 and 3.2 in 1914; and although this shows a persistent and considerable decline even in 1914 it compares very favourably with a Methodist Church membership of 603,100 in 1968, in a much expanded overall size of population for the country, with a density of 1.7. The same general pattern is discernable for all the other Nonconformist denominations. It seems that Nonconformity held its membership level as well as if not better than the Church of England. In addition, there was an overall widening of the national class constituency of Nonconformity which made it comparable in social composition to the established church. The 1903 *Daily News* religious census, under the directorship of Richard Mudie-Smith, revealed a slower Nonconformist rate of decline in the previous two decades in comparison with the Church of England. The Baptists, Methodists and Congregationalists could also take comfort from the fact that they achieved a greater membership in the early twentieth century than ever before.

The English Catholic Church of the first fourteen years of the twentieth century could feel even more pleased with its progress. The numbers of Roman Catholics appear to have continued on their upward path until they reached 1,357,000 in 1891 and 1,793,038 in 1913. In keeping with this very impressive growth, the number of churches and chapels seems to have increased from 597 in 1851 to 1,175 in 1881, 1,387 in 1891, 1,536 in 1901 and 1,845 in 1913. The supply of priests did not lag behind for it grew from 826 in 1851 to 1,551 in 1871, 1,979 in 1881, 2,604 in 1891, 3,298 in 1901 and 3,650 in 1913. And in the case of the Catholics the increases were not reversed during the remainder of the twentieth century. The Roman Catholic Church held its own in every respect. Of all the major religious traditions, 'it alone has managed virtually to escape a serious decline of manpower and material resources, and an accompanying drastic reduction of popular religious adherence'. [8]

Christianity in England in the early twentieth century did not only retain significance in the fairly explicit ways I have just indicated. There was the more subtle contribution it made to a sense of national identity, which was still as strong in the Edwardian, and immediate post-Edwardian world as it had been in late Victorian times. It is clear that 'during the second half of the nineteenth century the seamless intermingling of religion, art and patriotism was a widespread cultural phenomenon. Charles Kingsley glorified Christian English manhood; Gothic architecture and choral evensong came to be valued as pillars of "Englishness" even by those sceptical of Christianity.[9] In the early twentieth century, before the First World War, this welding together of cultural and spiritual impulses allowed people to think of themselves as 'Christian' although the nature and content of their belief systems had changed considerably and had superseded the dogmatic formulas of official Christianity.

But all these evidences of at least a residual spirituality masked an underlying decline and serious deterioration in the place religion held in the lives of individuals and of the nation as a whole, and in the status, standing and condition of the Protestant churches. Various sources and types of evidence, such as Charles Booth's elaborate survey of London in 1897–1900, Richard Mudie Smith's census in 1902–3, and C.F.Masterman's contemporary account and observations in *The Condition of England* (1909), combine to give a picture of escalating indifference to religious matters. There was 'a rapid decrease in the amount of time and thought which it was customary for laymen to bestow on religion'. It was not just a matter of the working classes not attending church. 'After Lord Selborne there were no more lord chancellors who spent their Sunday leisure in teaching Sunday schools. Family prayers as an aristocratic habit began to drop out; and though in the nineties it still largely continued in upper-class or middle-class households whose heads had started it long before, you seldom found young lay people starting it in new households.'[10] It became impossible to maintain the Victorian sabbath. 'Sunday after Sunday the doors of places of worship are thrown open, but the people do not enter. Churches are simply no attraction for them. Thousands are either hostile or indifferent to every kind of religious communion.'[11] Thus spake Richard Mudie Smith, and although he may have distorted the facts in his gloss about empty churches, even for London in the light of the statistics I have already cited, it shows with what pessimism an informed person viewed the situation. And he was probably more accurate when he referred to indifference rather than when he alluded to hostility, as there were very few contemporaries who described themselves as secularists or atheists. But even in this respect there were signs of things to come, for agnosticism was becoming more pronounced, especially in literary and academic circles. 'Whereas in the late Victorian period outright critics of Christianity, such as the poet Algernon Charles

Swinburne, still appeared to be the intellectual rebels; during the first quarter of the twentieth century agnosticism became increasingly the consensus of the cultural elite.'[12]

C.F.G. Masterman shared Richard Mudie Smith's morbid view of the contemporary scene. He thought that 'there can be no doubt that apart from any question of future revival, present belief in religion, as a conception of life dependent upon supernatural sanctions or as a revelation of a purpose and meaning beyond the actual business of the day, is slowly but steadily fading from the modern city race'.[13] And Masterman, perhaps rightly, gave particular importance to the gradual defection of the middle class, which he described accurately as 'the centre and historical support of England's Protestant creed'. Their 'drift away is', he stated, 'acknowledged by all to be conspicuous'.[14] In his study of Croydon, Jeremy Morris concluded that 'all denominations [and by this he meant all Protestant denominations] were seriously falling behind population growth in the late Victorian period', and this continued into the twentieth century. There were exceptional churches, but frequently their expansion in numbers was due to special prestige and impressive preachers, or a rapidly and greatly increased population in the locality. Stagnation or decline was especially evident in areas where the population was increasing but where there was a 'lowering' of the status of the district concerned from uniformly middle class to lower middle class and artisan; and in such areas Nonconformity fared as badly as Anglicanism. The overall impression gained by Morris was 'of an ebb tide of church attendance, punctuated here and there by a few solid rocks of continued growth'.[15] Hugh McLeod has drawn attention to the fact that even 'successful' churches probably achieved their growth at the expense of surrounding churches.[16]

The further development of leisure-time pursuits provided a counter-attraction to Sunday services. Leisure started to be organized in a national, co-ordinated and efficient way as an 'industry'. The National Sunday League tried to ensure that the urban demand for Sunday recreation was directed into healthy channels. It organized cheap-rate Sunday excursions. It persistently agitated for the Sunday opening of museums and art galleries, and in 1896 obtained government approval for the opening of the state's museums and art galleries to the public on Sunday afternoons. As the Edwardian age progressed this type of alternative use of Sundays became more common, with the Prince of Wales's Sunday dinner-parties helping to set a new pattern.

As far as the rites of passage are concerned, there is a somewhat enigmatic picture conveyed by statistics relating to the Church of England; and they may help us to discern some shifts in religious affiliation and practice. The proportion of marriages solemnized in an Anglican church is a good indicator of the degree of identity with the established church. Of course it does not take account of the large number of those for whom such a practice is almost entirely a social convention, or the staunch Nonconformist chapelgoer who liked to use the local church for such a ceremony; but it gives some impression of trends, and these were downwards in the forty years prior to the onset of the First World War. The number of marriages which took place in Anglican churches per thousand of the population was 747 in 1874, 707 in 1884, 686 in 1894, 642 in 1904 and 597 in 1919. But in parallel with this the number of baptisms and confirmations was on the increase. Anglican baptisms per thousand live births rose from 623 in 1885 to 641 in 1895, 678 in 1907, and 705 in 1917; and confirmations increased in absolute terms from 176,783 in 1881 to 214,531 in 1891, and 244,030 in 1914.[17] These statistics may illustrate the continued concern of many people to allow their children to undergo traditional services, hallowed in the community by centuries of acceptance as the right thing to do, while not being so prepared, when other options were open, to identify in some way with the church as adults in a very public service. A comment in the Visitation Returns for Canterbury for 1893 is more widely relevant than its immediate reference to St Nicholas at Wade in Kent, and is also applicable, perhaps more so, to the early part of the following century: 'Of those who are "chapel goers" many are baptized by the Church of England and bring their children to be baptized by the Church of England, and their dead to be buried by the Church of England. With the question, "Why am I, or why am I not a Churchman", the labouring man unfortunately concerns himself but little!'[18] It was all symtomatic of a pervasive theological and philosophical lack of sophistication and ignorance of or indifference to church matters which has characterized much of the population in every age but more particularly since the end of the nineteenth century, and is more prevalent in the less literate sections of the community. 'The religious historian ought really to bear in mind that the ordinary working-class population was too preoccupied with the needs of day-to-day living to spend much time on the niceties of religious doctrine. People's denominational sympathies, therefore, were likely to be determined by such practical matters as the location of churches and chapels in relation to their homes, the extent of religious charities, the availability of schools for the children, and the degree of influence exerted by landlords, farmers, and employers.'[19]

A further manifestation of weakness among the churches was the loosening of the Nonconformist ties with the Liberal Party and, more generally, the lessening of the influence of Nonconformity in moulding the national moral conscience.[20] The Liberal split over Home Rule in 1886 divided Nonconformists and thereby weakened Nonconformist aims. It also ushered in a protracted period of Conservative ascendancy sustained by further Liberal divisions over imperialism in the decade from 1895. The apparent revival of 1906, with a Liberal administration, had disappointing results for the Nonconformists. It was to be the last Liberal government of the twentieth century; and a further split in their ranks in 1916 over war policy presaged a decline which transformed British politics into an essentially two-party system, with the Labour and Conservative parties contending for power. The day of the 'Nonconformist conscience', if it had ever existed, was well and truly over.

Both Churchmen and Nonconformists were aware of a general drift away from Christian belief and commitment; and members of society as a whole were vaguely conscious of a shift away from the Christian presuppositions of the mid-Victorian age. 'By the years just prior to the First World War we find churchmen anxiously talking about the "modern age" as something not only quite distinct from the realm of organized religion but threatening it – and seeing it implicitly as the norm for the population. The new currents of social, cultural and political life were increasingly bypassing the Churches, which from now on manifested increasing signs of insecurity *vis à vis* society.'[21] Within the churches themselves at a national level the 'modern age' was perhaps most forcefully felt as a result of the impact of 'modernism' and 'liberalism' in theology. There had been many times before when wayward theology had disturbed the churches. But in the early twentieth century the new theological views were buttressed by being part of a wider 'modernism' embracing political, economic and social attitudes, the arts and the generally-accepted norms of society. In addition, although it could not necessarily be appreciated at the time, what was being experienced then was but the early stages in a theological movement which was to continue, with peaks and troughs, for the rest of the century. It was part of the transition from a pluralistic-type situation to a 'post-Christian', multi-faith pluralistic social and religious configuration.

In the early part of the twentieth century the main features of this theology were immanentism,[22] modernism and liberalism. Of crucial importance was the publication in 1901 of Adolf von Harnack's *Das Wesen des Christentums* (1900) in its English translation, *What is Christianity?* 'Suspicious of dogma, as the unwarrantable Hellenization of the Gospel, Harnack stressed the religion *of* Jesus, not the traditional religion *about* Jesus, and came to the conclusion that it was essentially the proclamation of the Fatherhood of God and the brotherhood of man.'[23] On his analysis Christianity was less mystical than moral in character. It became the duty of Christians, alongside and in co-operation with all men of goodwill, to bring in the kingdom of God. It was a notion which harmonized perfectly with the demands of Socialism. The New Theology, of which Harnack was a high priest, was a clarion call to the churches to undergo a moral awakening, in which social justice was to be an imperative of the Gospel in contradistinction to the ruthlessly impersonal ethics of industrialism. Such theology emphasized evolution rather than divine irruption, it rejected the verbal inspiration of the Bible and any materialistic after-death punishment. It generally accepted both the conclusions and the spirit of modern science with a stress on education, and on the kingdom of God rather than on the church.

The most prominent English exponent of this early twentieth-century theology was R.J. Campbell, minister at the City Temple, London, a citadel of Nonconformity, although he later lamented the chaos his teaching had created. He was greatly influenced by Harnack, but even more by the neo-Hegelian idealism of F.H. Bradley and Edward Caird, as well as by the writings of the mystics. His theology was 'born from a belief in the necessity of re-articulating the Christian faith in terms of the indwelling of God in the universe and in mankind'.[24] He started from a genuine concern about a dichotomy between Christian beliefs as traditionally taught and preached and the actual experience of people in their daily lives. There was a danger that modern man *en masse* would depart from Christianity, and such vital movements as socialism were dismissing Christianity on moral as well as on intellectual grounds. Campbell declared that the New Theology, with its placing of God's immanence decisively at the centre of its thought, would avoid the inherent dualism of traditional theology, and would be more comprehensible for modern man. It meant a new understanding of the relationship of God to the world:

When I say God, I mean the mysterious Power which is finding expression in the universe, and which is present in every tiniest atom of the wondrous whole. I find that this Power is the only reality I cannot get away from, for, whatever else it may be, it is myself.[25]

As with other liberal theologians, Campbell had a deep reverence for the person of Christ, but he had to revise the traditional understanding of the unique union of the divine and the human in Christ in view of his teaching that humanity and divinity were but parts of the same great consciousness. His views amounted to pantheism.

Campbell may be regarded as one voice, but a most important one, within a broad Modernist movement. It also encompassed Roman Catholic Modernism, which we have already examined, Anglican Modernism, and parallel movements among British Nonconformists and American and continental Protestants. In the next two chapters I will describe and comment on the various denominational manifestations of the movement and reactions to it by the majority of those who adhered to traditional theology.

In summary, the period 1901 to 1914 was a crucial time of transition. It contained elements from the preceding once highly religious but, especially in the last half of the century, greatly disturbed age of faith with its doubts, questionings and revolts; and it also clearly, in retrospect, contained seeds of future developments of quite alarming proportions. Like society at large it was good that those who lived at the time could not perceive what was in store in the short and long-term for the nation and for its churches.

Two World Wars

The attitudes and responses of the churches to the First World War were very similar and reflected the reaction in society as a whole. In the post-Victorian, pre-First World War years the nation, and the churches as part of the nation, regarded Germany with favour despite its challenge to England's naval and industrial supremacy and its expansionist policies; there was virtually no anti-German sentiment in the population at large or in the churches. Germany was portrayed as a country which was bound to England by both racial and dynastic ties. For Protestants there was the subliminal awareness that it had given the lead in throwing off the papal yoke in the sixteenth century; and it had shared with England almost four hundred years of Protestant history. It was perceived as a highly civilized nation which had produced some of Europe's finest artists, musicians, philosophers and men of letters. The Germans were portrayed as a people of the highest moral standards.

I will take two churchmen to illustrate the overall view of the churches, and then of the dramatic change of outlook once war was declared. The popular bishop of the people, Arthur Foley Winnington-Ingram of London, who was to be in the forefront of those during the war who hurled torrents of abuse upon the German nation, spoke up in the pre-war years in laudatory terms about its merits. In 1908 he was almost unrestrained in his effusive peroration:

> If you want to love Germans and Germany, go and live as I did in Germany. I will tell you some of the things that will make you love Germans and Germany. You will find there such kindly feelings toward England . . . I carried away first – and you would if you visited Germany – a sense of the genuine friendship of the people towards our country . . . I say, should we not love a nation like that? Why, it is akin to our own! We are cousins, nay, we are brothers to the Germans, and therefore, as a nation, I say, 'Wir alle lieben Deutschland und die Deutschen.'[26]

Such an attitude persisted until the very eve of the war. Canon Henry Scott Holland had no qualms in reprimanding governments when he thought they were at fault, but in August 1914 he was adamant about non-intervention, and he used his undoubted reputation to good effect by writing to the papers in a forceful and heartfelt plea for neutrality. When his advice was not heeded, 'with a violence uncharacteristic of this gentle, considerate scholar who enjoyed corresponding with children, he lashed out at the mass insanity that impelled rulers and subjects alike to cast civilization into the cauldron, all for the sake of a despicable little state like Serbia'.[27]

The following month, after war had been declared, his language was transformed. He wrote to a friend saying that 'every day reveals the black blind horror of Prussianism. It is the very devil. It has to be fought: and killed. It is the last word in iniquity. I could not have believed that men could be so diabolical.' By the end of 1914 he regarded war as not only a national duty but as involving issues of ultimate right and wrong. 'We are eschatologists. God must win. We cannot have anything else.'

From this it was a short step to what became characteristic of the note struck by church leaders of all denominations in declaring the war to be a crusade. We will examine this in more detail in the next two chapters, but for now our two spokesmen will indicate the message which was to become increasingly frenetic. By January 1915 Scott Holland was portraying the declaration of war as England's response to a summons from the Beyond, a fleeting glimpse of the Infinite:

> And under the sway of such a direct spiritual emergency we seemed for the moment to catch a sight of the eternal challenge which is the creative power behind all history - which is always there, always will be. Now it had blazed out, flung off all accretions and accumulations of time and chance, and we stood face to face with God, and we made our answer in His eyes. And we saw in an instant what He wanted, and so we took our place within His purpose. 'Come up hither', so the voice cried, 'and I will show you things that shall be.' And the world-drama was laid bare, and we saw the looms of God at work. We felt astir with the pressure and the tumult and the heat of those tremendous forces by which the energy of God is always driving our human story forward toward its great culmination.[28]

Likewise, Winnington-Ingram, whom we have encountered singing the praises of the German people and nation, made an equally sudden and dramatic volte-face. As early as 6 September 1914 he entitled a sermon to soldiers, 'The Holy War', and began with stories of German brutality. He quoted the Kaiser, Treitschke and Bernhardi from a recent issue of the *Daily Mail* and Rudyard Kipling's 'For All We Have and Are', made a brief and conventional confession of national and personal sins, and then continued:

> But when we have said all that, this is a Holy War. We are on the side of Christianity against anti-Christ. We are on the side of the New Testament which respects the weak, and honours treaties, and dies for its friends, and looks upon war as a regrettable necessity . . . It is a Holy War, and to fight in a Holy War is an honour . . . Already I have seen a light in men's eyes which I have never seen before.[29]

He reiterated this message in June 1915:

> I think the church can best help the nation first of all by making it realize that it is engaged in a Holy War, and not be afraid of saying so. Christ died on Good Friday for Freedom, Honour, and Chivalry, and our boys are dying for the same things. Having once realized that everything worth having in the world is at stake, the nation will not

hesitate to allow itself to be mobilized. You ask for my advice in a sentence as to what the Church is to do. I answer MOBILIZE THE NATION FOR A HOLY WAR.[30]

The response of the churches to the Second World War was remarkably muted in contrast to the high-pitched campaigning and jingoism of the First World War. In the 1930s the churches as a whole shared with society at large what seems in retrospect to be an astounding ambivalence, even nonchalance, in their attitude towards Germany and even Nazism. They may have been unduly influenced by the generally favourable attitude of Roman Catholicism to fascism; by the teaching of the Oxford Group movement, or Moral Rearmament, whose leaders supported pro-Nazi 'German Christians', and whose head, Frank Buchman, after meeting such leading Germans as Heinrich Himmler, thanked heaven for a man like Adolf Hitler who was building a front line of defence against the antichrist of Communism; or by the general public support for appeasement. But whatever the cause the reaction to the war when it came was restricted, restrained and reasoned compared with the responses to the First World War, and so it continued throughout the war, with a few notable exceptions, as we will see in the next two chapters.

The inter-war years

The First World War had a devastating and destructive effect on the nation and the churches in particular. There was the unprecedented 'loss of a generation'; the massive effect this had upon the politics, economics and social life of the nation as well as upon its religious life; and the unprecedented undermining of belief in divine providence, combined with a severe questioning of traditional Christian values. The England of 1919 was fundamentally different from that of 1913; and for the churches it was not an improvement.

At the national level there were further signs of the marginalization of the churches of which there had been hints in the pre-war years. 'The political role of the Churches was disappearing; their contribution to the social welfare had been largely taken over by the State; their provision for leisure activities was being increasingly supplied by secular bodies.'[31] They were being deprived of those functions which went beyond their purely liturgical and ecclesiastical activities, and were thus being denied those social roles which helped to integrate them into the community locally and nationally. At the same time that they were being reduced to religious teaching and witnessing they were, on the whole, able to attract fewer people.

There was also a widespread fear of socialism in church circles. As we will see there were some brave, and some somewhat foolish, attempts by the churches to engage in the new social and sociological issues, but there was a pervasive unrest among churchgoers about socialism in general. This was encouraged by the 'red scare' evident after the Russian Revolution of 1917, regarded by many as an 'atheistical outburst of blood and torture beyond description', which was the forerunner of industrial chaos in Britain 'engineered by the Communists in Moscow'.[32] All these factors combined to intensify the sense of Christian detachment from the political scene. They were symptomatic of a loss of political nerve among the churches.

And this alienation, or sense of irrelevance, was not confined to specific areas of life, either the political, social or economic. In the twelve years or so after the bloodiest war the country had ever experienced there was a pervasive ethos which was not favourable to the churches. The 'principal intellectual (as distinct from social) orthodoxy of England in the 1920s was no longer Protestantism, nor was it catholicism or any other form of Christianity. It was a confident agnosticism.' There was not 'a slow crumbling intellectually of religious belief' but rather 'an emphatic presupposition of disbelief, from which – if you were reasonably intelligent – only the clergy, Roman Catholics and a few eccentric neo-mediaevalists were expected to be exempt'.[33] Such a prevailing attitude in literary circles is encapsulated in the comment of Virginia Woolf on learning that the brilliant young American member of the Bloomsbury set T.S. Eliot had been baptized and confirmed in the Church of England in 1927:

> I have had a most shameful and distressing interview with dear Tom Eliot, who may be called dead to us all from this day forward. He has become an Anglo-Catholic believer in God and immortality, and goes to church. I was shocked. A corpse would seem to me more credible than he is. I mean, there's something obscene in a living person sitting by the fire and believing in God.[34]

In parallel, and in contrast to this intellectual alignment which was dominated by doubt, indifference, agnosticism and even atheism and hostility to the Christian faith as well as to the churches and all they represented, there was a noticeable change in the tone, content and focus of theology in academic circles, but also to some extent in the churches as well. In the first three decades of the twentieth century this shift in Christian thought was from theologies which were preoccupied with explanation, experience and concern for the social dimension to theologies which concentrated on redemption; the move was from a liberal confidence in man's automatic progress to perfection to confidence alone in the God who had wrought victory from the apparent disaster of the cross. It was, in short, 'a journey from immanence to transcendence, from general revelation to Biblical redemption'.[35] The central figure in this transition was Karl Barth. His theology of *Krisis*, in which every human act and achievement stands under the judgment of God and in which the church itself is in constant need of reformation, was an echo of the existential concern of Luther and the magisterial authority of Calvin. All human problems are ultimately insoluble apart from God, Creator, Judge and Redeemer.

Although it was some time before such thinking had an impact on English theology, and such influence was never widespread, it helped in the emergence of an English biblical theology. In England itself this was provided mainly by such New Testament scholars as Sir Edwyn Clement Hoskyns and Professor C.H. Dodd. In place of the futurist eschatology of liberalism with its stress on a realizable future utopia achievable by human effort, they substituted what Hoskyns termed 'fulfilled' eschatology or what Dodd called 'realized' eschatology, which asserted that the kingdom of God had been inaugurated by the life, teaching, death and resurrection of Jesus Christ, in whom God's new day had dawned. Such a sense 'of the Church's continuity and of its re-foundation on the basis of the recovered Gospel in the sixteenth century'[36] gained momentum in England as the 1930s progressed, and it remained an important strand in English theology for the rest of the century. In its early phase it was propagated by such Congregationalists as Nathaniel Micklem, John S. Whale and B.L. Manning; the Methodist R. Newton Flew; and the Baptist A.C. Underwood.

With hindsight the inter-war years may be regarded as a prolonged interlude between the two World Wars and, taken with those wars, a period when the pre-1914 world with all its residual Victorianisms was transmuted into the vastly contrasting post-1945 world in which rapid scientific and technological change was accompanied by equally significant shifts in values and attitudes. It was a time when the churches were largely occupied with their own internal issues and problems and were inevitably unaware of what was happening within this broader historical process. As I turn to a more detailed focus on the Church of England, the Nonconformists and the English Catholic Church during these years, with the concentration on detail that this entails, it is well that we do not loose sight of this wider context.

But before I take a closer look at the churches, a footnote on 'popular religion' will help as a reminder that the 'religion' of the country was not all confined to the institutional churches, to national movements, to headline-creating issues and events and to leaders of renown. Although, as I have indicated in this chapter, the two World Wars and the inter-war period are typically, and I think rightly, seen as a not very glorious time in the life of the churches, with considerable dislocation, internal dispute and not much evidence of creativity and progress, it appears that 'popular religion' did not suffer to such an extent. There seems to have been less disruption and more continuity than with the institutional churches in those beliefs and practices which I identified in the previous chapters as characteristic of urban working-class culture. Whereas the First World War had quite devastating effects on traditional, institutionalized, forms of religion in England the reverse was the case with popular working-class forms of religious belief and expression.

> If anything, the experience of international conflict acted as a catalyst to pre-existent trends of thought and feeling. During the war the religious responses of the people were marked by their incorporation of familiar and traditional aspects of behaviour, devotion and super-naturalism. A familiar folk theodicy was prominent in the use of charms, mascots and amulets both at home and at the front. The War encouraged the tendency to look beyond the churches for super-natural and superempirical explanations and solutions and strengthened the incorporation of a folk discourse within the popular religious repertoire.[37]

The war also resulted in the increased popularity of forms of belief which were condemned by the churches as unorthodox or even dangerous, such as popular spiritualism. A situation of heightened uncertainty and tension encouraged speculation and widespread beliefs about the character of the after-life which were varied and, from the point of view of the churches, often heretical. The war also vindicated moral principles which formed the bedrock of popular religion. 'Incidents of heroism and camaraderie appeared to offer conclusive evidence of the goodness of most men's instincts. "Active good will" thrived. It was independent of orthodox moral teaching and outside the sphere and influence of the church, and it was taken to indicate the prevalence and virtues of "latent Christianity".[38] At the same time that the war promoted quasi-orthodox, unorthodox or thoroughly heretical notions it also gave a renewed significance both at home and at the front to such traditional church-based practices as prayer and hymn singing.

One consequence of the war was the closer association of religion with the home and with the mother in particular. And this in turn accelerated the process of the 'privatization' and 'domestication' of religion which was increasingly to characterize religion, and especially Christianity, in a pluralistic, and later a multi-faith pluralistic, society. In the years from 1918 to 1939 such a trend was strengthened by a number of developments, most notably the wireless which 'provided a mechanism by which a private form of religious devotion was given a wider and more formalised expression'.[39]

Further reading

Bebbington, D.W., *Evangelicalism in Modern Britain. A history from the 1730s to the 1980s*, London 1989

Currie, R., Gilbert, A., and Horsley, L., *Churches and Churchgoers: Patterns of Church Growth in the British Isles Since 1700*, Oxford 1977

Davies, Horton, *Worship and Theology in England: The Ecumenical Century, 1900–1965*, Princeton 1965

Gill, Sean, *Women and the Church of England From the Eighteenth Century to the Present*, London 1994

Gray, John D.,*The Geography of Religion in England*, London 1971

Hastings, Adrian, *A History of English Christianity 1920–1990*, London 1991

Machin, G.I.T., *Politics and the Churches in Great Britain 1869–1921*, Oxford 1987

Marrin, Albert, *The Last Crusade. The Church of England in the First World War*, Durham, North Carolina 1974

McLeod, Hugh, *Religion and Society in England, 1850–1914*, Basingstoke 1996

Morris, Jeremy, *Religion and Urban Change. Croydon, 1840–1914*, Woodbridge 1992

Mowat, Charles Loch, *Britain Between the Wars 1918–1940*, London 1955

Ramsey, Arthur Michael, *From Gore to Temple. The Development of Anglican Theology between Lux Mundi and the Second World War, 1889–1939*, London 1960

Reckitt, Maurice B., *Maurice to Temple. A Century of the Social Movement in the Church of England*, London 1947

Royle, Edward, *Modern Britain. A Social History 1750–1985*, London 1987

Stephenson, Alan M.G., *The Rise and Decline of English Modernism*, London 1984

Taylor, A.J.P., *English History 1914–1945*, Oxford 1965

Wilkinson, Alan, *The Church of England and the First World War*, London 1978; reissued London 1996

Wilkinson, Alan, *Dissent or Conform? War, Peace and the English Churches 1900–1945*, London 1986

Williams, S.C., 'Religious Belief and Popular Culture: A Study of the South London Borough of Southwark (*c.*1880–1939)', Oxford D Phil. 1993

Wolffe, John, *God and Greater Britain. Religion and National Life in Britain and Ireland 1843–1945*, London and New York 1994

Wolffe, John (ed), *Evangelical Faith and Public Zeal. Evangelicals and Society in Britain 1780–1980*, London 1995

5

The Church of England 1901 to 1945

The pre-war years

At the dawning of the twentieth century the Church of England was in a rather parlous condition. It was aware that it had lost much ground to the Nonconformists, and even to English Catholicism which was manifestly more organized, unified and invigorated. As we have seen, ever since at least the acts of 1828 to 1832 the Church of England had been under attack for the privileges which it, in some people's view unwarrantably, enjoyed as the 'established' church. It could not claim to be the church of the nation when it was clear for all to see that such a high proportion of the population were not even nominal members of it, and an ever decreasing number of people were active and committed Anglicans. And yet it retained many of the benefits of establishment, and enjoyed a status, standing and esteem denied to other Christian traditions. Even some of its most sophisticated leaders had serious doubts about such a situation, and considered its perpetuation untenable. It was with much frustration and anger that Bishop Charles Gore asked Archbishop Cosmo Lang in 1912 how he could go on believing in an established church.[1] In the face of so many alternative denominational options, as well as the presence of substantial minorities of Roman Catholics, Jews, and those with no religious allegiance, the anomaly of establishment seemed to such critics to be blatantly obvious and in need of remedy. The nineteenth century had whittled away many of the Anglican privileges. Why, said some of its own members, let alone non-Anglican opponents of establishment, should the church-state link and all that went with it not now be severed once and for all? Randall Davidson, the long-serving, highly respected and influential Archbishop of Canterbury from 1903 to 1928, believed profoundly in establishment, and he managed to keep dissident Anglicans in check, and to resist pressure from without on this matter.[2] But erosion of its powers and prerogatives, and such questioning of its rights and advantages, was demoralizing and debilitating. It was especially irksome at a time of decline. It was destructive of Church of England confidence and self-respect, and undermined its efforts to fulfil its pastoral and evangelistic potential both nationally and locally. It was an important phase in that protracted and painful process whereby 'the Church was forced to shift from a monopolistic to a voluntaristic position, from the only officially recognized religious institution in England to a competing denomination'.[3]

A further cause of Church of England enervation in this period was internal friction. A large number of the most dedicated and ardent churchmen of that generation were at loggerheads, dissipating their energies in conflicts mainly over matters of liturgy and ritual. As we have seen, ritualism had been a major internal issue for the Church of England in the nineteenth century, and in 1903 it resurfaced.

In that year, as his first public act as Archbishop, Randall Davidson received a deputation of over one hundred Unionist Members of Parliament who were concerned about ecclesiastical disorders. They urged upon him the need for effective action in order to combat what was to them the alarming escalation of ritualistic practices of a Catholic nature in the Church of England. He conceded that stern, drastic and prompt measures were required, especially as there was widespread concern not only within the church but in the House of Commons. The following year a Royal Commission on Ecclesiastical Discipline was appointed.

The Commission concluded that the law relating to public worship in the Church of England was too narrow in order to accommodate the range of religious life, and its legitimate liturgical expression, as it had developed up to that time. It needlessly condemned much which was valued by a large section of church people, including many of the church's most devoted members. It did not take account of the quite remarkable changes in thought, care for ceremonial, and appreciation of liturgical continuity which had occurred since the law assumed its existing shape. In an age which had witnessed an extraordinary revival of spiritual life and activity there had not, the Commission asserted, been that power of self-adjustment in the matter of liturgical revision which was inherent in the concept of a living church. The Commission was also concerned that the machinery for exercising discipline had broken down. The means of enforcing the law in the ecclesiastical courts, even in matters which touched upon the church's faith and teaching, were defective and in some respects unsuitable.

The Commission made a number of recommendations, two of which were especially significant for the immediate and long-term life of the church. The first was a call to the bishops to ensure that certain unacceptable liturgical practices should cease forthwith, if necessary by proceedings in the ecclesiastical courts. The second was that which inaugurated the whole legislative process of Prayer Book revision.

In 1908 a Historical Report on Ornaments was presented to the Upper House of Convocation by a sub-committee of five bishops of whom Bishop John Wordsworth was the leader. It submitted a great deal of evidence in favour of the legality of vestments. It did not contain recommendations on the policy to be adopted, but it called forth a shower of memorials and protests.

Between 1908 and 1914 there was much animated discussion but no decision or action on Prayer Book revision; the policy was to do as little as possible. In the meantime the movement in favour of revision grew, and an advisory committee of liturgical scholars was appointed in July 1912. The critical question continued to be eucharistic vestments, and by the time war was declared there appeared to be a fair prospect that it could be resolved.

The onset of war did not terminate the debate. During the war, both at home and at the front, the eucharist assumed greater importance in the worship of churchmen, and it became increasingly prominent as a topic in the public discussion on the Prayer Book. Important debates took place on the matter of reservation[4] in the Upper House of Canterbury Convocation in 1915, 1917 and 1918; and in 1918 proposals for an alteration to the central part of the communion service were accepted from the Lower House. As we will see later in this chapter, from 1918 onwards the public and private discussion of Prayer Book revision became increasingly charged and culminated in the traumatic events of 1927 and 1928.

The main confrontation was between the High Churchmen and the Evangelicals. By the beginning of the twentieth century High Churchmen were committed to at least the weekly, and not infrequently the daily, celebration of communion or mass, the eastward position in conducting the service, candles on the altar, and, in the case of over two thousand churches, vestments. The reservation of the sacrament was accepted, and High Churchmen further stressed that if the consecrated bread was reserved for the sick it must signify an enduring sacramental presence of Christ, justifying reverence and prayer before it. There was a great desire among the resurgent High Churchmen for 'enrichment' of the Prayer Book services, usually by borrowing from the Roman Missal. The publication of *The English Liturgy* in 1904 showed how this could be done successfully without departing from the Anglican Communion. It was largely the work of Percy Dearmer and W.H. Frere, both of whom emphasized the continuity of the Church of England with the pre-Reformation Church. The Alcuin Club was founded in 1897 in order to promote this approach to liturgiology and church furnishings, and it produced some beautifully printed liturgical texts. All of this was abhorrent to Evangelicals.

In the pre-war years the more extreme opposition to ritualistic practices was spearheaded by militant Protestant bodies such as the Church Association, the National Protestant Church Union, the Protestant Truth Society, the Protestant Defence Brigade and the Wickliffe (*sic*) Preachers. Although most Evangelicals in the Church of England did not align themselves with the highly provocative actions of these organizations they very explicitly denounced what they regarded as quasi-Roman Catholic conduct symbolic of totally unacceptable doctrine. Some were even prepared to co-operate with non-Evangelicals in upholding what they believed to be an attack on the foundational beliefs of the Church of England. But in all their campaigning such objectors adopted rational and reasonable arguments and actions. Not so the more warlike, aggressive and uncompromising strand in Evangelicalism which was evident from the beginning of the century, when it was led by John Kensit and his Wickliffe Preachers. One example will indicate the tenor of the campaign undertaken by these vehement enthusiasts. On Sunday 14 January 1900 Kensit, accompanied by his son and some of the Preachers visited Christ Church, Belper, which was renowned for its ritualism. The following is the text of a letter from Kensit to the Bishop of Southwell:

My Lord Bishop – At the request of my own Diocesan, the Lord Bishop of London, I have in my crusade against the Mass and the confessional purposely abstained from any interference in the illegal services which have been, and are still being, conducted in our churches. His Lordship of London led me to believe that the Bishops intended to carry out their solemn promises made at their ordination to banish and drive away erroneous and strange doctrines. After waiting for sixteen months, being engaged with a band of my Wickliffe preachers in holding a Mission at Belper, I attended Christ Church being the district church where I am residing, and there to my disgust

I witnessed the Mass performed by the curate holding your licence, the Rev E.J. Scotcher. At the consecration of the bread a wafer was elevated high above his head. A server rang a bell, and all prostrated. The same illegality and idolatry were practised with the wine. I was compelled as a law-abiding Churchman to enter a protest and leave the building without partaking of the Holy Communion. The said curate, who holds your licence, is, I am informed, a member of the Confraternity of the Blessed Sacrament, an Association formed for restoring the Mass in our Church. The new Vicar who has accepted the living is also a member of the same society. On the Communion Table at Christ Church eight candles were burning, the curate several times kissed the table, and to all appearances ceremonially mixed the water with the wine. Now, my Lord Bishop, I call upon you to do your duty, and stop the Romanizing practices which have distinguished this and other churches in your diocese, especially at Derby, Sneiton, Buxton, and other places, and thus save me from the unpleasant duty of attending a service and entering in God's name a protest for my fellow-Churchmen, who are being driven out of the Church by this abominable idolatry – Awaiting your reply, yours for the truth (signed, John Kensit).[5]

The tactics adopted by the militants included similar disruptions, petitions, and the widespread distribution of literature. Some of the more moderate Evangelicals openly expressed their distress at such behaviour. A minority actually adopted a fairly elaborate ritualism themselves: they were usually part of a new liberal wing of Evangelicalism within the Church of England. This was a party within a party, and it added to the confusion within the church in the pre-war years.

These liberals were mainly young and they were very enthusiastic. They were discontented with what they regarded as the prevailing negativity of Evangelicals towards the various scientific and philosophical currents which had flowed since the middle of the previous century, and the Evangelical hostility, or at least lack of any sympathy, towards biblical criticism. They banded together between 1905 and 1907, arranged conferences of like-minded Evangelicals, and became known as the Group Brotherhood. Pamphlets were issued and there was a loose structure, but they remained for more than eighteen years a private, almost a secret, organization. They were concerned to 'think out afresh the doctrinal position of Evangelicals and to state in new terms the contribution which they had to make to contemporary life and thought'.[6] As we will see, the movement reached the height of its influence in the inter-war years, when it emerged into the full light of day and broadcast its views more self-confidently and effectively, but the foundations were laid in the pre-war years.

A far more radical movement assumed prominence in the early years of the twentieth century: modernism. It was represented by a totally new 'party' within the Church of England which can be dated with some precision back to 1898, for it was then that the Churchmen's Union for the Advancement of Religious Thought was founded, which in 1928 was renamed the Modern Churchmen's Union. Like Liberal Evangelicalism, it was to come to full flower in the 1920s, but the seeds were sown in the early years of the century. It was then that the main characteristics of Anglican Modernism became explicit. The typical English Modernist of that period and for some time to come was totally convinced of the existence of God and would have been horrified at the 'Death of God' school of the 1960s. He believed that God was in everything and that everything was in God. God worked only through the evolutionary process. Although God could be known to a certain extent in other religions he was supremely revealed in the Logos, Jesus Christ the Word of God. He did not doubt the existence of Jesus Christ, but if it could be proved that Jesus had never existed that would not demolish his religious faith. His Jesus was not an eschatological figure but rather the one who proclaimed the Fatherhood of God and the Brotherhood of Man. He accepted all that biblical criticism declared. He believed in the supernatural but not in the miraculous; and his Jesus did not perform miracles. Jesus was not born of a virgin, and his resurrection was spiritual rather than bodily. He wanted to keep dogma to the minimum, and ethics were more important than doctrine. He was unenthusiastic about the church, which he regarded as a necessary evil. Episcopacy was the best form of government, but the doctrine of apostolic succession was contemptible. He had concern for ritual, but later on, for example, did not like the Parish and People Movement (which was founded in 1949 in order to promote the liturgical movement as an organized force within the Church of England, with particular concern to make the eucharist the principal Sunday service).[7] He was not interested in pressing for the greater prominence of communion in the life of the church. Clerical subscription should be relaxed. He was well disposed to the Nonconformists and favourably inclined to reunion with them, but fought shy of Roman Catholics and the Orthodox Church. He championed the ordination of women and the marriage of divorced people in church. He advocated contraception, which was rigorously opposed by many churchmen. His focus was upon the life of the world to come, and he was frequently criticized for having insufficient interest in social questions.[8]

After 1898 the main pre-war landmarks in the history of Anglican Modernism were the founding in 1911 of the magazine The *Modern Churchman*, the publication of *Foundations* (1912), the first Conference of Modern Churchmen in 1914, and the influence throughout the period of Ripon Hall, the theological college founded in 1897 by Bishop Boyd Carpenter, which was a breeding ground for English Modernism.

Special mention should be made of *Foundations*, as it had both an immediate and long-term impact on the Christian community in England as a whole. The purpose of the volume was to expound and communicate a theology which was in harmony with modern science, philosophy, and scholarship in a number of other related fields.[9] The work promptly evoked a vigorous controversy, and generated a lively and widespread debate. It gave a fillip to modernism, so that in the following few years the movement agitated the theological world in a more profound way than it had in the past.

Although Anglican Modernists may not have been actively engaged in social thinking or social action, there were those in the established church who strove to articulate Christian political and social principles and implement them. Nineteenth-century Christian Socialism had a chequered history, but it bequeathed to the twentieth century a church concerned for social matters. Such bodies as the Christian Social Union (the CSU), established by Henry Scott Holland, Charles Gore and Brooke Foss Westcott in 1889, were small, but they taught the Church of England to think about social issues. By the first decade of the century 'there were very few Church leaders who did not adopt attitudes critical of industrial organization and social order – attitudes expressed in language, and according to a frame of reference, which was clearly furnished by the sort of atmosphere nurtured by the CSU . . . It was unusual, after 1900, to find a bishop who did not regard the declaration of social principles a primary duty.'[10]

One aspect of this spreading influence of social ideals was that the Christian Socialists themselves had by the beginning of the new century become more collectivist in their outlook than their forebears had been in the previous generation, with a definite belief in the rightful use of the state machinery to bring about a social and economic transformation. The founding of the Church Socialist League in 1906 reflected this, especially as it was bolstered in the same year by the possibilities which radical priests saw opening up as a result of the election of fifty-three Labour and Lib-Lab members to Parliament in the General Election. There was a mood of boundless optimism. The leaders of the League were mainly High Churchmen, and they were largely from northern England, where Mirfield was a centre of special importance and supplied such prominent Christian Socialists as Fr Paul Bull, Fr Samuel Healey and Fr Neville Figgis. The League was predominantly clerical, and it contributed some serious political and economic analysis to the current debate, as indicated by the inclusion of R.H. Tawney, Maurice Reckitt and A.J. Penny in its membership. In 1912 George Lansbury, later the Leader of the Parliamentary Labour Party, became its President. To the fore in the League were the Revd Frederick Lewes Donaldson and the persistent and durable upper-class leader Conrad Le Despenser Roden Noel. Noel had served under the distinguished 'slum priest' Fr Robert Dolling in Portsmouth, and from 1910 was incumbent of Thaxted, which he made the centre of Christian Socialism in England for the following thirty years. He was eccentric, and addicted to such gestures as flying a red flag from the tower of his church. He was an enemy of the rather comfortable armchair sort of liberal social reformation which was common among the CSU bishops. In its own distinctive way his socialism had impressive qualities.

It was unfortunate that the dedication and sacrificial work of those Anglicans engaged in urban ministry, and the sincere attempts by many Christian Socialists to construct a distinctively Christian theological social critique, did not result in any fundamental Christian social impact as measured by changes in government social policy, amelioration of the social and economic conditions of the mass of the submerged poor, or, it appears, a significant turning to the Christian faith of the religiously indifferent working classes. 'It is interesting that the Church of England, which contained a much larger number of clergymen attracted to "Christian Socialist" ideas than any other denomination, was also the Church that most noticeably failed to attract a working-class membership. A few slum priests who were Socialists achieved working-class congregations for a time because they were sympathetic pastors, not because of their politics. Working-class men, like all Englishmen, did not expect their clergy to preach political opinions, and did not like it when they did so.'[11] It has, however, to be granted that the extent of this failure 'to attract a working-class membership' is difficult to prove and to quantify. The Baptist denomination, which was perhaps the least concerned of all the Protestant denominations with a 'social gospel', actually grew in size around the turn of the century.

The Anglican failure to make the sort of social impact which was sought, and attract those estranged from the institutional church, can mainly to be attributed to long-standing structural causes, but there were immediate and more specific factors, among which the most significant was the matter of class. The social differences which separated the predominantly middle-class priests, with all their inherent social presuppositions and pre-dispositions, from the working classes who were, in most cases, geographically and socially living in different and alien worlds, were almost insurmountable barriers. Many 'forms of socialism and collectivism were unpopular because they were bourgeois in origin'.[12] There was widespread ignorance concerning the prevailing conditions in such areas as Bethnal Green, an unfamiliarity with the social and cultural mores and values of the working class, and not infrequently hostility to such values, lifestyles and patterns of behaviour in as far as they were known. Christian Socialists in general 'were unable to separate working-class values from the evil consequences of an appalling environment and economic hardship. Their simple instinct was to educate the working-classes into acceptance of their own cultural values. A chasm existed between styles of life which the Settlements did not bridge. They became little oases of upper-class life.'[13] The radical politics of many of the Anglican Christian Socialists was little related to the actual life situation of working-class people. Working-class autobiographies and city mission reports have corroborated research findings that 'any form of religion which reinforced rather than diminished class distinctions was unpopular with the urban poor. Indeed, the sheer "respectability" of much pre-First World War religion with its sabbatarianism and temperance, its clerical professionalism and opposition to popular recreations, excluded as many as it attracted. What was left has been described as "proletarian parochialism", which was founded on community solidarity and a homespun morality of not doing anybody any harm.'[14] A barrier existed between those who attempted to reach out to the urban working class and the very people to whom they longed to minister. Despite heroic and well-meaning efforts the urban working class therefore frequently proved to be 'largely beyond the reach of both the plebeian ultra-evangelicalism of Brethren, Baptists, Salvationists and city missioners, and the more colourful rituals of High Church Anglicanism and ethnic Catholicism'.[15] This was as true for the early years of the twentieth century as it had been for the latter part of the nineteenth century.

In the countryside class also played a major part in determining religious patterns of commitment and behaviour, but in rural communities immemorial custom still exerted considerable influence. The kind of situation so evocatively recounted by Flora Thompson in *Lark Rise to Candleford* remained accurate until at least the First World War. She reckoned that around the turn of the century nine out of ten of the inhabitants of Lark Rise would have declared themselves to be members of the Church of England, having been christened and married in the parish church. They buried their dead in the church graveyard, and while they lived they attended the festivals at Christmas, Easter and harvest time, visited the rectory on May Day, and paraded their finery and singing voices on Sundays. Most of them seldom entered the church other than at festival time or for rites of passage, and the majority, especially the men, resented clerical visits, and were particularly averse to any mention of religion. Their 'religion' was a 'delicate mixture of social utility, rural entertainment and moral consensus in which the parish church was closely enmeshed, albeit within certain defined limits set by the community'.[16]

It was not that the Church of England or the Nonconformists in town or country were lethargic. Masterman was probably right in reckoning them to be trying hard both pastorally and evangelistically. 'The Churches are extraordinarily active,' he wrote in 1909, endeavouring in this way and in that to influence the lives of the people. 'Their humanitarian and social efforts are widely appreciated. Their definite dogmatic teachings seem to count for little at all. They labour on steadily amid a huge indifference.'[17] Throughout the whole of the modern world, among all classes, he perceived a scene of gloom for the churches. 'The tide is ebbing within and without the Churches. The drift is towards a non-dogmatic affirmation of general kindliness and good fellowship, with an emphasis rather on the service of men than the fulfilment of the will of God.'[18] In town and country, at national and local levels, the Church of England was confused and divided. She struggled with a severe identity problem, and she had no vision or great sense of purpose and direction. It would have added to her sense of despondency if she could have foreseen that she was 'entering upon forty of the most difficult, exacting, and discouraging years of all her history'.[19] And just ahead was the first of two World Wars with a troubled and uneasy interlude between them.

The Church of England in time of war

In 1914 in the Church of England and more notably within the Nonconformist denominations there was a peace movement, but most members of the churches unhesitatingly and confidently asserted that Britain had no option but to take up arms against Germany in August 1914; it was a just and holy war.[20] Germany had set Europe ablaze for no other reason than that she might become a world power. In her mad lust her armies were guilty of foul atrocities. Such aggression must be resisted or it would mean the triumph of evil over righteousness; the victory of might over right. Not to have taken up arms in such a cause would have been a betrayal of sacred principles. Non-action would have meant dishonouring the name of Britain: it would have ensured that henceforth the country was held in righteous contempt, and Britain would have been dubbed a timorous, time-serving people, terrorized by the spectre of German militarism. The blatant wickedness and ungodliness of the German nation was proclaimed with no mitigating qualifications and with passion and indignation. The whole German philosophy and behaviour was declared to be a violent rejection of the Christian standard of righteousness and justice: it was a repudiation of the Sermon on the Mount and of the meekness and gentleness of Christ. Britain was launched on a godly crusade.

From within the ranks of the Evangelicals, the High Churchmen and the Liberals the call went out from the church to rally round the flag. Reference was made by some to the sinful state of the pre-war British nation, to the patience of God being exhausted, and to the angel of death having appeared over the land with his sword in his hand.[21] But such self-examination and self-condemnation soon gave way to a concentration on the sins of Germany.

Of course things did not appear in quite the same light to some German Christians. In September 1914 a group of eighty of the most renowned members of the German religious and academic communities led by Adolf von Harnack, Adolf Deissmann, Ernest Dryander and Rudolf Eucken issued an *Appeal to Evangelical Christians Abroad*, in which they enthusiastically supported their country's policies and defended 'the inner right of us and our Emperor to invoke the assistance of God'. They insisted that the Germans were fighting to save the West from Russian barbarism. They asserted that England was fully aware of this yet deliberately misrepresented the issues and endeavoured through its worldwide propaganda network to point a finger of guilt at Germany alone. Germany was, said the *Appeal*, fighting for its very existence against a host of hostile powers. 'No scruple holds back our enemies, where in their opinion there is a prospect of seizing for themselves an economic advantage or an increase in power, a fragment of our motherland, our colonial possessions or our trade. We stand over against this raging of the peoples, fearless because of our trust in the holy and righteous God.'[22] The *Appeal* was unacceptable to English churchmen, and it was made especially repugnant because it was published in England within four days of the burning of Louvain and the massacres at Dinant and Tremonde, in which dozens of defenceless civilians were machine-gunned in reprisal for guerrilla activity. Even Archbishop Davidson was incredulous.[23] Far from being sympathetically received, the *Appeal* further inflamed public opinion. The reply, *To the Christian Scholars of Europe and America*, which was signed by such leading churchmen as Charles Gore, Henry Scott Holland and Walter Lock, refuted the points raised in the *Appeal* one by one in polite but firm and uncompromising language. As a concluding and most telling counter blow the reply noted how Germany's actions spoke louder than all her paeans to Kultur and humanitarianism. In view of Louvain, 'will not the Christian scholars of other lands share our conviction that the contest in which our country is engaged is a contest on behalf of the supremest interests of Christian civilization?'[24]

As the war with all its horrors continued so the concept of a crusade became ever more passionately proclaimed. But there were restraining voices, most notably the High Churchman Bishop Gore. In the midst of an apathetic or hostile episcopate he denounced what to his mind was a shameful, unChristian upsurge of fanaticism. He chided the enthusiasts for resorting to language which was typical of that associated with the Crusades, not the most glorious period in English history. He was firmly convinced that England had no choice but to participate in the war; but he warned against self-righteousness and priggishness. Since the history of Britain was hardly immaculate, national repentance was more appropriate to the needs of the hour. To Gore the kingdom of God was more important than winning the war. 'The thoughts and feelings which patriotism inspires legitimately fill our minds and imaginations. But this is not enough. I am sure that if we simply yield ourselves to these thoughts and feelings we shall fall disastrously short of what our Lord would have us think.'[25] Protests were also registered by Walter Lock and Henry Scott Holland, both of whom maintained that notwithstanding their crimes, the Germans remained children of God; and clergymen should remember their calling as his servants, and not go about as 'Mad Mullahs preaching a Jehad'.[26]

As the war developed into an ever more bloody affair various specific issues surfaced. Pacifism was one of the first. Of course, to many of those who were loudest in proclaiming the conflict as a holy war conscientious objection was inconceivable. The biblical evidence against such non-participation seemed to them to be overwhelming, and the pacifists received little sympathy.[27] In the entire columns of the Anglican press for the whole of the war it is difficult to find presentations by conscientious objectors of their case, and where they were given a hearing what they said was typically dismissed with contempt. There was no debate, and the voice of moderation was seldom heard. The main exception was again Charles Gore. He spoke three times in the House of Lords in successive years against the ill treatment of the pacifists, despite not agreeing with what they believed. He thought that the genuine cases should be distinguished from those that were bogus, but he was adamant that every effort should be made to ensure that a fair and just system of appraisal and treatment was adopted. It was reprehensible that many of the tribunals set up to make assessments of individual cases had assumed that those trying to avoid military service were inevitably unpatriotic, and had therefore forfeited their rights under the law. It was, said Gore, inconsistent for the country to claim to champion freedom while at the same time it persecuted Quakers and others who rendered valuable service to society.

There was less unanimity of belief in the church over clergy enlistment than over conscientious objection. It was widely thought that ordination was a setting apart for a distinctive ministry, and was incompatible with military service; but many held that individual clergy should be given liberty to chose for themselves. A minority opinion saw no impropriety in the military involvement of clergy. There is also some evidence that the dogmatism of those opposed to clergy enlistment was somewhat moderated towards the end of the war.[28] In general the service chaplains were reckoned to have done a reasonable job in very difficult circumstances, although the Evangelical Chaplain-General, Bishop Taylor Smith, was heavily criticized for his extreme bias against High Churchmen, making it almost impossible for them to obtain commissions and to serve as chaplains, for his lack of university theological training, and for his unsophisticated, apolitical, atomistic approach in which he did not appreciate that conversion to a pietistic religion was an inadequate answer to the issues raised by the war both for faith and for society.[29] Archbishop Davidson neatly circumvented this particular problem by appointing the widely-known and well-liked Bishop L.H. Gwynne of the Sudan as Deputy Chaplain-General in charge of the chaplains in France, where most of them were serving.

Another agonizing ethical and moral question arising out of the war was that of reprisals. The zeppelin and aeroplane raids by Germany on British cities, the shelling of coastal towns, and the menace of U-boats intensified public animosity and popular hysteria, and evoked a wide-spread demand for reprisals against German civilians. But despite their typically unreserved and outspoken patriotism church leaders unambiguously condemned any retaliatory acts. Once more I will allow Gore to speak for many. On the occasion of the retaliatory British bombing of German towns in 1917 his protest was immediate: 'If we allow ourselves to be led by the Germans, the descent is easy and the end certain degradation.'[30] Also in 1917, at a most emotive burial of child victims of an air raid, Winnington-Ingram resolutely and courageously spoke out against reprisals, despite his frequent and more characteristic bellicose utterances. He said that he did not believe that the mourners would want sixteen German children killed to avenge the dead British children. But he balanced this with a call for just counteraction: 'What all demanded was strong deterrent naval and military action . . . on the places from which these attacks came, and that the strongest punishment should be given to the perpetrators and designers of these raids.'[31]

Some topics which surfaced during the war were of a more general nature, and not so clear cut. Foremost among these was the whole issue of suffering and death. Few ventured to attempt anything approaching a definitive answer. The Evangelicals retained a strong faith in the sovereignty of God and the Satanic origin of all evil, and remained convinced that good would ultimately triumph. By adopting such guidelines they were able to integrate suffering into their cosmic view, and reconcile it with their faith in a God of love. In the heat and trauma of battle, and faced with actual and highly distressing examples of individual pain and death, it was often found that differences of church tradition and theology among the chaplains lessened as all of them attempted to confront personal tragedy.

In the midst of war church leaders were mindful of the need to plan for peace. The mechanism adopted was a National Mission. It was a call both to individual conversion and national transformation. It enlisted the enthusiastic support of a broad range of churchmen of varying traditions, including those who inherited the Christian Socialist concerns. No one saw the potential of the Mission as a means to further social justice through Anglicanism more clearly than Percy Widdrington, who by that time was the strongest influence in the Church Socialist League. In April 1916 he wrote: 'The time of criticism is past. The day of action has come; it has been our misfortune to find ourselves in constant opposition to the authorities in the Church, and we have been out of sympathy with our fellow churchmen. We have been driven for our fellowship outside rather than inside the Church. We have almost become "aliens" to our mother's children. Such a state of things is to be deplored. It has been to some of us spiritually disastrous. Thank God the day of better things has come.'[32]

The Mission was succeeded by the establishment of five committees which reported in 1918. Their reports, and especially the last on *Christianity and Industrial Problems*, which appeared auspiciously in the month following the Armistice, provided a useful launching pad for the difficult inter-war years, as we will see in a moment.

There was a remarkable contrast between the whole reaction of the Church of England to the First World War and what happened immediately prior to and during the course of the Second World War. In the 1930s the church was complacent about events in Germany. This was epitomized by the trust placed by churchmen generally in the devout Anglican Lord Halifax as Foreign Secretary in the crucial months prior to the outbreak of war, that he 'would understand and moderate the wild men of Germany and Italy'.[33] At the Canterbury Diocesan Conference in 1939 the Archbishop of Canterbury, Cosmo Gordon Lang, paid tribute to 'the confidence of all parties in his spirit, his motives, his calmness, his steadiness of judgment'. But his background did not equip him to make accurate judgments about Hitler, Goering and the others with whom he had discussions. He was out of his depth, and he was unable to fathom the wickedness of such men. His faith had taught him a certain detachment from the world. The description by his biographer of his reaction to the Munich agreement is indicative of prevailing sentiments among the Church of England leadership at the time:

The belief in a Divine control over the affairs of the world led him to think that human beings could only move the course of events a little in certain directions, so that while prepared to do this, he was not ready to step in and stem the flood: and his profound belief in the future life made the disasters of this world seem by contrast transient and insubstantial. Thus armoured he could envisage human afflictions with an almost unearthly calm, and face war, when it came, with complete inner tranquillity . . .[34]

Lang gave the lead in the church's response to the Munich agreement; and it was disastrous. He ignored a request from Dean Duncan-Jones, one of the few priests in England who were well-informed about the state of Germany, that he should voice the conscience of England against what Duncan-Jones described as the 'most shameful betrayal in English history', and was effusive in his praise of what had been done. Both on the radio and in the House of Lords he adopted his most unctuous language in an oft-repeated expression of gratitude at once to God and to the Prime Minister. 'More than one member of Parliament said to me today as we all trooped into the lobby: "This is the hand of God".' With reference to Chamberlain, he declared in the Lords, 'no praise could be too great'.[35]

The views of the appeasers set the tone in the church as a whole, but they did not go unchallenged. For example, the East End priest Fr St John Groser was passionately opposed to the Mosleyites and the Munich agreement and expressed his indignation in a letter to the Anglican Guardian:

> Blackmail has succeeded. The threat of force has triumphed . . . That Mr Chamberlain should talk of 'peace with honour' when he has surrendered to this blackmail, torn up Article 10 of the League Covenant without reference to Geneva, and sacrificed the Czechoslovaks in order, as he says, to prevent a world war, is bad enough; but that the Archbishop of Canterbury should say that this is the answer to our prayers . . . is beyond endurance.[36]

But he and those of a similar point of view were but voices crying in the wilderness. 'In 1938, at least within the Church, both the right wing and the left, both the Establishment and the radicals, were appeasers. Only the odd man out questioned the wisdom of Mr Chamberlain. For the clergy as a whole, peace, to be pursued by all means and at almost any cost, was the overriding preoccupation of the thirties, whether or not they subscribed formally to Pacifism.'[37]

Partly because of these pre-war attitudes, the response of the Church of England leadership, and the church in general, to war when it came was very muted. Patriotism was as great as it ever was, but there was

We went on jigging He sletters.

never, either before or during the war, a wide-ranging, intense and heartfelt anti-Nazi, pro-British, sentiment to compare in any way to the passions aroused twenty-five years earlier. There were not the same appeals to promote a crusade, nor the same portrayal of issues in stark black and white terms. Attitudes were more restrained, and the language used was decidedly less aggressive. When Archbishop Lang exhorted people to pray for victory the appeal was issued in a very low key way, and he never attempted to rouse the nation. There was no dominant, powerful, charismatic figure who commanded national attention and who raised the anti-German temper to a high pitch of intensity.

There was not the jingoism of the First World War, but the restrained and reasoned Anglican reaction should not imply a lack of belief in the righteousness of the national cause. Far from it. William Temple typified the Church of England attitude in this respect, and indeed largely helped to mould it. He determined from the outset of the war that he could and would only speak for the Christian conscience. He proclaimed the war to be a 'divine judgment', and he upheld the national cause. In his first broadcast after the outbreak of war, on 3 October 1939, he declared that the country entered 'the war as a dedicated nation'. He went on to say that 'the prevailing conviction is that Nazi tyranny and oppression are destroying the traditional excellences of European civilization and must be eliminated for the good of mankind'. [38]

Temple's attitude was endorsed by others. To cite one: Hensley Henson, the then Dean of Durham, and later Bishop of Hereford, regarded Hitlerism as self-evidently standing for all that was evil. The country could make no terms with it. The issue was not merely political, or solely national, but essentially moral and spiritual. Two conceptions of human nature, two ideals of human destiny were in conflict, and no man could serve two masters. Henson and others even described the war effort of the nation as a crusade and a holy war, but they did so in more measured tones than their parents had done a generation earlier. [39]

and later Durham in the 1930s

The overall comparatively unemotional response was strange when there were more issues to inflame people than in the First World War, such as territorial expansion, the violation of people's rights, the torture and ill-treatment of prisoners of war, the wholesale bombing of towns and cities, and the horrors of the holocaust, and such technological advances as the radio made people more aware of what was going on than in the First World War. Perhaps it was a deliberate avoidance of the over-reaction a quarter of a century before, or the fact that the previous experience of world war had accustomed people more to the brutalities of modern warfare.

Nevertheless, there was one voice which sounded out with an authority and weight which could not be ignored: that of George Bell, the Bishop of Chichester.[40] His pronouncements on moral issues of the war were delivered with a transparent clarity and impartiality which was reminiscent of Charles Gore. He spoke out with boldness, penetration and courage on a variety of matters, and in the opinion of many thereby forfeited the opportunity of elevation to the archiepiscopate of Canterbury; for he was fearless in expressing views which were uncongenial to those charged with responsibility for the conduct of the war. He opposed any attempt by the church to project the idea of such an earthly war as a crusade; resisted any tendency of the church to make the victory of the national cause the supreme concern; and encouraged links between Christians of all nations, including the warring countries. He distinguished between Germany and National Socialism, and while he declared that the allies could never make terms with the latter, he held out the possibility of doing so with the former, under certain conditions. He attracted particular animosity from the managers of the war for his courageous renunciation of the bombing of German cities.

The inter-war period

The Report on *Christianity and Industrial Problems*, which arose out of the National Mission in the latter part of the First World War, became the charter of the Industrial Christian Fellowship, an organization which came into being in 1918 as a timely fusion of the Navvy Mission, which was an evangelistic agency which lacked a social message, and the socially orientated CSU, which had never achieved any successful contact with the working class. 'The ICF, with its great open-air "Crusades", its missioners at the street corners and in the factories, and its educational work through correspondence class and study circle, manifested in the post-war years, more effectively than had ever been done before, the concern of the nation's Church at once for the spiritual and the social condition of the masses of the nation.'[41] It was a measure of such Anglican involvement in the new organization that it managed to enlist a greater degree of episcopal patronage than any such Christian body had previously enjoyed. The new men who came forward to meet the challenge offered by this rekindled sense of mission and to serve in the ICF were for the most part those who had served overseas as chaplains with the citizen armies, and who, because of their sharing of the hardship and soul-searching experiences of ordinary people, gained an unusual insight into the physical, mental and spiritual needs of people whom they might not otherwise have known and understood so profoundly. Pre-eminent among these was Geoffrey Studdert-Kennedy ('Woodbine Willie') who, it has been well said, 'was in the true line of succession of Stanton, Dolling and Wainright'. They were all remarkably selfless lovers of God and man, 'impetuous and often it may be injudicious, but ready to burn their lives away without hesitation if the truth that is in them can but be spoken and the souls they yearn to rescue can but be reached and restored'.[42] William Temple said of Studdert-Kennedy, and it could have been said of many others in varying degrees, that 'the urging impulse was not in his thought but in his heart; it was the passion of sympathy with the victims of our present injustice'. His life was dedicated to making Christ known to individuals and in the social order, and he died in the midst of such service in 1929 at the early age of forty-six.

The social thrust, of which the ICF was one manifestation, was evident in a variety of ways. It showed itself in the way a group of ex-members of the Church Socialist League formed the League of the Kingdom of God in 1923 as an expression of their 'radical re-examination of the title deeds of the Church's social movement'.[43] It found a new form in the search for a Christian sociology, and the consequent publication in 1922 of *Is there a Catholic sociology?* by Egerton Swann, and of *The Return of Christendom*. In the former Swann answered his own question with a resounding Yes; and proposed that the three pillars of the church's own distinctive programme should be distribution of property, the just price, and a guild organization of industry. This did not ape the existing opinions of either the Labour movement or Socialism. It cut across all current cleavages, and it left the church in a position of sovereign independence which might require it to defy the Labour movement and the plutocracy alike.

The other publication was the product of several years work by the Christendom Group surrounding Percy Widdrington. This had first been assembled at Coggeshall in Essex in 1920, and had subsequently undertaken a comprehensive study of the ideals of mediaeval Christian society. It 'represented an elaborate, if not wholly satisfactory, exploration of the philosophical, theological and sociological foundations for a reformation of Catholic social teaching'.[44] In 1931 a quarterly journal was started entitled *Christendom: A Journal of Christian Sociology*, and the following year an annual conference was instituted. The 'Christian Sociology' which these enthusiasts did so much to foster was not sociology in the technical, scientific sense, for it was normative and propagandist, but it was a serious attempt to define distinctly Christian principles of society derived from Christian doctrine.

The group was identified with the English Catholic tradition in the Church of England, but it was not fiercely partisan. Indeed, it acquired an interdenominational dimension and drew upon various Protestant bodies. V.A. Demant was especially active, and his prolific writings furthered its ideals. Although he and others maintained that the prophetic duty of the church justified it in intervening in political affairs, the movement was ambivalent about its social aims. Widdrington and his friends in the League of the Kingdom of God, were determined to overturn the existing social order although they believed that to 'lose sight of the principles of Christian society in order to gain some political advantage was too high a price to pay'.[45] They strove to preserve the theological heritage of the nineteenth-century Christian Socialist movement, and they offered direction to churchmen who were eager to do battle with capitalism and yet were disenchanted with socialism. Although 'the very refusal to take sides in the day-to-day political struggle between Left and Right kept the Christendom Group from exercising much influence outside the small world of Anglo-Catholic intellectuals',[46] it was arguably the leading socialist movement in the Church of England in the inter-war years.

Nevertheless, of wider and more long-term importance in the life of the Church of England in the period 1918 to 1939 was the work associated with William Temple and COPEC. The new analysis and criticism of the social order which had been bequeathed to post-First World War England by the Christian Socialist movement in its various embodiments and manifestations became especially articulated in the inter-war years in the life, work and teaching of a block of Christian Social Union bishops; and their social thought received its clearest expression in the persuasive oratory and writings of William Temple, one of the most outstanding churchmen not only of the twentieth but of any century. Conditions of war, and especially the experience of the 3,000 Anglican chaplains, brought home to church leaders in a new and forceful way the extent of the alienation of the church from so many of the people, and the widespread lack of Christian knowledge among ordinary Englishmen. The social thinking of the church, and its concern to engage in debate over social issues and to find means whereby it could become more relevant to all sections of the public, found a focus in the inter-war years in the 1924 assembly in Birmingham of the Conference on Christian Politics, Economics and Citizenship (COPEC). It was a watershed in that it provided a more comprehensive, systematic and coherent statement than previously achieved of the Christian social radicalism of the preceding decade and more. The span of subjects embraced by the conference is indicated by the titles of the reports: *The Nature of God and His Purpose for the World, Education, The Home, The Relation of the Sexes, Leisure, The Treatment of Crime, International Relations, Christianity and War, Industry and Property, Politics and Citizenship, The Social Function of the Church*, and *Historical Illustrations of the Social Effects of Christianity*. The COPEC philosophy that 'the Gospel provides the Christian with the solution of all the problems involved in our earthly life' was widely accepted, but it was rejected by some, most notably Hensley Henson. He considered it a false assumption, and the true position to be exactly the reverse. For, he said, 'it is fundamental in Christ's religion that the redemption of the world must be effected through the redemption of individuals'.[47]

Another important reinforcement of the principles of social radicalism was the publication in 1926 of R.H. Tawney's *Religion and the Rise of Capitalism*.[48] It was a historical explanation of the transition from the mediaeval practice of Christian economic teaching to modern competitive individualism. Economics and religion had, according to Tawney, become separated. The unhappy result reported by every Christian Socialist, and many others not of that school was:

> a dualism which regards the secular and religious aspects of life, not as successive stages within a large unity, but as parallel and independent provinces, governed by different laws, judged by different standards, and amenable to different authorities.[49]

Tawney's other books, notably *The Acquisitive Society* (1921) and *Equality* (1931), became essential reading for those interested in social criticism.

To some extent Christian Sociology filled the gap left by the Christian Social Union in acting as an expression of Christian social radicalism, but it was the ascendancy of William Temple in the years after COPEC which most contributed to this. He symbolized the general acceptance by the church leadership of a respectable version of social radicalism. Even if the church as a whole lacked the social commitment which the radicals would have wished, there was in the inter-war years a growing social consciousness in church circles.

It was High Churchmen who were most active in these Christian socialist movements; and they also were responsible for the most successful and important inter-war attempts to achieve ecclesiastical and theological renewal: the Anglo-Catholic Congresses and two pub-lications, *Essays Catholic and Critical* (1926) edited by Edward Gordon Selwyn, and *The Gospel and the Catholic Church* (1936) by Arthur Michael Ramsey.

The idea for the congresses came from the little known East End priest, the Revd C.R. Deakin, and the chief organizer was the out-standing Marcus Atlay, vicar of St Matthew's, Westminster. At the head of the programme for the first of them in 1920 it stated that the purpose and aim was 'the extension of the knowledge and practice of Catholic Faith at home and abroad, and by these means to bring men and women to a true realization of our Lord Jesus Christ as their personal Saviour and King'. They were met by an overwhelmingly enthusiastic response. The numbers went up from one congress to another. According to the official reports there were 13,000 in 1920, 15,000 in 1923, 21,000 in 1927, 29,000 in 1930 and 70,000 in 1933.[50] A subsequent com-mentator has caught something of the atmosphere of worship and praise which characterized the 1920 congress, and no doubt it applies to the others:

I think on the whole that perhaps the Thanksgiving Services were in some ways the most striking feature of the congress. I am told that by 7.30 on Friday evening the queue of people waiting to get into Southwark Cathedral stretched from the Cathedral gates right across London Bridge to the Monument. It is the first time, surely, at any rate since the Reformation, that London Bridge heard a great crowd singing to the honour of the Mother of our Lord, as the waiting mul-titude sang again and again, 'Hail Mary, Hail Mary, full of grace'. These are some of the things which passed practically unnoticed in the newspapers; but which we shall never forget.[51]

There were a number of people, even among the leaders and organizers, who were not happy with the very open and explicit Catholic character of the worship and devotions at the congresses, and favoured forms of worship which would be more acceptable to a wider range of churchmen, or would at least not cause offence. There was particular concern about the Marian devotions, for instance in the hymns sung to the Blessed Virgin Mary, and objections were expressed by Winnington-Ingram, who had been persuaded to be President of the 1923 congress. He declared such a focus to be contrary to the doctrine and practice of the Church of England. But the less cautious, less inhibited advocates of the more extreme forms of Catholic devotion won the day.

'Perhaps the most important service the Congress movement rendered to the Anglo-Catholic Movement was to bring into the very forefront the need of missionary work not only in England but overseas.'[52] Partly because the Lambeth Conference of 1920 was due to be held shortly after the 1920 congress, six out of the eight chairmen at the congress meetings that year were bishops from overseas. In the following congress in 1923 Bishop Frank Weston of Zanzibar had a major influence in calling the participants to engage in the affairs of society and exercise their influence as Christians. Large sums of money were contributed through the congresses for the furtherance of world mission, and evangelism at home.

The five congresses engendered a sense of triumph, but it was perhaps inevitable that the euphoria could not be sustained, or the intensity of the emotional involvement maintained. Such effervescent gatherings have their day and pass away. In retrospect the magnificent high mass of the 1933 congress may be seen as a requiem for the exuberant, visionary type of Anglican Catholicism which the congresses represented.

Following the centenary year of the Oxford movement, the sixth Anglo-Catholic Congress was planned for 1940, to be the culmination of seven years evangelistic work in the parishes, and to coincide with the Lambeth Conference due for that year. The onset of war meant that both were postponed until 1948, and then they met under very much changed circumstances both for the nation, for the church and for Anglican Catholicism.

In the realm of theological thinking *Essays Catholic and Critical*[53] was an important publication. It was very consciously in the *Lux Mundi* tradition and was an attempt to do for theology, and more especially Anglican Catholic theology, what *Lux Mundi* had attempted to do about forty years earlier. It aspired to being 'a fresh exposition and defence of the Catholic faith'. As with *Lux Mundi*, a group of mainly academics who had 'been brought into close touch with the vigorous currents and cross-currents of thought and feeling amid which Christianity has to render its own life and truth explicit', felt 'compelled, both for themselves and for others, to think out afresh the contents and the grounds of their religion'.[54]

The essayists identified two main developments since the publication of *Lux Mundi* in 1889: a greater interest in the supernatural element in religion, and an expression of that in the context of Catholic unity and authority. The authors were attempting 'to bring into synthesis the Catholic and the critical movements'.[55]

The central issue was the source and nature of authority. The essayists were deliberately vague on this matter, as they were not prepared to recognize any single authority, whether that be an infallible Pope, an infallible Bible, or an infallible conscience. They identified the source of authority 'in the Spirit of God, who revealed and still reveals the unsearchable riches of Christ'; and the seat of authority 'in the common mind of the Church', with its normative expression 'in the Scriptures, and especially in the revelations of the Apostles and those who knew our Lord personally', but also in the Church's creeds, its dogmatic formularies, its liturgical forms and phrases – in short, in whatever has nourished and borne fruit in the lives of the saints.[56]

Essays Catholic and Critical did not reflect the biblical approach which was in the process of revival in English theology, and which I have already discussed. In fact the book was quite quickly to become somewhat dated, 'being later than the dogmatic theology of Gore and earlier than the return to the Biblical "theology of crisis"'.[57] This was not so with the contribution made to theological thinking in 1936 by Arthur Michael Ramsey in his book *The Gospel and the Catholic Church*, which was to have an enduring and stimulating influence.

The underlying conviction of the work was 'that the meaning of the Christian Church becomes most clear when it is studied in terms of the Death and Resurrection of Jesus Christ'.[58] The New Testament portrays the church as more than the 'extension of the Incarnation'. The disciples 'knew themselves to be the refounded Israel of God through being partakers in the Messiah's death'.[59]

Ramsey set forth the church not as a loose collection of believers in Jesus, but as a new nation with the solidarity of one race, brought to birth by a creative act of God, owing its existence to the death of Christ. 'Christianity therefore is never solitary. It is never true to say that separate persons are united to Christ, and then combine to form the Church; for to believe in Christ is to believe in One whose Body is a part of Himself and whose people are His own humanity, and to be joined to Christ is to be joined to Christ-in-His-Body; for "so is Christ" and Christ is not otherwise.'[60]

Ramsey believed that there was no fundamental conflict between the Evangelical and the Catholic elements in the Church of England. They were utterly one. The one gospel of God inevitably included the scriptures and the salvation of the individual; but as inevitably it included the order and the sacramental life of the Body of Christ, and the freedom of thought wherewith Christ has made us free. The two aspects of Anglicanism – Evangelical and Catholic – cannot really be separated. Anglicanism 'possesses a full Catholicity, only if it is faithful to the Gospel of God; and it is fully Evangelical in so far as it upholds the Church order wherein an important aspect of the Gospel is set forth'. [61]

Four of the final theological and ecclesiastical matters to consider in this review of the Church of England in the inter-war years were, unfortunately, causes of much strife and bitterness, as well as some benefits to the church in the short, medium and long-term: the high-water mark of modernism, the resurgence of Liberal Catholicism, the emergence of Liberal Evangelicalism into the full light of day, and the sequence of events which culminated in the abortive attempts at Prayer Book revision in 1927 and 1928. But I will then conclude with the largely successful struggle for changes in the government of the Church of England, its greater democratization, and the fuller involvement of lay people in its affairs, in all of which we once more encounter that remarkably energetic, able and creative churchman, William Temple.

In the inter-war years modernists communicated their core concerns and convictions more effectively to non-modernists than they had in the past, and modernism became more distinguishable and influential as a consequence. Although it was very varied, and it was a rebellion and an ideal rather than a system, common features are discernable in its various manifestations which allow us to treat it as one. The clearest of these were a determined effort to protect the right of free enquiry; an attempt to harmonize the findings of the modern sciences with Christian belief; and an insistence that there was development in the understanding of Christian faith. Between 1918 and 1939 the Modern Churchmen's Union became more aggressive in the promotion of its beliefs, largely as a result of the exertions of such men as H.D.A. Major, for many years Principal of Ripon Hall, and M.G. Glazebrook, first headmaster of Clifton and subsequently Canon of Ely.

Christology provided the focus for much of the modernist theological interest in the immediate post-First World War years, and that was the subject at the notorious Churchmen's Union conference at Girton College, Cambridge in 1921. The scene was set by the appearance in 1920 of the first volume of *The Beginnings of Christianity*, under the editorship of F.J. Foakes Jackson and Kirsopp Lake, in which Jesus was depicted as the bearer of an ethical message, prophetic in a mild sense, but extraordinarily jejune. The Conference came to conclusions, as reported and commented upon by Major, which caused a considerable stir in the church, and also to quite an extent in the country. Newspaper articles, quoting phrases out of context, created the impression that some of the modernists such as Hastings Rashdall were denying the divinity of Christ.

The following year, partly as a result of the Girton conference, the Archbishops appointed a commission to consider the nature and basis of Christian doctrine in order to demonstrate the extent of agreement within the Church of England, and to investigating how far it was possible to remove or diminish differences. It did not report until 1938, by which time other issues were occupying centre stage.

Charles Gore was both the foremost protagonist in the modernist controversy, hammering them unmercifully, and the chief proponent of Liberal Catholicism.[62] He set forth his brand of theology in a trilogy entitled *The Reconstruction of Belief*. Volume one, *Belief in God* appeared in 1921, the second volume a year later under the title *Belief in Christ*, and the final volume in 1925 with the title *The Holy Spirit and the Church*. *Essays Catholic and Critical*, which I have already considered, was the greatest monument to this Liberal Catholicism in the twenty years between the two wars. The spirit of the whole movement also appealed to those Evangelicals of a liberal inclination who decided it was time they went public with their views.

They did so in 1923 in a collection of essays under the title *Liberal Evangelicalism*. It was a plea that, in confident reliance on the basic Evangelical principles, Evangelicals, and Christians in general, should follow wherever the pursuit of truth led them. There should be no quarrel between science and religion and no divorce between religion and secular knowledge, which would most certainly happen if Christians rejected modern scholarship. Literary criticism, natural science and philosophy were not the enemies of Evangelicalism, but its three most powerful allies; its true enemies were the forces of worldly indifference, superstition, ignorance, and fear.

The leading representative of this new Evangelical strand was Vernon F. Storr. He and others of his cast of mind were also dissatisfied with some of the prevalent penal and substitutionary theories of the atonement, which they regarded as crude. They wanted to avoid a self-contained and closed twentieth-century Evangelical theological system which was not open to change. Storr was also among those who were fairly advanced in their liturgical views, being tolerant of the eastward position, and prepared to advocate elaborate vestments and the practice of reservation as long as there was no worship of the consecrated elements. Predictably all of this was anathema to many Evangelicals. They regarded it as a sell-out to modernism, and a retreat from true Evangelicalism.

The tension within the Evangelical ranks which the energetic and enthusiastic liberals precipitated was most poignantly and publicly demonstrated in the dramatic split in that bastion of Evangelicalism, the Church Missionary Society. As early as 1912 a number of clergymen presented a memorial to the general committee of the CMS deprecating the occasional invitation to Tractarian sympathizers to speak at the society's meetings. In the next few years the critics expressed particular concern that the evangelical basis of the society was being compromised and undermined in four specific ways: by the teaching given to CMS candidates; by the beliefs of some candidates; by co-operation with societies which, it was alleged, did not hold the basic CMS beliefs; and by some missionaries adopting the eastward position at communion services, whereby they stood between the congregation and the altar and, in the view of many contemporary Evangelicals, thus symbolized a mediatorial role for clergy. There was much exchange of correspondence, some of it in strong language, and battle lines were drawn. The climax came in 1922 when the incensed objectors broke away and formed the Bible Churchmen's Missionary Society. For the first few years after this the relationship between the two societies was at best tolerant and at worse hostile.

For the Church of England as a whole the inter-war years were to a great extent coloured by yet another feud, this time over Prayer Book revision.[63] In 1922 the House of Bishops of the new Church Assembly introduced the Revised Prayer Book (Permissive Use) Measure, which not only entailed three years of debates in the assembly, but produced a torrent of rival proposals, criticism, comment and protest. The revision stage began in October 1925 with a sitting in public; and for a year from January 1926 the House of Bishops met privately in forty or fifty full-day sessions.

During all this time there was much frantic, and often frenetic, activity in the various corridors of power and in less elevated places. Opinion about revision did not run exclusively along party lines. There was no single, identifiable Evangelical line. Although they were in the main averse to revision, there were shades of opinion. They were united in not wanting any revision which would involve a disturbance of the balance of doctrine contained in the existing Prayer Book.[64] And this stance was adopted by liberal and conservative Evangelicals alike. What aroused the passions of Evangelicals to fever pitch was the apparent assault on the tenets of faith most cherished by them; and they were determined to fight against changes that seemed to be in a Romeward direction. It was this fear, still dormant in even the most nominal churchmen, which particularly swayed opinion in general, and especially among churchmen, against the revisions.

Few Anglo-Catholics were enthusiastic for what was proposed. Lang thought the suggested alterations to the Order of Holy Communion were too meagre to be of much use to the church, but reluctantly concurred. Some, including the prominent High Church Principal of Pusey House, Oxford, Darwell Stone, argued for the rejection of the new book because it did not go far enough. Some thought that the intended changes were a threat to the traditional Anglican eucharistic theology.

At a crucial time, in the midst of an often heated debate, the archetypal Anglo-Catholic Viscount Halifax inadvertently dealt a severe blow to the whole revision process. He had been trying for some time to obtain Roman Catholic recognition of the validity of Anglican priestly orders with a view to the ultimate union of the Church of England with the Roman Catholic Church. He attempted to achieve his purpose in the 1920s through staggeringly audacious conversations with the Abbé Portal and Cardinal Mercier. The first of them took place entirely unofficially in 1921, but the three participants were subsequently successful in obtaining official authorization from both Rome and Canterbury. When the conversations resumed in 1923 the Church of England was represented by Halifax, W.H. Frere and Dean Armitage Robinson, all of them High Churchmen. The high point was 1925 when there seemed to be some possibility that Rome might acknowledge the true corporate existence of the Church of England as a church. But the moment passed, circumstances and attitudes rapidly changed, and it became evident that Roman Catholicism was moving in a quite different direction. The so-called Malines conversations were abruptly terminated. But they had fuelled pervasive anti-Roman fears, and aroused deep concern that the Church of England was over-inclined to move in a Romeward direction.

Nonetheless, despite this, and the strong opinions generated by skilfully directed Evangelical and Anglo-Catholic campaigns against the revised book, there was an overwhelming vote in favour of revision in all Houses of the Church Assembly. The Bill for revision was also passed by the Lords after a three-day debate of high quality and fine tone. But then it was twice defeated in the Commons in 1927 and 1928.

It is a sad commentary on the whole affair that the advocates of revision were themselves often lukewarm. 'The Prayer Book baby can hardly be said to have had very satisfactory godparents', one commentator wrote, 'since one Archbishop did not really want it at all and the other Archbishop would have preferred something else.'[65]

Lang, as Archbishop of Canterbury, had to lead the Church of England in the aftermath of this devastating blow. And it was a most unfortunate ten-year sequel. The real issue at stake had not been primarily liturgical or partisan; it was the question of the relationship of the Church of England to the state. The annulling by Parliament of such a major decision, duly arrived at by the church through its own legislative process, was a shattering blow to many churchmen. The Archbishops and other church leaders were not prepared to accept the decision of Parliament as a *fait accompli*; so they authorized the publication of the revised Prayer Book. And in so doing they stirred up a hornets' nest. The National Church League[66] indignantly retorted that this promoted lawlessness, and that the use of the communion service in the new book, encouraged by many bishops, was plainly illegal. Even the Church Pastoral-Aid Society, which normally avoided controversial matters, openly expressed its conviction that the church should accept and abide by the decision of Parliament.[67]

Liturgical confusion within the church and crisis in church-state relations helped to make the 1930s a somewhat miserable time for the Church of England. And Lang 'was neither the man to enforce the decision of parliament, nor to challenge it'.[68]

A sort of postscript was provided by a change in liturgical focus in the late 1930s. *The Parish Communion* edited by Fr A.G. Herbert was published in 1937. It helped to direct Anglican Catholics less towards the mass and more towards the parish communion which combined what

was best in both Catholic and Protestant traditions. It was an emphasis
which was to be taken-up with enthusiasm in many parishes at various
times in the post-Second World War decades.

I cannot leave the inter-war period without consideration of the moves
made to democratize the government of the Church of England. As the
First World War was drawing to a conclusion a group of Anglicans, of
whom the most important were H.R.L. Sheppard, the charismatic vicar
of St Martin-in-the-Fields, F.A. Iremonger, later Dean of Lichfield and
William Temple, banded together and formed the Life and Liberty
Movement. It has been described, perhaps with some degree of extravagance, as 'one of the most remarkable fellowships which ever changed
a Church's history'.[69] It certainly achieved much in a short time, for it
was largely due to the enthusiasm, energy and ability of its members and
leaders that the Enabling Act was passed in 1919. The following statement was printed on the first circulars of the Movement:

> The Life and Liberty Movement aims at securing for the Church with-
> out delay Liberty in the sense of full power to control its own life and
> organization. It does this in the belief that a unique opportunity is
> before the Church, which existing conditions prevent it from claiming
> to the full. The rising tide of Life within the Church demands Liberty,
> because Liberty is indispensable to the fullness of Life and its
> practical expression. It must no longer be necessary to wait for the
> convenience of Parliament before adaptations can be made and
> reforms effected. The opportunity is now, when our whole
> civilization has to be rebuilt. The Church must be able effectively to
> reform its own abuses and perform its part in the National and
> Ecclesiastical spheres. It is the Body of Christ, and must be free to
> obey spontaneously the command of its Divine Head, so as to make
> its witness obvious to the People, and effective for the extension of the
> Kingdom of God.[70]

The immediate child of the Enabling Act was the National Assembly
of the Church of England, or Church Assembly as it was commonly
called; and it met for the first time in 1920. It received powers delegated
to it by Parliament to deal with a range of matters, such as the creation
of new dioceses. Its lay members were to be chosen by those on newly
created electoral roles of baptized, but not necessarily confirmed,
members of the Church of England. Those enthusiasts of the Life and
Liberty Movement who had looked to the new body to be the organ for

revitalizing the whole church throughout the entire range of its life and witness were disappointed because it did not, by any stretch of the imagination or exercise of charity, meet such expectations. Even those who merely sought a way of facilitating organizational reform and increased efficiency may have harboured doubts when faced with the reality of the Assembly in action. But, for good or ill, it was a step which was to lead in the post-Second World War era to the establishment of the whole synodical system.

Further reading

Bell, G.K.A., *Randall Davidson Archbishop of Canterbury*, Oxford 1935

Chadwick, Owen, *Michael Ramsey. A Life*, London 1990; reissued London 1998

Davies, Horton, *Worship and Theology in England: The Ecumenical Century, 1900–1965*, Princeton 1965

Hylson-Smith, Kenneth, *Evangelicals in the Church of England 1734–1984*, Edinburgh 1989

Hylson-Smith, Kenneth, *High Churchmanship in the Church of England From the Sixteenth Century to the Late Twentieth Century*, Edinburgh 1993

Iremonger, F.A., *William Temple Archbishop of Canterbury. His Life and Letters*, London 1948

Lloyd, Roger, *The Church of England 1900–1965*, London 1966

Marrin, Albert, *The Last Crusade. The Church of England in the First World War*, Durham, North Carolina, 1974

Pickering, W.S.F., *Ango-Catholicism*, London 1989

Prestige, G.L., *The Life of Charles Gore. A Great Englishman*, London 1935

Thompson, K.A., *Bureaucracy and Church Reform: The Organizational Response of the Church of England to Social Change, 1800–1965*, Oxford 1970

Wilkinson, A., *The Church of England and the First World War*, London 1978

Wilkinson, Alan, *Dissent or Conform? War, Peace and the English Churches 1900–1945*, London 1986

6

The Free Churches and the Roman Catholics 1901 to 1945

The Free Churches – a general survey

The first forty-five years of the twentieth century was a period of consolidation, increasing respectability and social acceptance for the Nonconformists, or Free Churches as they can now be designated as they were increasingly characterized by their own independent, free life, rather than being those who simply did not conform to the established church; and they regarded themselves in this light. In the coronation year, 1902, the confidence of Nonconformists in their greater social status and acceptance by British society was immensely boosted when the new King personally commanded that they should send representatives to the coronation. It was the first time this had happened in their history. Between 1902, when Lord Salisbury left Downing Street, and the First World War there was not a genuine Anglican Prime Minister, and the leader of the nation in its confrontation with Germany was a Free Churchman. The Free Churches scored yet another first in November 1918 when King George V and Queen Mary attended their post-Armistice Thanksgiving Service in the Albert Hall. It was the first time that a reigning British monarch had ever been present at a Free Church service.

There were other signs of Free Church conformity and integration into society of a more continuous and long-term nature. For one thing while they did not account for half of the total population, although it was not far short of this, they did include a good half of those members of the nation who were committed and active participants in a church or chapel. They were also well entrenched in national life, with a long and distinguished history. The Congregationalists claimed in 1920 that 292 of their chapels dated back to the seventeenth century; for the Baptists the figure was 122; for the Presbyterians 22; and for the Unitarians 160.[1] And they were entering the strongholds of the establishment: in 1900 there was not a single Free Churchman in the House of Lords, but by 1920 there were several, and in 1920 they were admitted at Oxford to higher degrees in divinity.

But along with greater social acceptance went a decline in political influence. In the first decades of the twentieth century they did not have the cutting edge which typified the golden age of Nonconformist expansion, social impact and influence in the mid-nineteenth century. The ability of Nonconformists to command political and social attention and to exert an influence in political and social affairs was demonstrated for the last time in a very clear and identifiable way in the years 1902 to 1906 in the sphere of education and in the 1906 landslide Liberal victory at the General Election.

When Arthur Balfour introduced the government's massive Education Bill in 1902 he greatly offended Free Churchmen who saw it as a gross interference with the much-loved School Board system of 1870. They were almost hysterical in their opposition to the measure, and instituted a Passive Resistance Movement once the bill had become law. The Free Church fury did much to bring about the great Liberal victory four years later. This issue, combined with a renewed campaign against church rates, provoked thousands of otherwise respectable people to take action which bordered on illegality, and which brought them into court. Almost 200, including ministers, went to gaol.[2] A commentator observed in 1943 that subsequently, in the period since 1906, one of the greatest changes in the English religious and social scene had been the decline of Free Churchmanship.[3]

Although in 1910 there was further evidence of effective Free Church political engagement with Free Church support for the Parliament Act to limit the power of the House of Lords, it was merely a postscript to an influence that was really on the wane after 1906. It was 'the last great fling of Nonconformist politicization', and 1910 'witnessed a sharp turn to the tide'.[4] Free Churchmen were disillusioned with the Liberal alliance, yet its relationship with Labour was never institutionalized in the way it had been with the Liberal Party. So, paradoxically, in the first few decades of the twentieth century, while in fact the Free Churches were loosing power and influence, a high profile helped to give them confidence in their current importance and the expectation of a bright future. This optimism was reinforced by further evidence of health and grounds for hope. Their numbers at the very beginning of the century were still growing, there was an increase in their wealth, and a proliferation of well-built Gothic churches and large 'Central Halls'.

'Retrogression is not in our vocabulary. Forward is upon the banner of every organization of the Church,' wrote a Baptist minister in 1900.[5] A vitality was still apparent, but it was soon to be replaced by a more sedate and restrained tone for which the ever increasing number and proportion of middle-class members was largely responsible. And with this tendency went the social acceptance to which we have alluded. The Free Churches were rapidly assuming the sociological characteristics of a church. A professional ministry was accompanied by a reduced emphasis upon the gathering of the called-out faithful and a greater stress upon openness to a wide range of people; and there was a move away from evangelism and dogmatism to a more pronounced moral and ethical orientation.

This more predictable and very much more middle-class face of Free Churchmanship with its accompanying social concern and adoption of middle-class social mores was to be found in such leading Nonconformists as George Cadbury, C. P. Scott and John Scott Lidgett.[6] By 1920 Cadbury, the heir to an old Quaker family tradition and a highly successful manager of its chocolate factory in Birmingham, was a recognized patriarch, and his dictum that 'the service of God is the service of man' was widely accepted. He made Bournville a model factory and village, and the treatment of his work force was acknowledged by many as exemplary and to be followed. But he was also instrumental in the development of the Selly Oak colleges and was a pillar of Christian respectability in his community. This should not be taken as implying passive compliance with all socially acceptable policies, for he was able and willing to defy the prevailing public opinion when he felt this necessary as a Christian, as for example, when he refused to succumb to Joseph Chamberlain's highly charged imperialism, and bought the *Daily News* in order to oppose the Boer War. But his role as a pillar of society was indicative of the new integration of Nonconformists into the warp and weft of society.

C. P. Scott was editor of that queen of 'Free Church' newspapers, the *Manchester Guardian*, for forty-eight years. The '*Manchester Guardian*, like Manchester University and the greater part of Mancunian civic life, had almost grown out of Cross Street Chapel, the original Dissenters' Meeting House, turned over the generations Unitarian. Here was dissent at its most secular, its most assured, its most unparochial. It had generated the quintessentially liberal paper with an international reputation. It had retained its "conscience". Whether that was still a "Nonconformist conscience" was not quite so clear.'[7]

Some considered Scott Lidgett the personification of British Methodism and the greatest Methodist since Wesley. Remarkably, he laboured for fifty years in Bermondsey in a Settlement which he founded in one of the dreariest areas in 1890. And he, like the other two, was active in the social and political affairs of the community in which he served. He worked vigorously for the School Board of London County Council, and for the Senate of London University, acting as Vice-Chancellor in the 1930s when he was in his late seventies.

It is somewhat of a mystery why the new, more conformist Free Churchmanship of the early decades of the century should have coincided with an alarming decline in its power and influence in the land, and a shrinking of its numbers as a proportion of the total population, but this increased 'respectability' and conformity may have been an important factor. *Why?*

There were various other possible contributory causes. There was the immediate and devastating effect of the war. William Robertson Nicoll, described as the 'intellectual leader of Nonconformity', wrote in October 1914, 'The War has altered everything. One feels sure of nothing now. All the old foundations are shaken, and we do not know what we can keep.'[8] The First World War, in common with most wars, helped to relax moral standards. The Wesleyan Methodist Conference Address of 1920 lamented the 'swirl of rising dissatisfactions and disputings' and the 'ominous drift of untoward and foreboding things – the passion for pleasure, senseless extravagance, distaste for work, defiance of authority, ready resort to violence, lamentable laxity in sexual morals, flaunting disregard of the binding obligations of marriage and family life'.[9]

The war also seriously depleted the ranks of the churches. Of the 772,785 men killed a disproportionate number were officers, and of these many were church or chapel members. But the loss of church membership should not be exaggerated. Despite the drop in Free Church numbers as a proportion of the total population, between 1901 and 1931 there was an actual increase in the membership of each of the four main Free Church denominations.[10]

It has been suggested that urbanization may have been a significant factor.[11] It does appear that from 1901 onwards, at least until 1931, the growth of towns involved expansion both in population and in geographical spread from within and not, as previously, from rural migration. The towns were therefore not fed with rural Nonconformists as in former times. It has been said that in such towns 'Nonconformists

And that can be exaggerated too.

suffered from their own prosperity and with it, from their absorbtion into the mainstream of urban life. Here the majority of Englishmen did not regularly go to church or chapel. Here Nonconformity, with its own insistence on the "internalization" of the Christian religion suffered badly: people who believed that religion was essentially, and then completely, a way of life based on a regard for others and a private belief in God, had no need to go to church and even less, to chapels where the emphasis was on preaching.'[12] *(Munson)*

I would concur with this, but I would stress that this was but one part of a jigsaw. It was an element, but only one. At this point I simply draw attention to two other relevant considerations. First, the privatization of religion, and secondly the proliferation in towns particularly of institutional religious choice. One of the main components in 'the decline of institutional religion' in England, especially in the twentieth century, and in almost all occidental countries, has been this process of privatization. 'In modern society, in which men are highly individuated by diverse patterns of social experience, in which men have considerable choice of the influences to which they expose themselves, there is no longer a widespread community of feeling to which the Churches can minister.'[13] Allied to this is the quite astonishing multiplication of religious choice available to English people, and again especially to those in urban areas, in the twentieth century. As we will see, this process accelerated in the post-Second World War decades, but it was evident before 1945; and, of course, it was the multiplication of Free Churches which produced such a diversity of options. Denominational diversity 'has in itself promoted a process of secularization, in providing for the uncommitted a diversity of religious choice, in creating institutionalized expression of social differences and divisions, and in the very circumstance which, in extending choice, allows some to make no choice at all.'[14] And the proliferation of denominations was made even more confusing in the period 1901 to 1945 with the addition or rapid expansion of prospering small new sects such as Christian Science, Seventh Day Adventists, Jehovah's Witnesses, Assemblies of God, the Elim Foursquare Gospel Alliance and other Pentecostal churches.

From the late nineteenth century onwards there was first a gradual, then a steep downward slide for all Protestant churches and denominations. Some did better than others, but all were subject to 'decline'. Unless the wider historical process which I am presenting as the broad contextual framework for the history of all the churches is appreciated there is a danger that some more specific 'causes of decline' will not be seen, as they should, as only contributory factors and will be given too much weight. The various manifestations of 'modernism' which we have previously considered should be viewed as, albeit unconscious, reactions to the underlying transformation from pluralism to 'post-Christian' multi-faith pluralism. In trying to 're-state' Christian belief; in attempting to relate the age-old Christian faith to the thoughts and dispositions of 'modern man', and in the endeavour to confront 'man come of age' even before that particular phrase was coined, theologians were but responding to this fundamental transmutation of society of which they were at the time but dimly aware.

The particular denominations each illustrate some of the many characteristics of Nonconformist history in the period 1901 to 1945 which I have outlined in these brief introductory remarks.

Changes in the Free Churches

At the turn of the century the mainline Free Churches were still fairly robust and self-confident. Congregationalism was still showing signs of healthiness, growth and social impact. In 1875 there were 2,980 churches, branch churches and preaching stations.[15] By 1880 this had increased to 3,176[16] and by 1900 to 3,433.[17] The number of ministers had grown from 2,028 in 1880 to 2,161 by 1900. The census of London churches, undertaken by Richard Mudie Smith during the winter of 1902–03, showed that in most Congregational churches there was a penumbra of people who were not strictly church members but who attended the services. This was an important and considerable element in the life of the churches throughout the country. The days were soon to come when these people were to disappear from the churches.

The majority of Congregational churches were small in membership. The large and prosperous ones in such towns and cities as Birmingham, Bedford, Derby, Plymouth, Bristol, Bournemouth, Ashton-under-Lyne, Manchester, Liverpool, Wolverhampton, Halifax and Bradford attracted much attention, but over 61% of the churches had less than a hundred members.

During the fourteen pre-war years Congregationalists were actively engaged in political matters in support of the Socialists or as contributors to Liberal or Labour politics in local government; while others undertook Trade Union work. There was also an enthusiasm for Settlements in deprived urban areas. All of this was evidence of vitality, but it was also an indication that Congregationalism was moving away from its traditional prime concern for teaching and evangelism, especially as there was theological turmoil within the denomination. As we have previously seen the leading Congregationalist R.J. Campbell was the instigator of the 'New Theology' with its concentration on the immanence of God and its rejection of much traditional Christian dogma. Although P.T. Forsyth ably presented a counter emphasis on man's supreme need for the grace that alone can reconcile him to a holy God, and the redeeming and reconciling grace of God in Jesus Christ, especially in his book *The Person and the Place of Jesus Christ* (1909), Campbell seems to have shaken the doctrinal and spiritual foundations of Congregationalism and undermined the orthodox faith of many individual Congregationalists and others.

Immediately after the First World War, in 1919, the denomination embarked on a significant structural reorganization. The Scheme for Provinces and Moderators was adopted after a lively, and sometimes acrimonious, debate. It divided the country into nine provinces, each having a Provincial Committee composed of the County Unions concerned. Each Province was assigned a Moderator whose duties were to 'stimulate and encourage the work of the Denomination'. It was a far cry from the independency of the sixteenth and seventeenth centuries, and a further indication of the move in structure and ethos from a denomination to a church.

In the period 1918 to 1939 Congregationalists gained a reputation for participation in activities outside their own circles. Eighty-six representatives attended COPEC and they made valuable contributions to the work of the twelve preparatory commissions. Outstanding among them, and in the life of Congregationalism as a whole, was Alfred Ernest Garvie, who was especially active in the inter-war ecumenical movement. He served as Deputy-Chairman of COPEC and he was a prominent figure at the 1925 Stockholm Universal Christian Conference, which was an international and interdenominational gathering concerned with Christian social work.

But despite this alertness to the need to re-structure, and to engage in the broad sweep of Christian thinking, strategy and action which was going on around them, by the 1930s it was clear that the denomination itself was suffering from depressed numbers and declining spiritual vitality. Church membership was 257,435 in 1900, and was up to 291,128 by 1915. But by 1930, in spite of a population increase, it was down to 276,540, and the statistical rot had set in. 'For Congregationalism, as for the religious life of England generally, the Depression of the 'thirties was as much spiritual as it was economic.'[18]

In common with the Congregationalists and Nonconformity overall
the Baptists entered the twentieth century in a spirit of eager confidence.
In the *Daily News* census of 1903 they appeared as 'the one really growing religious body in the metropolis . . . wander where you may, there
is nowhere a symptom of Baptist decline'.[19] The optimism of the denomination was epitomized by the launching of the Twentieth Century Fund
in 1898, so that Baptists 'should greet the new century by raising a large
fund for a great advance'.[20] The target was £250,000, half of which
should be used for evangelization at home and for church extension in
districts where religious need was not met by other evangelical
churches, and the other half for the support of the weaker churches, the
augmentation of an Annuity Fund, and to help meet central administrative costs. The challenge to find such money was taken up with
enthusiasm.

The Baptists also adopted structural changes to improve ministerial
oversight. England and Wales were divided into ten districts, each under
a General Superintendent whose task was to watch over the interests of
the denomination in the area. They were not to be seen as bishops, for
the name did not imply anything more than moral and persuasive
authority. They were to be encouragers and advisers, and they were to
be at the service of the churches and ministers for all spiritual purposes.

The man responsible for executing both these schemes was John
Howard Shakespeare, who in 1898 had been appointed to the
secretaryship of the Baptist Union. And in 1905 he did another fine
piece of work by making the arrangements for the first Baptist World
Congress to meet in London.

Organizational matters increasingly assumed greater prominence as
the century advanced. Baptists were attracted by the Peace Movement,
plans for a World Alliance for Promoting International Friendship
through the Churches, and the beginnings of the Faith and Order
Movement.[21] It may be that the interest and involvement of
the Congregationalists, the Baptists, the Anglicans and others in the
ecumenical movement at this time was not a sign of strength but of
weakness. Bryan Wilson has detected such a significance in ecumenical
activity. 'The energy which churchmen have put into the ecumenical
movement has', he asserts, 'been perhaps in rough proportion as they
have lost hope of evangelization of the world.'[22]

The Baptists certainly had lost the high level of self-assurance and
expectancy which had been their hallmark at the beginning of the
century. The number of members continued to decrease in the 1930s;

there were serious divisions of opinion on basic issues such as whether they should abandon their traditional independent church polity in favour of a centralized connexionalism involving the development of the power and influence of the Baptist Union; and some of the key leaders died without men or women of comparable stature to replace them. 'The Second World War came upon a denomination troubled in mood and somewhat uncertain itself.'[23] This also quite well describes the disposition of the denomination in 1945 after the distress, trials, losses and exhaustion of the Second World War.

The Presbyterian Church of England continued to have close links with the Church of Scotland as it moved into the twentieth century. It was never very large, and it was concentrated in certain areas and towns rather than being spread throughout the country, but its influence was out of proportion to its size. This was partly because its ministers tended to be more academically qualified than those in other denominations, and to a greater extent than with other denominations it seems to have attracted a small but influential number of the more sophisticated and educated laity. But there were exceptions. One young man who transferred his allegiance from Presbyterianism to the Church of England, and later became an archbishop, Joost de Blank, declared: 'Becoming an Anglican meant for me the one word *liberation*. I was liberated from a narrow sectarianism; I was liberated from a bigoted anti-intellectualism; and I was liberated from an unreasoned and unreasonable puritanism.'[24]

The English Presbyterians made a conscious effort to recapture something of the theological emphasis and worship which had distinguished the denomination prior to the extended period from the early eighteenth century when it was almost annihilated by Socinianism and Unitarianism. In the late nineteenth century and then on into the twentieth they drew upon a notable lineage in service books which dated from the famous Westminster *Directory* of 1645. The Presbyterians claim to have been the first of the English Free Churches to have produced an official modern denominational service book, which they did in 1898. This was significantly revised in 1921, but it continued to be issued under the historic title of a *Directory of Public Worship*. In its turn, the 1921 book was the basis for *The Presbyterian Service Book* of 1948. This combined the older Puritan type tradition, which remained as a strong component of Welsh Presbyterianism, and the more liturgical tradition which was characteristic of Scottish and English Presbyterianism.[25]

There was quite a large Scottish element in English Presbyterian churches. This played its part in the natural sympathy between Scottish Presbyterians and English Free churchmen in their opposition to Episcopal pretensions south and north of the border.

The Quakers remained a numerically small denomination, and showed no sign of resurgence by 1945, but they maintained and even enhanced some of their inherited emphases. In the mid-nineteenth century there had been a distinct reinforcement of the social and welfare concerns of English Quakers. In America the Quaker interest had centred on the salvation of the soul, and the concern was primarily individualistic and theological.[26] Evangelical preaching became a matter of supreme importance, and there was an earnest seeking after definite conversions and sanctification. 'In England, on the other hand, the centre of interest among Friends, as the awakening to a new life and a new career became a fact, was emphatically humanistic and social rather than theological. English Friends felt more quickly and more keenly than did American Friends the intellectual and social currents of the time.'[27]

The continuing concern of Quakers for social and welfare work in the early part of the twentieth century was exemplified in the lives and labours of George Cadbury, who we have already considered; Seebohm Rowntree, whose *Poverty: A Study of Town Life* (1901) shocked people by what it revealed of the poverty and destitution of York, which was comparable with what Charles Booth had found in London; J. S. Fry; and the Storrs family. All of them had made a fortune in chocolate manufacture, and all of them gained a reputation for humanitarian concern.

The two World Wars also allowed Quakers to demonstrate their pacifist concerns and to put their principles into practice. The Fellowship of Reconciliation was founded in December 1914 and was predominantly Free Church and more specifically Quaker. It stood for the old pacifist tradition, most clearly associated with the Quakers, of personal conscientious objection, and refusal to take part in war whatever the circumstances and whatever the consequences. This was nobly carried into practice by Dorothy Buxton in the 1930s. She, more than anyone else in Britain, strove to make known the true facts about Nazi Germany by means of pamphlets and translations. She championed the Confessing pastors, but more generally was desperately concerned about the wider religious and humanitarian issues highlighted in Nazi tyranny. She was fervently pacifist but came to the conclusion that it had its limits, and that Nazism was so evil that resistance to it could justify another war. Prior to 1939 the Quakers were almost alone in working with British Jewry to help Jewish refugees from the Nazis. It was all part of the quiet engagement of Quakers in a host of social matters where there was a need, and where they thought that their unostentatious contribution could be of some use.

As they entered the twentieth century many Methodists, as with the Congregationalists and the Baptists, were optimistic; indeed a considerable number thought that the future was with their church. This exuberance was found locally as well as nationally, as in Nottingham where 'there was a mood of optimism and confidence'.[28] The Forward Movement had helped to reassure Methodists that they were addressing the real issues of the day, and that they had a bright future of evangelism and pastoral care ahead. *The Bitter Cry of Outcast London* of 1883, William Booth's *In Darkest England and the Way Out* (1890), and Charles Booth's pioneering surveys *Life and Labour in London* (c.1902) revealed something of the massive task facing any church which attempted to address social issues, but it did not deter the Methodists from continuing 'to provide centres of evangelism and social amelioration, the sacrament and the soup-ladle in hand, with a minister at the head of the enterprise who could remain long enough to be a social (and often political) force in the neighbourhood'.[29] Great faith was also placed in such centres as St James's Hall, the Manchester Mission and the Central Hall in Birmingham as large and impressive buildings and focusses for evangelism, social work and pastoral care in the vicinity. Such work was based on evangelistic preaching of a simple and powerful type; a social witness of a basically individualistic type despite avowals of collectivism; and 'the creation of cultural or semi-cultural interests around the church or hall building, which can be seen either as a broadening of the Church's outreach or as a creeping secularization of the Church's life'.[30] The Pleasant Sunday Afternoon Movement, the Band of Hope and Bright Hours continued to play a major part in the Methodist means of presenting the gospel in word and action to people in a non-churchy atmosphere.

In the space of the first forty-five years of the twentieth century Methodism became more theologically diverse; socially heterogeneous; southern based; and organically more unified.

Methodism was not unaffected by the 'social gospel' movement, modernism and the New Theology. Speaking to King George V, W. H. Lax stressed the traditional evangelical theology of Methodism. 'The Methodist Church', he told the king, 'is a loyal Church.' It stood for the 'great evangelical message of conversion', and also the 'absolute necessity of rendering service to the community'.[31] But that ideal was in conflict with the less orthodox views of the time, whether they were for a more all-embracing social theology and programme of social action, for a modification of received Methodist theology in the light of modern science and biblical criticism, or for a greater emphasis on the immanence of God.

Many ordinary Methodist members of perhaps theologically unsophisticated chapels would have enunciated a predominantly behaviour-centred theology which was coloured by the growing respectability of Free Churchmanship in general. In his study of Methodism in a Durham mining village Robert Moore discovered that 'Methodism was institutionalized as part of the community, not restricted to formal religious associations . . . the Methodists were so emphasizing traditional and communal values and activities that they became increasingly disconnected not only from current political issues but even from official Methodist policy discussions and liturgical changes.'[32] Methodism certainly did not speak with an undivided and unambiguous evangelical voice. Although it is right, as David Hempton has usefully remarked, that 'the concept of "popular religion", like its cousin "popular culture", is potentially misleading',[33] a number of themes do emerge from a range of local studies about the nature and content of popular Methodism.[34] These investigations have frequently unearthed ill-defined, Christian-related but not recognizably 'orthodox' clusters of belief or views which the churches in general, and the Methodists among them, had promoted by means of their educational and social activities.[35] Thoroughgoing scepticism was a rarity but, especially among the working class, there was a general vagueness about Christian beliefs. Most working-class people had only a dim perception of Christian doctrines or of the concept of eternal life, whether that related to heaven or hell. They were not orthodox Christian believers in any meaningful sense, neither were they anxious doubters. They did not confront and consciously reject or even ignore the Christian message; it was simply a world of thought and conceptualization which never entered their ken. The 'theology' of many ordinary Methodists was inevitably coloured by the prevailing social and cultural climate which they encountered. The whole thought-processes and orientation to theological issues, or the absence of such, was to a large extent dictated by the social situation in which those concerned found themselves. There is a common conviction arising out of many local studies 'that religion in industrial society is inseparable from the class, employment, community, ethnic and cultural interests of its adherents'.[36] This is not reductionism, but merely a recognition of historical and sociological facts.

As Methodism became more middle class, the same diffuseness, individual doctrinal ignorance and imprecision, although perhaps to a lesser extent, applied in the middle-class suburban and other ghettos. To this was added the thought-determining, conformist-engendering, pressures of middle-class respectability with all its emphasis on conduct and compliance with social mores.

Then there was the gradual shift from the predominance of the north to the pre-eminence of the south, which gained in momentum in the years from 1901 to 1945. 'After 1880 the "new" Methodist areas grew at disproportionately high rates compared with the old strongholds, much of the change being due to migration.'[37] This was reflected in the building of chapels, with a large proportion of both Wesleyan and Primitive Methodist new buildings being in the London area.

The first four and a half decades of the twentieth century were also notable for the drawing together of various branches of Methodism. For a long time a number of Methodists from the various Methodist traditions had considered the divisions in Methodism to be a scandal. 'The main sources of continued separation were at the top level, constitutional differences and, at the lowest, local pride and traditional snobbery.'[38] The Methodist Ecumenical Conference of 1901 encouraged negotiations on the topic of union, and this bore fruit in 1907 when the Methodist New Connexion, the Bible Christian Church and the United Methodist Free Churches joined forces to form the United Methodist Church. The new body consisted of 165,502 members, 903 itinerant preachers, 6,251 local preachers and 2,673 chapels. In 1912 the Wesleyan Conference expressed its conviction that the time had come for some appraisal about further union to be made. Negotiations took place in 1917 between a number of leading Wesleyan Methodists, Primitive Methodists and United Methodists, and in 1921 a scheme was drawn up. The Union took place in London on 20 September 1932. After a century and a half Methodism was once again a single entity, with the exception of the Independent Methodists and the Wesleyan Reform Union, which had a combined membership of about 25,000.

One of the first acts of the new, united, Methodist body was to accept a report which declared that 'there is no function of the ordained Ministry, as now exercised by men, for which a woman is disqualified by reason of her sex'.[39] It was perhaps indicative of a boldness and preparedness to tackle thorny issues which augured well for the future when, in the immediate post-1945 years, it was faced with and accepted the challenge of seriously debating a more ambitious, more comprehensive and far-reaching union with the Church of England.

The Pentecostalists

Pentecostalism in an international, institutionalized form originated in the twentieth century. The modern Pentecostal movement began in the United States in the first few years of the twentieth century. It was introduced into England in 1907 by an Anglican parish priest, Alexander A. Boddy, who soon made his church, All Saints, Sunderland, a centre for those in Britain who sought the experience of the baptism of the Spirit and speaking in tongues.[40] Among the early leaders were G. R. Polman, Smith Wigglesworth and Cecil Polhill. Boddy remained as a Church of England priest. He was a leading personality in the international Pentecostal movement. He regarded Pentecostalism as a revival within the churches, and in 1909 he therefore associated himself with the work of the Pentecostal Missionary Union, which was meant to be a body operating through the churches. By 1924, when the Union was dissolved and replaced by the Assemblies of God, organized as a free church, the Elim Pentecostal Churches and the Apostolic Church had already come into existence.

The Elim Pentecostal Churches were started by George and Stephen Jeffreys. George Jeffreys had founded the Elim Evangelistic Band as an evangelistic team to assist him in his missions. In 1926 the Elim Foursquare Gospel Alliance was established with the intention that it should be an umbrella organization for all Pentecostals in Great Britain; but the plan failed and only Elim members joined, so that the logical step was taken of changing the name from 'Alliance' to Elim Pentecostal Churches. By 1939 tension and strife between George Jeffreys and other leaders of the church resulted in his resignation, and in him founding the Bible Pattern Church Fellowship.

Of particular importance as an English Pentecostal leader in the pre-1945 era was Donald Gee. He was converted during the Welsh revival of 1904; was the vice-chairman of the British Assemblies of God from 1933, and from 1948 chairman. He wrote prolifically, and his works were translated into many languages, so he gained an international reputation. He was one of the foremost apologists for

Pentecostalism, and he co-operated with the World Council of Churches. It was symptomatic of the growth internationally and in England of Pentecostalism, which was to be a major force in world Christianity before the end of the century. We will be meeting Donald Gee again in the post-Second World War era of increased Pentecostal importance in the English religious scene.

The Roman Catholics

The triumphant progress of Roman Catholicism in the nineteenth century was not halted after 1900, but continued, latterly at a some-what moderated pace, until the end of the twentieth century. Of course the church experienced difficulties: internal problems and external opposition. The saga is not one of steady linear growth and uninter-rupted, mounting, influence and increasing acceptance by a principally Protestant country. But overall this is just what happened, and the two centuries' history is most impressive. Precise statistical information is not available. Yet the 'trend is clear enough. English Catholicism grew almost as rapidly as the Methodist and evangelical Dissenting com-munities during the early industrial era, albeit for different reasons, but unlike these Protestant competitors its growth continued unchecked throughout the Victorian era. And in the twentieth century, of all the major religious traditions, it alone has managed virtually to escape a serious decline of manpower and material resources, and an accom-panying drastic reduction of popular religious adherence.'[41] The only major blips in this growth pattern appear to have been a significant fall in the rate of adult conversions during the First World War, in the period between 1936 and 1946, and in the 1960s, which was not coun-tered by improvements in this respect in the 1920s and the 1950s.

By the Edwardian years English Catholicism had developed that dis-tinctive and unusual sub-cultural cohesion which has been its hallmark and an important contributory factor in its continued prosperity. Anti-Catholicism was not rampant and fierce during the closing decades of the nineteenth century, but the Catholics were still treated with suspicion and reserve; and their whole ethos and lifestyle was widely considered as un-English. Under Edward there was some relaxation of this stiffness and Catholicism 'gained a certain recognition and prestige which had been lacking under the somewhat rigid conventions of the Queen's reign'.[42] The King was the first English monarch since the

Stuarts who was not in some measure anti-Catholic. During his reign the old offensive phrases were removed from the coronation service, and the marriage of Alfonso XIII of Spain with the King's niece Princess Ena of Battenberg, accompanied by her reception into the Catholic Church, symbolized at least a lessening in the distaste for Catholics. The prestige of the peerage stood high, and there was considerable respect for the numerous and dignified Catholic peers headed by the Duke of Norfolk.

The Malines Conversations showed that antipathy to Rome and to Roman Catholic doctrines and practices was still present in the population, but they also highlighted 'the average Englishman's candid and impatient indifference'[43] of which all Catholics were aware.

By 1920 the English Catholic community numbered over two million, and it was served by almost 4,000 priests: 2,500 were diocesan and 1,400 regulars of whom Jesuits and Benedictines were the most important. The number of priests had amazingly doubled in the thirty years before the First World War. This was a key factor in the immense general strengthening of the institutional framework of English Catholicism; and it helped to cope with an increasing demand for priestly ministrations, for example, in the greater proportion of marriages performed in Catholic churches: from 42 per thousand in 1909 to 52 in 1919 and 60 in 1929. Although there continued to be rather more Methodist than Catholic marriages and eleven times more in Anglican churches, it was part of the fuller integration of the Catholic church into the wider community, and indicative of a church which was holding its own in the religious market place.[44]

A further sign of such Catholic penetration into English society was its wider social spread. Catholics were less concentrated in particular areas and cities than in the past. Such pockets still existed, but by the 1920s Catholics were more evenly distributed, still mainly, although not entirely, in urban centres. They were by then also more fully represented in all sections of the professional and business worlds. This gave greater variety to the Catholic community, and it also brought a cohesion which was formerly lacking in the southern counties. The Catholic Church grew impressively throughout the stretch of dormitory towns and urbanized countryside which developed between the southern outskirts of London and the Channel coast. In no part of England did the proportion of Catholic churches to the population mount so rapidly as prompt action was taken to provide for the tide of salaried Catholics, with their demands for comfortable Catholic preparatory schools and the Sunday Mass, when they pressed out farther and farther into the country.[45] The absence in their ranks of an extensive and influential middle and upper middle class was something which had deprived nineteenth-century English Catholicism of a much needed 'link to bind the older aristocratic Catholic families and the many converts who followed Newman from the Church of England to the Roman allegiance with the thousands upon thousands of impoverished Irish artisans and their families'.[46]

In addition to the army of priests, large secondary schools controlled by the Jesuits and the various orders of teaching brothers helped to build up a central core of Catholic life. Mention also needs to be made of the crucial part played by the laity and converts to Catholicism. In the earlier part of the century there had most notably been G.K. Chesterton, one of the most successful of Catholic protagonists, who expressed his religious views most interestingly in *Orthodoxy* (1908) and *The Everlasting Man* (1925). Compton Mackenzie was the doyen of English Catholic novelists whose works in the 1920s most explicitly portrayed his beliefs. There was a widening of such influence from the mid-1930s onwards. This can be appreciated simply by reciting the names of Lord Acton, the Duke of Norfolk, Friedrich von Hügel, Wilfred Ward, Hilaire Belloc, Graham Greene, Evelyn Waugh, Christopher Hollis and Lord Pakenham. *David Knowles,*

The more wholehearted engagement of the laity in general, and certain Catholics of outstanding political, literary or professional ability in particular, in the work of the English Catholic Church was in many ways a great strengthening of the Catholic community and an encouraging omen for the future. But it contained two unforseen potential or actual consequences. One was the danger of losing the solid working-class base which had been such a feature of nineteenth-century Catholicism, especially as a result of Irish immigration. The other was the feeding of the critical faculties of an extremely intelligent and articulate body of men and women. In the 'white collar' parishes in particular there was a noticeable impatience with the clergy in the late 1930s and thereafter for some time. There was an increasing lay desire to participate in the work of the parishes, to have a say in decision-making and, on a wider front, to have a voice in the councils of the church at national and international levels. It was but a cloud as small as a man's hand. But with our knowledge of the greater power which was later to be given to the laity at all levels in the church, the ever more insistent teaching of some 'rebel' theologians, and the pressure from some quarters for the ordination of women in the second half of the century, what was happening in the late 1930s and the 1940s can be seen as pregnant with meaning for the future.

Further Reading

Binfield, C., *So Down to Prayers: Studies in English Nonconformity 1790–1920*, London 1977

Brake, George Thompson, *Policy and Politics in British Methodism 1932–1982*, London 1984

Currie, R., *Methodism Divided*, London 1968

Davies, Horton, *Worship and Theology in England: The Ecumenical Century, 1900–1965*, Princeton 1965

Davies, Rupert E., George, A. Raymond and Rupp, Gordon (eds), *History of the Methodist Church in Great Britain*, 4 vols, London 1965–88

Hastings, Adrian, *A History of English Christianity 1920–1990*, London 1991

Hollenweger, Walter J., *The Pentecostals*, London 1972

Jones, R. Tudur, *Congregationalism in England 1662–1962*, London 1962

Nuttall, Geoffrey and Chadwick, Owen (eds), *From Uniformity to Unity 1662–1962*, London 1962

Part Three

Part Three

7

1945 to 1998: Context and General Situation

Numerical decline and multi-faith pluralism

There was undoubtedly a process taking place in England in the period from 1945 to 1998, which had its roots in the history of the country and of the churches from at least a century before, whereby Christianity became less central in the lives of individuals and in the life of the nation corporately. This was indicated by a marked decline in church membership taken as a whole, which included most of the mainline churches. There was a reduction in the number of people who used church and chapel rights of passage, which in some instances, as with marriage, were replaced by a secular substitute. There was less regard for distinctively Christian beliefs and values. Churches were treated with increasing disregard as institutions with clearly perceived functions and roles. Church leaders were held in less honour, given less respect and accorded less authority as representing the churches and the Christian faith. There was a widespread ignorance of the basic facts concerning the person of Christ, the Bible and what it contained and taught, Christian doctrines, and Christian practices, and such knowledge was in any case quite frequently considered unnecessary; and there was a pervasive indifference to all matters of the doctrine, and even of the morality, proclaimed by the churches.

The slide was well advanced by 1945. There was some minimal, short-lived upturn in the late 1940s and early 1950s, but this only interrupted an underlying drift downwards which became apparent during the following forty years. Such 'secularization' had been apparent in subtle as in more obvious ways for decades. Even as early as the 1920s the theological teaching of the institutional churches had, to an extent which was greater than for much of the past, become hazy, and without the authority and aura of relevance which it had commanded in the recent past. 'The accommodation of the modernists and the entrenched resistance of the conservatives both reflected an underlying sense that the prevailing cultural and intellectual climate had now turned decisively against Christianity.'[1] This less sympathetic cultural and intellectual environment, which was increasingly denuded of its Christian content and tone, was manifested in various ways more obvious in retrospect than at the time.

No longer were literature and the arts seen as ready vehicles for spreading official religious teachings: they were liable rather to be perceived as hostile or at best neutral. Art could be accepted with confidence as 'religious' only if it had been produced by conventional believers . . . in music the impression was, in contrast to the Victorian era, that innovation was occurring in spite of rather than because of the influence of the churches. Apart from Elgar, the leading English composers of the first half of the twentieth century were the atheist Delius and agnostic Vaughan Williams. Christians were also lukewarm towards the cinema, despite, or because of, their ready acknowledgment of its social and cultural importance. The aloofness of official religion from culture was an understandable reaction to the confusion of sacred and secular that had occurred in the previous generation, but still carried with it the converse danger of ghettoization.[2]

There were authors, artists and musicians who still found considerable inspiration in the Christian tradition, including, among those not already mentioned, Dylan Thomas, W. B. Yeats, W. H Auden, John Betjeman, Edwin Lutyens, Henry Moore, Dorothy L. Sayers, Graham Sutherland, J. R. R. Tolkein, and C. S. Lewis. But to 'say this is not to deny the extent to which by 1945 the majority of cultural activity occurred in an essentially secular context'.[3] And, of course, such leading cultural and intellectual figures lived during a time when the institutional churches were numerically in retreat.

At the beginning of the period we are about to consider it was currently estimated that only 10%–15% of the population were linked to some Christian church; that 25% or 30% were sufficiently interested to attend a place of worship upon special occasions; that 45% to 50% were indifferent to religion though more or less well disposed towards it, while 10%–20% were hostile.[4] In England the Easter Day communicants of the Church of England, taken as a proportion of the population over fifteen years of age, fell from just under 10% in the period just before 1939, to 6.5% in 1960, and 5% in 1968. Despite a greatly increased population in the country, the electoral roll of the Church of England dropped from 3,700,000 in 1930 to 2,700,000 in 1968. There were also ominous indicators of possible future woes in the statistics relating to Sunday schools. In 1939 there were 218 Church of England Sunday school children per 1,000 of the population aged three to fourteen years in England. By 1953 that figure was 177, and by 1960 it was 133. For the same three points in time the number of Sunday school teachers had likewise dropped from 127,000 to 98,000 and then to 85,000.[5]

A more recent analysis carried out by MARC Europe cast considerable light on this numerical decline. The survey was described by the Archbishop of Canterbury as 'the most thorough and comprehensive ever done of English churchgoing'.[6] It gave a most useful statistical 'map' of the state of the churches as they neared the end of the twentieth century. At the risk of a too wearisome recital of figures, its main conclusions may be briefly outlined.[7] All relate to four nodal points, 1975, 1979, 1985 and 1989; and they all show a downward drift. The total number of churchgoers in 1975 was 4,093,000, representing 11.3% of the adult population (not total population). By 1979 this had gone down 2% to 4,025,000, which represented 11% of the adult population. For 1985 the number was 3,755,00, showing a 7% reduction from the 1979 figure, and this represented 9.95% of the adult population. Finally, in 1989 the figure had declined even further to 3,706,900, a reduction of 1% over the total six years before, and this represented 9.5% of the adult population.[8] The surveyors in commenting on their own statistics qualify what appeared as an unmitigated picture of gloom for the churches. 'The figures do not', they said, 'suggest a major fall away from faith. There are always exceptions, but people, once converted and incorporated into a church, typically continue to be associated with it for most of their lives. The adult decline is caused by death: there are proportionately more elderly people (65 and over) in the church than in the population as a whole (19% against 15%) and they are not being replaced by younger people. One major reason for the decline in children is the reduced birth rate especially in the early 1980s.'[9]

The 1997 edition of *Church Statistics* painted an even darker picture for the Church of England. It showed an average total Sunday attendance for the established church of 1,045,000 in 1995. This was 36,000 lower than for the previous year; the biggest fall since the mid-1970s. There had been a downward figure every year during the 1990s, so this was only the most severe in a persistent downward trend. Other figures in the same report showed that the decline went across the board. Baptisms had dropped from 632,000 to 616,000 between 1994 and 1995; confirmations were down from 48,000 to 44,000; electoral roll numbers decreased from 1,479,000 to 1,468,000; and Easter communicants were down from 1,300,000 to 1,265,000. It was not tested whether the reductions in the attendance figures resulted from fewer members or fewer attendances by members than in the past.

It needs to be borne in mind that the reduced church attendance was not uniform throughout all theological traditions within the churches. The liberals seemed to have suffered the greatest losses, whereas the conservative and evangelical churches, or those traditions within any one church or denomination, had held their own. Those Protestant churches 'which emphasized adult commitment in membership showed rather less decline than Protestant churches with infant baptism'.[10] Some of the minor sects actually expanded; and most notably there was growth among the Pentecostal churches. There was also growth in the number of independent churches, house churches, and in the Orthodox Church.[11]

The evidence of overall numerical decline in commitment to the churches was reinforced by the findings of the *UK Christian Handbook*. These showed a drop in the number of those who might have been described as fringe or nominal members of churches and of the Christian religion. In 1980 68% of British people claimed some allegiance to Christianity, whereas in 1990 this was 65%. This residual strength was reflected in the millions of people who constituted audiences for certain religious or quasi-religious television and radio programmes. And here we are confronted with one of the main characteristics in late twentieth-century English society; the low and declining support and involvement in institutionalized forms of Christian faith running in parallel with a persistent, often vague and ill-defined, belief, or at least professed belief, in basic 'religious' tenets.

Two surveys will illustrate this. First, the 1970 Independent Television Authority's *Opinion Research Centre Survey of Popular Attitudes*. This found that 29% of British people who disclaimed membership of any church or denomination still described themselves as 'very' or 'fairly' religious. Although a smaller proportion of the total population in lower socio-economic groups attended church, a higher proportion than in the middle socio-economic groups assented to certain basic Christian beliefs. To the statement 'Jesus Christ is the Son of God',

89% of the former category said 'True', compared with 79% of the latter; and to the statement 'People who believe in Jesus as the Son of God can expect salvation', the response was respectively 71% and 59%.

Secondly, in 1980–83 Dr Robert Towler tested religious opinion among the population of West Yorkshire. Across the area as a whole he found that only 10% of the population went to church as frequently as once a month. And yet after questioning a random group of 2,000 people in Leeds, he discovered that over 66% of his sample believed in God; 61% believed in fate or destiny; and 40% believed in life after death.[12]

The religious scene in England was made infinitely more complex than ever before by the presence, and indeed growth, of a multitude of heterodox or unconventional Christian bodies, and the relatively new, but significant and expanding, non-Christian religious communities. Between 1975 and 1985 the number of Mormons increased from 80,000 to 102,000; and for Jehovah's Witnesses numbers grew from 80,000 to 92,000. The growth of non-Christian religions was even more striking, as believers entered the country bringing with them their cultures and faiths. In the decade after 1975 the number of Muslims increased from 400,000 to 900,000, which then represented over twice the number of Methodists. At that latter date there were also 175,000 Sikhs and 140,000 Hindus. In total the number of non-Christian believers in Britain rose from 811,000 in 1975 to 1,524,000 in 1985, when it compared with the 2,058,000 Anglicans.[13]

All these figures are indicative of a massive change in the pattern of religious allegiance in England in the fifty-three post-Second World War years. Four varieties of religion were to be found in this complex religious market situation. First, Christianity in its various institutional forms which, with a few very important exceptions such as Pentecostalism and the house church movement, was in decline. Secondly, the institutionalized expression of other faiths, which were growing rapidly, to a large extent because of the increasing size of the ethnic groups which practised the faiths concerned. Thirdly, residual Christianity which allowed a great number of people to subscribe to certain tenets of 'belief' and to accept certain 'Christian' codes of practice, without either attending any services of any institutionalized form of Christianity or without accepting the authority of any such religious body. Fourthly, a variety of explicit or implicit forms of agnosticism, atheism, or such a pronounced indifference that it amounted to one of these two. And all these religious alignments can only be fully understood in the context of a total transformation of society, locally nationally and globally.

Coping with change

Never before had England, or the world, experienced such rapid change as in the period from 1945 to 1998. It was quite overwhelming. And it was on so many fronts at the same time. There were rapid economic fluctuations, with the English economy having to adjust both to internal market and other changes, and, as at no time in the past, to all the currents of multi-national economies and world trade. Not only was it the USA which sneezed and England caught a cold; any of twenty or more countries could cause immediate and serious problems for England if they became subject to radical economic change, for whatever reason. One such cause of international economic problems was rapid political and constitutional change. This was no longer, if it ever had been, a matter of merely local and restricted interest and effect. The ripples went out all over the world. Then there were the advances in radio and television which gave remarkable vividness and immediacy to any event anywhere in the world. Equally astounding were the massive strides in transportation; so that it was easier and quicker to traverse the world than it had been two centuries before to travel the length of England. No country had ever been an island, in the sense of being able to live entirely unto itself, but now the world was a 'global village' with all that this implied. As for the micro-chip and its ramifications, it opened up a new world of achievement and possibilities of quite astonishing proportions and possibilities. And mention has not been made of the exploration of space, the potential for nuclear obliteration, and the manifold advances in various other branches of science and technology. Neither have I touched upon the infinite number of moral questions which medical science and many of the developments just mentioned raised afresh in an unprecedented and, in many cases, seemingly insoluble form.

Placed in a situation of such confusing issues and unparalleled pressures for the application of old and traditional beliefs and ethical standards to new and ever changing problems, it is of little surprise that the churches were frequently unimpressive in their responses, or non-responses, and often suffered from a sense of inadequacy. So many changes occurred within the span of one lifetime that what was experienced and taught in youth sometimes seemed ill-suited to the brave new world of forty years later. So it was no wonder that the age we are considering produced 'new moralities' and theologies of 'man come of age'. It had been and remained a severe test for the churches to hold fast to orthodox beliefs and apply them convincingly to new moral and ethical questions, and to proclaim old truths in ways and in a language which effectively communicated with men and women in such a transformed, and ever-changing, society.

One of the most devastating changes in terms of the need for adjustment and new attitudes was the remarkable redistribution of church and chapel goers in the latter half of the twentieth century. It took some adapting of attitudes and behaviour in all the churches to accommodate the unprecedented re-alignments as some churches or denominations shrank in size and others grew at a fast rate or appeared on the scene for the first time. I have already mentioned the surge in Pentecostalism, independent or house churches, and other new or much enlarged ethnic churches, but it is often not appreciated how much this entailed a psychological and emotional, as well as a rational and organizational, response. It was also bound up with the immigration of large numbers of Asians and West Indians, and the setting up of whole new communities, so that wider political, economic, social and racial issues were involved.

Many of the black immigrants who arrived in the twenty years after the Second World War, and continued to come but in lesser numbers after that, came from Christian backgrounds. Initially they joined existing English churches, and some found a spiritual home in that way. But a large proportion did not find indigenous churches congenial, and they set about establishing churches of their own. These included home churches, small new denominations, and churches affiliated to denominations with headquarters in the immigrants' home country. In most cases they were predominantly if not entirely composed of Africans or West Indians, with a leadership confined to local black people who emerged from among the immigrant communities. Such churches were usually in the Pentecostal-holiness tradition; and the worship commonly included speaking in tongues and prophecy, with a high degree of congregational participation. But there was considerable theological and ecclesiological diversity in the Afro-Caribbean traditions. Among the non-Pentecostal groups were the African Methodist Episcopal Church and the African Methodist Episcopal Zion Church, both of which came into existence in reaction to the racism of white Methodism in the United States at the end of the eighteenth century and the beginning of

*Kecius
gray
(d.c13) now
ta Pecticent
I was his
tutor.*

the nineteenth century. Likewise, the Wesleyan Holiness Churches, which had their origin in the United States in the nineteenth century, had the abolition of slavery as a major reason for their separate existence. There was also a resurrection of the Seventh Day Baptist Church, which had been established in Britain in the seventeenth century as a result of the influx of members from the West Indies, and of the Seventh Day Adventist Church.

I will be considering these Afro-Caribbean churches in some detail in chapter 9, but I mention them here as an illustration of the dramatic and traumatic changes in the domestic church scene locally and nationally in the post-Second World War half century in England.

Before turning to a full consideration of the Church of England, the Free Churches and the Roman Catholics I will briefly consider two matters which impinged on all the churches; new forms of evangelism and pastoral care and new manifestations of radical theology.

New forms of non-denominational evangelism and pastoral care

The life of the churches was greatly influenced by new forms of evangelism, or by old and well-tried methods used in new ways.

The first full-scale non-denominational evangelistic effort after the Second World War was by the British evangelist Tom Rees who conducted rallies in the Central Hall, Westminster, and then at the Royal Albert Hall, beginning just at the end of the war. They attracted thousands of people and resulted in innumerable conversions. Rees also extended his outreach into the provinces and, in 1945, opened Hildenborough Hall as a Christian conference centre.[14] Certain organizations such as Crusaders were active and others, such as Pathfinders, were started. There was also the London Mission of 1949 which I will be recounting in the next chapter; and there was the highly strategic enterprise of the Revd E. J. H. Nash in organizing 'Bash Camps' for boys at leading public schools, which touched the lives of such future Evangelical leaders as Michael Green (subsequently Principal of St John's College, Nottingham and rector of St Aldate's, Oxford), Dick Lucas (subsequently rector of St Helen's, Bishopsgate, London) and John Stott, the most significant Anglican Evangelical leader in the whole of the second half of the century. But the greatest evangelistic impact in the decades following the war was undoubtedly made by Billy Graham.

Billy Graham visited England in the spring of 1946 and addressed a number of public meetings.[15] He returned in October of the same year accompanied by Cliff Barrows, and the two of them spoke in twenty-seven cities and towns at 360 meetings in the ensuing five months, almost entirely to young people. At the conclusion of the tour a conference of 250 youth leaders gathered at Graham's initiative in Birmingham. Several of them wondered if Graham should return for a campaign not limited to youth. 'They had caught a gleam which could pierce war weariness and the defeatism, the littlemindedness which had settled on much of British religion.'[16]

That return came in 1954, and the results were extraordinary. The crusade was based on Harringay arena in London, but extended to various other centres by the novel means of Post Office landline relays, and concluded at Wembley stadium with what has been described as 'the greatest religious congregation, 120,000, ever seen until then in the British Isles'.[17] It captured the popular imagination and throughout the crowds attending were enormous. More than 38,000 people went forward at the meetings in response to the appeals by the evangelist.[18] It was an immense encouragement not only to the evangelicals who had organized and supported the venture, but to many other Anglicans and Free Churchmen who took hope for the future. Graham returned in 1966 for a crusade now supported by 1,800 ministers who involved their churches; and the results were once more dramatic. But for this crusade greater care was taken in the follow-up of individuals responding, and in the teaching and support afforded by the churches to which they went. Graham was to return on a number of occasions in the future, for by now he was a recognized figure, with international stature.

The Inter-Varsity Fellowship[19] was the evangelical body which worked in universities and other higher education institutions, and it enjoyed quite phenomenal success in the post-war decades. The numbers joining its local branches in the various colleges were high, it had an impressive unity of purpose and clear direction, and a self-confidence which most of the time did not degenerate into triumphalism. It had an incalculable impact on the lives of countless young people, and made an invaluable contribution to the surge of evangelicalism which persisted until the end of the century.

The Jesus movement and the charismatic movement powerfully influenced people of all ages and social backgrounds from many Christian traditions.[20] They provided a common, unifying element which bridged the Protestant and Catholic divide, the evangelical and non-evangelical camps and the Anglican and Free Church barriers. The charismatic movement began in England in a quiet and not very spectacular way between 1962 and 1964 with speaking in tongues in parishes like St Mark's, Gillingham, St Mark's, Cheltenham, and St Paul's, Beckenham, and with the founding in 1964 of the Fountain Trust by the Revd Michael Harper to help all Christians in all the denominations who had been 'baptized in the Spirit' to be taught more about this individual and corporate experience and its implications. It spread throughout the country, and in many countries worldwide. In 1971 the first international conference was held under the auspices of the Fountain Trust in Guildford; and for the first time ever Roman Catholics, traditional Protestants and members of designated Pentecostal churches shared the same platform.

During the 1970s the movement manifested itself publicly in prayer meetings and conferences and in various churches experiencing 're-newal'. Music and drama assumed an important place in the worship of such churches; and overtly charismatic collections of hymns appeared, such as *Sound of Living Waters* (1974) and *Fresh Sounds* (1976), which were also used in non-charismatic, mainly evangelical, churches. The distinctively charismatic form of church worship, known to many by the raising of arms and hands with open palms during the singing of hymns and at other times, continued into the 1990s. And the Toronto experience of the 1990s was but one particular form of what was a most remarkable, prolonged, pervasive and powerful influence throughout the churches of England.

Non-denominational events appealed especially to teenagers who had little sympathy with denominational divisions. Spring Harvest and Greenbelt provided opportunities annually for thousands of Christian young people, and some who were not so young, to gather in a relaxed fashion, to share their faith, and to worship, laugh, learn and eat together. They did not concentrate solely on somewhat emotional acts of worship but combined informality with serious Bible study and teaching sessions. The gatherings seemed to catch the mood of the age and to be attuned to what many were seeking in a period when evangelicalism was thriving.

Lastly, mention needs to be made of the use by Christians of all types and traditions of the media as a means of evangelism and teaching. An impressive number of Anglicans, Free Churchmen and Roman Catholics were able to make thoroughly professional and yet uncompromisingly Christian contributions to radio and television programmes. The daily service, the Sunday morning service, and the BBC Sunday evening broadcast *Songs of Praise*, which continued through many years to be one of the most popular television programmes of the week, attest to the fact that in the latter part of the twentieth century Christianity was far from dead.

Theological radicalism

Some of the theologians in the second half of the twentieth century, and especially around the 1960s, propounded views which were radical, and in some cases seriously at variance with Christian orthodoxy as understood by well-informed conservative churchmen. I will avoid discussion of John A. T. Robinson's *Honest to God* (1963) as this will be considered in some detail in the next chapter. I will briefly focus on four theologians.

Paul van Buren's *The Secular Meaning of the Gospel* was published in 1963. In it he dismissed theism 'on the logical positivist's premise that statements about God, who is beyond empirical experience, are meaningless. Jesus Christ, however, still had great meaning for the world, not in religious or theistic terms, but as the perfect expression of freedom, for in him alone there is seen perfect freedom – freedom from tradition, from fear, from the pressures of society, from self. Herein lay his authority, and Easter was the moment when the followers of Jesus awoke to the fact of his freedom and were liberated so as to share in it among themselves and with others.'[21]

A further, equally influential, book of the same genre was published two years later. *The Secular City* by another American, Harvey Cox, described modern technological culture 'not as a contradiction of biblical truth but as its genuine fulfilment. The doctrine of creation liberates man from superstition and Jesus is the bestower of freedom to all men in every situation and is the personification of the kingdom of God. Man's fulfilment is now to be found in the secular city.'[22] The church as the servant of the city must be a community undergoing liberation from rigid and compulsive patterns of behaviour which arose out of mistaken images of the world. Misleading metaphysics and irrelevant other worldliness were a hindrance to people seeking to meet God in the normal daily human duties and relationships of secular life – which was the only place where he could be found – and must therefore be discarded. It is of note that Harvey Cox, like some others involved in this secular style of theology, later revised his opinions and placed a much higher value on orthodox Christianity.

Then there were the ultimate articulations of radical theology in the works of T.J.J. Altizer and William Hamilton. They were the chief proponents of the 'death of God' theology and, although their works were not as widely read, and their ideas not so readily acclaimed in England, as those of van Buren and Cox, they helped to produce the theological climate in which the works of John A.T. Robinson, Maurice Wiles and Don Cupitt were able to flourish. Altizer asserted that God died when Jesus came, as there was then no further need for him. Since that time he has been wholly immersed in history, and has become progressively incarnate in the universal body of humanity. Hamilton placed the death of God in the twentieth century. There was no longer any point in waiting for God, for he will never come. Man must create his own meaning and in doing so Christ can still provide the key.

Some of these views influenced theologians within the English churches; and the churches increasingly harboured a variety of theological convictions. It was but the culmination, at least up to that time, of what had been taking place for well over one hundred years. This was particularly evident in the Church of England. Writing in 1986, one acute observer commented that 'Since *Essays and Reviews* (1860), which first signalled the fact that the methods of German biblical criticism had penetrated the Church of England, there has been a steady broadening of permitted theological opinion until we have reached the point where there exists a diversity of fundamental Christian world views within a single church.'[23] The Church of England continued to pride itself on its ability to bring a range of theological convictions within its very ample umbrella. But there were many who questioned whether there was a limit to such a policy of tolerance. 'It is', one commentator remarked in 1989, 'stretching credulity beyond reasonable limits to maintain that such a diversity is an expression of comprehensiveness understood in terms of complementarity. Such diversity is not an expression of multi-faceted complementarity. It is an example of pluralism. The contemporary Church of England contains a number of different Anglicanisms.'[24]

Further Reading

Bebbington, D.W., *Evangelicalism in Modern Britain. A history from the 1730s to the 1980s*, London 1989

Brierley, Peter, '*Christian' England. What the English Church Census Reveals*, London 1991

Chadwick, Owen, *Michael Ramsey. A Life*, London 1990; reissued London 1998

Currie, R., Gilbert, A., and Horsley, L., *Churches and Churchgoers: Patterns of Church Growth in the British Isles Since 1700*, Oxford 1977

Davies, Horton, *Worship and Theology in England: The Ecumenical Century, 1900–1965*, Princeton 1965

Gill, Sean, *Women and the Church of England From the Eighteenth Century to the Present*, London 1994

Gray, John D., *The Geography of Religion in England*, London 1971

Hastings, Adrian, *A History of English Christianity 1920–1990*, London 1991

Peart-Binns, John S., *Wand of London*, London 1987

Robinson, John A.T., *Honest to God*, London 1963

Royle, Edward, *Modern Britain. A Social History 1750–1985*, London 1987

Sandhurst, B.G., *How Heathen is Britain?*, London 1946

Welsby, Paul, *A History of the Church of England 1945–1980*, Oxford 1984

Wolffe, John (ed), *Evangelical Faith and Public Zeal. Evangelicals and Society in Britain 1780–1980*, London 1995

Davie, Grace: Religion in Britain Since 1945.

Brown, Callum: The Death of Christian Britain.

8

The Church of England 1945 to 1998

A new era

'New' periods of time in the continuous historical process are often not easy to identify or justify; but the end of major wars frequently provide exceptions, and 1945 was most certainly one. This was so for the nation as a whole, and in a very special way for the Church of England. Reconstruction was the order of the day. A new world had come into existence; and the magnitude of that newness can only be fully appreciated with hindsight. A new beginning was called for, and in the midst of such momentous times, when firm and yet inspirational leadership was essential, the Church of England was shattered by the early death of William Temple, the Archbishop of Canterbury in 1944.[1] He was a man of remarkable character and ability, regarded by some as the most outstanding person to occupy the seat of Augustine since the Reformation.

> Temple was a man who was listened to with respect by many in authority in Church and State and was loved by the common man, who regarded him as both champion and friend. He possessed exceptional intellectual power and prophetic insight. He was able to hold in synthesis theology, philosophy, politics, and economics and from this combination emerged his grasp of the nature of the Christian social principles which ought to guide the Church.[2]

welsby)

As the war drew to its close, and as the church looked to play its part in the massive task of post-war recovery, many of the principles which he held dear, and which he saw as needing to be implemented in the fields of housing, health, education, and social welfare, seemed to be on the verge of being put into practical operation. 'Never had an appointment to the archbishopric of Canterbury been so universally acclaimed as that of William Temple and, because expectations were so high, it is understandable that his death was viewed in catastrophic terms.'[3] 'We are burying the hopes of the Church of England,' Joseph McCulloch reflected at the funeral on 31 October 1944.[4]

The new leader, Geoffrey Fisher, was a remarkably different man. He had been headmaster of Repton, where he succeeded William Temple, from 1914 to 1932; and it showed![5] His forte was administration, and some thought that he ran the Church of England like a school. Efficiency, organizational ability and indefatigable work were useful qualities for such a time. It is questionable if they represented an adequate replacement for the higher order attributes of the charismatic and energetic Temple. But they helped the church to face and partially meet the mighty tasks of administrative and financial reform, recovery from devastating war damage to churches and vicarages, and the provision of pastoral care which were priorities in the aftermath of war.

While Fisher and the Church of England in general were active in literally rebuilding, Bishop George Bell of Chichester used his wide contacts with German and other continental church leaders in an intense effort to assist with the reconstruction of Europe. It was all part of the post-war involvement of the church in international and national action to restore what had been so ruthlessly and sadly destroyed. But the Church of England also had its distinctive areas of activity, most notably in evangelism, pastoral concern, liturgy and theological debate.

Evangelism

In 1945 the Church of England Commission on Evangelism, chaired by the Evangelical Bishop of Rochester, Christopher Chavasse, produced its widely circulated and much debated report *Towards the Conversion of England*. It read like an evangelical treatise and it helped to give prominence and official Church of England endorsement to the particular evangelical emphasis which pervaded it. It had many of the merits and the shortcomings of current evangelicalism. It provided a realistic appraisal of the problems, frustrations, and spiritual lethargy of many of the clergy, and called for opportunities to be made available for spiritual renewal. The laity were embraced as part of the 'Apostolate of the Church'. The report saw them as essential in the work of evangelism as they were most in contact with lay people at work and socially; and it asked for appropriate training to be made available for them. It advocated the use in full by the church of modern agencies of propaganda such as the cinema, drama, television, the press and literature, but seemed to be over-impressed and naive about the extent to which such channels of communication could aid in the furtherance of evangelism. It called, somewhat unrealistically, for enormous expenditure on advertising over a five-year period. It concluded with specific proposals such as schools of preaching for the clergy, a new short Catechism, diocesan groups for study, Christian cells, the better ordering of liturgical worship and the provision of 'popular services'. Most importantly it recommended that the archbishops should establish a permanent Council on Evangelism. The report was strong in its confident assertion of the message to be proclaimed, and on some of its ideas for encouraging personal commitment. It was weak in that it showed little appreciation of the social dimension of the work and witness of the church as part of a truly conceived and comprehensive evangelism in which the church ministered to the whole person and the whole range of social needs which were so urgent and demanding at the time.

Although it was severely criticized by many churchmen, and the Church Assembly refused to set up a Council on Evangelism, the report stimulated a serious reassessment of the importance being accorded to evangelism; it prompted dioceses, deaneries and parishes to organize missions, and some dioceses to appoint Diocesan Missioners; it resulted in schools of evangelism for clergy and laity; and it helped to inspire Walter Carey, the retired Bishop of Bloemfontein, and Brother Edward to found the Village Evangelists in 1948.

Then there was the great Mission to London of 1949, led by the High Church Bishop of London, William Wand.[6] Under the motto and rallying phrase 'Recovery Starts Within' he enlisted thousands of helpers from the worst-bombed parts of the East End to the residential districts of Middlesex, from the cities of Westminster and London, from Paddington and Tottenham, and from all types and shades of churchmanship. He defined the Mission's targets clearly, showing that he had a comprehensive view of evangelism:

There were to be three points of attack. We were to make our main endeavour that of winning the outsider, the person who hitherto had been either indifferent or mildly antagonistic to religion. As a by-product of this effort we hoped at the same time to stir up new interest in those who had lapsed . . . The third aim was more unusual. It was felt that in society as at present constituted under a Welfare State it was very important to show how Christianity applied not only to the individual, but also to the common life . . . We felt that if a Mission was to have a really good and lasting effect, it must show that Christianity had a message for every common concern of mankind.[7]

In May 1948 8,000 church people gathered in the Royal Albert Hall and committed themselves to prepare for the Mission one year later. 'It was no ordinary mass rally. There was an air of excitement and tautness. Little wonder, as those attending were about to be transformed into the Church's shock troops.'[8] By the turn of the year 15,000 were in preparation. Publicity was widely distributed, the media was kept alerted, missioners were commissioned. During the Mission itself meetings abounded. 'The Church was everywhere, in pub and club, factory, street and shop.'[9] Lectures were given simultaneously in St Paul's Cathedral, Westminster Abbey and Southwark Cathedral. 'All London seemed to be talking about God and many lives were being changed.'[10] Of course there was some dimming of the vision, and some falling away after the Mission was ended, but it was a mammoth evangelistic effort, and a significant turning point; and it was masterminded by a man who was dubbed a Liberal Catholic!

Wand gives some further insight into his concept of evangelism at that time:

We must make the whole environment in which we live capable of expressing the beauty and splendour of Almighty God. I believe that in the parishes where that effort is consciously made there is a beauty, a power, and a splendour that comes out from the Church, flowing from the altar, penetrating every home, and kindling a fire on every domestic hearth. The greatest gain we have made in the religious sphere in the last century has been the renewed grasp of the sacramental principle and the endeavour to work it out in every detail of our daily lives. If we in these days can reinforce that lesson and adapt our teaching of it to the needs of our generation, then I believe we shall be able to give to the men and women of our day something which they very sorely need. We have the answer to our questions in the Gospel of the Kingdom. That is the Gospel we must preach, and today is our day of opportunity.[11]

Liturgy and theology

Dom Gregory Dix owed his incredible influence to his brilliance as a scholar, his unconventionality and good humour as a controversialist, and his most distinguished work, *The Shape of the Liturgy,* which appeared in 1945. The book opened a new era in English liturgical studies. It was a study of the 'ritual pattern' of the eucharist. Abandoning the search for an archetypal eucharistic prayer, Dix set out to show that underlying all the older liturgies is to be found 'a single normal or standard structure of the rite as a whole'.[12] He called this the 'shape' of the liturgy, and said that it was based on Christ's actions at the Last Supper.

> Our Lord (1) took bread; (2) 'gave thanks' over it; (3) broke it; (4) distributed it, saying certain words. Later He (5) took a cup; (6) 'gave thanks' over that; (7) handed it to His disciples, saying certain words. We are so accustomed to the liturgical shape of the eucharist as we know it that we do not instantly appreciate the fact that it is not based in practice on this 'seven-action' scheme, but on a somewhat drastic modification of it. With absolute unanimity the liturgical tradition reproduces these seven actions as four: (1) The offertory; bread and wine are 'taken' and placed on the table together. (2) The prayer; the president gives thanks to God over bread and wine together. (3) The fraction; the bread is broken. (4) The communion; the bread and wine are distributed together.[13]

Dix then elaborated on this theme in great detail in his massive book. It reached an unexpectedly wide readership and played a part in all subsequent revisions for many years during a period of considerable liturgical activity. *And students still lap it up.*

Whatever view was taken on the form of the communion service, there was a group within the Church of England which sought to make that service the central act of worship in all parishes. The Parish Communion movement had received an initial impetus to action by the publication in 1937 of *The Parish Communion,* a series of essays edited by A. G. Herbert. Its object was neatly summed up in the phrase 'The Lord's own service on the Lord's day for the Lord's people'. The pioneer of the movement was Henry de Candole, who became Bishop of Knaresborough in 1949. And it was in that year that the Parish and People Movement was launched.[14] Its ideas were to percolate through to many parishes in the following decades.

In liturgical matters in the immediate post-war period Dix and *The Shape of the Liturgy* were outstanding, and very constructive. In the realm of theology E. W. Barnes made the most important contribution with his book *The Rise of Christianity* (1947), but it was destructive.

CH Dodd 'destroyed' it
— a devastating review!

His was the voice within the church which lauded modern science to an unseemly extent and contrasted the orderly universe of science with the, by inference, disorderly and therefore unacceptable miraculous elements in the Gospels. 'Its inadequacies of scholarship minimized its influence, and in fact it marked a theological dead end. But it was one call of the warning trumpet that the day of major theological restatement was coming, and with this task the Church has been occupied ever since.'[15] The tenor of the whole work was to discredit the authority of the New Testament books, and to weaken confidence in their accuracy by dating them well in the second century. In eliminating the miraculous Barnes dismissed the virgin birth and the resurrection. He expressed the highest appreciation of the character and teaching of Jesus, but minimized the duration of Jesus' ministry and downplayed the crucifixion. He pronounced the narrative of Paul's early life as unreliable, and declared his letters to be a patchwork of miscellaneous documents and fragments.

The book caused distress and indignation and Fisher, the Archbishop, was obliged to make a statement. In his presidential address to the Convocation of Canterbury he acknowledged Barnes' intended honesty in writing the book and his devotion to Christ, but he went on to list the faults and inadequacies of the work and concluded by saying that it 'so diminishes . . . the content of the Christian faith as to make the residue which is left inconsistent with the scriptural doctrine and beliefs of the Church in which he holds office . . . If his views were mine, I would not feel that I could still hold episcopal office in the Church.'[16] Barnes later demurred from such a view. 'I believe', he stated, 'the conclusions reached in my book to be true and I hold them to be entirely compatible with my position as a Bishop in the Church of England.'[17] And there the matter rested.

In the 1950s the foremost theological debate was around the issue of fundamentalism. It was mainly aroused by the growing influence of the Inter-Varsity Fellowship represented by Christian Unions in the universities, the Billy Graham crusade of 1954–55, which included an invitation to conduct a mission in the University of Cambridge, and the increase in the number of evangelical candidates for the ministry. In a letter to *The Times* Canon H. K. Luce, headmaster of Durham School, said that the Billy Graham invitation raised an issue which did not seem to have been squarely faced in this country. Universities exist for the advancement of learning: on what basis, therefore, he asked, could fundamentalism claim a hearing at Cambridge? A considerable correspondence ensued, which was later published. One bishop sharply disagreed with another, and all kinds of views were expressed, sometimes in trenchant and hard-hitting language.

The attack on 'fundamentalism' was most comprehensively elaborated in Gabriel Herbert's *Fundamentalism and the Church of God* (1957). Herbert considered the type of fundamentalism he was addressing to be 'a grave menace to the Church of God'.[18] He especially abhorred the rigid evangelical doctrine of the Bible; objected to the assertion that the Bible was literally true; and denounced an evangelical self-righteousness which condemned all who disagreed with them. The rigidity and all-or-nothingness of the evangelicals was dangerous. When Christians who were nurtured on such teaching were confronted with proof that the biblical account of the creation was unscientific, or when they were faced with biblical discrepancies, they might then suspect that they were not being told the whole truth about the Bible. Having been told that they must believe everything, they might end by believing nothing. He was answered in measured tones by the evangelical John Stott in a succinct leaflet entitled *Fundamentalism and Evangelism*, and by J.I. Packer in a more extended version of the conservative evangelical case, *Fundamentalism and the Word of God* (1958).

It was, however, in the 1960s that a theological storm occurred which was fiercer and more protracted than any since that over *Essays and Reviews* almost exactly one hundred years before. The book of theological essays under the title *Soundings*, which was published in 1962, provided vague rumblings. John A. T. Robinson's *Honest to God* 'set all the fireworks and thunderings of the long-pent storm free to rage in fury'.[19]

The essays in *Soundings* were by ten theologians. They set out not to provide confident answers, but rather to identify pertinent questions which needed to be explored. It seemed to them that

the great problem of the Church (and therefore of its theologians) is to establish or re-establish some kind of vital contact with that enormous majority of human beings for whom Christian faith is not so much unlikely as irrelevant and uninteresting. The greatest intellectual challenge to faith is simply that thoroughly secularized intelligence which is now the rule rather than the exception, whether it expresses itself in science or philosophy or politics or the arts. It is by no means clear that anything like Christian faith in the form we know it will ever again be able to come alive for people of our own time or of such future time as we can imagine. It is just as uncertain that Christian ideals and ways of thought, as we know them, will be able to re-engage an intelligence and imagination now so far separated from them.[20]

Except for the fact that the book gave the first public airing to what has been christened the New Morality, it produced little reaction. It was a very scholarly work by a group of academics who always wrote with caution and restraint; but it heralded a revolution. It at least implied a radical questioning of traditional theology. It was a foretaste of what was to come in a more controversial, sensational and popular (but not necessarily easy to understand) form the following year.

When Robinson wrote *Honest to God* he made publishing history. 'The book appears to have sold more quickly than any new book of serious theology in the history of the world.'[21] In the first three months of the book's life its author received over a thousand letters of response. In television programmes and on the radio, by means of cartoons and satirical jokes, newspaper articles and reviews, sermons and letters to editors, the debate it provoked was perpetuated for a long time.

Honest to God was inspired by three German theologians: Rudolf Bultmann, Dietrich Bonhoeffer and Paul Tillich. Bultmann, with his concern to 'demythologize' the gospel, was a challenge to the 'biblical' theologians. Bonhoeffer, with his vision of a 'religionless' Christianity, was a challenge to Christian escapism and undue pietism. Tillich, with his philosophy based on faith as 'ultimate concern' with the 'ground of our being', was a reminder of the call of the church to embrace all mankind in its concern.

In order to communicate Christian doctrine Robinson believed that the church was being called not merely to a restatement of traditional orthodoxy in modern terms, but to a much more radical recasting 'in the process of which the most fundamental categories of our theology – of God, the supernatural, and of religion itself – must go into the melting'.[22] The lay world, Robinson said, found traditional orthodox supernaturalism largely meaningless.

Indeed, Robinson identified with this incomprehension. His concern was that those, like him, who radically questioned the established religious frame, should be accepted as no less genuine, or in the long run necessary as defenders of the faith, than the orthodox; but he was not sanguine. He anticipated increasing alienation 'both within the ranks of the Church and outside it, between those whose basic recipe is the mixture as before (however revitalized) and those who feel compelled above all to be honest wherever it may lead them'.[23]

Man, Robinson asserted, had come of age, and the old images of God were no longer adequate. Pictures of God 'up there' or 'out there' were unhelpful. More appropriate was the terminology of depth psychology, in which God was thought of as 'the ground of our being'. Jesus was the 'man for others', who is united with 'the ground of his being' because of his utter concern for other people. The test of worship is how far it makes us more sensitive to the beyond in our midst, or to Christ in the hungry, the naked, the homeless and the prisoner. In the sphere of morals the radical 'ethic of the situation' was advocated, in which nothing was prescribed except love.

The reactions to the book from within the Church of England were, as would be expected, extremely varied. The liberal wing understandably saw merits in the work which High Churchmen and evangelicals denied. Many liberal evangelicals, like Max Warren, who completed a distinguished career as Secretary of the Church Missionary Society in 1963, welcomed the publication. Indeed Warren had encouraged Robinson to publish it; and after it appeared he defended its honest attempt to re-examine the Christian vocabulary and see if it could be used to commend Jesus Christ to those who did not know the kind of religious shorthand characteristic of orthodox Christianity. It was, said Warren, not a dogmatic book. The author was gentle and sensitive, and was asking himself questions: he was an explorer. It was not an easy book to read, but 'honest to goodness', Warren declared, it was worth reading.[24] And in 1968, despite all the trauma it had caused, he joined with others in celebrating the fifth anniversary of the book's publication.

J. I. Packer was once again the chief spokesman for the more conservative evangelicals, and he couched and concentrated his response in a leaflet entitled *Keep Yourselves from Idols* (1963). I will give a quite full account of what he wrote because it not only reflects the evangelical attitude at the time to *Honest to God*, but the stance taken by evangelicals generally to the liberal theology which was to be prominent in the life of the churches for the remaining part of the century. For the same reason I will do likewise with the High Church reaction and response.

Packer paid tribute to the book as a most frank and, for that reason, most engaging work.[25] Nonetheless, in common with evangelicals at large, he wished the book had not come from a bishop. 'No doubt the church needs its gadflies and even its heretics . . . But it is not to the office and ministry of a gadfly that a bishop is consecrated.'[26] Packer accepted that *Honest to God* legitimately raised questions which needed to be addressed and answered. He also recognized that it was not, and did not claim to be, a definitive answer to such profound theological and philosophical questions: it was a tentative exploration. Indeed, considering the originality of Robinson's mind, Packer thought the book bore 'the marks of unfinished thinking on page after page'.[27]

Packer was critical of Robinson's proposal that we should stop thinking of God as a person separate from ourselves, and should give the name 'God' to the 'ground of our being'. Such a God, Packer asserted, could not meaningfully be called 'Father'. Robinson's real message was not that God is love, but that love is God, and the bishop's Jesus (whose pre-existence and virgin birth he certainly denied, and apparently his bodily resurrection, present dominion and future return also) could not really be called either Saviour or Lord.

Packer considered that the saddest thing about *Honest to God* was its genuine pastoral and evangelistic intent, but its unhelpful and inept attempt to meet such pastoral and evangelistic needs. The cure was worse than the disease. The God offered by Robinson was no less, but no more, than the deepest thing within us. The God of creation, providence, and revelation, the God in whose image we were made, the Lord of history, self-existent and tri-personal, vanished from the scene. Nor was there any place in the picture for the incarnation, the atoning sacrifice of Christ, the resurrection, the second coming, the law and the promises.

A gospel for intellectuals (or anyone else) that was bought at the price of such a loss was not worth having. By mutilating the Christian message in this fashion, Packer continued, the bishop had not, as he thought, rescued the perishing, he was 'merely sinking the lifeboat'.[28] The choice was not 'between two images of the same God, but between two Gods, two Christs, two histories, and ultimately two religions'. The God portrayed by Robinson was no longer recognizable as 'the God and Father of our Lord Jesus Christ', and when that point is reached one has 'changed the truth of God into a lie and started to worship a false God'.[29] The admonition of the Apostle John to 'keep yourselves from idols'[30] applied in the case of *Honest to God*, and the warning should be heeded.

In his concluding remarks Packer identified the true radicals in the post-Christian world. They were not those who changed the gospel under the shallow delusion that man had changed, but those who were bold enough to face 'modern man' and maintain that the Bible was still right, that God was still on the throne, that the risen Christ was still mighty to save. Man remained the sinner he had always been. The apostolic gospel was still 'the power of God unto salvation', and not even such great mistakes as those Packer had been examining could finally 'stop its course, or thwart its triumph'.[31]

The distinguished High Church theologian E. L. Mascall recognized the significance of the publication, and then went on to a thorough analysis of the book. 'Whatever its other merits may be', he wrote, 'Dr J. A. T. Robinson's best-selling paper-back volume *Honest to God* has at any rate attracted attention to a movement in present-day theology which, while it has not perhaps the monopoly of enlightenment and constructive thought with which some of its more fervent exponents have credited it, may be more widespread than has been commonly recognized in English-speaking religious circles.'[32]

Mascall identified *Honest to God* as the product of a process which he termed 'the secularization of Christianity'. He was categorical in his assertion that one 'of the most imperative duties with which the Christian theologian is confronted is that of relating the revealed datum of Christian truth, final, absolute and fundamentally permanent as he must by his Christian commitment believe it to be, to the essentially incomplete, relative and constantly changing intellectual framework of the world in which he lives'.[33] He considered that the new school of Protestant theology represented by *Honest to God* was a reaction to the long reign of the biblical school of Karl Barth, but he resented the fact that it took as its starting-point the outlook of contemporary secularized man, and demanded that the traditional faith of Christendom should be completely transformed in order to conform to it. He considered this particularly deplorable at a time when Western civilization was, at least in its outlook, radically irreligious. It was said by the new theology that contemporary man was so radically secularized that he simply could not accept supernatural Christianity; therefore we must completely desupernaturalize Christianity in order to give him something he can accept. Such an approach Mascall declared to be utterly untenable and unacceptable. It discarded the essentially unchanging gospel.

He dismissed the 'demythologizing' of the new theology, inaugurated by Bultmann, as an undesirable and unjustifiable manifestation of the new theological reductionism. He was outspoken in his criticism. 'One might be pardoned', he wrote, 'for supposing that Robinson had despaired of trying to convert the world to Christianity and had decided instead to convert Christianity to the world.'[34] It was over-simplistic and inaccurate for Robinson to assert that Christians naively believed in a 'three-decker universe'. The Christian belief in God as the absolute necessary Being could validly be expressed analogically in such spatial terms, but this was supplemented by the equally analogical notion of God as being everywhere.

Mascall concluded his review of *Honest to God* on a positive note; very similar in essence to that of Packer. He wrote:

> What we are called to in this twentieth century is not the abandonment of the accumulated treasures of our Christian heritage, but their putting at the service of the contemporary world. This will involve us in tasks of interpretation which will tax us to the uttermost as we try to interpret Christian truth not only to Western industrialized, secularized man, but also to the people of the East and of Africa, with their own great heritage of philosophic thought and religious practice. After this long, and I fear, extremely tedious examination of Dr Robinson's programme, I can only repeat, though in a sense presumably different from that which he intended, that, in its exclusive concern with one small section of our community, it is not too radical but not nearly radical enough. It does not get down to the roots.[35]

Michael Ramsey commented as a pastor charged with pastoral responsibility of a high order as Archbishop of Canterbury, as well as from the point of view of an eminent High Church theologian. It was therefore very appropriate that his most widely-read response to *Honest to God* took the form of a small pamphlet which had in mind people who had been perplexed by the ferment of ideas about God and religion.

'It is', said Ramsey, 'the putting of our own feeble little grasp of God, or our own individual picture of God himself which is the peril of "religion".' But he saw a greater peril still. Religion could mean 'a set of pious attitudes and practices within which we look for God, forgetting that God may sometimes be found less amongst them than amongst the things we call non-religious or secular'.[36]

Ramsey pointed out that some Christian thinkers, for instance Paul Tillich, had asked modern man not to look for God in religion at all, as had been the way in the past, but to look for God in the midst of the human relationships of everyday life in our secular world, and he

One recalls endless debates on all this — Sheffield in 1962–5

showed some sympathy for this view. He thought that there was validity in helping a man who was estranged from ordinary religious talk to find God by thinking in depth about himself and his own meaning. He suggested that many who had tried to commend Christian belief in recent years, including himself, had been advocating such an approach. Dietrich Bonhoeffer had, however, gone further and suggested that all religion was obsolete and must go. It was part of man's immaturity and must be replaced by man's own discovery of purpose, love and ultimate reality in the depth of his being and in the concrete context of human relationships. In *Honest to God* the Bishop of Woolwich had asked that Christianity should be separated from religion, and had declared the prevailing traditional image of God to be outmoded.

Ramsey asserted that even if the frame of a Christian's relation to God is to be set within the secular it will still be a relationship to a Beyond. 'Call it deep down, but it always means a Beyondness.' And he asked if, despite any possible radical changes in terminology and presentation, religion will not remain with us: 'reverence, awe, dependence, adoration, and penitence'.[37]

On the matter of Christ's divinity, Ramsey said that he had 'never met either a "simple" Christian or a theologian who believed that God travelled through space to visit the planet'. The background of the orthodox doctrine was the contrast between Creator and creature and it was in that contrast that the imagery about 'coming down' was used. 'One who is divine, the Creator, by an act of divine humility took upon himself our creaturely human existence.'[38]

He was concerned that much in Robinson's treatment of the New Testament was left obscure, especially in relation to the atonement and the resurrection, because they were demythologized.

He also argued for the centrality in the Christian life of withdrawal; and while he acknowledged the dangers of worship and prayer becoming unrelated to the world and not being set within the common life, he believed that the new way of thinking, which gave such a prominent place to engagement in and with the world, was liable to miss out on a whole dimension of truth – an inescapable strain of asceticism and renunciation was to be found both in the Gospels and in a long line of great exponents of the Christian way.

Although Ramsey expressed appreciation of the new approach to morals, for example in its concern to avoid legalism, he stressed that Christ came to fulfil and not to abolish the law, and the teaching of Paul made it clear that love did not supersede the law but profoundly expressed its meaning.

This whole debate highlighted a process of coalescence into 'parties' which had been gaining momentum in the post-war period and was to become central to the life of the Church of England at national and local levels as the century progressed. So it is to this that I now turn.

The Evangelicals

The fifty years and more after the ending of the Second World War saw an Evangelical resurgence in the Church of England. It was in the immediate aftermath of the war that the Evangelicals started in a significant way to emerge from the 'ghetto in which they had incarcerated themselves'[39] since the turn of the century or earlier.

At first the indications of a renaissance were somewhat faint and dispersed. In 1944 Tyndale House was opened in Cambridge as an evangelical centre for biblical and theological study and research, and its undramatic influence was to increase as the Tyndale Fellowship was inaugurated to encourage postgraduate evangelical students to think more seriously about biblical and theological matters. Then in 1945 there was the evangelical impact of the report *Towards the Conversion of England*, which I have already reviewed. Three years later, in the year of the Lambeth Conference, a representative gathering of all shades of evangelicalism issued a book of papers under the title *Evangelicals Affirm* which, despite its serious omissions and deficiencies, at least showed a degree of evangelical concern for effective involvement in the efforts towards post-war recovery and reconstruction.

The 1950s opened with the Evangelical response to Archbishop Fisher's invitation to contribute to an assessment of the existing state of the church. It took the form of a publication in 1950 entitled *The Fulness of Christ: the Church's Growth into Catholicity*. In the same year John Stott began his twenty-five year tenure as rector of All Souls church, Langham Place in London. He more than anyone else was to be at the heart of the impending and extended Anglican Evangelical revival. In 1954 the 'first major co-operative evangelical effort in the biblical field for many years',[40] resulted in the publication by the Inter-Varsity Fellowship of the long-lasting and immensely influential *New Bible Commentary*. The same year saw the Billy Graham crusade which so stimulated and strengthened Evangelicalism; a secondary result being the publication by John Stott of *Fundamentalism and Evangelism* and by Jim Packer of *'Fundamentalism' and the Word of God*, both of which gave reasoned and biblically-based replies to the current heavy criticism of evangelical evangelism. In the following year, 1955, Stott founded the Eclectic Society as a forum for Evangelical clergy under forty years of age. In 1959 two leading Evangelical laymen purchased the *Church of England Newspaper* which, under the editorship of John King, rapidly developed into a vigorous organ for the promotion of an outward-looking Evangelicalism. And in the following year Latimer House began its life as an Evangelical research centre in Oxford. It was in the 1950s that Gervase Duffield took a leading part in organizing the Evangelicals in the House of Laity of the Church Assembly into a cohesive group; and during that decade also that Evangelicals were increasingly appointed to official Church of England commissions.

The strides forward continued into the 1960s. In 1960 the Church of England Evangelical Council (CEEC) was established as the English group of the newly-formed Evangelical Fellowship in the Anglican Communion. It provided a means whereby Evangelical leaders nationwide could confer and plan strategically, and it encouraged inter-national awareness among Evangelicals as it spoke out on a number of issues. By the mid-1960s the Evangelical theological colleges were full. An active and fruitful work by the Scripture Union in schools and the Inter-Varsity Fellowship in the universities and colleges helped to pro-duce a steady stream of ordinands. In the ever-multiplying Evangelical parishes rigid adherence to the 1662 Prayer Book and a Sunday pattern of 8.00 am communion, 11.00 am morning prayer and 6.00 or 6.30 pm evening prayer started to give way to the use of the various alternative services, and to the holding of parish communions or family services as the main Sunday morning gathering for worship. It was also during the mid-1960s that Evangelicals were in the forefront of the charismatic movement; and Evangelicalism was invigorated and energized once more by a Billy Graham crusade in 1966. Then came a major landmark for Evangelical evolution: the National Evangelical Anglican Congress at Keele University in 1967.

By 1967 the Evangelicals were beginning to discover something of the maturity, power and effectiveness reminiscent of former years long ago, and the Keele Conference gave expression to this. The distinctive marks of the gathering were a willingness to give greater consideration to the views of non-Evangelicals; a concern to relate the Christian faith to contemporary political, economic and social issues; and a desire to take the ecumenical movement seriously. But the most far-reaching and controversial effect was to set Church of England Evangelicals squarely within the historic, established church.[41] This was not evident to many of the participants or observers at the time, but it soon emerged as a fundamental consequence of a reinvigorated Evangelicalism determined to give priority to its Anglicanism alongside its evangelicalism. This was provocative. An influential body of non-Anglican evangelicals led by the able, immensely respected and energetic minister of Westminster Chapel, Dr Martyn Lloyd Jones, were of the opinion that membership of doctrinally 'mixed' churches such as the Church of England was incompatible with evangelicalism, and that it compromised those concerned, or even removed their right to be called evangelical.

Keele was a watershed for Evangelicalism. 'The Church of England now had to take the evangelicals seriously, with the result that they have played a full part in the life of the Church at both diocesan and national level,'[42] wrote one commentator in 1984. In many ways the promise of Keele was not fulfilled, but it remained an important staging post in the Evangelicalism of the second half of the twentieth century; and the following decades saw further considerable advance. Evangelical theological colleges continued to flourish. The number of Evangelical clergy so increased that by the late 1970s there were not enough benefices with Evangelical patronage to accommodate them all. Some went into parishes with other traditions, and this over-supply persisted until the end of the century. Evangelical parishes became some of the most vigorous in the country with large congregations and a wide range of thriving activities. Evangelicals became Archbishops of Canterbury and York and were increasingly appointed to the episcopal bench. Some such as Colin Buchanan and Professor Sir Norman Anderson played a full part in the central councils of the church, Sir Norman being lay chairman of the general Synod for many years. Some competently participated in the Methodist-Anglican unity discussions, and others such as the Revd Julian Charley were active in ecumenical consultations. Evangelicals took a full and distinctive part in the debates engendered by the publication of James Barr's *Fundamentalism* (1977) and John Hick (ed), *The Myth of God Incarnate* (1977). They were also in the forefront of liturgical debate and change, and in the blossoming of hymnology. The Grove booklets and other more extended works provided an evangelical comment on a wide spectrum of ecclesiastical, social and ethical issues. The charismatic movement in its various manifestations brought increasingly widespread renewal. Non-denominational developments such as the lively, varied and imaginative forms of evangelism undertaken by Youth for Christ, the well-supported National Festival of Light, and the burgeoning work of the Evangelical Alliance, all helped in different ways to stimulate the life of Church of England Evangelicalism. And on the international stage, John Stott in particular spearheaded a movement for evangelical unity, co-operation and concerted effort on a number of fronts which found its focus in such gatherings as the Lausanne Congress on World Evangelization in 1974.

Such new life, growth and achievements were a result of immense efforts and at the cost of some tensions. The steadily growing sense of Anglican Evangelical identity, strength and accomplishment sometimes resulted in a neglect by the Church of England Evangelicals of their evangelical brethren in the Free Churches, and a refusal to participate in pan-evangelical enterprises or to support them fully; and this engendered a sense of resentment among Free Church evangelicals. The charismatic movement produced divisions as well as renewal both nationally, locally and in individual churches. Because of this and the variety of expressions of evangelicalism, Church of England Evangelicals were more diffuse and the Evangelical base less sharply defined in the late 1970s than it had been in the late 1960s.

Evangelicalism was strengthened, and its acceptance and influence in the wider church was furthered by the Evangelical Anglican Assemblies which first took place in 1983 and 1984. Their institution meant that

> for the first time in its long and varied history the evangelical movement in the Church of England had brought into being a representative structure in which its various constituent parts could find a voice through delegates responsible to the movement at its grass-roots level.[43]

The prominence and influence of Evangelicals continued with little abatement in the 1990s. There were internal problems, for example the formation of a group under the title 'Reform' which opposed the ordination of women and was critical of the main body of Evangelicals for not being clearer and more decisive on a number of issues such as their attitude to priests who were practising homosexuals, and there were differences of opinion about the charismatic movement, but such things did not prevent the Evangelicals as a whole exercising a remarkable and sustained influence in the Church of England, and to an extent acting as a force in society.

High Churchmanship

We have already seen that High Churchmen played leading parts in the immediate post-Second World War Church of England with the magisterial work by Gregory Dix on the liturgy and J.W.C. Wand's London Mission being outstanding. In 1945 Dix was also asked by Geoffrey Fisher 'to convene a group of Anglicans of the "Catholic" school of thought to examine the causes of the deadlock which occurs in discussions between Catholics and Protestants and to consider whether any synthesis between Catholicism and Protestantism is possible'.[44] A high calibre team was assembled and in 1947 issued its report: *Catholicity. A Study in the Conflict of Christian Traditions in the West, being a Report presented to His Grace the Archbishop of Canterbury*. It usefully made clear their distinctive High Church view of the nature of the Church, which was highly coloured by the particular emphases of one of the group members, Michael Ramsey. They wrote:

> . . . it is a distortion of the apostolic doctrine to say that men are first united to Christ, through faith, within an invisible society of the truly faithful, and then find admission to the visible Church. The right order is not: Christ – faithful individuals – the Church; but: Christ – the Church – faithful individuals. It is Christ-in-His-Body who justifies men, and their justification is their deliverance into His body. The visible Church is part of the Gospel: there is no Scriptural sanction for the view that the Gospel is something that is complete, without the Church, and that the Church is a further stage that follows after the acceptance of the gospel.[45]

'The "wholeness" of the visible Church manifests itself in its outward form.'[46] It embodies itself, they said, in the apostolate and in the apostolic succession, in baptism as the rite of initiation and in what was from the early days of the Christian faith the central act of worship, the eucharist. The English Catholics were prepared to seek a synthesis within the Anglican ideal of comprehensiveness, as this was largely unrealized, but this was not possible without the minimal theological consensus required. 'If theologians are not agreed from the outset in believing the Church to be a Divine fact prior to the individuals who composed its membership, in believing its outward order to be part of its being, in affirming the unity of the faith, in recognizing the authority of "Tradition" together with that of Scripture, then they have not reached agreement about the first principles of the unity they are seeking.'[47]

The post-war influence of High Churchmen and the particular

theological emphasis which characterized them reached its height when the main force behind the report just considered, Michael Ramsey, became Archbishop of Canterbury in 1961. 'No biographer, not even a Boswell, could write Michael Ramsey's life. It needs the mannerisms, the tone of voice, the unspoken humour which is not communicable.'[48] He had been an outstanding undergraduate; had gone as a curate to Liverpool after theological college; left parochial work to become sub-warden of Lincoln Theological College; had returned briefly to parish work as a curate in Boston, Lincolnshire, then moved back to Cambridge for only a few months, as vicar of St Benet's, before becoming Professor of Divinity at Durham University and Canon of Durham Cathedral. In 1950 he was appointed Professor of Divinity at Cambridge, and two years later Bishop of Durham, where he remained until his translation to Canterbury in 1961.

Ramsey was Archbishop for thirteen years, and it was a full, varied and eventful archiepiscopate. He disliked, and was bored by administration, except when it entailed vital matters such as the choice of bishops, or personal correspondence; and with about fifty letters a day to which to respond there was plenty of scope for that. 'The greater part of my time as a Christian pastor', he said, 'is spent in helping ordinary people.'[49] His predecessor, Fisher, had been a gifted administrator, and Ramsey's shortcomings, and especially his ineptness at man-management, made staff relations difficult.

Prominent among the moral issues on which he was expected to pronounce were homosexuality, the re-marriage in church of divorced people and the question of the grounds on which divorce was acceptable, abortion, euthanasia, capital punishment and race relations; and on all of these he gave a lead which was well considered and, in some instances, as for example on the matter of race relations, unambiguous, fearless and uncompromising. He had not lost his concern for, and even passion for, social justice, which at one stage in his life had made him think seriously about the possibility of entering politics as a career. He was still a Liberal politician at heart, and his yearning for a just and fair society led him to forthright condemnations of South African apartheid and the Rhodesian regime of Ian Smith; and this provoked violent criticism from some politicians and civic leaders. At one point he found that as a consequence of his pronouncements he was suddenly at the centre of what was described as 'the windiest political storm endured by an Archbishop of Canterbury since the revolution of 1688'.[50] In retrospect he wondered how he survived 1965, when the storm was most fierce, and thought that he had been helped by a kind of interior peace which he had learned at Cuddesdon Theological College.

Ramsey was an ecumenist by conviction and in practice. As an illustration of this, he was not against the ordination of women to the priesthood, but he was against the Church of England taking such an unusual and fundamentally contentious and divisive step without reference to other churches. He wanted it to be an act of the whole church. He rejoiced in his spiritual affinity with such leaders as Athenagoras, the Ecumenical Patriarch of Constantinople. In 1956 he visited Moscow and experienced a spiritual empathy with Orthodox believers as he joined with them in worship, and he developed a close friendship with Patriarch Alexei. The subsequent visit of Alexei to Lambeth in 1964 was the first such ever of a Patriarch of Moscow to Britain. It was a high point of harmony between Canterbury and Moscow.

The outcome of the Vatican Council of 1962 to 1965, with the new openness to Protestants which it introduced, was welcomed by Ramsey. Fisher had visited the Vatican in an unofficial capacity; in 1966 Ramsey made an official visit. There were demonstrations against the move, led by Dr Ian Paisley, but to no avail. He had a warm rapport with Pope Paul VI; they worshipped together, and when they parted the Pope gave Ramsey the most precious gift he was able to bestow, for he slipped off his episcopal ring and placed it on Ramsey's palm, and Ramsey put it on his own finger. 'No Pope could have said anything louder about the vexing sore over the validity of Anglican Orders. It spoke more loudly than any bull or encyclical.'[51] Ramsey wore it for the remainder of his life, and after his death his wife, Joan, gave it to Archbishop Runcie so that it should become the permanent property of the see of Canterbury. Not all was harmony between Rome and Canterbury, and despite the joint commission of theologians to discuss matters uniting and dividing the two churches, which was one of the results of the visit and was subsequently called ARCIC, there were not infrequent moments of crisis, friction and irritation, but a new era had been inaugurated in Anglican-Roman Catholic relations.

The Anglo-Catholic lover of Eastern Orthodoxy and friend of Roman Catholics was deeply committed to the concept of Anglican-Methodist unity, and worked hard for its achievement.[52] The Church of England rejection of the scheme (which will be described in detail in the next chapter) was one of the most painful experiences of his life. It came near to shattering his faith in the Church of England and his enthusiasm for it.

Ramsey was above all else a man of God, with all the profound sense of vulnerability of one who was sensitive to suffering in himself (for many months while at theological college he was under a psychiatrist) and in others, and all the humility of one who was constantly aware of his own human frailty. He loved silence and contemplation, but he also loved the complementary pastoral activity of caring for others and service in the world. He greatly appreciated Taizé as a religious community, full of young, questioning people, with Catholics and Protestants worshipping and praying together.

Ramsey retired in 1974, and died peacefully in 1988. By then English Catholics were divided and besieged. The main reason was the often fierce and bitter difference of theology, outlook and opinion on specific topics between the more conservative High Churchmen and the ever more influential and growing liberal element. The conservatives were led by the redoubtable Graham Leonard, the Bishop of London.[53] From the 1960s onwards he was the most prominent figure in championing the catholicity of the Church of England. He was forthright, with an admirable clarity of conviction and purpose, and he was prepared to take unpopular and controversial stands on a range of divisive issues. He was convinced that the Church of England in general, and more especially its leaders, had for decades failed to speak out fearlessly, declaring God's absolute, and to many unpalatable, standards, in opposition to the spirit of the age.

Between the early 1970s and the late 1990s three matters in particular aroused the emotions of Anglican Catholics, highlighting and making public the tension between their conservative and liberal wings: the whole debate over homosexuality, the question of remarriage in church of divorced people, and, most emotively of all, the worldwide, highly contentious, divisive and well-publicized matter of the ordination of women to the priesthood and to the episcopate.

By the late 1980s the Anglican Catholics were plagued by this disagreement and discontent, and they were quite severely demoralized. This was compounded by the suicide of Gareth Bennett in 1987, and the emergence of Affirming Catholicism, a formalized group of liberal Anglican Catholics. Bennett was an ordained Oxford don who was found to be the author of the 'anonymous' 1987/88 *Crockford's Preface*. In it he was highly critical of what he regarded as the liberalization of the Church of England, and Archbishop Runcie's personal responsibility for such a state of affairs.[54] His article, and his suicide in the face of the storm which his comments had aroused, somehow epitomized the confusion and concern of a significant body of like-minded High Churchmen at the time. Affirming Catholicism was established in 1990 by a group of Anglican Catholics who were becoming more and more disgruntled with what they regarded as the over-negative, hidebound, inflexible theological and social outlook of traditional, mainstream Anglican Catholicism in the face of rapid theological and social change.

Anglican Catholics at the end of the twentieth century were still a force in the Church of England, and they played a full part in its life. But the divisions in their ranks persisted, and it remained a question for the twenty-first century whether they would experience a further diminution of their unity, power and influence, or undergo some form of rejuvenation.

Radicals and Liberals

Radicals and Liberals in the Church of England probably had more of a voice, and were more listened to, in the fifty years after the ending of the Second World War than at any time before. I recognize that there is a great difference between the 'radical' theologian, whether clergyman or layman, who appeared to discard so much of the basic Christian doctrines and perspectives that it is questionable if the remaining theology could rightly be called 'Christian', and the theologian, whether clergyman or layman, who genuinely wished to retain the essential Christian dogma but to present it in a way which took account of intellectual frames of reference which may have been alien or hostile to the Christian outlook. It is sometimes difficult to know into which category any particular person fell.

We have already seen how much attention was given in 1947 and the following years to E. W. Barnes's *The Rise of Christianity*, and the stir caused by *Soundings* in 1962, followed far more sensationally by *Honest to God* in 1963.

The next major theological agitation precipitated by the radical theologians was the publication fourteen years later of a book edited by John Hick under the title *The Myth of God Incarnate* (1977). It was part of an extended debate on christology. In 1973 there had appeared a book by John Robinson entitled *The Human Face of God* in which the historical Jesus was frankly presented as 'an entirely human personality through which divinity was manifested'. Jesus, Robinson wrote, was 'different from other men, not in kind, but in degree'.[55] Even more radical was the book by Maurice Wiles which appeared in 1974 with the title *The Remaking of Christian Doctrine*, in which it was maintained that incarnational theology was difficult if not impossible; we must either discard traditional christology or accept incoherence. In 1975 Don Cupitt, the Dean of Emmanuel College, Cambridge, declared that 'the Eternal God, and a historical man, are two beings of quite different ontological status'. It was, Cupitt asserted, 'simply unintelligible to declare them identical'.[56] *who ever did?*

The debate was fuelled yet further by Professor G.W.H. Lampe in his 1976 Bampton Lectures, *God as Spirit*. He controversially declared that God as Spirit was always and everywhere at work, and the only exceptional thing about Jesus was that he provided 'the focal instance and key to God's dealings with the world and with men and women. God acted as Spirit in Jesus decisively and in unparalleled fashion, but this activity was in a totally human Jesus'.[57] Much more concern was, however, generated by the Church of England Doctrine Commission under the chairmanship of Maurice Wiles when in 1976 it produced a document entitled *Christian Believing*. The Christian faith and life for all believers was depicted as 'a voyage of discovery', rather than an assurance, and, in the opinion of many, the Commission pushed the limits of comprehensiveness to such an extent that it downgraded the standards of orthodoxy.

The Myth of God Incarnate was launched amid great publicity, and 30,000 copies were sold in the first eight months. It consisted of a series of essays in which the New Testament and the development of Christian doctrine were declared to be culturally conditioned. The conception of Jesus as God incarnate, the second person of the Trinity, living a human life, was declared to be a mythological or poetic way of expressing his significance for us. The Chalcedonian definition of christology was rejected as incomprehensible to modern man. The whole matter of the incarnation and 'orthodox' christology was brought into question.

In the same year, 1977, James Barr, 'one of the most penetrating minds at work in biblical study in Britain',[58] published his controversial book *Fundamentalism*. In it he identified the most pronounced characteristics of fundamentalist belief as:

(a) a very strong emphasis on the inerrancy of the Bible, the absence from it of any sort of error;

(b) a strong hostility to modern theology and to the methods, results and implications of modern critical study of the Bible; and

(c) an assurance that those who do not share an identical religious viewpoint are not really 'true Christians' at all.

He found the clearest embodiment of fundamentalism in Britain to be the Universities and Colleges Christian Fellowship (UCCF, formerly the Inter-Varsity Fellowship), and his critique was based largely on its publications. Although he wrote the book with the declared goal of understanding, he unhesitatingly expressed his disagreement with fundamentalism as he defined it. 'Its doctrinal position . . . especially in regard to the place of the Bible, and its entire intellectual apologetic' seemed to him 'to be completely wrong'.[59]

Liberalism in the 1980s and 1990s was epitomized by four churchmen: Don Cupitt, David Jenkins, David Edwards and John Habgood. Cupitt represented the most theologically extreme of this quartet. He described himself as 'a thoroughgoing Christian heretic and dissident' who 'cannot endure any attempt to control interpretation or finalize truth'.[60] In rejecting any creed or set of beliefs to which he was asked to conform Cupitt went to the extreme of saying that theological interpretation must be an individual matter. 'The only truly religious God is and has to be a man-made God. Your God has to be, let's be blunt about it, your own personal and temporary improvisation.'[61] For Cupitt man had come of age and would no longer accept beliefs to which he was asked to agree. 'The trouble with believing today, then, is that the churches persist and our own psychology persists in clinging to ideas of fixed meaning, authoritative interpretation, orthodoxy and final Truth. In an age when language has become completely enhistorized and humanized these ideas are no longer tenable, but we hold on to them because of our obsession with power, our desire to be governed and our reluctance to grow up.'[62]

David Jenkins caused furore and consternation because it was thought by many that he did not hold to certain basic beliefs which it was incumbent for him to accept and proclaim as a bishop in the Church of England. This was so from the moment in 1984 when it was announced that he was to be the new Bishop of Durham. And he was unequivocal in his attitude to the two main causes of such concern: the virgin birth and the resurrection. What he had to say on those issues tells us about his whole approach to Christian belief. It was very different from the attitude of Cupitt, but was still a cause of perturbation and even anger for the conservative, orthodox Christian.

I do not deny any basic Christian doctrines. What I have openly declared, and shall continue to maintain, is that literal belief in the Virgin Birth or the Empty Tomb are not basic Christian doctrines.

The basic Christian doctrine is that God became Man in Jesus (in shorthand, the doctrine of the Incarnation). The story of the Virgin Birth is told to make that point. The basic Christian doctrine is that God raised up Jesus so that Jesus is alive for evermore. I have been trying to separate the basic Christian doctrines – in which I firmly believe – from the stories which have been told to get those doctrines over. The stories are very useful as a means of getting the point across, but only so long as people do not miss that point and get stuck on the stories.[63]

David Edwards was even more orthodox than Jenkins, yet he laid considerable stress on the freedom to question received doctrines and to take account of contemporary intellectual discoveries and perspectives when assessing Christian dogma. He identified himself with the radical theological movement in the Church of England from the inception of its modern phase in the 1960s, and even sympathized with some of its more iconoclastic features, while at the same time he maintained a foot firmly in the orthodox camp.

Essentially this deeper movement results from a desire to honour and to hear the secular modern world. The Church must *listen* to the world before it attempts to interpret the world's own spiritual experience – experience which the world already enjoys, but which it may not acknowledge as in any sense Christian. Here, the whole emphasis is on the Church as mankind's servant. At the centre is a vision of Christ as the man alongside his fellow-men, speaking to them of a God they are already beginning to know. In order that the Church may help the world to see God through Christ, some Christians are quite ready for a wholesale revision of the Church's doctrines and customs, worship and work, organization and architecture, morals and politics, and are ready to declare themselves in favour of change even when they do not see exactly where the process of change will end. If I had to put a label on this movement, as the Evangelicals or the Anglo-Catholics were labelled in their days, I would call it Christian radicalism.[64]

Lastly, there was John Habgood, the scientifically-trained theologian who obtained the ear of many as the Archbishop of York. As a man with an acute intellect and a passion for honesty and the avoidance of humbug, hypocrisy, the use of stereotyped answers to intractable problems and glib pronouncements in response to complex issues, he often interpreted theology in ways which more conventional churchmen found irritating. Some considered him indecisive, evasive and imprecise in his affirmation and declaration of fundamental Christian beliefs. But he took pleasure in a theological approach characterized by 'the unfamiliar angle, the unexpected shaft of light, the revealing silence which conveys more than could have been said in words'.[65]

He once described himself as a 'passionate moderate'. And he regarded this as a virtue and a strength:

> To live with opposites, not in a weak compromise, but constantly allowing different convictions, different emphases, different insights to react fruitfully on each other, entails a kind of death. We have to let others be themselves. If need be, we have to let them wound us. We have to reject utterly the sort of touchiness and pettiness and narrow-mindedness which can so quickly make us all scurry away from one another behind our defences, We have to bear the pain of difference if we are to know the joy of discovery.[66]

Of course the groupings just described should not be taken to imply that the Church of England in the last half of the twentieth century was neatly arranged into three compartments. Far from it, for it was thoroughly mixed to include conservative Evangelicals, Evangelical Liberals, Liberal Evangelicals, traditional Church of England Catholics, Catholic Liberals, Liberal Catholics and, accounting for a considerable proportion of church members, what may be designated Broad Churchmen who would not identify themselves with any of these clusters. At the end of the twentieth century the established church was as comprehensive as it had ever been.

Dioceses, parishes, clergy, people and 'popular religion'

As I conclude this review of the Church of England in the half-century after the end of the Second World War, it is appropriate to focus not so much on the matters of 'high politics', of national and international issues, and of prominent personalities, but upon the life of churches and people at the local level. Certain changes in the central government of the Church of England helped to determine what went on right through the system to the parishes.

The Church Assembly, which had been inaugurated by the Enabling

Act of 1919, had various shortcomings, and most notably the lack of full participation by the laity in discussions and decisions on the church's doctrine and worship. In 1969 the Synodical Government Measure received the Royal Assent. It provided for a General Synod and synodical government throughout the Church of England at diocesan and deanery levels. The General Synod was to consist of three houses: bishops, clergy and laity. It was to have power to make canons and to pass Measures, and it was to have wide-ranging responsibilities relating to the national and international life of the Church of England. It was to encourage and facilitate full participation by the laity; and the diocesan and deanery synods were to give the laity the opportunity for a greater involvement in local church life than they ever had before.

In the meantime, in 1964, Leslie Paul had presented a report commissioned by the Church Assembly entitled *The Deployment and Payment of the Clergy*, usually known as 'the Paul Report'. It accused the Church of England of being a bad steward of its resources. The church required more clergy but had little right to ask for them until it had some efficient machinery which permitted it to deploy them and pay them effectively and equitably. The sixty-two recommendations of the report included proposals that the parson's freehold should be replaced by a leasehold arrangement, and that the distinction between beneficed and unbeneficed clergy should be abolished; proposals that patronage should be replaced by regional appointment bodies, together with a central Clergy Staff Board, and that there should be a new type of parochial unit called the 'major parish', which would be staffed by a college of clergy, all of whom would be of incumbent status, to cope with the high density urban areas and widely scattered rural parishes. It advocated a national salary structure with the stipends of the clergy kept in step with those of the teaching profession, and proposed that there should be increments for long service together with salary loadings for posts of special responsibility. Clergy should retire at the age of sixty-five on full pension. The report also stressed the need for the laity to exercise ministry, and it recommended a pastoral lay apostolate with street organizations based on house communions. It was a tragedy that reform did not take place in the wake of the report; and it took twenty years to implement its recommendations even in a much modified form.

The major proposals of the report were considered by a commission under the chairmanship of Canon Fenton Morley. This produced a report in 1967 entitled *Partners in Ministry*, with suggestions which were largely in harmony with what the Paul Report had recommended.

Paul was at QCB until 1970.

I knew Morley well when he was Vicar of Leeds.

But its recommendations were received with the same mixture of enthusiasm, disapproval and a final unwillingness to take comprehensive and
radical action.[67]

Part of the national context against which the local scene should
be viewed was the crisis in the theological colleges because of lack of
funding and a reduced number of students. The consequence was a
reduction in their numbers, leaving those with an evangelical tradition
even more dominant at the end of the century.

Then there were the liturgical changes, the various new versions of
the Bible and the surge in the composition of new hymns, all of which
had an incalculable impact on local church life. The 1960s and 1970s
introduced a progressively accelerating process of liturgical experimen-
tation which reached a high point with the acceptance of the Alternative
Service Book (ASB) of 1980. During the last two decades of the century
the charismatic movement made the situation even more complicated
as churches added pentecostal-type and charismatic-type features to
services which were already almost unrecognizable as distinctively
Anglican.

In 1946 a committee of thirty-two American scholars produced the
Revised Standard Version of the New Testament, and the whole Bible
appeared in 1952. Overall it avoided 'Americanisms', and its modern
but dignified language made it popular. It signalled what was surely the
most prolific period ever for the publication of different versions of the
Bible in part or in whole. In 1949 Ronald Knox introduced his transla-
tion of the entire Bible, which was intended for private use only. In the
meantime J.B. Phillips had caused much excitement with his *Letters to
Young Churches* (1947), *The Gospels in Modern English* (1952), *The
Young Church in Action* (1955) covering the Acts of the Apostles, and
The Book of Revelation (1957). Dr E.V. Rieu produced a translation of
The Four Gospels (1952), and his son C.H. Rieu followed this with *The
Acts of the Apostles* (1957). A 'major event in the world of scholarship,
of printing and of ecumenical co-operation'[68] came to fruition in 1970
with the publication of the *New English Bible*. It was well received and
many millions of copies were sold. Also immensely popular was *The
Bible in Today's English Version* (1976), usually known as 'The Good
News Bible'. This aimed to provide a faithful translation of the original
text expressed in standard, everyday, English, avoiding words and
forms not in current and widespread use. An English edition of
The Living Bible appeared in the early 1970s. English-speaking
Roman Catholics produced *The Jerusalem Bible* (1966). It was an

annotated version of the whole Bible based on the work of French biblical scholars. It was appreciated by many Anglicans who used it in public worship. It was revised in 1985. Both the *Revised Standard Version* and the *New English Bible* were revised in 1989.

Accompanying these astonishingly productive few years of Bible translation was a remarkably creative period from about the middle of the century onwards in the composition of hymns. Up to 1950 most Church of England churches used one of a small range of hymn books, all of which were probably at least fifty years old, with their roots set deeply in Victorian soil. In the post-war period composers of the eminence of Sir Arthur Bliss and Benjamin Britten composed church music. Contributions were also made by Edmund Rubbra, Michael Tippett, Malcolm Williamson, Geoffrey Bush, William Matthias and Peter Anson. The Royal School of Church Music, founded in 1927, was particularly effective in promoting high standards of teaching for church musicians, enthusing choirs and stimulating church music generally. Its influence became both worldwide and ecumenical. Credit for this must go largely to Dr Gerald Knight, the Director from 1952 to 1973, and his successor, Dr Lionel Dakers.

It was in the 1950s that the major hymn books of the immediate post-war years were published. *Hymns Ancient and Modern Revised* (1950), *Congregational Praise* (1951) and *The BBC Hymn Book* (1951) soon established their place in the worship of English churches. The same decade also saw the first serious questioning of accepted axioms about church music, and the appearance of a radically new and freer type of music. In 1956 Geoffrey Beaumont produced his *Folk Mass* as a means 'whereby those unfamiliar with traditional forms might enter into the worship of the Church'.[69] It attracted considerable attention, and it led to the formation of the Twentieth Century Church Light Music Group which produced its own books and a number of popular hymns. Sydney Carter was prominent in writing and popularizing new songs for church worship, among which were 'Lord of the Dance', 'When I needed a neighbour', and 'No use knocking on the window'. It was also during these years that vocal and instrumental (usually guitar) groups were re-introduced to lead worship.

The 'explosion of modern hymn writing',[70] accompanied by new hymn books, supplements to standard hymn books and a multiplicity of home-grown parish booklets continued into the 1960s and beyond. The innovations were not confined to the Church of England. New Roman Catholic hymn books appeared, and there were various denominational and non-denominational productions. Special mention should perhaps be made of the *Anglican Hymn Book* (1965), *Youth Praise* (Vol. 1, 1966; Vol. 2, 1969), the *New Catholic Hymnal* (1971), *Psalm Praise* (1973) and *Hymns for Today's Church* (1982). To these and other widely recognized and acclaimed works must be added the countless individual church song books. The introduction of new hymns in modern language and style, and the adaptation of familiar well-established hymns, was not accomplished without much protest. This was especially so with *Hymns for Today's Church*. In such hymn books as the *New Catholic Hymnal* there was modernization of some of the texts into a 'you' form, but *Hymns for Today's Church* broke new ground by consistently applying the principle to all hymns. And it was not just a matter of language, for the new approach entailed questions about theology, sexism, syntax, thought-form and imagery. The whole subject had many ramifications, and by the late 1990s, although the storm had subsided, the issues were far from being resolved.

Lastly, in this review of matters at national level which impinged on local church life, there was the whole fraught issue of the ordination of women. Throughout this most active period of liturgical revision, new Bible translations and new hymnody, the question of the ministry of women, and more especially their right to ordination, became increasingly urgent and central to the thinking of the Church of England. In 1947 Convocation discussed the possibility of authorizing qualified women to 'take special services in church and to speak at them'. It was, however, not until the 1960s that the Church Assembly opened up the debate on the ordination of women, and women began to participate more fully in services – conducting them, reading the Bible, preaching and assisting with the holy communion. The Lambeth Conference of 1968 declared that the theological arguments as then presented for and against the ordination of women to the priesthood were inconclusive. In 1975 the General Synod expressed the view that there were 'no fundamental objections to the ordination of women to the priesthood', but it did not proceed to any consequent action. The bishops at the 1978 Lambeth Conference, recognizing that some Anglican provinces had women clergy, agreed to respect each other's discipline in that matter. In 1984 the General Synod resolved that legislation for the ordination of women should be prepared. Meanwhile, in the Anglican Communion worldwide changes were taking place. The diocese of Hong Kong ordained women in 1971 and was followed by the Church of the Province of New Zealand in 1974, the Anglican

Church in Canada the following year and the Episcopal Church of the USA in 1976. Finally, after extended and furious debate at national and local levels, the General Synod agreed in 1995 that women should be entitled to ordination.

All this ministerial, liturgical, biblical and musical activity combined to have a very considerable impact on all the parishes in the land. No congregation was unaffected. And when one adds the influence of the charismatic movement and such general developments in society as changing attitudes to authority, to the role and function of women and to marriage and the family, as well as an increasing indifference to institutional forms of religion, it all amounted to a need for major readjustments by local churches in their forms of worship and corporate life, and in their relationship to the community in which they were located.

And there were many and varied attempts to make appropriate adaptations. A few examples will give something of the flavour of what efforts were made. One of the first and most inspiring endeavours was the rebuilding of Coventry Cathedral which had been devastated by German bombing in 1940. The reconstruction work was more than a bricks and mortar exercise, for by design, careful planning and much dedicated service by bishops, clergy and laity the new building, which literally arose out of the ashes, established itself as a centre not only for reconciliation, but for engagement with contemporary society.

While this was going on a remarkable work was being undertaken in industrial mission in Sheffield by E. R. Wickham. He was appointed with a very specific but most difficult task: to attempt to penetrate the industrial wasteland of East Sheffield so that the Christian faith might become more pertinent to the work, family, social and individual lives of the many thousands of workers there whom the churches had never been able to attract in substantial numbers. Wickham mobilized the laity and clergy in a valiant programme of action. It was an inspiration to others, and was followed by the planting of industrial missions in many other conurbations, including London and Teesside. He also embodied his thoughts and analysis of the historical and sociological factors most relevant to an understanding of the contemporary situation in a book entitled *Church and People in an Industrial City*, which soon became the charter document of industrial mission.

Another, somewhat less heralded, pioneer in 'downtown' mission was Ernest Southcott of Leeds, who laboured with immense commitment in his slum clearance area parish of five estates which lacked any sense of community. In keeping with the insights of the Liturgical Movement the

Parish Communion on Sunday was the centre of worship. But in order to help in mission and as a means of introducing people to a teaching, worshipping and caring fellowship Southcott created two kinds of house churches; one for those members of the local community who were more fully integrated and committed churchgoers, where the holy communion was celebrated, and the other for the less committed which usually consisted of prayer, study and discussion.

At a national level the concern of the Church of England to understand the problems of ministry facing it and to address them was reflected in the publication in 1985 of the report *Faith in the City*, with its sequel *Faith in the Countryside* appearing in 1990. Both attracted considerable attention within the churches, in political circles, where there was pointed criticism that the Church of England was becoming unduly influenced by left wing views, in the media, and among the public in general. The debate they engendered continued into the 1990s in the General Synod, and locally in synods and parishes.

Further Reading

Brierley, Peter, *'Christian' England. What the English Church Census Reveals*, London 1991

Chadwick, Owen, *Michael Ramsey. A Life*, London 1990; reissued London 1998

Davies, Horton, *Worship and Theology in England: The Ecumenical Century, 1900–1965*, Princeton 1965

Hylson-Smith, Kenneth, *Evangelicals in the Church of England 1734–1984*, Edinburgh 1989

Hylson-Smith, Kenneth, *High Churchmanship in the Church of England From the Sixteenth Century to the Late Twentieth Century*, Edinburgh 1993

Jasper, Ronald C.D., *George Bell Bishop of Chichester*, London 1967

Lloyd, Roger, *The Church of England 1900–1965*, London 1966

Peart-Binns, John S., *Wand of London*, London 1987

Robinson, John A.T., *Honest to God*, London 1963

Welsby, Paul A., *A History of the Church of England 1945–1980*, Oxford 1984

useful survey not excellent.

9

The Free Churches and the Roman Catholics 1945 to 1998

'Church', 'denomination' and 'sect': the changing face of the Free Churches

The process of increasing social acceptance and integration into society for the old, mainline denominations, combined with decreasing membership, which was well under way by 1945, continued between 1945 and about 1970. But subsequently there was a variable pattern of decline, stagnation and growth. The greatest expansion was among the new, informal, largely unstructured, groups and new 'sects'.

The numerical decline was quite alarming for the Free Churches up to 1970, and it went right across the board to cover all the denominations except various Pentecostal and Afro-Caribbean churches and some of the 'fringe' sects such as Mormons and Jehovah's Witnesses. They lost about one third of all their membership in England and Wales in the period 1914 to 1970. There were variations between the denominations with, for example, an approximate 40% drop for the Congregationalists and a 26% reduction for the Methodists. In the period between 1914 and 1939 the average decline in England and Wales was 6%, and slightly above that figure for England alone, whereas between 1939 and 1970 it was 30%, being somewhat less in England alone. And these figures understate what was an even worse position, because Free Church attendance was reckoned to be larger than the official membership in the years up to 1914, even as much as twice as large; whereas in the following decades through to the end of the century the church attendance was less than the official membership.[1]

Between 1975 and 1998, however, this overall decline did not apparently persist.[2] The Methodist Church and the United Reformed Church (the denomination formed in 1972 by the uniting of the Congregational Church in England and Wales and the Presbyterian Church of England, which was enlarged in 1981 by the accession of a majority of the

Disciples of Christ in Britain) declined quite dramatically; the Baptists grew slightly and the Afro-Caribbean and Pentecostal churches at a higher rate; and there was a massive increase in Independent churches. This latter, heterogeneous, group included the House Church Movement, the open and closed Brethren, the Fellowship of Independent Evangelical Churches (FIEC), the Union of Evangelical Churches (UEC), the Congregational Federation Churches (initially consisting of those which did not combine to form the United Reformed Church), the Evangelical Fellowship of Congregational Churches (EFCC), the majority of the Churches of Christ, the New Apostolic Churches and the Liberal Catholic Church. Taken as an aggregate this group represented a significant proportion of the total attendances for the Free Churches: in 1989, 292,800 adult churchgoers out of a total of 1,249,000. In 1989 they also seem to have had a greater membership by far than the Baptists (199,400) and the United Reformed Church (114,00), and were almost as large as the Methodists (396,100) who, given the respective rates of increase and decline, they would overhaul by the end of the century.

It is significant that the growth was almost entirely among the smaller evangelical groups. This is consistent with what I suggest in the Introduction. As Bryan Wilson predicted the sects have prospered to a greater extent than other religious collectivities.[3] The 'sects' or 'denominations' which fared best had a clear evangelical character which allowed a full and varied expression of personal faith in worship and witness. It appears that those Free Churches which had gained most in social 'respectability' were the ones which experienced the most serious numerical decline, while the less inhibited, less socially conformist, 'sects' flourished.

I can highlight the general pattern I have outlined by focussing on particular Free Churches.

By 1945 there was a widespread sense of gloom pervading Congregationalism as a denomination. The 1930s had seen the number of members in England drop from 276,540 to 251,331; a decrease of over 9% and at an average loss of 2,801 members per year.[4] Even more alarming as a portent for the future was the loss of Sunday school scholars as the total numbers shot down from 366,861 in 1930 to 260,746 in 1939, representing a 29% decline at an average annual rate of 11,790 scholars. The Congregationalists were aware that they could not take refuge in the plea that the war made this drift downwards exceptional; it was the continuation of a decline which had been evident for two decades and more, and there was little hope expressed that the trend would be reversed. The post-war year forecasts were morbid.

The Report of the Congregational General Purposes Committee in 1950 complained not only that 'we are weaker by over 100,000 members than we were twenty years ago' but that 'Congregationalism as a specific and identifiable church order is fast disappearing in many parts of the world.'[5] A three-year Forward Movement launched at that time did little to stem the tide.

During the course of the next three decades there was an attempt to meet the crisis by organizational rationalization. The Congregational Union both consolidated and centralized its power. There was a multi-plication of committees. The ministry of women had been recognized from the early part of the century, and the first woman was ordained in 1917. But despite this the number of trained ministers became fewer. Laymen and laywomen played an increasingly important part in the life of the local churches. The forms of worship conducted by the ministers also became more formal and 'Anglican' in character. *A Book of Public Worship compiled for the use of Congregationalists* was published in 1948. A number of able Congregationalists worked vigorously in the Ecumenical Movement, and the Congregational Union became closely identified with the ecumenical cause.

High on the agenda for this rationalization programme were talks with the Presbyterian Church of England about possible union, which had been taking place since 1932. At the suggestion of the Presbyterians a new series began in 1945.

The Presbyterian Church of England had, like the Congregationalists, been experiencing decline and consequent demoralization. By 1961 they had only 71,329 members, 283 ministers and 52 local and lay preachers.[6] At the time the union actually took place in 1972, with the formation of the United Reformed Church, the main areas of Presby-terian concentration were a triangle formed by the Scottish border, the north-east coast of England, and a line taken from Sunderland to the Solway Firth; Merseyside; south-east Lancashire; and the Greater London area. There was an increase of numbers in the South East at that time, undoubtedly due in part to the settlement of Scottish immi-grants in the region. But this focus on Scottish origins and a Calvinistic theology was lessened very considerably with the 1972 union.[7]

The creation of the United Reformed Church did not prove to be a panacea for the ills of the constituent parties. Not all former members of the two denominations concerned joined; and, as we have seen, the numbers of the new church declined during the remaining part of the century. One interesting, but abortive, consequence was the prompt call by the new church for a wider union. The leaders of the United Reformed Church took up the idea first accepted by the British Council of Churches' Faith and Order Conference at Nottingham in 1964, and invited other churches to join in talks planned to lead to a covenant to work and pray for unity. The outcome was the establishment of the Churches' Council for Covenanting, which produced its proposals in 1980. Once more, as in the Anglican-Methodist discussions, which we will consider later in this chapter, the chief problem was the validity of ministries and the form which any service of reconciliation should take. Although the plans were accepted by most churches they were defeated in 1982 by a combination of Anglo-Catholics and Evangelicals in the Church of England, largely because of deliberate ambiguity on the question as to whether re-ordination was intended.

Between 1911 and 1965 the proportion of Baptist members to the total population almost halved. And, like the Congregationalists, the drop in the number of Sunday school scholars was even more dramatic, from 131 per 10,000 of the total population in 1901 to 40 in 1961.[8] But unlike the other mainline Nonconformist denominations the decline appears to have been checked, at least to some extent, and turned into gain in the period 1975 to 1989, when the adult membership went up from 193,000 to 199,400.[9] The explanation for this may well be that the growth figures hide an actual drop in the Baptist Union numbers, from 174,300 to 166,100, whereas the more 'free', 'independent' Baptists, which were included in the grand total, increased: from 1979 to 1989 the Grace Baptist Assembly went up from 12,000 to 12,500, the Jesus Fellowship (also called Jesus Army) from 300 to 900, and the other (free) Baptist churches from 9,400 to 14,100.[10] Although these are small absolute figures they reinforce the picture of expansion in the smaller 'sect-type' groups, which is one of the features of the multi-faith pluralistic phase of the religious history of the country.

Since the 1851 census there have been several significant changes in the Baptist distribution pattern. By 1970 the main area of Baptist strength ran from Leicestershire to Suffolk and included the counties of Northamptonshire, Buckinghamshire, Bedfordshire, Hertfordshire and Cambridgeshire. There was by then a second concentration of Baptists centred round the Bristol Channel in the counties of Herefordshire,

Gloucestershire and Somerset. Baptists were to be found in considerable numbers in all the counties of southern and south-eastern England, with the exception of Cornwall. They were noticeably thin in the whole of northern England, the West Midlands and Lincolnshire.

Methodists in the latter half of the twentieth century could draw very little comfort from any set of statistics relating to them as a denomination; such figures were a cause of almost unmitigated despondency; they all told the same story of massive deterioration. Just a few will illustrate this. From the date of the union in 1932 to 1974 the membership fell from 817,429 to 557,249, and the proportion of members to each 1,000 of the population from 27 to less than 15; and this continued with a reduction of the adult membership from 454,000 in 1975 to 396,100 in 1989. The *rate* of decline of the membership was slowing down, but the rate of decline in attendance was increasing: it was 0.4% per year from 1975 to 1979, 1% per year from 1979 to 1985, and 1.5% per year between 1985 and 1989. The losses were even more severe in the ranks of Local Preachers, where there was a drop from 34,948 in 1933 to 17,291 in 1973; and in Sunday school scholars, where the numbers went down from 1,297,953 in 1933 to 332,129 in 1974. And, as a last statistic, the number of men offering themselves for the ordained ministry plummeted from over 200 a year in the immediate post-union years to less than 50 by 1970. After that there was a slight increase in the number of ordinands, but mostly because of the admission of women.[11]

Some of the hopes of those who advocated Methodist union were not realized. Not only did numerical decline continue after the union, and for extended periods accelerate, but rationalizing measures were frustrated. Thus the anticipated drastic reduction in the number of chapels and the amalgamation of circuits was effected in places but was not universally achieved. A large number of trustees turned a deaf ear as attention was drawn to the blatantly obvious financial, ministerial and operational unviability of chapels which they cherished as 'theirs'. Nostalgic attachment to a chapel or a defiant refusal to allow the Wesleyans to continue while the nearby Primitive or United Methodist Church was closed down, helped to perpetuate a most unsatisfactory situation. 'During the years of numerical decrease, therefore, the ratio of chapels to members has remained absurdly high, and has given the impression that the Methodist Church is even weaker in numbers than it actually is.'[12]

The only shred of consolation for Methodists was evidence that the number of workers was on the increase from about the mid-1970s onwards, which was in addition to the slight upward trend in the number of ordinands. This may have been a result of improved methods of attracting workers, and to the care and training given in cultivating a wide range of skills; but it may also indicate that a shrinking membership and reduced numbers of attenders was paring the church down to those who were more fully committed. This may apply in a more general way to the churches as a whole. 'The penumbra of the churches has so contracted that now even part of the churches' own membership must be regarded as belonging to the fringe. On the other hand, the devotional practice of some church members has changed and possibly intensified despite the general decline.'[13]

The overall weakness and declining numbers and influence in society of the Free Churches, including the Methodists, has, as we have seen, led to plans for union within their own ranks or between a particular denomination and another denomination or church. But union in itself is not revival. Some sociologists assert that it is 'the turning in on itself of institutionalized religion, as its hold on the wider social order has diminished'.[14] It certainly appears that reunion schemes in the twentieth century in England have been motivated largely by concern about deteriorating and even desperate church situations, and that they have arisen in the main as a result of initiatives by lay, and more especially ordained, leaders, rather than as a consequence of pressures from below. There is considerable force in the argument that the healing of divisions 'is something which restores the morale of churchmen – and in a secular society a larger proportion of churchmen are professional churchmen – in a period when the external influence of the Church is declining either in terms of numbers of Church supporters in the wider population, as in England, or in terms of Christian influence over behaviour and morality, politics, education and other institutions, as in the United States.'[15] It may well be true that schemes of reunion are triggered by a corporate sense of defeat, and the analysis of Bryan Wilson may be accurate for churches in a multi-faith pluralistic situation, if we assume that the 'ecumenical movement' to which he refers includes all the types of union schemes to which I have referred, and that 'churchmen' embraces those of all denominations and churches. He writes:

The energy which churchmen have put into the ecumenical movement has been perhaps in rough proportion as they have lost hope of evangelization of the world. Essentially this has been a movement directed inwards into the life of the Church, not outwards into the wider society, which remains essentially unmoved by ecumenical achievement, and perhaps even rather suspicious of it. The laity who remain committed to their various denominations appear markedly less enthusiastic for actual assimilation with other bodies than do the clergy. Nor does ecumenism achieve much in the way of increasing the influence of reunited bodies.[16]

Union has at least one major disadvantage in that it can lessen the impact on individuals of the history and traditions of the denomination to which they belong. A union creates a new body without any accumulated traditions and values, and without the identity which is familiar to members of the bodies involved. Because of this those who participate in the union may experience a loss of ardour and commitment. 'Ecumenism may be a policy not only induced by decline, but one encouraging decline.'[17]

The Anglican-Methodist union scheme

Of course the most public and prominent attempt at union in the period 1945 to 1998 was that between the Anglicans and the Methodists. It covered a long period of negotiation and finally ended in failure amid much bitterness and recrimination.

When the Archbishop of Canterbury, Geoffrey Fisher, delivered his sermon in the university church in Cambridge on 3 November 1946 he reopened the whole question of union between the Church of England and the Free Churches in England, and he gave a much-needed impetus to the ecumenical movement. He did not believe that the English churches were ready for constitutional reunion, but thought that they should grow towards full communion with one another. In particular, since the Free Churches had often accepted that any future united church would be episcopal, Fisher suggested that they could 'take episcopacy into their system' and explore its nature and value.

It was a new, imaginative and hopeful concept and received a positive response. The Free Churches agreed to send delegates to a joint conference with Church of England representatives to assess the implications of the Cambridge sermon. The conference published *Church Relations in England* (1950). It concluded that 'negotiations for the establishment of intercommunion would have to be conducted in a parallel series between the Church of England and the individual Free Churches on the other side'.[18]

The Methodist Church was alone in its willingness to proceed further, and in 1955 official 'Conversations' were initiated. An *Interim Report* was published in 1958. Both churches accepted it, and organic union thus became the official goal. In 1963 the report *Conversations between the Church of England and the Methodist Church* proposed a plan for uniting the two churches, and asked for decisions on this in 1965. For the first time since discussion on home reunion started, following the Lambeth *Appeal to all Christian People* of 1920, a definite scheme was proposed for reintegrating the national episcopal church with one, and that the largest, of the non-episcopal Free Churches.

The report did not carry the consent of all the Methodist members of the group producing it. A 'Dissentient View' was appended signed by four Methodists. It was an ominous sign, for their case 'was clearly the tip of an iceberg of dissent'.[19] The Methodist opposition incorporated those who, for various reasons, had a distaste for the whole concept of union with the established church. Such opponents often rejected episcopacy on the grounds that it was not laid down in scripture. There was concern that Anglo-Catholics would interpret the service of reconciliation as the ordination for the first time of Methodist ministers; and that in any union the Methodists might be absorbed into the Church of England. In their dissenting note the four dissidents drew attention to this last possibility, perhaps with some disregard for the range of theological views contained in current Methodism. 'To move', they said, 'from a church committed to the evangelical faith into a heterogeneous body permitting and even encouraging unevangelical doctrines and practices would be a step backward which not even the desirability of closer relations would justify.'[20]

Episcopacy and mutual recognition of ministries was at the core of the discussions from the outset, and they continued to be central issues in the 1960s. Related to this was the suggested Service of Reconciliation. Some Anglicans, in line with the Methodist dissidents, objected to the proposed service because it implied, as stated in an Open Letter from some leading Evangelicals, 'the ordination to a priesthood not hitherto exercised of Methodist ministers' who were 'already true ministers of God's word and sacraments'. The signatories of the letter were 'whole-hearted' in their 'desire for the unity of the visible church' and they warmly welcomed the report of the Conversations, but they could not accept any service which failed to declare the unambiguous and unqualified acceptance of the validity of the existing Methodist ministry. They were 'convinced that the right way to unite ministries' was by 'mutual recognition, with episcopal ordination thereafter, as in the Church of South India'.

Some leading High Churchmen also objected to the apparently deliberate imprecision which, it seems, was intended to encourage an openness and liberty of interpretation of what was stated. Graham Leonard issued a statement with which many other Anglican Catholics would probably have concurred in which his convictions were clear and his accusations set forth in unequivocal language:

> The report is suspect in general and in particular with regard to the honesty of what it advocates. The proposals for reconciliation involve an intentional ambiguity which makes the prayers of the service of reconciliation irrelevant. Many of us cannot see how, with a clear conscience, we can take part in prayers to God which are deliberately disingenuous. This is not a matter of a fine point of theology – it is a matter of common honesty. We believe that true Christian unity can only be achieved with the help of the Holy Ghost, the Spirit of Truth, and that this is completely incompatible with any deliberately determined disingenuity . . . The proposals, as they stand, present a device to escape reality and a formula to avoid clarity. Far from achieving true unity, they will cause further divisions.[21]

In spite of the opposition and criticism the Methodist Conference approved the scheme on 8 July 1969 by a majority of 76%. The Church of England General Assembly decided that it must command a 75% approval. After a debate of high quality the joint convocations, voting by houses, in total voted 263 for and 116 against, a 69% vote in favour. To some that appeared to be the end. But advantage was taken by the proponents of the scheme of the opportunity to reintroduce it for a decision by the newly inaugurated General Synod. In the event this was merely a prolongation and intensification of the agony.

In the meantime, in 1970, three Church of England Evangelicals, Colin Buchanan, Michael Green and James Packer, and two Anglo-Catholics, Graham Leonard and E.L. Mascall, published *Growing into Union*, which produced fast and furious reactions. The Anglo-Catholic authors differed from the Evangelical contributors in their perceptions and reasons for opposing the scheme, but all of them found much common ground. They advocated

> a one-stage procedure, the nub of the matter being expressed in this way: [we recommend] the simple expedient of inaugurating a united

Church in a piecemeal way territorially, leaving the existing denominations to exist alongside each other in every place where conscience, even untutored conscience, might so decree. This is the conclusion, novel in the history of English ecumenical discussion, to which we have come. This will do justice to the various principles on which we wish to build far better than any other procedure which has suggested itself to us. And it is a principle which, if novel in England, has some precedent in South India. As South India is the only existing union in which Anglicans have joined, we may well look cautiously in that direction for help.[22]

Their goal was a reintegrated English church which would embrace diversity while at the same time being genuinely national and comprehensive within explicit limits set by biblical essentials.

The authorities decided not to pursue the book's recommendations but to go ahead as they had previously planned. They were bent on reintroducing their own scheme. The day for a final decision was 3 May 1972. The vote was 333 for and 173 against, which gave a somewhat reduced majority, compared with the previous vote, of 65.8%. The scheme was dead. The Church of England and the Methodists went on their separate ways.

The Pentecostals, independent and Afro-Caribbean churches

The justification for grouping these churches is that they had features in common, including their somewhat uninhibited styles of worship, their appeal to those who valued spontaneity of worship, their emphasis on the charisma of person rather than office, their lack of extensive and rigid structures, and their short history in England compared with the mainline Free Churches. And they were exceptional in that they experienced growth in membership in the last decades of the century when all around them there were churches losing the numbers battle. In describing these three groups their inter-relatedness will soon become apparent. And I will first focus on the West Indians.

From 1951, when there was a catastrophic hurricane in Jamaica, to 1962, when the Commonwealth Immigrants Act was passed, there was a mass immigration of about 260,000 West Indians to Great Britain.[23] Sixty-nine per cent of them regularly attended church in their home countries, a proportion which grew rapidly smaller as they settled in their country of refuge.[24] On their arrival they were shocked to find that the white host population were both extremely racist and largely a-religious or anti-religious. It was especially painful for them to discover almost the same racism and discrimination within the churches as outside. They were typically treated with curiosity, ignored, or shown varying degrees of hostility. There were other factors such as their unrealistically high expectations of English Christianity, the contrasting cultural temperaments of the immigrants and the conservative white English, the difference between the generally young West Indians and the more elderly inner city congregations, and the contrasting styles of worship and church life. Most white congregations 'lacked characteristics which black Christians considered concomitants of authentic faith and spirituality: demonstrable love, life and spiritual power; a high degree of visible Christian commitment; a strong sense of community and a full opportunity to participate at every level'.[25]

Many of the migrants were already Pentecostals, and some were ordained. At first they joined the English Pentecostal churches. But it was not long before they founded their own churches with West Indian pastors and elders. These West Indian churches, in addition to providing the kind of worship which the migrants were seeking, became sanctuaries for the black community in the face of many dangers and prejudices, and they served as succours 'for the physically uprooted, the emotionally displaced, the socially and culturally bereaved, and the spiritually bankrupt'.[26] The function served by these churches tended to change somewhat as the migrant population became settled and established themselves. But for all generations the black Pentecostal congregation provided 'a focus for ingroup solidarity as a protection against the disdain and rejection of white society and the white churches'. It was a participative community which drew 'all its members together – both adults and children – into active involvement', created a sense of belonging and worth, and affirmed black personhood and dignity. The Pentecostal community was also 'a sympathetic milieu for the development and expression of creativity, artistry and leadership in the black liturgical tradition'.[27]

One characteristic of these black Pentecostal churches was their extreme proneness to internal dissentions. This split them into a multiplicity of groups which were doctrinally identical or very similar. In 1989 the adult membership in England was 68,500 in 164 specific churches, each a mini-denomination, some with many congregations but most with just one, and with more than one thousand congregations in total. The largest two of these were the Church of God of Prophecy with 9,200 attenders and the New Testament Church of God with 8,500 attenders. Others included the First United Church of Jesus Christ (Apostolic) UK, the New Testament Assembly, the United Pentecostal Church and the Wesleyan Holiness Church.[28]

And in parallel with this the mainline Pentecostal churches such the Elim Pentecostal Church and the Assemblies of God in Great Britain continued to prosper. These two together accounted for 88% of Pentecostal churchgoers in England, although there were substantial smaller groups such as the Apostolic Church, and two holiness groups, the Emmanuel Holiness Church and the Church of the Nazarene.

But far more prolific and with a vastly greater rate of growth than either the Afro-Caribbean or the Pentecostal Churches, or indeed of these two categories combined, were the various Independent Churches. Their numbers went up from 167,000 in 1975 to 292,800 in 1989; and from 14% of all Free Church attenders in the former year to 23% in the latter year. In addition to residential schools, which I will discount as being a 'special case', there were three main components of the Independent Church category: the Fellowship of Independent Evangelical Churches (FIEC), the Brethren (Open) and the House Church Movement. The dynamic behind the Independent Group as a whole was the latter, and behind that the charismatic movement was a crucial factor.

The 1950s and the 1960s were the years when the charismatic movement in Britain emerged from being a random range of unco-ordinated manifestations of the 'baptism of the Holy Spirit', many unknown to others undergoing the same experiences, to being a consciously single movement. It appears to have been the time when this new development of Pentecostal-type experiences outside the Pentecostal churches was seen as 'a *movement* in a way that the ordinary expansion of Pentecostal churches was not'.[29] The leading figures in the new movement did not want outsiders to view it as simply an extension of Pentecostalism. It was considered that such an association would impede its spread and acceptance within the historic churches. This did not mean that they were hostile to the Pentecostals or deny their role in the overall Pentecostalism of the country; but the charismatic movement was perceived by its leaders as richer and more significant than the prevailing Pentecostalism. The Pentecostals on their part were, at least initially, both fascinated by the vitality and growth of the new movement, but suspicious about its authenticity.

By the mid-1960s there were a number of charismatic house

fellowships in which those baptized in the Spirit sought deeper fellowship than they could find in the existing church structures. The subsequent expansion of house churches was quite sensational. Many of
them in the 1960s were outside the mainline denominations. They were
evangelical and pentecostal, but they were different in style and
organization from existing groups, sects or demononitations.[30] As they
mushroomed a large number remained extra-denominational, but a vast
number operated within both the Protestant churches and the Roman
Catholic Church. And many of the churches in which these charismatic
groups settled were neither charismatic nor evangelical: so the
charismatic movement became associated with churches representing a
large spectrum of theological and attitudinal positions. In total the
charismatic groups and house churches attracted tens of thousands of
people in England; and they established themselves as a prominent
feature in the religious landscape of England on the eve of the twenty-
first century.

The Roman Catholics

In spite of declining numbers of worshippers at Mass, in 1989 the
Roman Catholics were the largest of the four main divisions of the
English churches. Measured in terms of adult churchgoing they had
experienced a greater reduction between 1975 and 1989 than the other
three categories but they just retained their numerical edge. For 1989
the figure was 1,335,900, compared with 1,181,000 for the Church of
England, 1,229,700 for the Free Churches and 8,400 for the Orthodox
Church. These figures may not have had the same meaning and
significance for each of the four Christian traditions concerned, but they
are valid as a broad indication of the situation.

The English Roman Catholic community of 1989 was different
in many respects from what it had been in 1945. This was a result of
internal changes and external pressures over those forty years and more.
The first instrument of a changed social and religious climate for English
Roman Catholics was the universal provision of secondary education as
a result of the 1944 Education Act. This enormously benefitted the
largely working-class Catholic community and helped to promote that
process of transformation into a more middle-class church which was a
feature of English Catholicism in the latter half of the century. The Act
was particularly effective in this way as it was followed by the Robins
Report of 1963 and the subsequent impressive expansion of tertiary
education. 'By the late 1970s the social class background of English

Catholics was little different from that of the population as a whole.'[31] The tailing off in the 1960s of the number of Irish migrant workers, partly as a result of the entry of the Irish Republic into the EEC and the expansion of the Irish economy, helped in this changing class structure.

The increased social mobility was manifested in a decided movement of Catholics out of the old, traditional, working-class, mainly Irish, inner-city parishes into the new suburban estates which were springing up in all major conurbations. It was also a contributory factor in the changing distribution pattern of Roman Catholics throughout England; most notably in the relative growth of Catholicism within a radius of sixty miles of the centre of London. In 1851 only the County of London stood out above the general sea of low density. By 1989 the picture was very different. Catholicism remained strong in the North West and the North East with, for example, one person in eleven in Merseyside going to Mass each Sunday; but the Catholic community was considerable in central London, where one person in sixteen attended Mass in Inner London Northwest, and one person in nineteen in Outer London Southeast. [32]

Then there was the impact upon the English Catholic community of the Second Vatican Council (1962–65). In the post-war years prior to Vatican II Rome maintained a tight control over the worship, lifestyles and beliefs of its English flock. Up to the late 1950s the Roman Catholic Church in England, as elsewhere, was not allowed any discussion on theological matters with non-Catholics, or any sharing of prayer or worship.[33] The Encyclical *Mystici Corporis Christi* of 1943 reaffirmed that the Roman Catholic Church and the Church of Christ were identical; and seven years later there was the dogmatic definition of the Assumption of the Blessed Virgin Mary. In the same year, 1950, the Encyclical *Humani Generis* condemned any attempt to deny the identification of the Mystical Body of Christ with the Roman Catholic Church. The following year these exclusive claims were reinforced by another Encyclical, *Sempiternus Dei*, which asked rhetorically if it was not 'holy and salutary and according to the will of God that all at long last return to the one fold of Christ'.

But a drastic change in this rigid authoritarianism was about to be initiated. It was heralded when the seventy-seven year old Giuseppe Roncalli was elected Pope in 1958 as John XXIII. Within the first year of his pontificate he announced the calling of an 'Ecumenical Council of the Universal Church', and established a new Secretariat for the Promoting of Unity among Christians as part of the preparation for this.

As we have seen, Geoffrey Fisher took advantage of this new openness and became the first Archbishop of Canterbury to visit the Pope in Rome since 1397. With the agreement of the Vatican a Church of England representative, Canon Bernard Pawley, was appointed in 1961 to live in Rome in order to act as a two-way link between the Archbishops and the Pope and to promote mutual understanding.

During the Second Vatican Council Pope John died and was succeeded by the liberal and open-minded Cardinal Montini as Paul VI. In March 1966 Michael Ramsey paid his official visit to the Pope. The Pope and Archbishop issued a joint declaration in which they expressed their intention 'to inaugurate between the Roman Catholic Church and the Anglican Communion serious dialogue which . . . may lead to that unity in truth for which Christ prayed'.[34] Within a month of the visit the Anglican Institute was established in Rome as a meeting-place for members of the Anglican Communion and other churches, particularly the Roman Catholic Church.

The Second Vatican Council was perhaps the most important ecclesiastical event of the century.[35] It was a watershed in modern Roman Catholic history. It created a great sense of liberation and redefinition. It introduced measures and ideals which were seemingly copied from traditional Protestant churches. It initiated a process for decentralizing the administration and power of the Roman Catholic Church which was so firmly concentrated on Rome, for reducing the hierarchical autocracy of the clergy and the bishops, and for guarding more carefully against the potentially corrupting effects of accumulated wealth and power. Scripture was reinstated to a more central role in the life of the church.

The changes in the liturgy were especially significant for Catholics in their local situations. They were remarkable for a church which hitherto had claimed to be the bastion of traditionalism, conservatism and orthodoxy. The previous, apparently sacrosanct, practices and cults of the Counter-Reformation, which a large number of Anglican Catholics had so much admired and copied, now suddenly became out of fashion, even forbidden. There was an overnight reversal of attitude and policy: that which a moment before had been regarded as sacred and inviolate was, without warning, profaned, derided and abandoned. The rigid structure of the Tridentine mass, which was universally recognized and respected, which was seen as an ideal by many sympathetic non-Catholics, was suddenly swept away. It was replaced by a new, variable structure, new musical settings and accompaniments, and the use of the vernacular. What had hitherto been a solemn, awesome service, with a profound sense of mystery pervading it had, with alarming rapidity, been permeated by Protestant ideals and customs, making it 'a simple and direct, homely and even folksy, gathering'.[36] Evening masses in apparent imitation of the previously much despised Protestant evening communion services, were also introduced. The former seemingly immovable liturgical fixed points were being discarded, and Anglican Catholics were placed in a dilemma: whether to follow the example being set, or to diverge from the church which had hitherto provided them with a model in order to preserve their long-established liturgical principles and practices.

The main components of the liturgical change were few but radical and far-reaching. A redressing of the balance between the authority of the Bible and that of tradition was to be achieved not only by the introduction of the vernacular or new versions into the liturgy, but by giving greater importance to the Bible in the interpretation of doctrine, and by granting more freedom to biblical scholars. The Council proposed a new strategy for the training and redeployment of clergy and laity to make them more effective in meeting the needs of the contemporary world. The 'liturgical revival' was to be implemented as an enrichment of the life of the church. The theology of the church was reviewed and the escalation of Marian doctrines halted. There was a declaration on religious liberty; and greater freedom was granted to take up 'dialogue with the contemporary world'. Lastly, a new ecumenical spirit was made explicit.

Writing in 1989 one commentator described some of the effects of these changes on the worship of local English Catholics:

> In Britain the ordinary "Catholic in the pew" first experienced these changes in the Sunday liturgies. The Latin of the Mass was replaced by English. The priest no longer said Mass with his back to the laity in a way which had emphasized his key mediatory role and his "apartness" from lay people. Now he faced the congregation in order to stress the community dimension of worship. Lay people read from scripture and led the new bidding prayers, brought up the gifts at the Offertory, and, more recently, have served as special ministers in the distribution of Holy Communion.[37]

The effect of Vatican II on the pattern and tone of local worship was a direct result of agreements at the Council. What were less predictable were the long-term consequences. Foremost among these was the extent to which there was a move away from the acceptance of clerical authority and the dictates of the pope. Increasingly Catholics made up their own minds on a range of matters of personal morality, and more especially on the issue of contraception. And this individual or collective decision-making extended even to issues such as intercommunion. Just as significant was the process of 'normative convergence' to the values of society among English Catholics in general and young Catholics in particular who seemed to become increasingly alienated from institutional religion.

A further unforseen consequence of Vatican II, and in part a result of the growing stress on private judgment rather than on the collective body, was the declining political power of Catholicism. This was demonstrated in the failure of the Catholics to prevent the passage of the 1967 Abortion Act. It was epitomized by the unassuming, largely pastoral, leadership of the widely popular and respected Cardinal Basil Hume in contrast to such princely primates as Nicholas Wiseman and John Heenan.

Other non-Anglican churches and Christian or quasi-Christian bodies

By the late 1990s there was a bewildering array of Christian and quasi-Christian churches, denominations, sects and groups, as well as a countless number of other non-Christian religious communities, places of worship and organizations too numerous even to list in a work such as this. But some of them need to be mentioned as they were an important part of the Christian scene.

The Quakers had undergone a massive reduction in numerical strength since their halcyon pioneer days of growth in the seventeenth century. By 1800 they had declined to 20,000 in England and Wales, and in the subsequent two centuries of phenomenal population expansion they had shrivelled to 1,500 adult churchgoers.[38] In the period 1975 to 1989 they, together with the Salvation Army, the Lutheran Church and the Moravian Church experienced a miserable diminution of membership. Among these smaller Free Churches the Seventh Day Adventists stand out as being exceptional in that they grew from 9,800 in 1979 to 12,300 in 1989.[39]

Another notable example of expansion was the Orthodox Church. The number of Orthodox adult churchgoers leapt from 6,000 in 1975 to 9,400 in 1989. Churches from nine different Patriarchates[40] had been established in Britain by 1989, as well as representative congregations from eleven other countries. It is remarkable how much interest the church aroused, not least among young, intelligent people, including undergraduates. It also catered for the significant minority of the population who had migrated from countries where the Orthodox Church was dominant. The membership, which was 232,100 in 1989, far exceeded the number of attenders.

Lastly, there were a number of very active bodies outside the Trinitarian Christian tradition, such as the Jehovah's Witnesses and the Mormons, which expanded considerably in the latter part of the twentieth century. So also did the non-Christian religious traditions such as Buddhism, Hinduism and Islam.

Two features stand out above all else when confronted by this staggering kaleidoscope of Christian and other religious traditions and institutional forms of religion, many of which have not even been mentioned. First, 'religion', however defined, was not dead in England at the end of the twentieth century, even in its institutional form. Secondly, within that institutional expression of the Christian religion there appears to have been a significant shift from the old-established, more formal, more restrained, conventional, and more traditional churches and denominations to churches and denominations which appeared to those who were drawn to them to offer a different, more attractive spirituality.

Further reading

Brake, George Thompson, *Policy and Politics in British Methodism 1932–1982*, London 1984

Brierley, Peter, '*Christian' England. What the English Church Census Reveals*, London 1991

Currie, R., *Methodism Divided*, London 1968

Davies, Horton, *Worship and Theology in England: The Ecumenical Century, 1900–1965*, Princeton 1965

Davies, Rupert E., George, A.Raymond and Rupp, Gordon (eds), *A History of the Methodist Church in Great Britain*, 4 vols, London 1965–88

Hastings, Adrian, *A History of English Christianity 1920–1990*, London 1991

Jones, R. Tudur, *Congregationalism in England 1662–1962*, London 1962

Nuttall, Geoffrey and Chadwick, Owen (eds), *From Uniformity to Unity 1662–1962*, London 1962

Part Four

Global Mission 1833 to 1998

The gospel for all nations and all peoples

The churches in England made more effort and achieved more success in extending the Christian faith beyond the confines of their own country in the late eighteenth century and in the nineteenth century than at any previous time. In the twentieth century they did even better. The penetration into every quarter of the world in less than two hundred years was astonishing. The contribution of English Christians to the task of worldwide mission bears comparison with what any other nation of comparable size has ever accomplished. It is a remarkable story of initiatives taken, of courage, dedication, persistence, faith, hope and charity.

If one date can be taken as a nineteenth-century nodal point for this heroic saga it would not be 1833 but 1841.[1] Up to that point the tradition of evangelization which had characterized a few insightful, far-sighted enthusiasts in the last years of the eighteenth century and the first two decades of the nineteenth century, and which had led to the founding of the London Missionary Society (LMS), the Baptist Missionary Society (BMS), the Church Missionary Society (CMS) and the Wesleyan Missionary Society (WMS), was sustained with great difficulty. The early years of the pioneer societies just mentioned were marked by tentative yet bold ventures and experiments, grievous mistakes, tragic waste of life, and limited success. But the societies and the intrepid early missionaries had above all else given a lead and inaugurated an enterprise; they had set an example and furnished a few shining names.

A start had been made, and a momentum generated, but it had all gone a little flat in the late 1820s and the 1830s. It was not that there was no support for mission. The income of the CMS had doubled during a period of sixteen years and the fruit of past efforts had been garnered. High Churchmen also transformed the Society for the Propagation of the Gospel (SPG) in the 1830s 'from a colonial church society financed by parliamentary grants and royal letters (directives inviting collections in parish churches) to a missionary society prepared to press its claims on the voluntary support of the Anglican public'.[2] Nonetheless, there had been little expansion, and there was not that vision for what could be achieved and that determination and energy to set to work which was soon to be so much in evidence. 'Consolidation rather than extension is the note of the period.'[3]

In 1841 there were clear signs that this was about to change. They were quite small indications of an impending age of missionary endeavour, but significant none the less. In that year the Colonial Bishoprics Fund was instituted, the Peninsular and Orient line opened the Red Sea route to India, the ill-fated Niger Expedition was undertaken, and, probably most important of all, David Livingstone arrived in Africa.

Livingstone was enthused by the accounts of the African scene and the challenge to evangelization which came from Robert Moffatt, whose daughter he was afterwards to marry. 'In 1840 Moffatt had described to him how he had often seen the smoke of a thousand villages rising in the morning air, and the gospel had not been preached in one of them. This picture Livingstone never forgot, and the various expeditions which gave him a deathless name as an explorer were undertaken in order to open up ways along which the gospel might travel.'[4]

Soon after Livingstone arrived the CMS started its work in Africa using as its agents two Germans, J.L. Krapf and J. Rebmann. In parallel with this Bishop Gray of Cape Town undertook a very effective work of organizing missions among the natives in South Africa where the LMS and the WMS also flourished. Africa then and to an extent during the whole of the rest of the century was to be the primary focus for missionary effort by the English churches; and it was the one area which more than any other fired peoples' imaginations. It was also the 'Dark Continent' which provided the archetypal setting for a crusade to rescue the heathen. At this stage and throughout the nineteenth century probably the majority of the missionaries were impelled by a conviction that idolatry was 'the master-sin of Heathenism'.[5] The 'grave moral seriousness of idolatry seemed to allow only one conclusion with regard to the eternal destiny of the "heathen": unless they believed in Christ they must be presumed lost for all eternity'.[6] Many Christians agonized over the lost, and were haunted by the enormity of the disaster of millions who were without Christ and without hope. The more thoughtful and sensitive among the missionary-minded Christians were also aware of the moral dilemma of a theology which consigned the lost heathen to eternal damnation, and they struggled with conflicting convictions and emotions. This is captured by Robert Moffatt in a sermon in London in 1843:

> Who can look to the East Indies now, and to China now; who can look to those interesting portions of the globe, because the most populous, the most dense, without yearning with compassion over the teeming millions that are there moving onward every day like some vast funeral procession; onward and downward, sadly and slowly, but certainly to the regions of woe? 'Oh, you are a hard man,' some might say; 'do you think they will go to hell?' Where do they go? Do they go to heaven? All idolaters, we are told, have their portion in the lake that burneth with fire and brimstone. I wish that someone would enlighten my mind, if it wants light on this subject, and tell me whether or not all the heathen have perished, all idolaters have perished. But we know that nothing that is unclean, or that loveth and maketh a lie, can enter the holy place.[7]

This belief in the eternal perdition of the 'heathen' imparted a sense of absolute urgency and priority to the missionary imperative.[8] The divine command loomed large in the consciousness of the Victorian missionary and of those evangelicals and others who enthusiastically supported the missionary enterprise. 'Evangelical understanding of the doctrine of divine providence provides the most telling illustration of the confluence of biblical and Enlightenment influences in fashioning the evangelical world-view in the nineteenth century. The biblical revelation of God as the sovereign Lord of history was married to the Newtonian concept of God as the supreme governor of the universe, so that human history was regarded as an ordered process, moving according to fixed rules of operation towards the fulfilment of the purposes of the divine architect.'[9] One example of this belief in divine providence was the acceptance, as in the case of Livingstone, of imperialism and commercial expansion as part of a general historical process. The flag did in many situations prepare the way for the Bible, but the promotion of the gospel was supreme, and gospel values were most typically applied to imperialist and commercial policies and actions by the ministers and missionaries concerned. There was an unrelenting insistence on the overriding moral and spiritual responsibility of those privileged to open up and develop new, hitherto unexplored and technologically unadvanced territories, and to bring countless spiritual and practical benefits to innumerable benighted people.

The surge in missionary interest and activity from the 1840s onwards was also underpinned by an eschatological conviction known as post-millennialism, which postulated that Christ would return in glory after the thousand years of the millennium on earth. This interpretation of the Second Coming was shared by most missionaries and supporters of missionary work until about the 1880s. There was a quite widespread belief that the church stood on the brink of the last days of history. 'Christians expected that the work of foreign missions would initiate a turning of the "heathen" to Christ on such a scale that the kingdoms of this world would become in actuality the kingdom of Christ. The biblical vision of the rule of Christ and his saints over the earth for a thousand years – the millennium – was understood to refer to the era of world-wide gospel triumph which missionary evangelism would inaugurate.'[10] There was considerable optimism, with a prevailing belief that evangelism was destined to succeed on an unprecedented scale, and that Britain had a special divinely appointed role in this global outreach. Such a view was bolstered throughout the Victorian era by the remarkable expansion of British rule over more and more of the world. Missionaries were buoyed up by such assurances. They showed outstanding tenacity and persistence although they often laboured for many years and even a lifetime with little visible fruit in terms of conversions. Later in the century a premillennialist theology was to become more influential, and this emphasized that the moral and spiritual state of the world would deteriorate before the cataclysmic intervention of the second coming. But in the meantime the fervour and exuberance induced by postmillennialism had its effect in promoting a new missionary endeavour.

Advance in many directions

The first missionary enterprise in the 1840s, and the one which attracted the greatest public attention, was Sir Thomas Fowell Buxton's Niger Expedition of 1841. It was a dismal failure but it was successful in arousing awareness and concern for such issues as heathenism, the evils of the still existing slave trade in Africa, and the opportunities for both commercial expansion and the propagation of the gospel awaiting those prepared to take advantage of them. Buxton had hoped to extinguish the West African slave trade by means of legitimate commerce. Livingstone was motivated by a similar concern in his advocacy of 'commerce and Christianity', but in his more reflective moments he acknowledged the strictly limited value of commerce by itself:

> Commerce has the effect of speedily letting the tribes see their mutual dependence. It breaks up the sullen isolation of heathenism. It is so far good. But Christianity alone reaches the very centre of the wants of Africa and of the world. The Arabs or Moors are great in commerce, but few will say that they are as amiable as the uncivilized negroes in consequence. You will see I appreciate the effects of commerce much, but those of Christianity much more.[11]

The missionary outreach of the years from the 1840s to the 1880s embraced the Nonconformists and the Church of England, but it was the latter which gave the strongest lead. And the drive forward was by both Evangelicals and High Churchmen.

Catholic Anglicans and Evangelicals shared a concern about mission. Both were engaged in overseas mission, and both looked for conversions. But they differed in their modes of belief and action in undertaking the missionary task. Raoul Allier, in his monumental work, *La Psychologie de la conversion chez les peuples*, posited two types of approach to the conversion of preliterate peoples.[12] The object of mission and conversion is, he said, the same for both Catholic and Evangelical. But whereas the Evangelical missionary is often a lay person, usually sent by a society, who makes converts individually by his own preaching and contacts, then draws the converts together in a church, and administers baptism to those who are converted, the Catholic missionary is most often a priest who erects a building, a chapel or a church, and invites non-Christians in the neighbourhood to enter it with the hope that by their continuing presence in it they will gradually become Christians and, after instruction, will seek baptism and so will enter the Christian fold. In overseas missionary work the Anglican Catholics adopted the Catholic model, and also gave great importance to the missionary bishop who is sent forth by the church, going before to organize the church, rather than being sent only after the church has been partially organized: bishops were seen as the *sine qua non* of the church. 'From the emphasis on the bishop as possessing the fullness of Apostolic ministry, from whom all other ministry derived, there emerged the idea of the missionary bishop as the characteristic means whereby the mission of the Church should be forwarded. Episcopacy was not a desirable addition to already established churches, but the Apostolic foundation-stone.'[13]

The Evangelicals and world mission

'It was the Evangelicals who taught the Church of England to be missionary.'[14] They, together with their evangelical brethren among the Dissenters, were the initiators in the 1790s of that remarkable leap forward in world mission consciousness and action to which I have referred. In the nineteenth century the main vehicle through which they made an astounding advance in realizing the vision of global mission with which they opened the century was the Church Missionary Society.

In the first years of its life the Society faced many difficulties. No wave of missionary enthusiasm swept over English Christendom in the late eighteenth century and early nineteenth century as is often implied. It was difficult for the new society to attract the interest and support of the church, and impossible at first to enlist English missionaries. Various scandals, and a high death rate among the first pioneers, was demoralizing. There was no previous experience to give precedents for action, and errors abounded. But under the magnificent leadership of men such as John Venn, Thomas Scott, Josiah Pratt and Edward Bickersteth, progress was made. In spite of innumerable setbacks the work went forward in India, Sierra Leone and New Zealand, and new mission fields were opened up, including Ceylon (1818), Egypt (1826), British Guiana (1827) and Abyssinia (1830) before we come to the opening of our period.

During the Victorian era the CMS extended its activities to a wide range of other centres, including Ibadan (1851), Lagos (1852), Mauritius (1856), Hong Kong (1862), Madagascar (1863), Japan (1868), Persia (1875), the Seychelles (1875), Uganda (1875) and Mombasa (1887). But merely to list such new spheres of operation, although it gives a sense of impressive achievement, does not convey what this story of expanding missionary effort entailed in terms of human effort, heroism and self-sacrifice. I will focus on one area, Eastern Equatorial Africa, as a sample of what was involved, and of the kind of activities which stirred the imaginations of those at home. The sort of events I am about to recount had long-term consequences for the worldwide spread of Christianity and the character of countless communities and countries. Such missionary enterprises also contributed significantly to the whole tone and tenor of 'Victorianism'.

As Ludwig Krapf at the time of Victoria's accession and then the mid-century explorers penetrated the interior of Eastern Africa there were reports of an inland kingdom called Buganda.[15] It was finally reached by John Speke in 1861 and H.M. Stanley fourteen years later. In 1875, in a remarkable letter to the *Daily Telegraph*, Stanley, writing from Buganda, challenged Christendom to send a mission to the country. Two days later the CMS received an anonymous letter in which £5,000 was offered as an initial fund for such a project. The CMS made its plans with urgency and yet with great care. Special contributions poured in, and soon £15,000 had been donated. In deference to the political situation in Eastern Africa the enterprise was called the Nyanza Mission, leaving its precise locale an open question.

The missionaries set sail in 1876 and journeyed inland. Two mechanics and one of the leaders, Alexander Mackay, had to return to England because of ill health; porters deserted, and Dr John Smith died of fever, thus creating the first missionary grave on the shores of the Nyanza. By then only three of the party were left. Soon after their arrival in Buganda two of them were murdered. In 1878 the one survivor, the Revd C.T. Wilson, was joined by Alexander Mackay. By 1882 the first Protestant baptism took place. In 1884 James Hannington sailed for Buganda as the first Bishop of Eastern Equatorial Africa. In the meantime the small Bugandan church was facing persecution. Native Christians were banished and imprisoned. Three of them were put to death – cruelly cut about with long curved knives, and then thrown on a large fire. When Hannington and his group of fifty men arrived on the borders of the country they were held in a miserable hut, led out after eight days, surrounded, and all but four were slain. It was subsequently reported that the white man, before he fell, had given a message for the kabaka that he died for Buganda, and that he had purchased the road to Buganda with his life.

After this the church underwent great persecution. Some of the finest converts were burnt or tortured to death in horrific ways. A member of the church council was unmercifully clubbed and thrown into the flames. Another had his limbs cut off one by one and roasted before his eyes. Thirty-two others were burnt on one huge pyre. About 200 perished in all. The kabaka, Mwanga, was the first instigator of much of this persecution, suffering and death. In England voices were raised counselling despair and the abandonment of the mission, but the CMS resolutely continued on its course. A period of quiet succeeded the onslaught. Mwanga was plotting the death of the leading Christians, but he was deposed. Religious liberty was proclaimed and there was a rush of Ganda to receive Christian instruction. But the pendulum was to swing again. The Muslims expelled CMS and other missionaries in a determined effort to win the country for Islam, and once more the voices of despondency were raised in England. Ironically, Mwanga was reinstated on the throne and presided over a policy of evicting the Muslims. He then issued a declaration of religious liberty. By the end of the century there were thousands of native Christians in Buganda with their own churches, clergy and teachers; an eloquent testimony to twenty-five years of quite epic endeavour. And many another tale could be told of other areas of the world to which missionaries were sent under the auspices of the CMS.

In the growth and consolidation of the CMS, and in the evolution of the nineteenth-century overseas missionary enterprise of the Church of England, as well as in the development of a theology and philosophy of mission, a special place of significance and honour should be given to Henry Venn.[16] The events of his life were not dramatic, but he was arguably the greatest missionary statesman of the Victorian church, and as such he has suffered undeserved neglect from historians in the past.

He became Honorary Clerical Secretary of the CMS in 1841. In 1847 he resigned his incumbency of St John's Drypool, Hull; and from then until his retirement in 1872 his public life was entirely devoted to the service of the CMS.

Throughout his Secretaryship Venn had to grapple with the often uneasy relationship between the CMS as a voluntary body within the Church of England and the developing ecclesiastical structures abroad, as he and his society sought to promote evangelism and church development. As a missionary strategist he had one leading idea: 'the euthanasia of missions'. He was concerned that the non-departure of European missionaries would result in native churches becoming missionary-dominated. The foreign missionary should always be primarily an evangelist. Venn's aim was to plant indigenous churches which would be self-supporting, self-governing and self-extending. The missionary society should work in a country in such a way that the removal of the missionaries left the national church standing unassisted. The European and missionary presence should be interim only. Once brought into existence the national church should be allowed to develop according to its own national character, with indigenous leadership and episcopate unencumbered by the continuing European personnel. Perhaps inevitably Venn had to compromise his own principles in certain situations, and even when that distinguished African Samuel Crowther was consecrated bishop in 1864 he was not so much bishop of a developed local church as a kind of pioneering evangelist in episcopal orders.

Venn challenged the High Church notion that the episcopate was of the *esse* of the church, and that the church was not present without a bishop. He was concerned that bishops should be provided for the young churches, to confirm believers, to ordain and to exercise oversight, but he did not believe that they were indispensable for mission work and the establishment of a church.

He wanted to initiate commercial enterprises in West Africa to make the inhabitants more self-supporting. He arranged for Africans to spend three months at Kew Gardens, where they learnt modern methods of cultivation. He established cotton gins at Abeokuta; he promoted the training of Africans in industrial employments and he helped them to establish themselves in profitable trade and commerce.

At home Venn avoided controversy, insisting on the essentially positive character of Evangelicalism. Matters of ecclesiastical dispute were not allowed to be mentioned at anniversary meetings and he seldom engaged in contentious issues. Evangelism was imperative and time should not be squandered on fruitless disputes.

The CMS was to a great extent dependent on the Evangelicals for support; but this home support was subject to considerable fluctuations. In the period 1850 to 1875 the income of the Society did not keep pace with the cost of the expanding activities.[17] But in the last quarter of the century there was a resurgence of missionary enthusiasm. A period of strident imperialism helped to stimulate a global perspective among people generally, and encouraged churchmen to consider afresh the possibility of world evangelization. The Moody-Sankey mission in Cambridge and the Keswick movement produced new and zealous converts and helped to heighten missionary awareness and concern.

Extraordinary interest was aroused in the autumn of 1884 by the announcement that the captain of the Cambridge cricket eleven, C.T. Studd,[18] and the stroke of the Cambridge boat, Stanley Smith, were going out as missionaries with Hudson Taylor to China. Soon they were joined by the Revd W.W. Cassels; Montagu Beauchamp, a nephew of Lord Radstock, and also well known as a rowing man; D.E. Hoste, an officer in the Royal Artillery; and the sons of the late MP for Bedford, C.H. and A.T. Polhill-Turner, the former an officer in the 6th Dragoon Guards, and both prominent Eton and Cambridge cricketers. A series of meetings, culminating in the valedictory gathering in Exeter Hall, London, in 1885, generated wide-ranging and intense missionary ardour. Possibly 'no event in the century had done so much to arouse the minds of Christian men to the tremendous claims of the Field, and the nobility of the missionary vocation'.[19]

At the same time the death of General Gordon in Khartoum focussed attention on Africa. Shortly afterwards the murder of Bishop Hannington and the persecution of Christians in Buganda in 1886 caused an uproar in the British press, and sales of missionary literature escalated. The extent to which the missionary cause came to life in the Christian world in the years covered by these various trends, activities and events can be seen in the creation of the new Boards of Mission, and in the great interdenominational missionary conferences of 1878 and 1888. In 1886–87 thirty-five offers of service were accepted by CMS, of which eighteen were university graduates, twelve of them Cambridge men. Of the 514 men who passed through the Evangelical theological college, Ridley Hall, during the time of Handley Moule (1881–99) 117 became foreign missionaries, while a further 76 served abroad in other capacities.[20]

This was the age of the missionary meetings, with lantern slides, speakers, or an exhibition, and deputation work with missionaries touring the country. It was also the time when the Keswick Convention exercised a powerful influence in the call to missionary work. Hudson Taylor, who started the China Inland Mission,[21] reckoned that two-thirds of his workers had come via the Convention. From 1888 the Convention also provided the finances to send out and support its own missionaries; of whom the most famous was Amy Wilson Carmichael who went to Japan in 1893 and later worked in Ceylon and South India. The Student Volunteer Missionary Union of Great Britain and Ireland (founded in 1892) was a further most effective agency for inciting missionary interest and commitment. The greater acceptance of world-wide missionary responsibility is indicated by the fact that the average recruitment of the CMS which had been less than eight a year in the first half of the century, rose in the period 1848 to 1880 to sixteen and a half, and from 1881 to 1894 to thirty.

Among the new Evangelical initiatives of the nineteenth century the South American Missionary Society holds a distinguished place.[22] It probably had 'the most tragic birth in the history of modern missions'.[23] Allen Gardiner reached the rank of Commander in the British Navy. He experienced an evangelical conversion during one of his voyages, and at the age of forty left the navy in order to devote himself to missionary work. His first efforts were in Natal. Arriving there in 1835 he visualized the possibility of a chain of mission stations stretching up the whole of the east coast of Africa as far as Zanzibar and beyond. But he was 'stronger in imagination than in execution'.[24] He had ideas of a mission to New Guinea, but then turned his attention to South America.

Having failed to undertake a work in Paraguay and Bolivia he went in 1850 with six companions to Tierra del Fuego, the desolate archipelago which forms the southernmost point of South America, one of the bleakest and most tempestuous regions in the world. The ship with their provisions failed to arrive; the natives would not feed them; the drifting ice broke their nets so that they could not fish; and during the severe winter on that inhospitable shore the whole party died of starvation. In his diary Gardiner had written: 'Poor and weak as we are, our boat is a very Bethel to our souls, for we feel and know that God is here. Asleep or awake, I am, beyond the power of expression, happy.'[25]

After seventeen years of hard and valiant missionary work, without having seen a single convert or any fruit from his labours, Gardiner's death was to achieve what his passionate appeals had failed to accomplish. When the bodies were found the words in his diary echoed around the world, and the churches in England were stirred to take an interest in South America. A schooner named after Gardiner landed a party of missionaries. But the tragic saga continued. In 1859 the mission was almost wiped out when eight of its workers were murdered.

It only became evident many years later that the labours of Gardiner and the other pioneers had not been in vain. Before the mission began, Charles Darwin had described the inhabitants of the area as the most degraded beings in the world. In 1870 he wrote to the South American Missionary Society saying that 'the success of the Tierra del Fuego Mission is most wonderful, and charms me, as I always prophesied utter failure. It is a grand success. I shall feel proud if your committee think fit to elect me an honorary member of your society.'[26] And he subscribed to the work from that day until his death. In 1872 the first group of Tierra del Fuegans was baptized. Gradually the society extended its work widely among Indian peoples never reached by the Roman Catholic Church. In Chile the society laboured among the Araucanian Indians; in Paraguay the mission concentrated on the violent Legua people; and in Brazil it was again the Indian tribes to which the missionaries were sent.

The Evangelical missionary zeal, with its preaching and publicity at home and its heroic exploits abroad, undoubtedly had a considerable influence upon the whole process of colonization in the nineteenth century; and in turn it was affected by the onward march of Britain as an imperial power.[27] As Stephen Neill has pointed out, the greatest expansion of Christianity coincided in time with the worldwide and explosive expansion of Europe; the colonizing powers were the Christian nations; and this entailed a variety of compromising relationships between missionaries and governments. In the main, Christianity was carried forward on the wave of Western prestige and power.[28] It might be added that this was perpetuated in the twentieth century, with the leading role taken over by the United States of America.

The cry of such Evangelicals as Charles Grant and Thomas Fowell Buxton was for Britain to assume a total civilizing role and to develop commerce in produce as an alternative to the slave trade. This inspired many to work not only for the conversion of the natives to Christianity, but also their conversion 'to animal husbandry, double-entry book-keeping and all the other accomplishments of Western civilization'.[29] The association between 'commerce and Christianity was clear to such a church leader as Bishop Samuel Wilberforce. 'The providence of God . . . has ordained that when Christianity is placed in any great centre, it should be borne everywhere by the natural power of commerce itself . . . commerce . . . is intended to carry, even to all the world, the blessed message of salvation'.[30] Wilberforce was also aware of another nuance of the link between Christianity and commerce. According to him Christianity has 'the effect of training the human race to a degree of excellence which it could never attain in non-Christian countries', giving 'value to life', 'dignity to labour' and 'security to possessions', with the consequence that a Christian people would tend to be 'a wealth-producing people, an exporting people and so a commercial people'.[31]

One not too sympathetic commentator concludes that for the Victorians

> the overwhelming purpose of empire was the conversion of the native inhabitants within it, whether to the doctrines of free trade, representative government or revealed religion. This was the enduring legacy of the missionary outlook which the Evangelicals had given to nineteenth-century Britain.[32]

There is much truth in this, but it should not imply that it was always a matter of direct cause and effect; as if all missionaries consciously adopted such an outlook. Many of them went out simply 'to proclaim the gospel'. But it has to be acknowledged that the 'imperial' demands of the gospel were often prominent in the thinking of missionaries and may frequently have distorted their view of Christian mission.

Their vision was frequently clouded by national and racial pride, and in certain essential respects was distorted by the mechanistic world-view which they had inherited from Enlightenment thought. As a result, they sometimes failed to apply the ethical demands of the kingdom of God as rigorously to their own nation as they did to the non-Western societies to which they were sent. Their relationship to the diverse forces of British imperialism was complex and ambiguous. If it was fundamentally misguided, their error was not that they were indifferent to the cause of justice to the oppressed, but that their perceptions of the demands of justice were too easily moulded to fit the contours of prevailing Western ideologies. In this respect, our predecessors reflect our own fallibility more closely than we care to admit.[33]

It is perhaps not surprising that there was a measure of late nineteenth-century disillusionment about the whole policy and strategy of linking commerce and Christianity.

The failure of commerce to materialize and of Christianity to advance according to expectations were associated with both criticism of existing missionary strategies and the search for alternatives. A profound reaction against missionary methods involving any measure of westernization, and the growth of missionary bodies marked by simplicity of organization, intense personal faith, and a commitment to itinerant evangelism, were features of the years 1865–90. Old-established societies like the Wesleyans and CMS were deeply split by these developments.[34]

The Anglican High Church contribution to nineteenth-century mission

Although the Tractarians became influential in the Society for Promoting Christian Knowledge (SPCK), which had been founded in 1698, and helped the Society for the Propagation of the Gospel (SPG), which had been founded in 1701, they were not as greatly concerned with overseas mission as the Anglo-Catholics later in the century. There were various efforts to promote overseas mission by a number of High

Church bodies during the century, but the societies founded and the work undertaken was small and unambitious; it made little impact on the public imagination, and it elicited little support. 'Beyond any shadow of doubt the greatest contribution to missionary work came with that unequivocally Anglo-Catholic society . . . the Universities' Mission to Central Africa.'[35]

The UMCA originated with David Livingstone's famous appeal in the Senate House, Cambridge, on 4 December 1857. He had stirred the nation with the portrayal of his adventures, and turned the thoughts of many to Central Africa. In his writings and speeches he made it clear that he regarded himself not so much as an explorer as a pioneer missionary. In unforgettable concluding words at the Cambridge gathering he challenged his audience: 'I go back to Africa to try to make an open path for commerce and Christianity. Do you carry on the work which I have begun. I leave it with you.'[36] The following year an association was formed, which took the name The Oxford and Cambridge Mission to Central Africa, with the object of sending out at least six missionaries under a leader who should, if possible, be a bishop. The mission field would be in the region of the upper waters of the Zambesi, and the Mission was placed under the general oversight and care of the Bishop of Cape Town and Metropolitan of South Africa.

The committee worked and waited for a year, and finally Charles Frederick Mackenzie was chosen to be the leader of the proposed mission. He was a Cambridge graduate, was Second Wrangler, a Fellow of his College, and in 1859 was Archdeacon in Natal. The Universities of Dublin and Durham agreed to co-operate in the work, so the association was re-named the Oxford, Cambridge, Dublin and Durham Mission to Central Africa. Before he departed it was arranged that Mackenzie should be consecrated bishop by the South African bishops, in order that he and his party would be 'truly missionaries sent out on their mission by the Church'.[37] Some details of the early experiences of this courageous band and their successors will help to reinforce our appreciation of the nature of nineteenth-century missionary work, and the sense of adventure which must have conveyed itself to the churches and the public in general in England.

The small company of seven set sail from Plymouth on board the SS *Cambrian* prepared for a hard life. They included a carpenter and agricultural labourer as well as two priests, as they anticipated having to build their own homes and provide much of the food for themselves. On 1 January 1861 Mackenzie was consecrated bishop: the first missionary bishop to be sent out by the Church of England for a thousand years. Travelling up the Zambesi and its tributary the Shere the missionaries, who had been augmented by some local volunteers, first settled in the territory of the most important chief in the district, Chibisa. The whole region had been plunged into turmoil by the slave raids and the cruelty of the slave trade. The expedition pressed on further into the interior accompanied by Dr Livingstone. They encountered a party of armed Yaos, a local tribe, with a train of eighty-four captive slaves, disarmed them and freed the slaves. Those freed included men, women and children, so a new village was established at Magomero, which became the first headquarters of the Mission. They built their own houses and started to construct a church. The daily offices were said and an ordered routine of life was begun. But all around them was a continual state of war. There was famine and disease and the ever present threat of invasion and death. In an attempt to relieve the shortage of supplies the bishop, together with a local priest recruit, H.W. Barrup, set out to meet Livingstone who was on his way up the river. Then tragedy struck. One night the canoe in which they were travelling ran on to a sandbank and overturned. Although righted, their food was all soaked and they lost their medicine box, including all the quinine. As they waited for Livingstone on a mosquito-infested island the bishop fell ill of fever, and with no quinine he died on 31 January 1862. The party struggled back to Magomero with the sad news, and within three weeks Barrup too had died. In the next year or so they had to withdraw from Magomero, two more of the missionaries had died, and another was so desperately ill that he had to return to England. It was a dark hour for the Mission.

In 1863 a new bishop, William George Tozer, was consecrated. He had to cope with a deplorable situation. He moved the headquarters to Morambala, which was more healthy, and soon after that to Zanzibar. In 1865 there was the first baptism of adults.

Though it was now away from the Zambesi the Mission never lost sight of its original objective to reach the tribes in the neighbourhood of Lake Nyasa, and in 1867 a new attempt was made to penetrate the mainland with a base being established at Magela or, as it was later called, Msalabani. In 1872 a violent storm destroyed much of the Zambezi headquarters, and soon after that one of the most devoted of the gallant five missionaries, and a particular friend of the bishop from their college days, died. It was a terrible blow to the bishop on top of repeated trials, and more than he could bear with his failing health, so he returned to England and resigned his bishopric.

It was another testing time, but change was soon to come. In 1873 a treaty was signed between the British government and the Sultan of Zanzibar which entailed the closure of the slave market in Zanzibar. The site was purchased by the Mission, a thatched mud hut was built, and at the place where the whipping post had stood, and where abominable cruelties had been perpetrated for countless years, the gospel was preached. A church was constructed which later became the cathedral.

Bishop Tozer was replaced by his faithful friend and fellow worker Dr Edward Steere, a Doctor of Laws, and a very able, energetic, resolute and inspiring leader. His episcopate from 1874 to 1882 marks a great expansion in the work of the mission. He called for volunteers who were to be paid a pittance and were asked to dedicate themselves to the work in a self-sacrificing way. The response was immediate and generous, and from that time onwards a stream of them carried the Christian message from the base at Zanzibar far and wide into East Africa. Gradually the mainland was evangelized. A station was established at Magela, a freed-slave village was started at Masasi and, in 1879, John Swedi became the first African in the UMCA to be admitted to Holy Orders. In the same year the first sixteen freed slaves to be baptized were admitted to their first communions.

But with progress went further blows. In 1881 Bishop Steere died, and in 1882 the Angoni tribe made a terrible raid on Masasi, setting fire to the houses, looting, desecrating the church and killing seven people. Nonetheless, the missionaries carried on the work despite the tragedy and the threat of the Angoni to return again to slay all the Europeans they met and to take the heart of their leader as a charm to bring victory over the white men. Such courage and endurance was to be rewarded, for the mission was ready for a great advance in the next few years.

Before he died Bishop Steere had commissioned Dr W.P. Johnson to undertake what was to prove an historic expedition into the Yao hills. It was the beginning of mission work around Lake Nyasa itself. Johnson was faced with the warlike Angoni, slaying and plundering villages, but with astonishing bravery he boldly went out alone to meet them, won their trust and friendship, and set up missionary work in the area of Chief Chityi in 1882.

After a long vacancy Bishop Steere was succeeded in 1883 by Charles Alan Smythies. To his episcopate belongs the establishment of a theological department in the Kinngani school for the training of clergy, and the use of a steamer on the lake to reach the lakeside villages.

As the mission reached the end of the nineteenth century and moved into the twentieth century the process of consolidation went on. The hearts of the pioneers would have been gladdened to have witnessed the consecration of the first Bishop of Nyasaland in 1892; the arrival of Bishop Hine as the first Bishop of Northern Rhodesia in 1910; the consecration in 1926 of the first Bishop of Masasi; the many African bishops, priests and laymen who were to play such a distinguished part in the life of their homeland churches and in the wider councils of the church; and the multitude of Christians who would come to faith and grow in grace because former generations so cared that they went, and so loved that they gave themselves in the service of God, the church and their fellow men.

This work in East Central Africa shows that High Church Anglicanism in the last half of the nineteenth century had within it a passionate concern for world mission; a concern that was translated into outstanding and sacrificial service. Other examples may be cited. It will suffice to mention very briefly New Zealand as represented in the life and labours of George Augustus Selwyn, and Melanesia as depicted in the missionary zeal of John Coleridge Patterson.

In 1841 the Tractarian George Selwyn was made missionary Bishop of New Zealand, and over the next twenty-six years established himself as one of the most notable ecclesiastics of the century. The situation confronting him on his arrival was somewhat fraught. After British sovereignty was declared in 1840 the number of settlers greatly increased, and with this growth in the expatriate population came inter-racial mistrust. Under his leadership the great majority of the Maori race professed acceptance of the Christian faith. It was also under the inspiration of Selwyn that New Zealand became the first of the new style of independent province within the Anglican Communion in 1857. What he did in the country was of massive significance, and he made a further major contribution to mission in the Pacific with the establishment of the Melanesian Mission and the involvement in 1861 of John Patterson as the first Bishop of Melanesia.

Patterson was a man of great charm and Christian affection, and he had an exceptional linguistic faculty which enabled him to master the many languages of his island world. He was also genuinely humble. His strategy was to disturb the manners and customs of the people as little as possible in propagating the gospel. He hoped to achieve this by such methods as taking some of the more able boys from many islands and sending them for training, first to New Zealand and later to Norfolk

Island, so that they might later return to their home islands as teachers. On a fateful day in 1871 he landed alone and unsuspecting on the island of Nukapu in the Santa Cruz group, and was immediately set upon and killed, possibly in revenge for the kidnapping of some of the inhabitants by white men a few months earlier. His body was placed in a canoe, and was found to have five wounds in the breast, on which a palm branch tied in five knots had been placed: 'Christians could not but be reminded of the five wounds of another innocent Victim.'[38] In his death Patterson made more impact in England than he had done in his life, for the news of it made a profound impression and called forth a new wave of support for the work of the church in the South Seas.

The Congregationalists

Congregational support for foreign missions was a prominent feature in the life of the denomination in the first half of the nineteenth century.[39] Congregationalists co-operated with other denominations in assisting the British and Foreign Bible Society, which had been founded in 1804, the Religious Tract Society, started in 1799, the British and Foreign Sailors Society, established in 1818, the British Society for the Propagation of the Gospel among the Jews, and the Evangelical Continental Society. Then there were the specifically Congregational societies: the Irish Evangelical Society, founded in 1814 and, most importantly, the London Missionary Society.

The latter was one of those pioneer societies of the 1790s which launched the modern missionary movement. It was distinctive among these in that it was non-denominational, and had tried to unite Anglicans and Dissenters, Calvinists and Arminians, Baptists and paedobaptists under one missionary umbrella. But gradually it lost its ecumenical comprehensiveness, and by the 1820s it had assumed its historical identity as the missionary organ of the Congregational denomination. More than anything else it widened the horizons of the Congregationalists and helped to raise their world mission consciousness during the 1820s and the following decades. The mounting enthusiasm for it and its work is reflected in the financial contributions which rose from £115,619 in the five years ending in 1820 to £293,172 in the five years ending in 1850.

By 1850 the society had 170 missionaries at work, assisted by 700 native agents.[40] Between 1816 and 1850 a total of 356 missionaries went out, and this included men of outstanding ability and tenacity.

Among this noble band of pioneers were such heroes of the faith as the intrepid John Williams who laboured in Tahiti for many years, built a ship when bereft of almost all the necessary tools and was brutally murdered at Erromanga; the Revd Dr John Philip, minister of Union Chapel, Cape Town, and superintendent of the society's work from 1820 to 1847, who strove against many odds in his fearless advocacy of the rights of the black inhabitants; Robert and Mary Moffat who served strenuously in South Africa for many years, and who, as we have seen, were instrumental in attracting David Livingstone to work in Africa; and John Wray who demonstrated iron will and more than common resolution in his leadership of the Congregationalist work among slaves in British Guiana when slavery was rampant, and who rejoiced to witness the end of both the evil trade and slavery itself. And of course there was the life and activities of the greatest of the LMS missionaries, and a national hero, Dr David Livingstone.

It was workers such as these who quickened the pulse of Congregationalists in the home country, and who made such a magnificent contribution to the whole nineteenth-century missionary enterprise. But there was a marked tailing off in the missionary zeal and support from about the 1880s onwards. As the century drew to a close the Congregationalists strove almost feverishly to maintain interest in missionary work and support for it by means of teas, sales of work, house-to-house collections, the holding of meetings, a network of 'auxiliaries', the publication of the LMS *Missionary Chronicle*, and the publication of a large number of books. But the desperate struggle was to a large extent in vain. 'The romantic age in missions had passed. No missionary could hope to be lionized in massive rallies after 1900. Heathenism at home was alarming; social evils nearby were more poignant than those in Africa or India.'[41]

The Baptists

The Baptists, to an even greater extent than the Congregationalists, put their missionary eggs in one basket: the Baptist Missionary Society (BMS).[42] The last decade of the eighteenth century and the first two decades of the nineteenth century had been a golden age for Baptist missionary work, even if this had not been fully recognized at the time. During those years the BMS had been founded (in 1792), William Carey had gone out to serve in India, the Serampore missionaries had done some marvellous pioneer work, and the activities of the missionaries and the BMS as an organization had enthused many Baptists in England to give support. 'Their labours and achievements had lifted the whole Baptist community in the esteem of the public. The Missionary Society had, moreover, acted like a magnet upon the Baptist churches, drawing them together, as never before, in a common purpose and putting new life into them. This new feeling of unity was endangered but, mercifully, not destroyed by the controversy which broke out between the Serempore missionaries and the Society's committee.'[43]

But by the 1820s there was a certain lagging behind as measured by previous standards and compared with other denominations. This can be measured by the income to the BMS which in 1821 was £11,600, well behind the Wesleyan Missionary Society, the LMS and the CMS which ranged from £27,000 to £33,000.[44] Nonetheless, the work of the Society went ahead in many lands throughout the century.

In the Indian sub-continent the progress was slow. In 1843, fifty years from the time William Carey and John Thomas arrived in Bengal, the total membership of the BMS churches was only 1,449.[45] The greatest pressure militating against conversions was, of course, the Hindu religion, but also the caste system. 'Whereas the early converts of the Serampore mission had included a disproportionate number of high-caste people, from the 1830s the caste system operated in such a way as to exclude nearly all who possessed means and influence from the Christian community.'[46] Towards the end of the century there was still little sign that the BMS had built up a church which was remotely capable of operating independently without external leadership and help. It was only after the World Missionary Conference of 1910 strengthened the spirit of co-operation between Protestant missions that momentum was given to the moves towards autonomy for the Indian churches.

The degree of success in other countries was patchy. In China there was a tentative, short-lived, and not very effective attempt to found a mission in 1845; but in 1859 a new effort was made which put down roots and was well enough established to survive the onslaught of the Boxer Rising of 1899–1900 when there were mass killings of Christians. In West Africa the continuing crusade against slavery became in turn the catalyst for a new BMS mission which was started in 1840. The progress was slow, and a number of the Baptist missionaries or members of their families died as a result of the unhealthy conditions in fever-ridden areas. The Congo mission was inaugurated in 1877. Livingstone had died in northern Zambia in 1873, and there were subsequent moves to continue and extend the work he had initiated. The Baptists wanted to be part of this initiative. It was twelve years before the first baptisms took place on the upper river, and even these candidates were young people who had worked for the missionaries. By 1900 the upper river stations could boast only fifty church members between them.[47]

In the other sphere of activity, the West Indies, the situation contrasted remarkably with the countries just mentioned. The BMS missionaries went not primarily as evangelists, for the territory was not wholly unevangelized, but as pastors and teachers of an existing Christian negro community. And the work was crowned with great success. 'In no other Baptist field during the nineteenth century was church growth so spectacular, and nowhere else was progress towards the autonomy of the indigenous church so rapid, nor so firmly insisted on by the Society. Perhaps most notable of all, Baptist missionaries in the West Indies exercised a more decisive influence on the course of secular history than they did in any other part of the world.'[48]

The Methodists

From the moment in 1784 when John Wesley 'set apart' Thomas Coke and others for work in North America, and the British Methodist Church finally and formally shouldered its overseas missionary responsibility, the worldwide extension of Methodism was astounding; and of course missionary activity in countries which had not 'heard the gospel' was part of this global expansion and activity. The Methodist Missionary Society, founded in 1813, was to become the largest Protestant missionary society in Europe. Methodist mission was therefore an important part of the total nineteenth-century missionary enterprise of the English churches.

It took some decades to promote interest in world mission among English Methodists and to establish and develop what was later called the Home Organization Department. This was far more than a money-collecting body, although it undertook that task with astonishing efficiency, so that the income from contributions and legacies was £90,182 in 1840. It was concerned with educating Methodists about 'the deplorable condition of many nations of the earth yet destitute of evangelical light and privileges'. There was widespread ignorance about the geography and current situation in countries outside Europe, partly because so very little was known even by those most informed. It was the age of exploration. Repeated expeditions went out from Britain to seek for the source of the Niger. And Englishmen were exploring and tentatively 'opening-up' country after country, although it was all at a very early stage, and most of the world was unexplored and mysterious. In 1838 the Revd John Hawtrey spoke to the Methodists at the Exeter Hall, London, of the prevailing lack of knowledge and information:

> . . . comparatively little . . . has, up to the present time, been done. We have yet but approached the confines of the enemy's territory. It is but little we know of the interior of Africa; it is little we know of the empire of China; it is little we know of even our own immense colonial possessions in the eastern world.[49]

And of course even the little that was known had to be communicated, and a concern generated to send out Christians who would work for change and evangelism.

A corpus of missionary hymns helped to arouse and sustain a high level of consciousness among English Methodists of their evangelical obligation to support overseas mission. At a time when public meetings were of great importance as a means of communication, the impact of powerful speeches and a vigorous rendering of appropriate hymns was considerable. Such gatherings as the annual missionary meeting provided an immense impetus for the cause and often aroused tremendous enthusiasm. And behind this often quite spectacular façade there grew up a pyramid of committees which descended from the Conference, through district and circuit to local church level, offering a superb instrument for adult education. By 1838, the centenary of the conversion of the Wesleys, this structure was working with great effectiveness. 'If the vast sums of money raised by the Methodist Missionary Societies in subsequent years were gathered at a financial cost in terms of administrative and advertising expenses so low as to be the envy of all other charities in the country, this was because the Connexional system of voluntary workers – connected by personal links through committees to headquarters – opened channels of communication at the minimum expense.'[50]

The Methodists also made good provision for the training of ministers, with a training college and a Theological Institution in two branches, one at Didsbury, Manchester, and one at Richmond, Surrey. It was typical of the systematic way mission was organized by the Methodists in the Victorian era. Missionary societies also emerged within each of the divided sections of Methodism. The English Methodists as a whole provided one of the most impressive examples of response to opening opportunities for world mission in the nineteenth century.

Nevertheless, even for them the work was slow and painstaking. Once the Missionary Society was launched the fields of activity multiplied with great rapidity but then it was mostly a matter of dedicated, typically not sensational, service over a long period. In the early years of the Society Sierra Leone and Canada were priority areas. A small start was made in Namaqualand, north-west of Cape Town, in 1816; and by 1881 Methodism was so strongly established in South Africa that a separate South African Conference was instituted. In the Gold Coast the pioneer in 1838 was Thomas Birch Freeman, the son of a negro and a white woman. In India the work was confined to Mysore and Madras until the last decade of the century, and the utter failure of the attempt to reach the high-caste Indians meant that evangelism was pursued in an indirect way by means of schools, colleges and hospitals. The number of converts remained depressingly low throughout most of the century. But then suddenly, about 1880 and continuing into the twentieth century, there were mass movements to Christianity among the outcastes over large areas of South India, mostly in Hyderabad, accompanied by many outbursts of persecution. In Ceylon there were very few converts for a century; and the same was true for China, where Methodist missionaries laboured with little evident result until a mass movement among the Miaos people started in 1904. It was typical of the chequered history of Methodist missions during the whole course of the nineteenth century. What was being laid, however, was the foundation for a most impressive worldwide Methodism which was to assume gigantic proportions in the following century.

The Roman Catholics

It is not possible to describe and discuss the overseas mission of the English Catholic Church in the same way as I have done for the Church of England and the Nonconformists. This is because that church differed from the others in two fundamental ways. First, the focus for mission policy and strategy, and for its implementation, rested in general outside the bounds of the country, mainly in Rome or the headquarters of the main Catholic orders involved in mission in various parts of the world. This became increasingly so with the growth of Ultramontanism. Secondly, England was for most of the nineteenth century, and indeed the twentieth century also to a lesser extent, the object of Catholic mission rather than the instigator, or even channel, for mission to other countries. Catholic religious orders engaged in mission were sent to England to help strengthen and extend Catholicism in the country. England was a receiving rather than a sending country as far as mission was concerned. Even the powerful United States was regarded until the beginning of the twentieth century as a mission field in which few priests were produced locally; and it was only in 1908 that the Pope withdrew the country from the jurisdiction of the Propaganda, thus indicating that it was no longer a mission field. English Catholicism was smaller and weaker, and even after the establishment of the hierarchy in 1850 control largely remained in Rome.

It was mainly because of this centralization that the Roman Catholic Church was able to give a high measure of coherence and direction to its massive army of missionaries throughout the world. It is probable that by the 1960s the Catholic missionaries in countless countries numbered more than 60,000, which was more than all the non-Roman churches combined. As an illustration of the scale of the Catholic missionary enterprise, in 1957 one single missionary body, the White Fathers of Cardinal Lavigerie, had more than 2,000 ordained missionaries in Africa, together with 1,200 White Sisters in a parallel organization for women.[51]

If any Englishman or woman wanted to serve as a Catholic missionary in the nineteenth or twentieth century they sought acceptance and training through one of these international Catholic missionary bodies. English missionary work was therefore internationalized. It was exceptional to have an arrangement, as instituted in 1911 in the United States, of a national seminary, or its equivalent, for foreign missions.

Of considerable secondary importance in the nineteenth century, and continuing to quite an extent into the twentieth century, was the indirect influence of Roman Catholic mission as an inspiration for Anglo-Catholics in establishing such bodies as the Community of the Resurrection. This particular society and brotherhood was very active in world mission and, among others of note, was responsible for training and sending out Trevor Huddleston for his invaluable work in South Africa.

The twentieth century

Four aspects of world mission stand out in the twentieth century. There was first the transformation of the world mission scene characterized by international, inter-church co-operation, the growth of nation states and national, indigenous churches, and the transforming effect of the world becoming a 'global village' as a result of technological developments. Then there was the international development of the theory and practice of Christian mission, so that missiology became a recognized academic discipline. Thirdly there was the ecumenical movement. And lastly there was the coming into prominence on the world scene of a multiplicity of non-Christian religions, and most notably Islam, Hinduism and Buddhism. The four together constituted a revolution. I will, of course, be viewing them as they influenced the missionary outlook and activities of the English churches.

The English churches and world mission from 1900 to 1998

The century opened with the two most impressive and massive demonstrations ever of Christian missionary confidence: the 1900 New York Ecumenical Missionary Conference and the Edinburgh World Missionary Conference of 1910. Both declared unmistakably that the Christian mission to the world had become internationalized. The former was designed to demonstrate and inspire, and to show the worldwide nature of the Christian mission, and it achieved its aims; the latter was more for the purpose of planning and reflecting, and it most certainly accomplished its objective. In addition, in these formative years for twentieth-century world mission and ecumenicalism, there was the charismatic figure of John Mott. He had brought the Young Mens' Christian Association and the Student Volunteer Movement in America into an integrated programme in the 1890s, and campaigned under the slogan of 'the evangelization of the world in this generation', which had fired the imagination of countless young people. He had been largely responsible for the founding of the World Student Christian Federation in 1895. The 1900 Conference served to reinforce his stature as the greatest international statesman for Christian mission. Mott was a leading evangelist among students across the world. He was a brilliant chairman at the Edinburgh Conference; for its Continuation Committee and its successor the International Missionary Council; and at the two succeeding conferences at Jerusalem in 1928 and Tambaram, Madras, in 1938. He was instrumental in the birth of National Christian Councils in India, China and Japan in the 1920s. Here, in these conferences, and in this man, was epitomized the new missionary enterprise of the twentieth century. Throughout the remainder of the century international conferences, travelling evangelists and teachers, and the increasing power of the media changed the mission scene beyond all recognition. The contrast with the nineteenth century could hardly have been greater, or the changes more suddenly introduced.

In the wings at Edinburgh, as stewards and members of the Student Christian Movement, were such figures as William Temple, William Paton, John Baillie, Kenneth Kirk, William Manson and Neville Talbot; men of immense future influence in the spheres of mission, English church life, theological debate and ecumenical affairs who had caught a vision of a world church in which Indian, Chinese, Japanese, African and other New World leaders of distinction would serve and work together. It was the phenomenon which William Temple as Archbishop of Canterbury would one day refer to as the 'great new fact of our time'. [52]

In England by the 1920s one man in particular was responsible for the shape and direction of the evolving missionary movement: J.H. Oldham. There were outstanding missionaries who were having an impact not only in their own countries of work, but on the missionary movement as a whole, such as Arthur Shearly Cripps in Rhodesia,[53] who was fighting for the rights of Africans; C.F. Andrews in India, who was a thorn in the flesh of the church leadership whom he regarded as too complacent and colonialist;[54] and Norman Grubb and C.T. Studd who laboured heroicly in the heart of Africa.[55] They were enthusiasts, whether mystical, political or evangelical, but Oldham had his vital part to play; and it was hardly less remarkable. 'By 1920 he was the spider at the heart of almost every non-Roman missionary web, the mind who could best interpret the future, the tactician who could handle both C.F. Andrews and the Colonial Office, the international ecclesiastical statesman in comparison with whom almost every bishop appeared immeasurably provincial in outlook.'[56] He it was who in 1919 drew the attention of Randall Davidson to the omission in the League of Nations covenant of any reference to freedom of conscience or religion, allowing the Archbishop to raise the matter and have the necessary reference inserted in the Article on the Mandated Territories. It was Oldham who ensured that German missionary property was exempted at Versailles from confiscation for reparations. He it was who was most involved in negotiations to enable the missionaries expelled from the colonies during the war to be permitted to return. Oldham was the one who successfully marshalled the archbishops and Church of England opinion when there was a famous furore over the misuse of Kenyan labour, and subsequently over a wide range of other Kenyan problems in the early 1920s. This was the type of man, and these the kind of issues, which were to typify the much more widely defined missionary work of the churches in the twentieth century. In Oldham, as in Mott, 'we see emerging quietly and efficiently the new consensus: an explicit gospel most certainly at its heart, indeed in a fairly uncomplicated way, but it was now embedded within the recognition both that "the message" carried with it, in one way and another, responsibility for a vast range of other matters – education, political, economic, racial – and that most of these matters simply could not begin to be tackled effectively other than in an inter-denominational way'.[57]

A more concerted approach was imperative in face of the growth of churches in all the continents, and with the emergence of a host of independent countries set on running their own affairs, not least in the ecclesiastical sphere. Take Africa as an example. The continent began the century with rather less than 10,000,000 Christians, but by 1980 this had become 230,000,000 or more, and the number was escalating.[58] 'This represents one of the most extraordinary phenomena of human history.'[59] And to sheer numerical increase was added the effect of rampant nationalism and the quite staggering increase in the number of churches, denominations, sects and groups. An early indication of what was to come were the 'Ethiopian' movements and 'Zionism', both of which combined religious enthusiasm, the desire for indigenous Christianity and political aspirations.[60] But the increase in such demands, and the proliferation of Christian groups with the post-Second World War release from Western controls and cultural accretions, could not have been foreseen. There was a veritable explosion of indigenous independent movements. In Nigeria, as an example, the Church of the Cherubim and Seraphim gave rise to some 200 additional denominations or sects, one of which alone (the Church of the Eternal Sacred Order of Cherubim and Seraphim) had 300,000 affiliated members in 1980.[61]

Confronted by quite staggering national and international political, economic, social and religious changes, especially in the second half of the century, the English churches, as with churches throughout the world with few exceptions such as the Orthodox Church, felt compelled to make radical changes in their missionary strategy.

'Mutual responsibility and interdependence in the body of Christ' was a concept which dominated Anglican thinking during the decade after its conception in 1963, and had a major effect on missionary activity among Anglicans and others. It was an attempt to communicate to both clergy and lay people the awareness that mission should be central in the life of the church at home and not viewed as something to be done in far-off lands. John V. Taylor, who succeeded Max Warren as General Secretary of the CMS, was a fervent advocate and able interpreter of such a global perspective. In 1973 the Anglican Consultative Council launched 'Partners in Mission' to promote the principle that there is one mission in the world shared by the worldwide Christian family. Simon Barrington-Ward, who succeeded Taylor as General Secretary of the CMS in 1975 (and who was to become Bishop of Coventry in 1985), shared the same vision and clarified the aims of the Society within the overall framework of 'interchange' and 'interdependence'. He emphasized that sharing was to be expressed in evangelism, in renewal and in the search for social justice. It was not a matter of 'spirituality and renewal or social action, but spirituality and renewal and social action, with the Cross central to all'.[62] Such a view was endorsed increasingly by Evangelicals in the Church of England. It found evangelical expression in the Lausanne International Congress on World Evangelisation in July 1974.

The Lausanne Conference was a pivotal event. It has been said that to read the official account of it 'is to be transferred from a world of polemics into an international gathering of Christian leaders which can stand comparison with any of the great missionary conferences of the century, whether the Edinburgh Conference of 1910, the Jerusalem Conference of 1928 or the Tambaram Conference of 1938'.[63] Half of those present, including 50% of the key planning committee and of the speakers, were from Third World countries. The Congress put the Third World on the map of Evangelical Christianity in a new way. The Lambeth Conferences had, of course, brought together bishops from such countries, but here were more grass-roots leaders and participants. It was yet another acknowledgment that Western domination of the church was over. It contributed new insights into the nature and purpose of Christian mission in the modern world, which was seen as including both evangelism and socio-political action, but with priority being given to evangelism.[64] Evangelicals began to show a new concern for human rights, and for such matters as government aid to developing countries. The mounting support for The Evangelical Alliance Relief Fund (TEAR Fund) amply demonstrated this enlarged concept of world mission. TEAR Fund was one of a number of non-denominational world mission and relief societies which commanded support from a range of people, but mostly Evangelicals. Indeed, Evangelical enthusiasm was often greater for such pan-evangelical missionary enterprises than for the more restricted Anglican-based enterprises.

An additional sign of flexibility in the face of such gigantic changes in the world scene as I have already indicated was the increased concern for co-operation between various missionary societies. In some cases this resulted in amalgamation, as with the CMS and the Church of England Zenana Missionary Society in 1957, and the merger of the Universities Mission to Central Africa and the Society for the Propagation of the Gospel in 1965. The societies also worked together in Partnership for World Mission and the Board of Mission and Unity; and various missionary organizations negotiated up to the last years of the century about how they could share buildings. Such planning envisaged the continued separate identity and independence of each society, but with shared resources and closer contact in order to improve effectiveness and eliminate some of the problems experienced in the past.

By the end of the century many Church of England parishes and local Free Churches had become more outward-looking and conscious of their membership of a universal church than in former times. The function and purpose of missionary societies, their relationship to one another in the light of their different churchmanship and historic connections, their integration into the network of worldwide inter-church activities, and their role within independent, self-governing nations and churches had, in the last quarter of the twentieth century, become matters of intense debate. Churches and missionary societies were also confronted by frequently fierce opposition from non-Christian religions, or by local strife and civil war. Many problems remained unresolved as the century neared its end.

Missiology

The theory, philosophy, theology and sociology of Christian mission have assumed a prominence in the twentieth century which, I suspect, they never enjoyed before. For one thing world mission had never been such a massive sphere of activity, and had not loomed so large in the life of the churches. It was also more clearly part of the total evolution of nation-states. It was an integral element in a process of national development and indeed international relations which was of concern to many people other than those immediately engaged in the mission task.

It was also becoming far more 'professional' and efficiently organized. It was an area of high profile activity. The kind of developments which I have just considered helped to provide a 'context' for the changing theology of Christian mission.[65]

In the first two decades of the century the prevailing concern was expansion and the theology of mission assumed that this was the case. It touched on such matters as the relationship of Christianity to other faiths, but there was widespread willingness to follow what D.S. Cairns declared in the report on the 'Missionary Message and the non-Christian Religions' for the 1910 Edinburgh Conference, that the approach to non-Christian religions was to be sympathetic and charitable while holding to the claim of finality and what he termed the absoluteness of Christ. There was still the residue of the Victorian confidence in the supremacy of the Christian faith. But the First World War cast a shadow over all this. It undermined the faith of people in the unquestioned superiority of the Christian faith and the values of Christianity, and helped to introduce a more reflective and thorough appraisal of the purpose and rationale of Christian mission; and this mood was paramount in the 1920s and 1930s

The English thinker who most carefully scrutinized current mission practice in the early 1920s was Roland Allen. He was fearful of the potential dominance of large 'national' churches, or of the imposition by missions, as external authorities, of predetermined forms of orthodoxy with regard to doctrine or practice. He believed that the apostle Paul set the pattern to be followed by merely giving guidelines to the communities he established before leaving them to the Holy Spirit and their reason. He had a deep belief in the inner vitality and giftedness of the local church.

At the 1928 Jerusalem Conference, which was a follow-up to the 1910 Edinburgh Conference, great anxiety was expressed that in mission circles there had been a discernable shift into syncretism, and that the whole missionary movement was in danger of drifting towards the 'social gospel' position which was so prevalent in North America.

In the ten years separating the Jerusalem Conference from its successor at Tambaram, Madras, in 1938 the main focus of missiology was the relationship of the Christian faith to other religious traditions. The key work in the debate was that prepared for the Tambaram Conference by Hendrik Kraemer entitled *The Christian Message in a Non-Christian World* (1938). The great divide in the continuing debate and at the conference was the degree to which it was appropriate to accommodate to other religious traditions. It was the kind of issue which would never be finally resolved, but it was especially divisive at a time when other world religions were coming into prominence and more clearly presenting a challenge to Christianity.

At this time, and well into the post-Second World War period, missiology in England as elsewhere was especially invigorated by two able Dutchmen, Hendrik Kraemer, whom we have just met, and W.A. Visser 't Hooft. Kraemer emphasized the theocentricity of the Bible and the imperative of the God-given command to the church to bear true witness to the gospel. The same note was struck repeatedly, that missionary manifestations 'can only legitimately be called Christian and missionary when they issue directly from the apostolic urgency of gladly witnessing to God and his saving and redeeming Power through Christ'.[66] He endorsed the call for a 'pristine enthusiasm for evangelism' to which the Japanese Christian T. Kagawa had recalled missions in the 'present complicated world'.[67]

But in the immediate aftermath of the Second World War, and well into the succeeding decades three Anglicans were also immensely important in applying their special brand of theology and ecclesiology to thinking on world mission; Max Warren, Stephen Neill and Kenneth Cragg. Warren was firmly of the opinion that the interpreter of missionary history who wished to understand the meaning of some of the things happening within and to the church in his day and generation 'should insist that Christian missions must always be studied in their political, social and economic context'.[68] He gained a wide audience by expressing his views in a series of CMS *Newsletters*. In the later 1950s he especially advocated the 'Christian presence' whereby understanding of relationships with other great religions was fostered. This was an approach which he shared with a friend and fellow Anglican, Kenneth Cragg, who expounded his views in *The Call of the Minaret*.

Cragg was sure that in regard to mission the church had no option: 'as long as Christ is Christ and the Church knows both itself and him, there will be a mission to Islam'. He insisted that 'we present Christ for the sole sufficient reason that he deserves to be presented'. He remained convinced that 'we cannot neglect that Christ claims discipleship and that his Gospel is something expecting a verdict'.[69] Nonetheless he saw in Muslim society, and in individual Muslims, qualities which he admired and respected and wanted to be retained and preserved, such as hospitality, simplicity, discipline, dignity, family affection and sensitivity to the poor.

Stephen Neill had immense experience in various capacities: as a missionary in India, in important church posts in England, as a bishop in India, and as a professor, writer and speaker of renown. He admired Kraemer, and like him found the relativism of the modern world disturbing. It was inevitable that in holding to the truth Christians would be faced with the need for exclusiveness and intolerance of alternatives. Pluralism was a fact of the contemporary world, but it must not lead to a relativist view of truth.

The key words in the world mission debate in the 1960s were dialogue and liberation. The great thing was for those with different views within the Christian tradition to enter into dialogue, and such a procedure was recommended between Christians and non-Christians. Even the Roman Catholics talked in these terms. In the Vatican II document *Nostra Aetate* (the Declaration on the Relation of the Church to non-Christian Religions) for the first time non-Christian religions were portrayed as bodies which the Church should respect and with which the Christian should enter into dialogue; and words such as 'pagan', 'idolatry' and 'error' were notably absent.

Liberation theology, which originated in South America, which came to the fore in the late 1960s, and which flowered in the 1970s, offered a radical new approach to Christian mission and theological method. It required religion to be inextricably intertwined with political, economic and social action in which the poor, disadvantaged, alienated and downtrodden members of society should be the prime concern of a church which existed for such unrepresented and misused sectors of the population. The Christian purpose should be to change society, to make it more righteous, just and equitable. Two foundation texts were Gustavo Gutiérrez, *A Theology of Liberation* (1974) and J.L. Segundo, *The Liberation of Theology* (1976). The ripples from the stone cast into the theological and missiological pool by the Liberation theologists had not subsided by the 1990s. Issues were raised or highlighted which would not go away; and they remained on the missiological agenda.

In the 1960s and 1970s evangelical perspectives on world mission came to the fore. These were given a public face in a series of highly important world gatherings such as the Berlin Congress on Evangelism in 1966, the Wheaton Congress on Christian World Mission in the same year and the Lausanne Congress of 1974, to which I have already made reference. The latter was notable for the maturity of judgment of its participants, 'the breadth of its engagement internationally and missiologically and its success in holding together the evangelistic note, mission as proclamation, with the stress on social justice, concern for the poor and socio-political involvement'.[70] The English Evangelical, John Stott, was most influential in the conference. He was the one mainly responsible for the drafting of the Covenant which emerged from the gathering. And the principles which it enshrined proved to be an important source of mission thinking and strategy for a generation to follow. It was also notable that evangelical leaders on the whole were anxious to disavow any attempt to replace the International Missionary Council, which was the official organ of the World Council of Churches movement, or to express any hostility to the approach taken by that body in its missiology. This did not prevent well-intentioned criticism and comment as, for example, John Stott's observations after the World Council of Churches gathering in Nairobi in 1975, when he expressed regret that in the ecumenical movement it appeared that evangelism had 'become largely eclipsed by the quest for social and political liberation'.[71]

As the 1970s gave way to the 1980s another conservative evangelical, Donald McGavran from the United States, greatly helped to mould English missiology, especially by his views on church growth. He stressed the importance of numerical increase and questioned mission thinking and strategy which did not result in such expansion or which resulted in massive funding for areas of low response, often to the detriment of more responsive, but under-resourced, alternatives.

McGavran failed to convince the distinguished English missiologist Lesslie Newbigin whose emphasis was upon the need for a 'genuinely missionary encounter between scriptural faith and modern culture'.[72] Despite a full life, including being a bishop in India and General Secretary of the International Missionary Council, Newbigin was a missiologist of the top rank. His focus was upon the mission of the church which lived in the shadow of the European Enlightenment. He thought that Western Christianity was in certain respects constrained by the rarefied atmosphere of pure Enlightenment rationality, and that the consequent somewhat atomized and unduly rational and cerebral Christianity of the post-Christian societies of the West could greatly benefit from the greater stress upon aesthetic experience and emotional integration to be found in some of the so-called less advanced societies of Asia and Africa. This was in accord with much of the missiology of the 1990s which had to address a world so much more open to the insights and orientations of a multiplicity of cultures than ever before.

A measure of the change which had taken place in the nature of world mission, and in the missiology which underpinned it, in the course of the twentieth century was the fact that the debt burden on Third World countries topped the agenda in the planning for the 1998 Lambeth Conference. Previous Lambeth Conferences had tended to be dominated by the churches of Europe and North America and other more developed countries of the world. For some bishops of developing countries the apparent preoccupation of the churches in the occident with sexual matters, and such ecclesiastically domestic issues as the ordination of women, important as these topics were, seemed almost obscene when compared with problems of mass poverty, starvation and suffering in various forms. The agenda of the churches was literally being set by a world church in which countries which had so recently been the scenes of missionary activity were taking a prominent part.

The ecumenical movement

The twentieth-century ecumenical movement had deep roots,[73] although three ecumenical initiatives in the latter part of the nineteenth century were especially significant. The first of these was the 1888 Lambeth Conference proclamation known as the Lambeth Quadrilateral. It declared that home reunion could be based on the acceptance by any participating church of four Articles:

(a) The Holy Scriptures of the Old and New Testaments as 'containing all things necessary to salvation', and as being the rule and the ultimate standard of faith.
(b) The Apostles' Creed, as the Baptismal Symbol; and the Nicene Creed, as the sufficient statement of the Christian faith.
(c) The two Sacraments ordained by Christ Himself – Baptism and the Supper of the Lord – ministered with unfailing use of the words of institution, and of the elements ordained by Him.
(d) The Historic Episcopate, locally adapted in the methods of its administration to the varying needs of the nations and peoples called of God into the unity of His Church.

The proposals were discussed at most of the denominational annual assemblies, and the general response was that, useful as they were, the article on the historic episcopate presented an insuperable barrier.

The second initiative was the holding of a series of six conferences at Grindelwald on home reunion, the first of which took place in 1892. They were arranged chiefly at the instigation of Henry Lunn, a

Methodist missionary. A wide range of denominations was represented, and every shade of theological belief. The conferences highlighted the problem of ministerial orders as being especially crucial to both Anglicans and Free Churchmen. It was also evident that, in addition to some High Churchmen, one section of Church of England Evangelicalism, and that not the narrowest, was reluctant to admit the Free Churches to full communion with the Church of England.

The last initiative was the conversations between Viscount Halifax, the Abbé Portal and Cardinal Mercier which we have previously considered.

As we enter the twentieth century the ecumenical atmosphere noticeably changes. The opening up of the world gave greater opportunities for interchange of ideas; and interaction between individuals from different Christian traditions helped to enlarge understanding and break down barriers. This was typified in the Conferences of 1900 and 1910. Denominational differences also appeared particularly irrelevant in missionary situations, and a major hindrance to the presentation of the gospel of love and reconciliation.

A crucial date was 1920. It was the year of the Lambeth Conference's *Appeal to All Christian People*: 'one of the rare ecclesiastical documents which does not get forgotten with the years: probably the most memorable statement of any Lambeth Conference'.[74] It called for a new initiative in the wake of the First World War: 'We do not ask that any one communion should consent to be absorbed in another. We do ask that all should unite in a new and great endeavour to recover and to manifest to the world the unity of the Body of Christ for which He prayed.' In the two-and-a-half decades that followed little came of the *Appeal* despite the warm Free Church response to its tone and general tenor. The obstacle of the 'historic episcopate' remained, for it was still retained as part of the Lambeth vision of unity, and it continued to be unacceptable to the non-episcopal churches as a condition for any great advance in the institutional relationship of Free Churches with the Church of England. Although the *Appeal* was couched in terms which made it not too prelatical or monarchical the substance, especially as it related to episcopacy, continued to be a stumbling block. As one distinguished Free Church scholar said some years later, the *Appeal* 'seemed to alter things, but in cold, actual fact it did not. With the magnificent and unconscious sleight of hand that comes from centuries of practice in the *via media* the Anglicans took back what they seemed to give, and, as usual, wanted it both ways.'[75] Perhaps the *Appeal* had more

Hastings.

significance for the long rather than the short term, as a prophetic finger pointing to futures far beyond the lifetime of the bishops gathered in conclave in that post-war dawn.

Nonetheless, it did appeal to some Free Churchmen at the time. There were those who increasingly came to accept the need to find new ecumenical ways ahead. Prominent among such was J.H. Shakespeare, the energetic and able secretary of the Baptist Union, and 'the most deeply and consistently ecumenical of all the Church leaders of the time'.[76] He became more and more convinced that denominationalism was outmoded, had outlived its usefulness, and was increasingly destructive of religious effectiveness; and that a divided church could not speak effectively to a divided world. Even before the *Appeal*, in 1918, he published *The Churches at the Crossroads*, in which he showed that he was in many respects ahead of his time. 'It is in principle one of the most important books of twentieth-century Christianity because it sets out so clearly the logic of the forthcoming ecumenical movement.'[77] He called not only for full unity between the Free Churches, which he had advocated for many years, but for unity between the Church of England and the Free Churches. The division of 1662 was a mistake; and the Free Churches must be prepared to accept episcopacy. Few Free Churchmen concurred, and many strongly disagreed. If intercommunion was to come, they asserted, it should be without preconditions. It was an impasse which was to be encountered repeatedly during the remainder of the century.

Within the churches in England little more of ecumenical significance occurred during the next twenty-five years. There were somewhat vague expressions of polite goodwill expressed by church leaders, but it was all rather hollow and platitudinous. On the international stage there was the continuing work of 'Faith and Order' and 'Life and Work', the supporting movements out of which the ecumenical movement was made. Most importantly there was the Oxford Conference of Life and Work in 1937. It resolved to establish a World Council of Churches which came into being and had its first Assembly in Amsterdam in 1945. In all of this William Temple was prominent, and through him the Church of England was deeply engaged in the whole worldwide ecumenical debate. But the next major ecumenical leap forward on the domestic front came immediately after the ending of the Second World War.

The precipitating event was the 1946 Cambridge sermon of Geoffrey Fisher. I have alluded to his initiative in the previous chapter, but it was of such immediate and long-term importance that I will look somewhat closer at what he had to stay. He set forth his credentials and outlined his motives:

There is a suggestion which I should like in all humility to make to my brethren of other denominations. We do not desire a federation: that does not restore the circulation. As I have suggested, the road is not yet open, we are not yet ready for organic or constitutional union. But there can be a process of assimilation, of growing alike. What we need is that while the folds remain distinct, there should be a movement towards a free and unfettered exchange of life in worship and sacrament between them as there is already of prayer and thought and Christian fellowship . . . My longing is not yet that we should be united with other Churches in this country, but that we should grow to full communion with them. As I have said and as negotiations have shown, no insuperable barrier to that remains until we come to questions of the ministry and government of the Church. Full communion between Churches means not that they are identical in all ways, but that there is no barrier to the exchange of their ministers and ministries.

The Archbishop then defined and made explicit what he was proposing:

The non-episcopal Churches have accepted the principle that episcopacy must exist along with other elements in a reunited Church. For reasons obvious enough in church history they fear what may be made of episcopacy. But they accept the fact of it. If they do so for a reunited Church, why not also and earlier for the process of assimilation, as a step towards full communion? It may be said that in a reunited Church they could guard themselves in the constitution against abuses of episcopacy. But they could do so far more effectively by taking it into their own system. The Church of England has not yet found the finally satisfying use of episcopacy in practice; nor certainly has the Church of Rome. If non-episcopal Churches agree that it must come into the picture, could they not take it and try it out on their own ground first?

Fisher had launched his ship. He had boldly charted a possible course ahead. It was a red-letter day for the ecumenical movement. 'How much is owed to the Cambridge sermon preached in 1946 it is hardly possible even to guess, but it did take the movement out of the deep freeze and got inter-Church discussions started again.'[78] It was one factor in stimulating the conversations and the scheme for organic unity between the Methodist Church and the Church of England which finally foundered in 1972.

Many people in these years when church unity in England was high on the agenda of various denominations, and when the failure of the unity scheme between the Church of England and the Methodists was causing such agony, thought that a model had already been provided by the Church of South India.[79] It had been born after long negotiations in 1947. No re-ordination of the non-Anglican clergy had been required but all the church's bishops shared in the Anglican succession, and all future ministers were to be episcopally ordained. A 'Pledge' was provided whereby no congregation would be compelled to accept a ministry about which its members objected on grounds of conscience. The Faith and Order conference at Nottingham in 1964 was strongly convinced that this South India scheme had not been fully and fairly considered and assessed, and many Church of England members and Free Churchmen endorsed that view.

The most significant ecumenical advances in the remaining part of the century were the formation of the United Reformed Church in 1972; the visits by Archbishops Fisher, Runcie and Carey to the Pope, the latter taking place in 1996; the work of the Anglican-Roman Catholic International Commission; a variety of official and unofficial contacts between the Church of England and the Roman Catholic Church; and, perhaps most importantly, clear evidence of a local working together of individuals, groups and churches across denominational boundaries in many areas of the country as in the Free Church Councils and in other community-based, less formal ways. At the national and international levels, and in the relationship of churches one with another as institutions, major obstacles remained. There was the divide between the Church of England and the Roman Catholic Church over the ordination of women, the reluctance of the Roman Catholic Church to accept the validity of the Church of England bishops and clergy, and differences of attitude and policy between the Church of England and the Roman Catholic Church on such ethical and moral issues as birth control, abortion and euthanasia; there continued to be such questions as attitudes to episcopacy, the mutual acceptance of ministries, and matters relating to baptism and church order which hindered organic union between the Church of England and the Free Churches; and there were theological and church government issues which were problems in the way of unity between different Free Churches. But at the local level different criteria often applied. Confronted with declining congregations, considerable local apathy towards any institutional form of Christianity, and a not very high level of concern or sophistication among church or chapel membership regarding those theological and ecclesiological matters which so troubled some of their national leaders, local churches often understandably emphasized the practical desirability of working together. And they frequently took action in advance of any denominational mergers.

In 1969 the Sharing of Church Buildings Act was passed which allowed the use of existing Church of England buildings by other denominations and made it lawful for new churches to be constructed on a shared basis, with certain limitations and conditions.[80] Areas of ecumenical co-operation were established, especially in new towns and housing estates where there was no entrenched denominational pattern. In other areas where such patterns already existed there was often a concerted effort to discover imaginative alternatives to institutional independence and rigidity, especially when institutional inflexibility was considered to be a barrier to effective evangelistic and pastoral work. As early as 1946 in Cobham, Bristol, a joint Baptist, Congregational and Methodist Church was started, while in 1968 at Desborough in Norfolk, a small town of 5,000 inhabitants, Anglicans and Methodists began working towards a united congregation, a team ministry and a single church complex. In 1969 the British Council of Churches published *The Designation of Areas of Ecumenical Experiment*, and by 1973 all the main churches had established a Consultative Council for Local Ecumenical Projects in England, which acted as an advisory body. By 1977 there were 289 designated areas in Great Britain, 241 of which involved sharing buildings, 191 the joint working of congregations and 194 a sharing of ministries. The Church of England was a partner in 188 such projects, the Methodists were engaged in 241, the United Reformed Church in 153, the Baptists in 41 and the Roman Catholics in 26. Tensions and problems were inevitable because of reconciling different ecclesiastical practices and beliefs, and because so many individuals with their own views and personalities were involved. A high profile was given to local co-operation by the sustained and highly commendable working-together of the Anglican Bishop of Liverpool David Sheppard and the Roman Catholic Archbishop of Liverpool, Derek Worlock. By 1997 the concept of co-operation was so well accepted that the Church of England launched a debate under the umbrella title, 'Working Together'. This provided a mechanism whereby the possibility of ecumenical co-operation could more readily be explored at all levels from the parish to the national synod.

Non-Christian religions

A unique feature of the world situation from the mid-twentieth century onwards for Christians in so-called Christian countries was the presence in their midst of believers representing all the other major world religions. Such adherents of non-Christian faiths were no longer 'out there', and securely confined to their own countries of origin or areas which the 'Christian' countries had proselytized. They were no more just part of 'heathenism' to which missionaries were sent. These non-Christian world religions were now not so mysterious and unknown, allowing the imagination to run wild in picturing lurid and often exaggerated extremes of primitive and 'uncivilized' behaviour by their practitioners. They were on the doorstep of the 'home' churches, embodied in real people, seen at close quarters, and increasingly treated with tolerance by the state as part of a religiously mixed population. What is more, because of immigration, they were expanding in the host countries in the last three decades of the century while the Christian churches taken as a whole were contracting. When this is set alongside the situation in the 'home' countries of the other world faiths, where, in general, the Christian faith remained a small minority body, struggling to hold its own, the global transformation from the pioneer 'missionary' days in the 1830s was stark and sensational.

It was a situation which raised for the churches a whole new range of theological, ecclesiological and practical problems. What was the relationship between Christianity and more particularly the person of Christ as 'the' way, 'the' truth and 'the' life, and the claims of other religions? How far should the churches in England go in tolerating and accommodating non-Christian beliefs and practices out of neighbourly love for the practitioners of those faiths, and in order not to be bigoted? Where should the line be drawn between charity and the determination to remain faithful to the distinctiveness of Christianity and the exclusivity of the claims of Christ? And, more specifically in this respect, what attitude should be taken to multi-faith services or the use by the followers of other religious traditions of Christian churches for their own worship? What a contrast from the *ancien regime* of the late eighteenth century and early nineteenth century when the Christian faith, although buffeted and attacked, seemed to be at the very centre of the life of the nation.

When we cast our eyes backwards even further perhaps we can discern the process outlined in the Introduction: with the transmutation from the early sixteenth-century monopolistic configuration to the pluralism which was well advanced in the latter part of the nineteenth century, and on to the multi-faith pluralism of the late twentieth century. And by appreciating this transformation perhaps it is possible to glimpse the changes we have reviewed as dramatic and yet not leading to the inevitable demise of the Christian faith.

But it is also possible to stand back and place the life, worship, witness and work of the English churches in a context which goes far beyond the confines of one country, England, or the one hundred and sixty-five years on which we have focussed. The English churches with all their imperfections and oddities can be viewed as part of an immeasurably greater unfolding drama which we can but vaguely perceive and understand; one which spans all the fullness of time, and encompasses the whole world.

Further reading

Goodall, N., *The Ecumenical Movement*, 2nd edn, Oxford 1964

Jones, R.Tudur, *Congregationalism in England 1662–1962*, London 1962

Neill, Stephen, *A History of Christian Missions*, Harmondsworth 1964

Newbigin, Lesslie, *The Other Side of 1984. Questions for the Churches*, Geneva 1984

Rouse, R., and Neill, S.(eds), *A History of the Ecumenical Movement, 1517–1948*, 2nd edn London 1967

Stanley, Brian, *The Bible and the Flag. Protestant missions and British imperialism in the nineteenth and twentieth centuries*, Leicester 1990

Stanley, Brian, *The History of the Baptist Missionary Society 1792–1992*, Edinburgh 1992

Stock, Eugene, *The History of the Church Missionary Society*, 4 vols, London 1899–1916

Stott, John R.W., *Christian Mission in the Modern World*, London 1975

Thompson, H.P., *Into All Lands. The History of the Society for the Propogation of the Gospel in Foreign Parts 1701–1950*, London 1951

Wilson, George Herbert, *The History of the Universities' Mission to Central Africa*, London 1936

Yates, T.E., *Venn and the Victorian Bishops Abroad*, London 1978

Yates, Timothy, *Christian Mission in the Twentieth Century*, Cambridge 1994

Abbreviations

Bibliography

Adams, Pauline A., 'Converts to the Roman Catholic Church in England, circa 1830–1870', Oxford B Litt. 1977

Ainsworth, A.J., 'Religion in the working-class community and the evolution of socialism in late nineteenth century Lancashire: a case of working-class consciousness', SocH, 10, 1977, pp. 354–80

Allchin, A.M., The Silent Rebellion. Anglican Religious Communities 1845–1900, London 1958

Altholz, J.L., 'The Mind of Victorian Orthodoxy: Anglican responses to "Essays and Reviews", 1860–1864' in Parsons (ed), Religion in Victorian Britain, Vol IV

Altholz, Josef L., 'The Warfare of Conscience with Theology' in Parsons, Gerald (ed), Religion in Victorian Britain, Vol IV: Interpretations, Manchester 1988

Altholz, Josef L., The Liberal Catholic Movement in England. The "Rambler" and its Contributors 1848–1864, London 1960

Anderson, G.H., 'The Theology of Missions 1928–58', Boston Ph.D 1960

Anderson, Olive, 'Women preachers in mid-Victorian Britain: some reflections on feminism, popular religion and social change', HJ, 12, 3, 1969, pp. 467–84

Anglican Evangelicals and their New Assembly. A Forum for United Thought and Action in the Church of England, London 1983

Anglican–Roman Catholic International Commission, The Final Report, London 1981

Anson, P., The Call of the Cloister: Religious Communities and Kindred Bodies in the Anglican Communion, London 1955

Archbishop of Canterbury's Commission on Urban Priority Areas, Faith in the City. A Call for Action by Church and Nation, London 1985

Armstrong, Anthony, The Church of England, the Methodists and Society 1700–1850, London 1973

Avis, P., 'The Tractarian challenge to consensus and the identity of Anglicanism', KTR, 9, 1986, pp. 14–17

Badham, Paul (ed), Religion, State, and Society in Modern Britain, Lampeter 1989

Baker, D. (ed), The Church in Town and Countryside, Oxford 1979

Balleine, G.R., *A History of the Evangelical Party in the Church of England*, London 1908

Barnes, John, *Ahead of His Age. Bishop Barnes of Birmingham*, London 1979

Barr, James, *Fundamentalism*, London 1977; 2nd edn 1981

Barrett, D.B. (ed), *World Christian Encyclopaedia*, Nairobi 1982

Battiscombe, Georgina, *John Keble. A Study in Limitations*, London 1963

Beales, D. and Best, G. (eds), *History, Society and the Churches*, Cambridge 1985

Bebbington, D.W., 'The city, the countryside and the social gospel in late Victorian Nonconformity', *SCH*, 16 ,1979, pp. 415–26

Bebbington, D.W., *The Nonconformist Conscience: Chapel and Politics 1870–1914*, London 1982

Bebbington, D.W., *Evangelicalism in Modern Britain. A history from the 1730s to the 1980s*, London 1989

Bell, G.K.A., *Randall Davidson Archbishop of Canterbury*, 2 vols, Oxford 1935

Bennett, G.V and Walsh, J.D. (eds), *Essays in Modern English Church History*, London 1966

Bentley, Anne, 'The Transformation of the Evangelical Party in the Church of England in the Later Nineteenth Century', Durham Ph.D 1971

Bentley, James, *Ritualism and Politics in Victorian Britain. The Attempt to Legislate for Belief*, Oxford 1978

Berger, Peter L., *The Sacred Canopy*, New York 1967

Berger, Peter L., *A Rumour of Angels*, London 1979

Best, Geoffrey, *Mid-Victorian Britain 1851–75*, London 1971

Binfield, C., *So Down to Prayers: Studies in English Nonconformity 1790–1920*, London 1977

Binfield, Clyde, ' "We claim our part in the great inheritance": the message of four congregational buildings', *SCH*, Subsidia 7, 1990, pp. 201–23

Bossy, J., *The English Catholic Community 1750–1850*, London 1975

Bowen, D., *The Idea of the Victorian Church: A Study of the Church of England 1833–1889*, Montreal 1968

Bradley. I., *The Call to Seriousness: The Evangelical Impact on the Victorians*, London 1976

Bradley, J., *Religion, Revolution and English Radicalism*, Cambridge 1990

Braithwaite, R., *The Life and Letters of the Rev. William Pennefather*, 2nd edn, London 1878

Brake, George Thompson, *Policy and Politics in British Methodism 1932–1982*, London 1984

Bready, J. Wesley, *Doctor Barnardo Physician, Pioneer, Prophet*, London 1930

Brent, Richard, *Liberal Anglican Politics. Whiggery, Religion, and Reform 1830–1841*, Oxford 1987

Brierley, Peter, 'Christian' England. What the English Church Census Reveals,

Bebbington J. W. Victorian Nonconformity. Headstart History. 1992.

London 1991

✓ Briggs, John and Sellers, Ian (eds), *Victorian Nonconformity. Documents of Modern History*, London 1973

Briggs, J.H.Y., *The English Baptists of the Nineteenth Century*, Didcot 1994

✓ Brilioth, Yngve, *The Anglican Revival. Studies in the Oxford Movement*, London 1933

✓ Brogan, D.W., *The English People: Impressions and Observations*, London 1943

✓ Brose, O.J., *Church and Parliament: The Reshaping of the Church of England 1828–1860*, Stanford 1959

. Brown, Ford K., *Fathers of the Victorians: The Age of Wilberforce*, Cambridge 1961

Brown, K.D., 'Ministerial recruitment and training: an aspect of the crisis of Victorian Nonconformity', *VS*, 30, 1987, pp. 365–83

Brown, K.D., 'College Principals – a cause of Nonconformist decay?', *JEH*, 38, 2, 1987, pp. 236–53

Brown, Kenneth D., *A Social History of the Nonconformist Ministry in England and Wales 1800–1930*, Oxford 1988

Bruce, Steve, *A House Divided. Protestantism, Schism, and Secularization*, London and New York 1990

Bruce, S. (ed), *Religion and Modernization: Sociologists and Historians Debate the Secularization Thesis*, Oxford 1992

Buchanan, C.O., *Encountering Charismatic Worship*, Nottingham 1977

✓ Buchanan, C.O., Mascall, E.L., Packer, J.I. and the Bishop of Willesden, *Growing into Union. Proposals for forming a United Church in England*, London 1970

Budd, Susan, 'The Loss of Faith. Reasons for Unbelief among Members of the Secular Movement in England, 1850–1950', *P&P*, 36, April 1967, pp. 100–125.

Budd, S., *Varieties of Unbelief: Atheists and Agnostics in English Society, 1850–1960*, London 1977.

✓ Buren, Paul van, *The Secular Meaning of the Gospel*, New York and London 1963

Burns, R.A., 'The Diocesan Revival in the Church of England c.1825–1865', Oxford D Phil. 1990

Butler, Cuthbert, *The Life and Times of Bishop Ullathorne*, 2 vols, London 1926

Butler, Perry (ed), *Pusey Rediscovered*, London 1983

✓ Butterfield, Herbert, *Christianity and History*, London 1949

Calder, Angus, *The People's War. Britain 1939–1945*, London 1969

Canon, Walter F., 'Scientists and Broad Churchmen: an Early Victorian Intellectual Network', *JBS*, 4, 1, November 1964, pp. 65–88

Capon, John, *Evangelicals Tomorrow: A Popular Report of Nottingham 77, the National Evangelical Anglican Congress*, London 1977

Carpenter, Edward, *Cantuar. The Archbishops in their Office*, Oxford 1971

Carpenter, Edward, *Archbishop Fisher – His Life and Times*, Norwich 1991

Carpenter, S.C., *Church and People, 1789–1889. A History of the Church of England from William Wilberforce to 'Lux Mundi'*, London 1933

Carpenter, S.C., *Winnington-Ingram. The Biography of Arthur Foley Winnington-Ingram Bishop of London 1901–1939*, London 1949

Carwardine, R., *Transatlantic Revivalism: Popular Evangelicalism in Britain and America*, London 1978

Catherwood, Christopher, *Five Evangelical Leaders*, London 1984

Catholicity. A Study in the Conflict of Christian Traditions in the West, being a Report presented to His Grace the Archbishop of Canterbury, London 1947

Chadwick, Owen (ed), *The Mind of the Oxford Movement*, London 1960

Chadwick, Owen, *The Victorian Church*, 2 vols, London 1966, 1970; reissued London 1987

Chadwick, Owen, *The Secularization of the European Mind in the Nineteenth Century*, Cambridge 1975

Chadwick, Owen, *Michael Ramsey. A Life*, London 1990; reissued London 1998

Chadwick, R.E., 'Church and People in Bradford and District, 1880–1914; the Protestant Churches in an Urban Industrial Environment', Oxford D Phil. 1986

Charles, C., 'The Origins of the Parish Mission in England and the Early Passionist Apostolate, 1840–1850', *JEH*, 15, 1964, pp. 60–75

Christensen, T., *Origins and History of Christian Socialism 1848–54*, London 1962

Christensen, Torben, 'F.D. Maurice and the Contemporary Religious World', *SCH*, 3, 1966, pp. 69–90

Church, R.W., *The Oxford Movement 1833–1845*, London 1892

Clark, G. Kitson, *Churchmen and the Condition of England 1832–1885. A study in the development of social ideas and practice from the Old Regime to the Modern State*, London 1973

Clark, J.C.D., *English Society 1688–1832. Ideology, social structure and political practice during the ancien regime*, Cambridge 1985

Clarke, C.P.S., *The Oxford Movement and After*, London 1932

Clarke, W.K. Lowther, *A History of the SPCK*, London 1959

Clements, Keith W., *Lovers of Discord. Twentieth-century theological controversies in England*, London 1988

Clifford, Paul Rowntree, *Venture in Faith: The Story of the West Ham Central Mission*, London 1950

Coad, F.R., *A History of the Brethren Movement*, London 1968

Cockshut, A.O.J. (ed), *Religious Controversies of the Nineteenth Century. Selected Documents*, London 1966

Commission on Evangelism, *Towards the Conversion of England*, London 1945

Connolly, G.P., ' "With more than ordinary devotion to God": the secular missioner of the North in the Evangelical age of the English mission', *NWCH*, 10, 1983, pp. 8–31

Connolly, G.P., 'The Transubstantiation of Myth: towards a New Popular History of Nineteenth-Century Catholicism in England', *JEH*, 35, 1, 1984, pp. 78–104

Connybeare, W.J., 'Church Parties', *The Edinburgh Review*, 98, 1853, pp. 273–343

Conversations between the Church of England and the Methodist Church. A Report, London 1963

Coombs, Joyce, *George and Mary Sumner. Their Life and Times*, London 1965

Cornish, *A History of the English Church in the Nineteenth Century*, 2 vols, London 1910

Cowherd, Raymond G., *The Politics of English Dissent. The Religious Aspects of Liberal and Humanitarian Reform Movements from 1815 to 1848*, New York 1956

Cox, Harvey, *The Secular City*, New York and London 1965

Cox, J., *The English Churches in a Secular Society: Lambeth, 1870–1930*, Oxford 1982

Cox, Jeff, *The British Missionary Movement 1700–1950*, London and New York (forthcoming)

Cragg, Kenneth, *The Call of the Minaret*, 2nd edn London 1985

Creighton, Louise, *Life and Letters of Mandell Creighton sometime Bishop of London*, London 1905

Crowther, M.A., *Church Embattled: Religious Controversy in Mid-Victorian England*, Newton Abbot 1970

Cumming, G.J. and Baker, D. (eds), *Popular Belief and Practice*, Oxford 1972

Cupitt, Don, *Radicals and the Future of the Church*, London 1989

Currie, R., 'The division and reunion of British Methodism 1791–1932, with special reference to social and organisational factors', Oxford D Phil. 1966

Currie, R., *Methodism Divided*, London 1968

Currie, R., Gilbert, A., and Horsley, L., *Churches and Churchgoers: Patterns of Church Growth in the British Isles Since 1700*, Oxford 1977

Dallimore, Arnold, *The Life of Edward Irving. The Forerunner of the Charismatic Movement*, Edinburgh 1983

Dark, Sidney, *Wilson Carlile. The Laughing Cavalier of Christ*, London 1944

Davie, Donald, *A Gathered Church. The Literature of the English Dissenting Interest, 1700–1930*, London 1978

Davies, Horton, *Worship and Theology in England: From Watts and Wesley to Maurice, 1690–1850*, Princeton 1961

Davies, Horton, *Worship and Theology in England: From Newman to Martineau, 1850–1900*, Oxford 1962

Davies, Horton, *Worship and Theology in England: The Ecumenical Century, 1900–1965*, Princeton 1965

Davies, Rupert (ed), *The Testing of the Churches 1932–1982. A Symposium*, London 1982

Davies, Rupert E., George, A. Raymond and Rupp, Gordon (eds), *A History of the Methodist Church in Great Britain*, 4 vols, London 1965–88

Dewey, Clive, *The Passing of Barchester. A real life version of Trollope*, London 1991

Dews, D.C. (ed), *From Mow Cop to Peake*, Wesley Historical Society, Yorkshire branch, Occasional Paper 4 , Leeds 1982

Dillistone, F.W., *Into All the World. A Biography of Max Warren*, London 1980

Dix, Gregory, *The Shape of the Liturgy*, London 1945

Doyle, P., 'The Education and Training of Roman Catholic Priests in Nineteenth-Century England', *JEH*, 35, 2, April 1984, pp. 208–19

Drysdale, A.H., *History of the Presbyterians in England. Their Rise, Decline and Revival*, London 1889

Dunn, J.D.G., *Baptism in the Holy Spirit*, London 1970

Dunn, Sydney Alexander, *First United Church of Jesus Christ (Apostolic): a Caring Christian Organisation*, West Bromwich 1986

Dyos, H.J. and Wolff, M. (eds), *The Victorian City*, Vol II, Leicester 1973

Edwards, David L. (ed), *The Honest to God Debate*, London 1963

Edwards, David L., *Leaders of the Church of England 1828–1978*, London 1978

Edwards, David L., *Tradition and Truth. The Challenge of England's Radical Theologians 1962–1989*, London 1989

Edwards, M.L., *After Wesley 1791–1851*, London 1935

Edwards, Maldwyn, *Methodism in England 1850–1932*, London 1943

Elliott-Binns, L.E., *The Evangelical Movement in the English Church*, London 1928

Elliott-Binns, L.E., *Religion in the Victorian Era*, London 1936

Elliott-Binns, L.E., *English Thought 1860–1900. The Theological Aspect*, London 1956

Ellis, Ieuan, '"Essays and Reviews" Reconsidered', *T*, 74, 614, August 1971, pp. 396–404

Ellis, Ieuan, 'Dean Farrar and the Quest for the Historical Jesus', *T*, 89, 728, March 1986, pp. 108–115

Ellsworth, L.E., *Charles Lowder and the Ritualist Movement*, London 1982

England, Edward, *The Spirit of Renewal*, Eastbourne 1982

Ensor, Robert, *England 1870–1914*, Oxford 1936

Evans, E.J., 'Some reasons for the growth of English rural anticlericalism, 1750–1830', *P&P*, 66, 1975, pp. 84–109

Evans, Eric J., *The Forging of the Modern State. Early Industrial Britain 1783–1870*, London 1983

Ewing, John W., *Goodly Fellowship: A Century Tribute to the Life and Work of the World's Evangelical Alliance 1846–1946*, London 1946

Faber, Geoffrey, *Oxford Apostles. A Character Study of the Oxford Movement*, Harmondsworth 1933

Field, C.D., 'The Social Structure of English Methodism, Eighteenth-Twentieth Centuries', *BJS*, 28, 1977, pp. 199–225

Flindall, R.P. (ed), *The Church of England 1815–1948. A Documentary History*, London 1972

Foster, J., *Class Struggle and the Industrial Revolution: Early Industrial Capitalism in Three English Towns*, London 1974

Fox, Adam, *Dean Inge*, London 1960

Froude, Richard Hurrell, *Remains of the late Rev Richard Hurrell Froude*, MA, 2 vols, ed John Henry Newman and John Keble, London 1838, 1839

Fullalove, B., 'The Ministry of Women in the Church of England (1919–1970)' Part II, *MC*, 29, 3, 1987, pp. 41–50

Furey, F.E., 'The Theology of Mission in the Writings of Max Warren', Louvain Lic. ST 1974

Gartrell-Mills, C.F., 'Christian Science: an American religion in Britain, 1895–1940', Oxford D Phil. 1991

Gay, John D., *The Geography of Religion in England*, London 1971

Gilbert, A.D., *Religion and Society in Industrial England: Church, Chapel and Social Change 1740–1914*, London 1976

Gilbert, Alan D., *The Making of Post-Christian Britain. A history of the secularization of modern society*, London and New York 1980

Gill, R., *The Myth of the Empty Church*, London 1993

Gill, Sean, *Women and the Church of England From the Eighteenth Century to the Present*, London 1994

Gilley, Sheridan, 'Papists, Protestants and the Irish in London, 1835–70', *SCH*, 8, 1972, pp. 259–66

Gilley, Sheridan, *Newman and his Age*, London 1990

Gillispie, Charles Coulston, *Genesis and Geology. A Study in the Relations of Scientific Thought, Natural Theology, and Social Opinion in Great Britain, 1790–1850*, New York 1959 *Reprinted 1986.*

Gilley, Sheridan & W J Sheils.
a History of Religion in Britain. Blackwell 1994
pp 2/54

Golby, J.M. (ed), *Culture and Society in Britain 1850–1890. A Source Book of Contemporary Writings*, Oxford 1986

Goldingay, John, 'James Barr on Fundamentalism', *Churchman*, October 1977

✓ Goodall, N., *The Ecumenical Movement*, 2nd edn Oxford 1964

Gordon, James M., *Evangelical Spirituality from the Wesleys to John Stott*, London 1991

✓ Gore, Charles (ed), *Lux Mundi. A Series of Studies in the Religion of the Incarnation*, London 1889

✓ Gowland, D.A., *Methodist Secessions. The Origins of Free Methodism in Three Lancashire Towns: Manchester, Rochdale, Liverpool*, Manchester 1979

Green, Roger Lancelyn and Hooper, Walter, *C.S.Lewis. A Biography*, Glasgow 1974

✓ Green, S.J.D., 'Religion and the Industrial Town, with special reference to the West Riding of Yorkshire c.1870–1920', Oxford D Phil. 1989 *Published*.

Grisewood, Harman (ed), *Ideas and Beliefs of the Victorians*, London 1949

Groves, C.P., *The Planting of Christianity in Africa*, 4 vols, London 1948–58

Grubb, Norman, *C.T. Studd. Cricketer and Pioneer*, London 1933

Gunstone, John, *Pentecostal Anglicans*, London 1982

Haakonssen, Knud (ed), *Enlightenment and Religious Rational Dissent in eighteenth-century Britain*, Cambridge 1996

Haigh, A., *The Victorian Clergy*, London 1984

Hampson, M.D., 'The British Response to the German Church Struggle 1933–39', Oxford D Phil. 1973

Hardman, B., 'The Evangelical Party in the Church of England, 1855–1865', Cambridge Ph.D 1964

Hardman, Keith J., *Charles Finney 1792–1875. Revivalist and Reformer*, New York 1987

Harford, John Battersby and Macdonald, Frederick Charles, *Handley Car Glyn Moule Bishop of Durham. A Biography*, London 1922

Harper, Michael, *A New Canterbury Tale*, Nottingham 1978

Harper, Michael, *Bishop's Move*, London 1979

Harrison, Brian, 'For Church, Queen and Family: The Girls' Friendly Society 1874–1920', *P&P*, 61, November 1973, pp. 107–38

Harrison, J.F.C., *The Second Coming: Popular Millenarianism 1780–1850*, London 1979

Harrison, P., '*Religion*' *and the Religions in the English Enlightenment*, Cambridge 1990

Harvey, G.L.H., *The Church and the Twentieth Century*, London 1936

✓ Hastings, Adrian, *A History of English Christianity 1920–1990*, London 1991

✓ Hastings, Adrian, *Robert Runcie*, London 1991

✓ Heasman, Kathleen, *Evangelicals in Action. An Appraisal of their Social Work in the Victorian Era*, London 1962

Hebert, Gabriel, *Fundamentalism and the Church of God*, London 1957

Heiman, M.E., 'English Catholic devotion 1850–1914', Oxford D Phil. 1992

Helmstadter, Richard J. and Lightman, Bernard (eds), *Victorian Faith in Crisis. Essays on Continuity and Change in Nineteenth-Century Religious Belief*, London 1990

Hempton, D.N., 'Bickersteth, Bishop of Ripon: The Episcopate of a Mid–Victorian Evangelical', *NH*, 17, 1981

Hempton, D., *Methodism and Politics in British Society 1750–1850*, London 1984

Hempton, David, *Religion and Political Culture in Britain and Ireland From the Glorious Revolution to the Decline of Empire*, Cambridge 1996

Hempton, David, *The Religion of the People. Methodism and popular religion c.1750–1900*, London and New York 1996

Hennell, M., *Sons of the Prophets: Evangelical Leaders of the Victorian Church*, London 1979

Henry, B., 'Women's Struggle for Professional Work and Status in the Church of England, 1900–1930', *HJ*, 26, 1983

Henson, Hensley, *Retrospect of an Unimportant Life 1869–1939*, 3 vols, Oxford 1942

Heyck, T.W., 'From Men of Letters to Intellectuals: The Transformation of Intellectual Life in Nineteenth-Century England', *JBS*, 20, August 1980

Heyck, T.W., *The Transformation of Intellectual Life in Victorian England*, London 1982

Hick, John (ed), *The Myth of God Incarnate*, London 1977

Hill, Michael, *A Sociology of Religion*, London 1973

Hilton, Boyd, *The Age of Atonement. The Influence of Evangelicalism on Social and Economic Thought 1785–1865*, Oxford 1988

Hobsbawm, E., *The Age of Revolution*, London 1962

Hocken, Peter, *Streams of Renewal. The Origins and Early Development of the Charismatic Movement in Great Britain*, Exeter 1986

Hodder, E., *The Life and Work of the Seventh Earl of Shaftesbury, KG*, 3 vols, London 1886

Hole, R., *Pulpits, Politics and Public Order in England, 1760–1832*, Cambridge 1989

Hollenweger, Walter J., *The Pentecostals*, London 1972

Hornsby-Smith, Michael, 'The Roman Catholic Church in Britian since the Second World War' in Badham, Paul (ed), *Religion, State, and Society in Modern Britain*.

Hornsby-Smith, M.P. and Lee, R.M., *Roman Catholic Opinion: A Study of Roman Catholics in England and Wales in the 1970s*, Guildford 1979

Horridge, G., 'The Salvation Army in England 1855–1900', London Ph.D 1989

Horridge, Glenn K., *The Salvation Army: Origin and Early Days 1865–1900*, Godalming 1993

Huxley, Thomas Henry, *Science and Christian Tradition*, London 1894

Hylson-Smith, Kenneth, *Evangelicals in the Church of England 1734–1984*, Edinburgh 1989

Hylson-Smith, Kenneth, *High Churchmanship in the Church of England From the Sixteenth Century to the Late Twentieth Century*, Edinburgh 1993

Hylson-Smith, Kenneth, *The Churches in England from Elizabeth I to Elizabeth II*, Vol I: *1558–1688*; Vol II: *1689–1833*; Vol III: *1833–1998*, London 1996, 1997, 1998

Inglis, K.S. 'Patterns of Religious Worship in 1851', *JEH*, 11, 1960, pp. 74–86

Inglis, K.S., *Churches and the Working Classes in Victorian England*, London 1963

Iremonger, F.A., *William Temple Archbishop of Canterbury. His Life and Letters*, London 1948

Isichei, Elizabeth, *Victorian Quakers*, Oxford 1970

Jaeger, Muriel, *Before Victoria. Changing standards and behaviour 1787–1837*, Harmondsworth 1967

Jagger, Peter, *A History of the Parish and People Movement*, London 1978

James, Eric, *A Life of Bishop John A.T. Robinson, Scholar, Pastor, Prophet*, London 1987

James, William, *The Varieties of Religious Experience*, 2 vols, London 1902

Jasper, Ronald C.D., *George Bell Bishop of Chichester*, London 1967

Jay, Elisabeth (ed), *The Evangelical and Oxford Movements*, Cambridge 1983

Jenkins, David and Jenkins, Rebecca, *Free to Believe*, London 1991

Johnson, Douglas, *Contending for the Faith: A History of the Evangelical Movement in the Universities and Colleges*, Leicester 1979

Jones, P. d'A., *The Christian Socialist Revival, 1877–1914. Religion, Class, and Social Conscience in Late-Victorian England*, Princeton 1968

Jones, Rufus M., *The Later Periods of Quakerism*, 2 vols, London 1921

Jones, R. Tudur, *Congregationalism in England 1662–1962*, London 1962

Joyce, P., *Work, Society and Politics*, Brighton 1980

Kent, John, *Jabez Bunting: The Last Wesleyan*, London 1955

Kent, John, *The Age of Disunity*, London 1966

Kent, J.H.S., 'The Role of Religion in the Cultural Structure of the Later Victorian City', *TRHS*, 5th series, 23, 1973, pp. 153–73

Kent, J., *Holding the Fort: Studies in Victorian Revivalism*, London 1978

Kent, John H.S., *The End of the Line. The Development of Christian Theology in the Last Two Centuries*, London 1982

Kent, John, *The Unacceptable Face. The Modern Church in the Eyes of the Historian*, London 1987

Ker, Ian, *John Henry Newman. A Biography*, Oxford 1988

King, John C., *The Evangelicals*, London 1969

Knight, Frances, *The Nineteenth-Century Church and English Society*, Cambridge 1995

Knox, Edmund Arbuthnott, *Reminiscences of an Octogenarian 1847–1934*, London 1934

Kraemer, Hendrik, *The Christian Message in a Non-Christian World*, London 1938

Lamb, C., 'The Call to Renewal: Kenneth Cragg's Vocation to Islam', Birmingham Ph.D 1987

Lampe, G.W.H., *God as Spirit*, Oxford 1977; reissued London 1983

Lancelot, J.B., *Francis James Chavasse Bishop of Liverpool*, London n.d.

Laqueur, T.W., *Religion and Respectability: Sunday Schools and English Working-Class Culture, 1780–1850*, Yale 1976

Lathbury, D.C. (selector and arranger), *Correspondence on Church and Religion of William Ewart Gladstone*, 2 vols, London 1910

Leaver, Robin, *A Hymn Book Survey 1962–80*, Nottingham 1980

Lax, W.H., *His Book: The Autobiography of Lax of Poplar*, London 1937

Leech, Kenneth and Williams, Rowan (eds), *Essays Catholic and Radical*, London 1983

Lewis, C.S., *Surprised by Joy. The shape of my early life*, London 1955

Lewis, Donald M., *Lighten Their Darkness: The Evangelical Mission to Working-Class London 1828–1860*, Westport 1986

Lewis, Donald M., '"Lights in dark places": women evangelists in early Victorian Britain, 1838–1857', *SCH*, 27, 1990, pp. 415–27

Liddon, H.P., *Life of Edward Bouverie Pusey*, edited and prepared for publication by Johnstone, J.O. and Newbolt, W.C.E., 4 vols, London 1893–97

Lightman, Bernard, *The Origins of Agnosticism. Victorian Unbelief and the Limits of Knowledge*, Baltimore and London 1987

Linberg, D.C. and Number, R.L. (eds), *God and Nature: Historical Essays on the Encounter between Christianity and Science*, Berkeley 1986

Livingstone, David N., *Darwin's Forgotten Defenders. The Encounter between Evangelical Theology and Evolutionary Thought*, Grand Rapids 1987

Lloyd, Roger, *The Church of England 1900–1965*, London 1966

Loane, Marcus, *John Charles Ryle 1816–1900*, London 1983

Lockhart, J.G., *Cosmo Gordon Lang*, London 1949

Longford, Elizabeth, *Victoria R.I.*, London 1964

Lucas, J.R., 'Wilberforce and Huxley: A Legendary Encounter', *HJ*, 22, 2, 1979, pp. 313–30

Luckmann, Thomas, *The Invisible Religion: the Transformation of Symbols in Industrial Society*, New York 1967

Luker, D.H., 'Cornish Methodism, Revivalism and Popular Belief c.1780–1870', Oxford D Phil. 1987

Luker, D., 'Revivalism in Theory and Practice: The Case of Cornish Methodism', *JEH*, 37, 1986, pp. 603–19

Machin, G.I.T., *Politics and the Churches in Great Britain 1832 to 1868*, Oxford 1977

Machin, G.I.T., *Politics and the Churches in Great Britain 1869–1921*, Oxford 1987

MacLaren, A.A., *Religion and Social Class: The Disruption Years in Aberdeen*, London 1974

Magnus, Philip, *Gladstone. A Biography*, London 1954

Malmgreen, Gail (ed), *Religion in the Lives of English Women, 1760–1930*, London and Sydney 1986

Manwaring, Randle, *From Controversy to Co-Existence. Evangelicals in the Church of England 1914–1980*, Cambridge 1985

Mann, H., *Census of Great Britain, 1851. Religious worship in England and Wales, abridged from the official report*, London 1854

Marrin, Albert, *The Last Crusade. The Church of England in the First World War*, Durham, North Carolina 1974

Marsden, J.B., *Memoirs of Hugh Stowell*, London 1868

Marsh, P.T., *The Victorian Church in Decline: Archbishop Tait and the Church of England 1869–1882*, London 1969

Marsh, Peter, *The Conscience of the Victorian State*, London 1979

Martin, David, 'The Denomination', *BJS*, XIII, 1962

Martin, David, *The Religious and the Secular*, London 1969

Martin, David, *A General Theory of Secularization*, Oxford 1978

Martin, D. and Mullen, P. (eds), *Strange Gifts? A Guide to Charismatic Renewal*, Oxford 1984

Marwick, Arthur, *British Society Since 1945*, Harmondsworth 1982

Mascall, E.L., *The Secularisation of Christianity. An Analysis and a Critique*, London 1965

Masterman, C.F.G., *The Condition of England*, London 1911

Mathew, David, *Catholicism in England. The Portrait of a Minority: its Culture and Tradition*, London 1955

Mayor, S., *The Churches and the Labour Movement*, London 1967

McClatchey, D., *Oxfordshire Clergy, 1777–1869*, Oxford 1960

McCord, Norman, *British History 1815–1906*, Oxford 1991

McLeod, Hugh, *Class and Religion in the Late Victorian City*, London 1974

McLeod, Hugh, *Religion and the Working Class in Nineteenth Century Britain*, London 1984

McLeod, Hugh (ed), *European Religion in the Age of Great Cities, 1830–1930*, London 1995

McLeod, Hugh, *Religion and Society in England, 1850–1914*, Basingstoke 1996

McLoughlin, William G., *Modern Revivalism*, New York 1955

Medlicott, W.N., *Contemporary England 1914–1964 with epilogue 1964–1974*, London 1976

Miller, Donald E., *The Case for Liberal Christianity*, London 1981

Mole, David E.M., 'The Victorian town parish: rural vision and urban mission', *SCH*, 16, 1979, pp. 361–71

Moore, R., *Pit-men, Preachers and Politics: The Effects of Methodism in a Durham Mining Community*, Cambridge 1974

Moorhouse, Geoffrey, *The Missionaries*, Newton Abbot 1974

Morgan, Dewi (ed), *They Became Anglicans*, London 1959

Morgan, E.R. (ed), *Essays Catholic and Missionary*, London 1928

Morgan, Robert (ed), *The Religion of the Incarnation. Anglican Essays in Commemoration of Lux Mundi*, Bristol 1989

Morris, Jeremy, *Religion and Urban Change. Croydon, 1840–1914*, Woodbridge 1992

Mowat, Charles Loch, *Britain Between the Wars 1918–1940*, London 1955

Mozley, John Kenneth, *Some Tendencies in British Theology from the publication of Lux Mundi to the present day*, London 1952

Mudie-Smith, R. (ed), *The Religious Life of London*, London 1904

Munson, J.E.B., 'The education of Baptist ministers, 1870–1900', *BQ*, 26, 1978, pp. 320–27

Munson, J.E.B., 'The Oxford Movement by the End of the Nineteenth Century: the Anglo-Catholic Clergy', *CH*, 44, 1975, pp. 382–95

Munson, James, *The Nonconformists. In search of a lost culture*, London 1991

Murdoch, N.H., *Origins of the Salvation Army*, Knoxville, Tennessee 1994

Murphy, H.R., 'The ethical revolt against Christian orthodoxy in early Victorian England', *AHR*, 40, 1955, pp. 800–17

Murray, Jocelyn, *Proclaim the Good News. A Short History of the Church Missionary Society*, London 1985

Neill, Stephen, *A History of Christian Missions*, Harmondsworth 1964

Neill, Stephen, *The Interpretation of the New Testament 1861–1961*, Oxford 1964 *Rev. T. Wrigt. 2ᵈ Eᵈ.*

Newbigin, Lesslie, *The Household of God*, London 1953

Newbigin, Lesslie, *The Other Side of 1984. Questions for the Churches*, Geneva 1984

Newbigin, Lesslie, *Foolishness to the Greeks*, London 1986

Newman, John Henry, *Apologia Pro Vita Sua*, London 1846; Everyman edition London 1912

Newsome, David, *The Parting of Friends. A Study of the Wilberforces and Henry Manning*, London 1966

Newsome, David, *The Convert Cardinals. John Henry Newman and Henry Edward Manning*, London 1993

Newton, John A., *Search for a Saint: Edward King*, London 1977

Nicholls, David, *Church and State in Britain Since 1820*, London 1967

Niebuhr, Richard H., *The Social Sources of Denominationalism*, New York 1929

Nock, A.D., *Conversion: The Old and New in Religion from Alexander the Great to Augustine of Hippo*, London 1933

Nockles, P.B., 'Continuity and Change in Anglican High Churchmanship in Britain 1792–1850', Oxford D Phil. 1982

Nockles, Peter B., *The Oxford Movement in Context. Anglican High Churchmanship 1760–1857*, Cambridge 1994

Noll, Mark A., Bebbington, David W. and Rawlyk, George A. (eds), *Evangelicalism. Comparative Studies of Popular Protestantism in North America, the British Isles, and Beyond 1700–1990*, Oxford 1994

Norman, E.R., *Anti-Catholicism in Victorian England*, London 1968

Norman, E.R., *Church and Society in England 1770–1970. A Historical Study*, Oxford 1976

Norman, E.R., *The English Catholic Church in the Nineteenth Century*, Oxford 1984

Norman, E.R., *The Victorian Christian Socialists*, Cambridge 1987

Nuttall, Geoffrey and Chadwick, Owen (eds), *From Uniformity to Unity 1662–1962*, London 1962

Obelkevich, J., *Religion and Rural Society: South Lindsey 1825–75*, Oxford 1976

Obelkevich, J., Roper, L. and Samuel, R. (eds), *Disciplines of Faith: Studies in Religion, Politics and Patriarchy*, London 1987

Oddie, William, *The Crockford's File. Gareth Bennett and the Death of the Anglican Mind*, London 1989

Ollard, S.L., *A Short History of the Oxford Movement*, London 1915

Orr, J. Edwin, *The Second Evangelical Awakening in Britain*, London 1949

Orr, J. Edwin, *The Light of the Nations: Progress and Achievement in the Nineteenth Century*, London 1965

Otto, Rudolf, *The Idea of the Holy*, Oxford 1950

O'Tuathaigh, M.A.G.O., 'The Irish in nineteenth-century Britain: problems of integration', *TRHS*, 5th series, 31, 1981, pp. 149–73.

Packer, J.I., *'Fundamentalism' and the Word of God*, London 1958

Packer, J.I., *Keep Yourselves from Idols*, London 1963

Packer, J.I. (ed), *All in Each Place: Towards Reunion in England: Ten Anglican Essays with some Free Church Comments*, London 1965

Packer, J.I. (ed), *Guidelines: Anglican Evangelicals Face the Future*, London 1967

Parsons, Gerald (ed), *Religion in Victorian Britain*, 4 vols. Vol I: *Traditions*,

Vol II: *Controversies*, Vol III: *Sources*, Vol IV: *Interpretations*, Manchester 1988

Parsons, Gerald, 'Reform, Revival and Realignment: The Experience of Victorian Anglicanism' in Parsons (ed), *Religion in Victorian Britain*, Vol I, Manchester 1988

Parsons, Gerald, 'From Dissenters to Free Churchmen: The Transition of Victorian Nonconformity' in Parsons (ed), *Religion in Victorian Britain*, Vol I, Manchester 1988

Parsons, Gerald, 'Introduction: From Centre to Periphery. Victorian Religious Controversies in Perspective' in Parsons (ed), *Religion in Victorian Britain*, Vol II, Manchester 1988

Pawley, Bernard C. (ed), *The Second Vatican Council: Studies by Eight Anglican Observers*, London 1967

Payne, E.A., *The Baptist Union: A Short History*, London 1958

Peart-Binns, John S., *Ambrose Reeves*, London 1973

Peart-Binns, John S., *Wand of London*, London 1987

Peart-Binns, John S., *Living with Paradox. John Habgood, Archbishop of York*, London 1987

Peart-Binns, John S., *Graham Leonard Bishop of London*, London 1988

Peel, A., *Three Hundred Years: A History of the Congregational Union of England and Wales*, London 1931

Pelling, Henry, *Popular Politics and Society in Late Victorian Britain*, London 1968

Penhale, Francis, *The Anglican Church Today: Catholics in Crisis*, London 1986

Phillips, Thomas, *The Welsh Revival. Its Origin and Development*, London 1860, Edinburgh 1989

Pickering, W.S.F., *Anglo-Catholicism*, London 1989

Polkinghorne, J., *One World. The Interaction of Science and Theology*, London 1986

Pollock, J.C., *A Cambridge Movement*, London 1953

Pollock, J.C., *The Cambridge Seven*, London 1955

Pollock, John, *Moody without Sankey*, London 1963

Pollock, John, *The Keswick Story: The Authorised History of the Keswick Convention*, London 1964

Pollock, John, *Billy Graham. The Authorised Biography*, London 1966

Pope, Liston, *Millhands and Preachers*, New Haven, Conn. 1942

Porter, Andrew, ' "Commerce and Christianity": the rise and fall of a nineteenth-century missionary slogan', *HJ*, 28, 3, 1985, pp. 597–621

Prestige, G.L., *The Life of Charles Gore. A Great Englishman*, London 1935

Pugh, D.R., 'The Church and Education: Anglican Attitudes 1902', *JEH*, 23, 3, July 1972, pp. 219–32

Purcell, William, *Fisher of Lambeth. A Portrait from Life*, London 1969

Quebedeaux, R.A., 'Charismatic Renewal: The Origins, Development and Significance of Neo-Pentecostalism as a Religious Movement in the United States and Great Britain, 1901–74', Oxford D Phil. 1975

Quinn, Dermot, *Patronage and Piety. The Politics of English Roman Catholicism, 1850–1900*, London 1993

Rack, H.D., 'Domestic Visitation: a Chapter in Early Nineteenth Century Evangelism', *JEH*, 24, 4, 1973, pp. 357–76

Ralls, W., 'The Papal Aggression of 1850: a study in Victorian anti-Catholicism', *CH*, 43, 1974, pp. 242–56

Ramm, A., 'Gladstone's religion', *HJ*, 28, 1985, pp. 327–40

Ramsey, Arthur Michael, *The Gospel and the Catholic Church*, London 1936

Ramsey, Arthur Michael, *From Gore to Temple. The Development of Anglican Theology between Lux Mundi and the Second World War, 1889–1939*, London 1960

Ramsey, Arthur Michael, *Image Old and New*, 1963

Reardon, B.M.G., *Liberal Protestantism*, London 1968

Reardon, Bernard M.G.(ed), *Roman Catholic Modernism*, London 1970

Reardon, Bernard M.G., *From Coleridge to Gore. A Century of Religious Thought in Britain*, London 1971

Reckitt, Maurice B., *Maurice to Temple. A Century of the Social Movement in the Church of England*, London 1947

Rees, Jean, *His Name was Tom: The Biography of Tom Rees*, London 1971

Reynolds, M., *Martyr of Ritualism: Father Mackonochie of St Alban's, Holborn*, London 1965

Robbins, Keith, 'Religion and Identity in Modern British History', *SCH*, 18, 1982, pp. 465–87

Robbins, Keith, *The Eclipse of a Great Power. Modern Britain 1870–1992*, 2nd edn London 1994

Roberts, M.J.D., 'The Role of the Laity in the Church of England c.1850–1885', Oxford D Phil. 1974

Roberts, M.J.D., 'Private patronage and the Church of England 1800–1900', *JEH*, 32, 2,1981, pp. 199–223

Roberts, M.J.D., 'Pressure-Group Politics and the Church of England: the Church Defence Institution 1859–1896', *JEH*, 35, 4, October 1984, pp. 560–82

Robinson, John A.T., *Honest to God*, London 1963

Robinson, John A.T., *The Human Face of God*, London 1973

Robson, Geoffrey, 'Between town and countryside: contrasting patterns of churchgoing in the early Victorian Black Country', *SCH*, 16, 1979, pp. 401–14

Rogers, Alan, 'When City speaks to Country: the emergence of the town as a focus for religious activity in the nineteenth century', *SCH*, 16, 1979, pp. 335–59

Rogerson, J., *Old Testament Criticism in the Nineteenth Century: England and Germany*, London 1984

Rosell, Garth M. and Dupuis, Richard A.G. (eds), *The Memoirs of Charles G. Finney. The Complete Restored Text*, Grand Rapids 1989

Rosman, D., *Evangelicals and Culture*, London 1984

Rouse, R., and Neill, S. (eds), *A History of the Ecumenical Movement, 1517–1948*, 2nd edn London 1967

Rowdon, Harold H., *The Origins of the Brethren*, London 1967

Rowell, G., *Hell and the Victorians: A Study of the Nineteenth-Century Theological Controversies Concerning Eternal Punishment and the Future Life*, Oxford 1974

Rowell, G., *The Vision Glorious: Themes and Personalities of the Catholic Revival in Anglicanism*, Oxford 1983

Rowell, Geoffrey (ed), *Tradition Renewed. The Oxford Movement Conference Papers*, London 1986

Rowlands, John Henry Lewis, *Church, State and Society. The Attitudes of John Keble, Richard Hurrell Froude and John Henry Newman 1827–1845*, Worthing 1989

Rowley, H.H., *The Old Testament and Modern Study*, Oxford 1951

Royle, E., *Radical Politics, 1790–1900: Religion and Unbelief*, London 1971

Royle, E., *Victorian Infidels: The Origins of the British Secularist Movement, 1791–1866*, Manchester 1974

Royle, E., *Radicals, Secularists, and Republicans: Popular Freethought in Britain, 1866–1915*, Manchester 1980

Royle, Edward, *Modern Britain. A Social History 1750–1985*, London 1987

Ruse, Michael, 'The Relationship between Science and Religion in Britain, 1830–1870', *CH*, 44, 1975, pp. 505–22

Russell, George W.E., *Edward King, sixtieth bishop of Lincoln*, London 1912

Rycroft, P., 'Church, Chapel, and Community in Craven, 1764–1851', Oxford D Phil. 1988

Sack, James J., *From Jacobite to Conservative. Reaction and Orthodoxy in Britain c.1760–1832*, Cambridge 1993

Sanderson, Michael, 'Literacy and social mobility in the Industrial Revolution in England', *P&P*, 56, August 1972, pp. 75–104

Sanderson, Michael and Laqueur, Thomas W., 'Debate. Literacy and social mobility in the Industrial Revolution in England', *P&P*, 64, August 1974, pp. 96–112

Sandhurst, B.G., *How Heathen is Britain?*, London 1946

Saward, Michael, *The Anglican Church Today: Evangelicals on the Move*, London 1987

Sellers, I., *Nineteenth Century Nonconformity*, London 1977

Selwyn, Edward Gordon (ed), *Essays Catholic and Critical By Members of The Anglican Communion*, London 1926

Shiels, W.J. (ed), *The Church and Healing*, Oxford 1982

Shiels, W.J. and Woods, D. (eds), *Voluntary Religion*, Oxford 1986

Simes, D.G.S., 'The Ultra Tories in British Politics 1824–1834', Oxford D Phil. 1975

Skeats, H.S. and Miall, C.S., *History of the Free Churches of England 1688–1891*, London 1891

Smith, M.A., 'Religion in Industrial Society: The Case of Oldham and Saddleworth 1780–1865', Oxford D Phil. 1987

Smith, M.A., *Religion in Industrial Society: Oldham and Saddleworth 1740–1865*, Oxford 1994

Smyth, Charles, *Cyril Forster Garbett Archbishop of York*, London 1959

Snead-Cox, J.G., *Life of Herbert Vaughan*, 2 vols, London 1910

Snell, K.D.M., *Church and Chapel in the North Midlands: Religious Observance in the Nineteenth Century*, Leicester 1991 STOKE

Soloway, Richard Allen, *Prelates and People. Ecclesiastical Social Thought in England 1783–1852*, London 1969

Spinks, G. Stephens, *Religion in Britain since 1900*, London 1952

Stanley, Arthur Penrhyn, *Life and Correspondence of Thomas Arnold*, London 1844

Stanley, Brian, *The Bible and the Flag. Protestant missions and British imperialism in the nineteenth and twentieth centuries*, Leicester 1990

Stanley, Brian, *The History of the Baptist Missionary Society 1792–1992*, Edinburgh 1992

Stephens, W.R.W., *The Life and Letters of Walter Farquhar Hook*, London 1881

Stephenson, Alan M.G., *Anglicanism and the Lambeth Conferences*, London 1978

Stephenson, Alan M.G., *The Rise and Decline of English Modernism*, London 1984

Stevenson, John, *British Society 1914–45*, Harmondsworth 1984

Stiles, Andrina, *Religion, Society and Reform 1800–1914*, London 1995

Stock, Eugene, *The History of the Church Missionary Society*, 4 vols, London 1899–1916

Stone, Lawrence, 'Literacy and Education in England 1640–1900', *P&P*, 42, February 1969, pp. 69–139

Stott, John R.W., *Christian Mission in the Modern World*, London 1975

Stott, John R.W., *Issues Facing Christians Today*, Basingstoke 1984

Streeter, B.H. (ed), *Foundations. A Statement of Christian Belief in Terms of Modern Thought: by Seven Oxford Men*, London 1912

Sumner, George Henry, *Life of Charles Richard Sumner*, London 1876

Supple, J.F., 'Ultramontanism in Yorkshire, 1850–1900', *RH*, 17, 1985, pp. 274–86

Supple, J., 'The Catholic Clergy of Yorkshire, 1850–1900: a Profile', *NH*, 21, 1985, pp. 212–35

Swift, Roger, 'Anti-Catholicism and Irish disturbances: public order in mid-Victorian Wolverhampton', *MH*, 9, 1984, pp. 87–108

Swift, Roland C., *Lively People. Methodism in Nottingham 1740–1979*, Nottingham 1982

Symondson, Anthony, *The Victorian Crisis of Faith*, London 1970

Tatlow, Tissington, *The Story of the Student Christian Movement of Great Britain and Ireland*, London 1933

Tawney, R.H., *Religion and the Rise of Capitalism* (1926), London 1944

Taylor, A.J.P., *English History 1914–1945*, Oxford 1965

Thompson, D.M. (ed), *Nonconformity in the Nineteenth Century*, London 1972

Thompson, David M., 'Church extension in town and countryside in later nineteenth-century Leicestershire', *SCH*, 16, 1979, pp. 427–40

Thompson, David M., 'The Emergence of the Nonconformist Social Gospel in England', *SCH*, Subsidia 7, 1990, pp. 255–80

Thompson, E.P., *The Making of the English Working Class*, Harmondsworth 1968

Thompson, H.P., *Into All Lands. The History of the Society for the Propagation of the Gospel in Foreign Parts 1701–1950*, London 1951

Thompson, K.A., *Bureaucracy and Church Reform: The Organizational Response of the Church of England to Social Change, 1800–1965*, Oxford 1970

Thompson, Phyllis, *An Unquenchable Flame: The Story of Cpt Allen Gardiner*, London 1983

Thomson, David, *England in the Nineteenth Century (1815–1914)*, Harmondsworth 1950

Toon, Peter, *J.C. Ryle: A Self Portrait*, Swengel, PA 1975

Toon, Peter, *Evangelical Theology 1833–1856. A Response to Tractarianism*, London 1979

Toon, Peter and Smout, Michael, *John Charles Ryle, Evangelical Bishop*, Cambridge 1976

Troeltsch, E., *The Social Teaching of the Christian Churches* (1912) ET (2 vols) London 1931

Tulloch, John, *Movements of Religious Thought in Britain during the nineteenth century*, Leicester 1971

Turner, Frank M., 'Rainfall, Plagues, and the Prince of Wales: A Chapter in the Conflict of Religion and Science', *JBS*, 13, 2, May 1974, pp. 46–65

Turner, F.M., 'The Victorian Conflict Between Science and Religion: A

Professional Dimension', *Isis*, 69, 1978, pp. 356–76

Turner, Frank M., *Contesting Cultural Authority. Essays in Victorian Intellectual Life*, Cambridge 1993

Turner, J.M., *Conflict and Reconciliation: Studies in Methodism and Ecumenism in England 1740–1982*, London 1985

Underwood, A.C., *A History of the English Baptists*, London 1947

Urquhart, Colin, *When the Spirit Comes*, London 1974

Vidler, A.R. (ed.), *Soundings. Essays concerning Christian Understanding*, Cambridge 1962

Vidler, Alec R., *The Church in an Age of Revolution: 1789 to the Present Day*, Harmondsworth 1961

Walker, Andrew, *Restoring the Kingdom*, 2nd revd edn London 1989

Walker, Peter, *The Anglican Church Today: Rediscovering the Middle Way*, London 1988

Walker, R.B., 'Religious Changes in Cheshire, 1750–1850', *JEH*, 17, 1966, pp. 77–94

Wand, J.W.C., *Recovery Starts Within: The Book of the Mission to London 1949*, London 1949

Wand, William, *Changeful Page*, London 1965

Ward, W., *The Life and Times of Cardinal Wiseman*, 2 vols, London 1897

Ward, W.R., *Religion and Society in England 1780–1850*, London 1972

Ward, W.R.(ed), *The Early Correspondence of Jabez Bunting, 1820–29*, London 1972

Ward, W.R., *Early Victorian Methodism: The Correspondence of Jabez Bunting 1830–1858*, London 1976

Ward, W.R., *Faith and Faction*, London 1993

Warren, M.A.C., *Social History and Christian Mission*, London 1967

Warren, Max, *Crowded Canvas. Some experiences of a life-time*, London 1974

Waterman, A.M.C., *Revolution, Economics and Religion. Christian Political Economy 1798–1833*, Cambridge 1991

Watkins, E.I., *Roman Catholicism in England from the Reformation to 1950*, London 1957

Watson, David, *One in the Spirit*, London 1973

Watson, David, *The Charismatic Movement in the Church of England*, London 1981

Watts, Michael R., *The Dissenters. Vol I: From the Reformation to the French Revolution*, Oxford 1978

Watts, Michael R., *The Dissenters. Vol II: The Expansion of Evangelical Nonconformity*, Oxford 1995

Wearmouth, Robert F., *Methodism and the Working-Class Movements of*

England 1800–1850, London 1937

Weber, Max, *The Protestant Ethic and the Spirit of Capitalism* (1904–5), ET London 1930

Weber, Max, *General Economic History*, New York 1963

Weber, Max, *The Sociology of Religion*, London 1965

. Welsby, Paul A., *A History of the Church of England 1945–1980*, Oxford 1984

Whale, John, *The Anglican Church Today: The Future of Anglicanism*, London 1988

Whitlow, Maurice, *J. Taylor Smith Everybody's Bishop*, London 1938

Wickham, E.R., *Church and People in an Industrial City*, London 1957

Wiles, Maurice, *The Remaking of Christian Doctrine*, London 1974

Wilkinson, Alan, *The Church of England and the First World War*, London 1978; reissued London 1996

Wilkinson, Alan, *Dissent or Conform? War, Peace and the English Churches 1900–1945*, London 1986

Willey, Basil, *More Nineteenth Century Studies. A Group of Honest Doubters*, London 1956

Williams, C.P., 'The Recruitment and Training of Overseas Missionaries in England between 1850 and 1900', Bristol M Litt. 1976

Williams, N.P. and Harris, Charles (eds), *Northern Catholicism. Centenary Studies in the Oxford and Parallel Movements*, London 1933

Williams, S.C., 'Religious Belief and Popular Culture: A Study of the South London Borough of Southwark (*c*.1880–1939)', Oxford D Phil. 1993

Wilson, Bryan R., *Religion in Secular Society. A Sociological Comment*, Harmondsworth 1969

Wilson, Bryan R., *Contemporary Transformations of Religion*, Oxford 1976

Wilson, George Herbert, *The History of the Universities' Mission to Central Africa*, London 1936

Wolffe, John, *The Protestant Crusade in Great Britain 1829–1860*, Oxford 1991

Wolffe, John, *God and Greater Britain. Religion and National Life in Britain and Ireland 1843–1945*, London and New York 1994

Wolffe, John (ed), *Evangelical Faith and Public Zeal. Evangelicals and Society in Britain 1780–1980*, London 1995

Woodward, Llewellyn, *The Age of Reform 1815–1870*, Oxford 1962

Worrall, B.G., *The Making of the Modern Church. Christianity in England since 1800*, London 1988

Yates, Nigel, 'Urban church attendance and the use of statistical evidence, 1850–1900', *SCH*, 16, 1979, pp. 389–99

Yates, T.E., *Venn and the Victorian Bishops Abroad*, London 1978

Yates, Timothy, *Christian Mission in the Twentieth Century*, Cambridge 1994

Yeo, S., *Religion and Voluntary Organisations in Crisis*, London 1976

Yeo, S., 'A New Life: The Religion of Socialism in Britain, 1883–1896', *HWJ*, 4, 1977, pp. 5–56

Yeo, S., 'Christianity in Chartist Struggle 1838–1842', *P&P*, 91, 1981, pp 109–39

Yinger, Milton J., *Religion, Society and the Individual*, New York 1957

Young, G.M., *Portrait of an Age*, Oxford 1936

Davie, Grace. Religion in Britain since 1945.

Jordan E.K.H. Free Church unity.

Grant, JW Free Churchmanship in England.

Holmes D. More Roman than Rome

Thomas T. the British — their Religions
Beliefs & Practices
1800–1986

Davies Rupert. the Church of England Observed.

Martin, David Associated of English Religion.

Davies, Rupert. the Church in our Times.

Jenkins, Daniel. the British — their Identity
and their Religion.

Paz D.G (Ed) Nineteenth Century English
Religious Traditions. 1995 USA

Turner JW Modern Methodism in England
1932 – 1998.

Brown, Callum The Death of Christian
Britain (2001)

Notes

In general, works will be referred to only by author's surname and shortened title. Publication details will be found in the Bibliography.

Introduction

1. Chadwick, *The Victorian Church*.
2. Parsons (ed), *Religion in Victorian Britain*.
3. Hastings, *A History of English Christianity*.
4. The period is covered by Worrall, *The Making of the Modern Church*, but that work concentrates on certain selected themes, and much work has been undertaken since its publication in 1988 which has greatly illuminated the history of the churches from 1833–1998.
5. Hylson-Smith, *The Churches in England from Elizabeth I to Elizabeth II*, 3 vols.
6. See Hylson-Smith, *The Churches in England*, Vol I , and Watts, *The Dissenters*, Vol I.

1. The Churches in England 1833 to 1901: An Overview

1. For the general history of the churches in the period 1833 to 1901, see especially Chadwick, *The Victorian Church*, Parsons (ed), *Religion in Victorian Britain* and Worrall, *The Making of the Modern Church*.
2. Cox, *The English Churches*, p. 5.
3. Parsons (ed), *Religion in Victorian Britain*, Vol I, p.5.
4. Hempton, *Religion and Political Culture*, p. 141.
5. For specific comments see Davies, *Worship and Theology in England: From Newman to Martineau* and Inglis, 'Patterns of Religious Worship in 1851'.
6. See Parsons, 'Introduction' in Parsons (ed), *Religion in Victorian Britain*, Vol I, p.7.
7. Cox, *The English Churches*, p. 94.
8. Chadwick, *The Victorian Church*, Vol I, p.6.
9. What follows owes much to Norman, *The English Catholic Church in the Nineteenth Century*.

10. Ultramontanism is a word widely used to denote a tendency in some sections of the Roman Catholic Church to favour the centralization of authority in the papal Curia rather than in the country concerned, or more locally the diocese.

11. See Wolffe, *The Protestant Crusade*.

12. Altholz, 'The Warfare of Conscience with Theology', p. 150.

13. McLeod, *Religion and Society*, p.1.

14. Ibid., p.3. Such an interpretation is also expounded by Gilbert, *Religion and Society*, Currie, *Methodism Divided*, and Kent, *Holding the Fort*.

15. See Cox, *The English Churches*; Callum G. Brown, 'Did Urbanization Secularize Britain?', *Urban History Yearbook*, Leicester 1988, pp. 1–14; and also Yeo, *Religion and Voluntary Organisations in Crisis*.

16. Rycroft, P., 'Church, Chapel, and Community in Craven, 1764–1851'.

17. Walker, 'Religious Changes in Cheshire, 1750–1850', p. 93.

18. Ibid., p. 94.

19. Smith, *Religion in Industrial Society*, pp. 270, 271.

20. Chadwick, 'Church and People in Bradford and District, 1880–1940'.

21. Ibid., pp. 341, 342.

22. Green, 'Religion and the Industrial Town'.

23. Ibid., p. 423.

24. Ibid., p. 423.

25. Ibid., p. 424.

26. Thompson, 'Church extension in town and countryside', p. 440.

27. I make mention at this stage of Kent, 'The Role of Religion in the Cultural Structure of the Later Victorian City'; Robson, 'Between town and countryside'; and Rogers, 'When City speaks to Country'; and of relevance Stone, 'Literacy and Education in England 1640–1900', with two further articles he stimulated, Sanderson, 'Literacy and social mobility in the Industrial Revolution in England', and Sanderson and Laqueur, 'Debate. Literacy and social mobility in the Industrial Revolution in England'.

28. See, for example, the cautionary remarks of Yates, 'Urban church attendance and the use of statistical evidence, 1850–1900'.

29. See Hylson-Smith, *The Churches in England*, Vol II.

30. Royle, *Modern Britain*, pp. 113, 114.

31. See, for example Rycroft, 'Church, Chapel and Community in Craven, 1764–1851' and Smith, *Religion in Industrial Society*.

32. Golby (ed), *Culture and Society in Britain 1850–1890*, p. 40.

33. Morris, *Religion and Urban Change*, p. 12.

34. Parsons, 'Emotion and Piety: Revivalism and Ritualism in Victorian Christianity' in Parsons (ed), *Religion in Victorian Britain*, Vol I, p. 219. For Moody and Sankey see especially Pollock, *Moody without Sankey*.

35. See Rogers, 'When City speaks to Country'.

36. For the early years of the Salvation Army see Horridge,*The Salvation Army*, and for the Church Army see Dark, *Wilson Carlile*.

37. Altholz, 'The Warfare of Conscience with Theology', p. 150.

38. In *The Condition of England* (1909), pp.14, 268. Quoted by Hastings, *A History of English Christianity*, p. 41.

39. Hempton, *Religion and Political Culture*, p. 142.

40. Cox, *The English Churches*, p. 92.

41. James, *Varieties of Religious Experience*, Vol II, p. 39.

42. Williams, 'Religious Belief and Popular Culture', pp. 295, 296. This is a work to which the present section is greatly indebted.

43. Ibid., p. 297.

44. Ibid., pp. 301, 302.

45. Ibid., p. 305.

46. Important works on the 'crisis of faith' include Budd, *Varieties of Unbelief*; Heyck, *The Transformation of Intellectual Life in Victorian England*; Lightman, *The Origins of Agnosticism*; Lucas, 'Wilberforce and Huxley'; Murphy, 'The ethical revolt against Christian orthodoxy in early Victorian England'; Royle, *Radical Politics*, *Victorian Infidels* and *Radicals, Secularists, and Republicans*; Tulloch, *Movements of Religious Thought*; Turner, 'Rainfall, Plagues, and the Prince of Wales' and 'The Victorian Conflict between Science and Religion'.

47. In this description and comment on science and religion the present work owes much to Gillispie, *Genesis and Geology*; Livingstone, *Darwin's Forgotten Defenders* and Worrall, *The Making of the Modern Church*.

48. Gillispie, *Genesis and Geology*, p. 121.

49. Ibid., p. 149.

50. Heyck, 'From Men of Letters to Intellectuals', p. 162. See also Canon, 'Scientists and Broad Churchmen'.

51. Quoted in Worrall, *The Making of the Modern Church*, pp. 74, 75, and in Chadwick, *The Victorian Church*, Vol II, p. 11. This present section is indebted to Worrall.

52. Wilberforce, S., *The Quarterly Review*, Vol cviii, pp. 255–64.

53. Lucas, 'Wilberforce and Huxley', p. 318.

54. For an investigation of the encounter between evangelicals and evolutionists see Livingstone, *Darwin's Forgotten Defenders*.

55. Sydney Eisen, 'Introduction' in Helmstadter and Lightman (eds), *Victorian Faith in Crisis*, p.1.

56. Ruse, 'The Relationship between Science and Religion in Britain, 1830–1870', p. 522.

57. Ibid., p.1.

58. Ibid., p.2.

59. James R. Moore, 'Theodicy and Society: The Crisis of the Intelligentsia' in Helmstadter and Lightman (eds), *Victorian Faith in Crisis*, p. 153.

60. Turner, 'Rainfall, Plagues, and the Prince of Wales', p. 65.
61. W.R. Ward, 'Faith and Fallacy: English and German Perspectives in the Nineteenth Century' in Helmstadter and Lightman (eds), *Victorian Faith in Crisis*, p. 39.
62. Willey, *More Nineteenth Century Studies*, p. 82.
63. Ibid., p. 81.
64. Altholz, 'The Warfare of Conscience with Theology', p. 157.
65. Rowell, *Hell and the Victorians*, pp. 79, 80. This is a book to which the present section owes much.
66. Ibid., p. 63.
67. Ibid., p. 83.
68. Altholz, 'The Warfare of Conscience with Theology', pp. 151, 152.
69. Ibid., pp. 150–69.
70. Reardon, *From Coleridge to Gore*, p. 60.
71. Ibid., p. 65.
72. Elliott-Binns, *English Thought 1860–1900*, p.7.
73. Ibid., pp.7, 8.
74. These comments are based on Tulloch, *Movements of Religious Thought*, pp. 205, 206.
75. See Harrison, *'Religion' and the Religions in the English Enlightenment*.
76. Altholz, 'The Mind of Victorian Orthodoxy', p. 28.
77. Worrall, *The Making of the Modern Church*, p. 102.
78. Altholz, 'The Mind of Victorian Orthodoxy', p. 29.
79. Ibid., pp. 39, 40.
80. Ibid. for an elaboration of this theme.
81. Ellis, '"Essays and Reviews" Reconsidered', p. 404.
82. Shaftesbury, MS Diary 12 May 1866.
83. A good account of 'liberalism', and one to which this present section is indebted, is to be found in Worrall, *The Making of the Modern Church*, pp. 115–33.
84. Ellis, 'Dean Farrar and the Quest for the Historical Jesus', p. 109.
85. Ibid., p. 111.
86. This is explored by Clark, for example in *Churchmen and the Condition of England 1832–1885*.
87. See Cox, *The English Churches*.
88. See Williams, 'Religious Belief and Popular Culture'; and also Callum G. Brown, 'The Mechanism of Religious Growth in Urban Societies' in McLeod (ed), *European Religion in the Age of Great Cities*, pp. 239–62, and Smith, *Religion in Industrial Society*.
89. See Joyce, *Work, Society and Politics*.
90. See Moore, *Pit-men, Preachers and Politics*.
91. Mudie-Smith (ed), *The Religious Life of London*, p. 13.
92. Bebbington, 'The city, the countryside and the social gospel in late

Victorian Nonconformity', p. 418.

93. Gill, *Women and the Church of England*, p. 76.

94. Anderson, 'Women preachers in mid-Victorian Britain', p. 484.

95. This account and analysis of Christian Socialism owes much to the standard works on the subject, Christensen, *Origins and History of Christian Socialism 1848–54* and Jones, *The Christian Socialist Revival, 1877–1914*; but see also Christensen, 'F.D. Maurice and the Contemporary Religious World'.

96. Christensen, *Origins and History of Christian Socialism 1848–54*, p. 24.

97. Ibid., p. 25.

98. F.R. Lamennais (1782–1854) was a French religious and political author who came to deny the whole supernatural order, and with this to reject the doctrinal beliefs of Catholicism and to adopt a vague pantheism. He was one of the greatest inspirers of new nineteenth-century political and social ideas and a forerunner of Modernism.

99. Christensen, p. 49.

100. *Autobiography*, ch. XVII, quoted in Christensen, *Origins and History of Christian Socialism 1848–54*, p. 58.

101. Ibid., p. 220.

102. Jones, *The Christian Socialist Revival, 1877–1914*, p.7.

103. This section owes much to the works of Royle, and especially *Radical Politics*

104. Ibid., p. 53.

105. Lightman, *The Origins of Agnosticism*, p. 121.

106. Huxley, *Science and Christian Tradition*, p. 268.

107. Budd, 'The Loss of Faith', p. 125.

108. Ibid., p. 125. See also Murphy, 'The ethical revolt against Christian orthodoxy in early Victorian England' for comments on the moral causes of the loss of faith of a few literary figures.

2. *The Church of England 1833 to 1901*

1. Evans, *The Forging of the Modern State*, p. 237. This is a book to which the present chapter is indebted.

2. The holding of more than one living at the same time.

3. Not being resident in the living for which the clergyman concerned is responsible.

4. The Test Act of 1673 required all holders of crown offices to receive the eucharist according to the usage of the Church of England, to take the Oaths of Supremacy and Allegiance to the sovereign, and to make a declaration against transubstantiation. The Corporation Act of 1661 required all members of municipal corporations to take an oath abjuring any rebellion against the sovereign, to declare the Solemn League and

Covenant null and unlawful, and to affirm that they had received communion according to the rites of the Church of England within the year preceeding their election.

5. The Swing Riots, named after a certain Captain Swing, took place in 1830 and 1831 as a protest against especially rural poverty arising out of economic developments and the imposition of rates etc.

6. Machin, *Politics and the Churches in Great Britain 1832 to 1868*, p. 28.

7. Ibid., p. 25.

8. Quoted in Chadwick, *The Victorian Church*, Vol I, p. 47.

9. Knight, *The Nineteenth-Century Church*, p.1.

10. Parsons, 'Reform, Revival and Realignment', p. 16.

11. Marsh, *The Victorian Church in Decline*, p.1.

12. Chadwick, *The Victorian Church*, Vol I, p.126.

13. Evans, *The Forging of the Modern State*, p. 241.

14. The comments and figures quoted in this paragraph are based on Evans, *The Forging of the Modern State*, pp. 241, 242.

15. Burns, 'The Diocesan Revival in the Church of England c.1825–1865', p. 4.

16. Chadwick, *The Victorian Church*, Vol I, p. 133.

17. Parsons, 'Reform, Revival and Realignment', p. 22.

18. Chadwick, *The Victorian Church*, Vol I, pp. 501, 502.

19. Elliott-Binns, *Religion in the Victorian Era*, p. 67. For a full account of his life see Sumner, *Life of Charles Richard Sumner*.

20. For his life and work see Balleine, *A History of the Evangelical Party in the Church of England*, and E.Roy Moore, 'John Bird Sumner, Bishop of Chester', Manchester MA thesis 1976.

21. Sumner, *Life of Charles Richard Sumner*, p. 135.

22. For a full account of the life of Ryle see Loane, *John Charles Ryle 1816–1900*; Toon, *J.C. Ryle*, and Toon and Smout, *John Charles Ryle*.

23. Loane, *John Charles Ryle 1816–1900*, p. 86.

24. Rowell, *The Vision Glorious*, p. 141. This book is the basis for the present short consideration of Bishop King.

25. Newton, *Search for a Saint*, p. 145.

26. Russell, *Edward King*, p. 149.

27. Rowell, *The Vision Glorious*, p. 151.

28. Bell, *Randall Davidson*, Vol I, p. 157.

29. Parsons, 'Reform, Revival and Realignment', p. 24.

30. Burns, 'The Diocesan Revival in the Church of England c.1825–1865', p.3; and for the figures on archdeacons cited in the previous paragraph, see Burns, p. 115.

31. Knight, *The Nineteenth-Century Church*, p. 180.

32. Chadwick, *The Victorian Church*, Vol I, p. 127.

33. Quoted in Parsons, 'Reform, Revival and Realignment', p. 24.

34. Haig, *The Victorian Clergy*, pp. 2,3.
35. See ibid., p. 27.
36. Ibid., pp. 48,49.
37. R. O'Day, 'The Men fom the Ministry' in Parsons (ed), *Religion in Victorian Britain*, Vol II, p. 264.
38. Ibid., p. 265.
39. Mole, 'The Victorian town parish: rural vision and urban mission', p. 370.
40. J.C. Miller, *The Church of the People*, London 1855, p. 14, quoted in ibid., p. 370.
41. Ibid., pp. 370, 371.
42. Roberts, 'The Role of the Laity in the Church of England c.1850–1885', p.i.
43. Parsons, 'Reform, Revival and Realignment', p. 27. This present account of the life and ministry of Hook is indebted to this article, but see also Stephens, *The Life and Letters of Walter Farquhar Hook*.
44. E.Humphries and E.C.Willoughby, *At Cheltenham Spa*, London 1928, p. 198.
45. Balleine, *A History of the Evangelical Party in the Church of England*, p. 162.
46. Leading article, *The Times*, 19 December 1882.
47. Balleine, *A History of the Evangelical Party in the Church of England*, p. 159.
48. Stock, *The History of the Church Missionary Society*, Vol I, p. 374.
49. Braithwaite, *The Life and Letters of Rev. William Pennefather*, p. 305.
50. See Laqueur, *Religion and Respectability*; Sanderson, 'Literacy and social mobility in the Industrial Revolution in England'; and Sanderson and Laqueur, 'Debate. Literacy and social mobility in the Industrial Revolution in England'.
51. Laqueur, *Religion and Respectablity*, p.186.
52. Ibid., p. 245.
53. Rack, 'Domestic Visitation', p. 357.
54. Ibid., p. 357.
55. Smith, *Religion in Industrial Society*, p. 272. This is a book to which the present comments are indebted.
56. Snell, *Church and Chapel in the North Midlands*.
57. Cox, *The English Churches*.
58. Lewis, *Lighten Their Darkness*.
59. McLeod, *Class and Religion, Religion and the Working Class* and *Religion and Society*.
60. Smith, *Religion in Industrial Society*, p. 274.
61. For these comments see Gay, *The Geography of Religion in England*, pp. 77, 78.

62. Dewey, *The Passing of Barchester*, p.2.
63. McLeod, *Religion and Society*, pp. 13, 14.
64. Knight, *The Nineteenth-Century Church*, p. 32.
65. Occasional offices are those services in the Book of Common Prayer which are for special occasions such as Baptism, Confirmation and Matrimony, as distinct from the regular and constant services of Mattins, Evensong and Holy Communion.
66. The churching of women is a form of thanksgiving by women for the birth of a child which was quite common in the nineteenth century.
67. McLeod, *Religion and Society*, pp. 20, 21.
68. This section on the 'slum priests' is based on my previous book, *High Churchmanship in the Church of England*.
69. Reynolds, *Martyr of Ritualism*, p. 39.
70. Ibid., pp. 240, 241.
71. Ibid., p. 92.
72. For a description of the team work under Mackonochie see Reynolds, *Martyr of Ritualism*.
73. Ibid., p. 94.
74. Munson, 'The Oxford Movement by the End of the Nineteenth Century', p. 384.
75. These opening comments are largely based on Nockles, *The Oxford Movement in Context*.
76. See for instance Bradley, *Religion, Revolution and English Radicalism*; Clark, *English Society 1688 to 1832*; Hole, *Pulpits, Politics and Public Order in England 1760–1832*; Sack, *From Jacobite to Conservative*; and Waterman, *Revolution, Economics and Religion*.
77. Rowlands, *Church, State and Society*, p. 223. This is a book to which this present section owes much.
78. Ibid., p. 58.
79. Ibid., pp. 63, 64.
80. Ibid., p. 66.
81. Ibid., p. 66.
82. Ibid., p. 128.
83. See Hylson-Smith, *High Churchmanship in the Church of England*; and Nockles, *The Oxford Movement in Context*.
84. See Hylson-Smith, *High Churchmanship in the Church of England* and *The Churches in England*, Vol II.
85. Quoted in Battiscombe, *John Keble*, pp. 152, 153.
86. Under its main provisions the bill abolished two of the four Irish archbishoprics and eight of the bishoprics by a process of amalgamation; it reduced the revenues of the two wealthiest sees, and abolished church cess, which was the tax paid by parishioners to maintain a parish church in repair.

87. Battiscome, *John Keble*, p. 154.

88. Ibid., p. 156.

89. Church, *The Oxford Movement 1833–1845*, p. 111.

90. Ollard, *A Short History of the Oxford Movement*, p. 43.

91. Newman, *Apologia Pro Vita Sua*, p. 77.

92. Church, *The Oxford Movement 1833–1845*, pp. 164, 165.

93. See 'Dr Hampden and the Oxford Malignants' in the *Edinburgh Review*, cxxvii, April 1836.

94. Key books on the Oxford Movement include Church, *The Oxford Movement 1833–1845*, Ollard, *A Short History of the Oxford Movement*, Brilioth, *The Anglican Revival*, Rowell (ed), *Tradition Renewed*, Nockles, *The Oxford Movement in Context* and Hylson-Smith, *High Churchmanship in the Church of England*.

95. Froude, *Remains*, Vol I, p. 336.

96. Ibid., p. 389.

97. Ibid., pp. 433, 434.

98. The Monophysite teaching emerged as a distinct form of doctrine in the fifth century. In essence the Monophysites taught that in Christ there was only the divine and not the human nature.

99. The Donatists were Christians who took a strict line in refusing reconciliation with those who had succumbed under the persecution in North Africa during the reign of the Emperor Diocletian.

100. See Allchin, *The Silent Rebellion* and Anson, *The Call of the Cloister*.

101. Davies, *Worship and Theology in England from Newman to Martineau*, p. 119.

102. See Prestige, *The Life of Charles Gore*.

103. See 'Preface' to Gore (ed), *Lux Mundi*.

104. See Norman, *Church and Society in England 1770–1970* and Jones, *The Christian Socialist Revival 1877–1914*.

105. In what follows, and in the rest of the present book, Evangelical(s), with an upper case 'E' will be used to denote the Evangelicals in the Church of England, and evangelical(s), with a lower case 'e' for evangelicals in general, not just those who were members of the Church of England.

106. For these and other revivals see Orr, *The Light of the Nations* and *The Second Evangelical Awakening*, McLoughlin, *Modern Revivalism* and Kent, *Holding the Fort*.

107. For the revival in England see Kent, *Holding the Fort* and Orr, *The Second Evangelical Awakening*. See also Bebbington, *Evangelicalism in Modern Britain* and Hylson-Smith, *Evangelicals in the Church of England 1734–1984*.

108. For an account of the Keswick movement see Pollock, *The Keswick Story*, and for a discussion of the wider holiness movement, including Keswick, see Bentley, 'The Transformation of the Evangelical Party in the Church

of England' and Kent, *Holding the Fort*.

109. Kent, *Holding the Fort*, p. 295.
110. For a description of work among students in the late nineteenth century see Tatlow, *The Story of the Student Christian Movement*.
111. For the life and work of Moody see Pollock, *Moody without Sankey*.
112. Hodder, *The Life and Work of the Seventh Earl of Shaftesbury*, Vol III, p. 47.
113. Anderson, 'Women preachers in mid-Victorian Britain', p. 484.
114. See Lewis, ' "Lights in dark places" '.
115. See Heasman, *Evangelicals in Action*.
116. For the early years of the Salvation Army see in particular Horridge, *The Salvation Army*.
117. Murdoch, *The Early Years of the Salvation Army*, p. x.
118. See Dark, *Wilson Carlile*.
119. Hodder, *The Life and Work of the Seventh Earl of Shaftesbury*, Vol II, p.3.
120. Of the various critiques special mention should be made of Bradley, *The Call to Seriousness*, Brown, *Fathers of the Victorians* and Norman, *Church and Society in England 1770–1970*.
121. Lewis, *Lighten Their Darkness*, p. 268.
122. See Ewing, *Goodly Fellowship*.
123. See for example Marsden, *Memoirs of Hugh Stowell*.
124. This is part of a 'Note on Liberalism' which Newman was asked to write after the publication of *Apologia Pro Vita Sua* in order to explain what he meant by that term.
125. Parsons, 'From Dissenters to Free Churchmen', p. 113.
126. Parsons, 'Introduction: From Centre to Periphery', p. 13.
127. Marsh, *The Victorian Church in Decline*, p. 289.
128. Roberts, 'Pressure-Group Politics and the Church of England', p. 560. The present section is indebted to this article.
129. Ibid., p. 561.
130. Ibid., p. 561.

3. *The Nonconformists and Roman Catholics 1833 to 1901*

1. Parsons, 'From Dissenters to Free Churchmen', p. 109.
2. R.J. Helmstadter, 'The Nonconformist Conscience' in Parsons (ed), *Religion in Victorian Britain*, Vol IV, p. 61. This is an article to which the present comments owe much.
3. Evans, *The Forging of the Modern State*, p. 304.
4. Machin, *Politics and the Churches in Great Britain 1832 to 1868*, p. 128.
5. Machin, *Politics and the Churches in Great Britain 1869 to 1921*, p. 31.
6. Ibid., p. 273.

7. For a full discussion of these issues see Thompson, 'The Emergence of the Nonconformist Social Gospel in England'. The present comments owe much to this article.

8. J.H.S. Kent, 'Hugh Price Hughes and the Nonconformist Conscience' in Bennett and Walsh (eds), *Essays in Modern Church History*, pp. 195, 204.

9. Bebbington, *The Nonconformist Conscience*, p.x.

10. Helmstadter, 'The Nonconformist Conscience' in Marsh (ed), *The Conscience of the Victorian State*, p. 167.

11. See Thompson, 'The Emergence of the Nonconformist Social Gospel in England'.

12. See Helmstadter, 'The Nonconformist Conscience' in Marsh (ed), *The Conscience of the Victorian State*, pp. 135–72, and Helmstadter, 'The Nonconformist Conscience' in Parsons (ed), *Religion in Victorian Britain*, Vol IV, pp. 61–95. (same article)

13. Helmstadter, 'The Nonconformist Conscience' in Parsons (ed), *Religion in Victorian Britain*, Vol IV, p. 61.

14. Ibid., p. 63.

15. Ibid., p. 66.

16. See Cowherd, *The Politics of English Dissent*.

17. Ibid., p. 163.

18. Gay, *The Geography of Religion in England*, pp. 108–17.

19. K.S. Inglis, 'English Churches and the Working Classes 1880–1900', Oxford D Phil. thesis 1956, ch. 2. See also Inglis, *Churches and the Working Classes in England*.

20. For the early history of the Salvation Army see Horridge, 'The Salvation Army in England 1855–1900', Ph.D thesis 1989, published as *The Salvation Army*.

21. Munson, *The Nonconformists*, p.2.

22. Ibid., p.7.

23. The most important works on the sociological distinction between church, denomination and sect are Weber, *The Sociology of Religion*; Troeltsch, *Social Teachings of the Christian Churches*; Niebuhr, *The Social Sources of Denominationalism*; Pope, *Millhands and Preachers*; Yinger, *Religion, Society and the Individual*; Martin, 'The Denomination'; Berger, *The Sacred Canopy* and *A Rumour of Angels*.

24. Davies, *Worship and Theology in England from Newman to Martineau*, p. 65.

25. Brown, 'College Principals – a cause of Nonconformist decay?', p. 236.

26. See Munson, 'The education of Baptist ministers, 1870–1900'.

27. This information is taken from McLeod, *Religion and Society*, p. 28.

28. Chadwick, 'Church and People in Bradford and District, 1880–1914'.

29. See Field, 'The Social Structure of English Methodism'.

30. See Snell, *Church and Chapel in the North Midlands*.

31. See Smith, *Religion in Industrial Society*.

32. See Binfield, *So Down to Prayers*.

33. Best, *Mid-Victorian Britain 1851–75*.

34. Chadwick, *The Victorian Church*, Vol I, p. 400.

35. For a history of the union see Peel, *Three Hundred Years*.

36. *Congregational Year Book*, 1856, pp. 44, 45.

37. Peel, *Three Hundred Years*, pp. 349–52.

38. The key work, on which the present account is based, is Payne, *The Baptist Union*.

39. Parsons, 'From Dissenters to Free Churchmen', p. 80.

40. Rowell, *Hell and the Victorians*, p. 32.

41. Parsons, 'From Dissenters to Free Churchmen', p. 80.

42. Rowell, *Hell and the Victorians*, p. 60.

43. Rack, 'Domestic Visitation'.

44. See Jones, *The Later Periods of Quakerism*, Vol I, pp. 490f., 505f.

45. Ibid., Vol II, p. 941.

46. Royle, *Modern Britain*, p. 313.

47. Ibid., p. 313.

48. Jones, *The Later Periods of Quakerism*, Vol II, p. 945.

49. For details of these schisms, and a useful account of the nineteenth-century Quakers, see Isichei, *Victorian Quakers*.

50. These details are based on Jones, *Congregationalism in England*, p. 222. This is the standard work on the history of Congregationalism in England.

51. Gay, *The Geography of Religion in England*, p. 139.

52. This list is taken from Jones, *Congregationalism in England*.

53. Briggs, *The English Baptists of the Nineteenth Century*, p. 74.

54. See ibid., p. 88.

55. See ibid., p. 89.

56. Ibid., p. 89.

57. Gay, *The Geography of Religion in England*, pp. 121, 122.

58. McLeod, *Class and Religion in the Late Victorian City*, p. 69.

59. Royle, *Modern Britain*, p. 320.

60. Currie, *Methodism Divided*, p. 33.

61. Quoted in ibid., p. 38.

62. Kent, *Jabez Bunting*, p. 18.

63. Jabez Bunting, *An Appeal to the Members of the Weslyan Methodist Societies in Great Britain*, (place and date of publication unknown), p. 6.

64. Davies, George and Rupp (eds), *History of the Methodist Church in Great Britain*, Vol II, p. 227.

65. Hempton, *Religion and Political Culture*, p. 28.

66. Peel, J.D.Y., *Herbert Spencer*, London 1971, p.40, quoted in Moore, *Pit-*

men, Preachers and Politics, p. 96.

67. Moore, *Pit-men, Preachers and Politics*, p. 96.
68. Ibid., p. 119.
69. Luker, 'Revivalism in Theory and Practice', p. 619.
70. See especially Thompson, *The Making of the English Working Class*.
71. See among a number of his works which touch on this theme, *The Age of Revolution*. *like*
72. See in particular Ward, *Religion and Society in England*.
73. Gilbert, *Religion and Society* and *The Making of Post-Christian Britain*.
74. See especially Hempton, *Methodism and Politics*, *Religion and Political Culture* and The *Religion of the People*.
75. Hempton, *Religion and Political Culture*, p. 27. See also Hempton, *Methodism and Politics*, pp. 55–84.
76. Hempton, *Religion and Political Culture*, p. 27. See also Ward, *Religion and Society in England*, and *Faith and Faction*, pp. 264–98.
77. For the life and teaching of Irving see especially Dallimore, *The Life of Edward Irving*.
78. This account of the Mormons is indebted to Chadwick, *The Victorian Church*, Vol I, pp. 436–39.
79. Norman, *The English Catholic Church in the Nineteenth Century*, p.1.
80. For an illustration of changing local Roman Catholic ministry see Supple, 'The Catholic Clergy of Yorkshire'.
81. Norman, *The English Catholic Church in the Nineteenth Century*, pp. 3, 4.
82. For discussions of the Irish Catholics in England in the nineteenth century see especially Gilley, 'Papists, Protestants and the Irish in London, 1835–70'; Swift, 'Anti-Catholicism and Irish Disturbances'; and O'Tuathaigh, 'The Irish in nineteenth-century Britain'.
83. The present comments on the Irish immigrants owe much to O'Tuathaigh, art.cit.
84. Swift, 'Anti-Catholicism and Irish Disturbances', p. 87.
85. Bossy, *The English Catholic Community*, p. 297.
86. Chadwick, *The Victorian Church*, Vol I, p. 274.
87. Norman, *The English Catholic Church in the Nineteenth Century*, p. 242.
88. Chadwick, *The Victorian Church*, Vol I, p. 283.
89. Connolly, 'The Transubstantiation of Myth', p. 94.
90. A Letter on Catholic Unity addressed to the Right Hon. the Earl of Shrewsbury, by Nicholas Bishop of Melipotamus, London 1841, quoted in Charles, 'The Origins of the Parish Mission in England', p. 75.
91. Adams, 'Converts to the Roman Catholic Church in England', p.6.
92. Gilley, 'Papists, Protestants and the Irish in London, 1835–70', p. 259.
93. Ibid., p. 260.
94. Quoted in Evans, *The Forging of the Modern State*, p. 305.

95. For nineteenth-century anti-Catholicism see especially Norman, *Anti-Catholicism in Victorian England* and Wolffe, *The Protestant Crusade*.

96. Goldby (ed), *Culture and Society in Britain 1850–1890*, p. 38.

97. These quotations are taken from Ralls, 'The Papal Aggression of 1850', p. 256.

98. See especially Reardon, *Roman Catholic Modernism*.

99. Norman, *The English Catholic Church in the Nineteenth Century*, p. 333.

100. See especially Newsome, *The Convert Cardinals*.

101. For the life of Ullathorne see Butler, *The Life and Times of Bishop Ullathorne*.

102. Mathew, *Catholicism in England*, p. 196.

103. For the life and teaching of Wiseman see especially Ward, *The Life and Times of Cardinal Wiseman*.

104. For the life and teaching of Manning see Newsome, *The Convert Cardinals*.

105. See Snead-Cox, *Life of Herbert Vaughan*.

106. For the debate about secularization see Berger, *The Sacred Canopy* and *A Rumour of Angels*; Bruce (ed), *Religion and Modernization*; Hill, *A Sociology of Religion*, ch. 11; Luckmann, *The Invisible Religion*; Martin, *The Religious and the Secular* and *A General Theory of Secularization*; Wilson, *Religion in Secular Society* and *Contemporary Transformations of Religion*.

4. *1901 to 1945: General Decline for All the Churches*

1. Gilbert, *The Making of Post-Christian Britain*, p. 76.

2. Ibid., p. 76.

3. See essay by C. Brown in Bruce (ed), *Religion and Modernization*.

4. For religion in England in the period 1901 to 1914 see especially Lloyd, *The Church of England*.

5. McLeod, *Religion and Society*, p.2.

6. These figures are taken from Gilbert, *Religion and Society*, p. 28.

7. Ibid., pp. 31–42.

8. Ibid., p. 46.

9. Wolffe, *God and Greater Britain*, p. 187.

10. Ensor, *England 1870–1914*, pp. 307, 308.

11. Robbins, *The Eclipse of a Great Power*, p. 154.

12. See Wolffe, *God and Greater Britain*, pp. 199, 211.

13. Masterman, *The Condition of England*, pp. 219, 220.

14. Ibid., p. 222.

15. Morris, *Religion and Urban Change*, p. 182.

16. D.H. McLeod, 'Membership and Influence of the Churches in Metropolitan London, 1885–1914', Cambridge Ph.D 1871, pp. 115, 116, to

which reference is made in Morris, *Religion and Urban Change*, p. 182.

17. These figures are taken from contemporary censuses and quoted in Hastings, *A History of English Christianity*, pp. 35, 36 and Chadwick, *The Victorian Church*, Vol II, pp.221–22.

18. Quoted in Pelling, *Popular Politics and Society*, p. 24.

19. Ibid., p. 18.

20. For an elaboration of the political associations of Nonconformity at this time, and the whole matter of the churches and politics see Machin, *Politics and the Churches in Great Britain*.

21. Clements, *Lovers of Discord*, p. 17.

22. Immanentism stressed the nearness of God rather than his sovereign power and 'otherness'.

23. Davies, *Worship and Theology in England: From Newman to Martineau*, p. 124. The present section owes much to this work.

24. Ibid., p. 125.

25. Clements, *Lovers of Discord*, p. 35, and his ref. 27.

26. Quoted in Marrin, *The Last Crusade*, pp. 86, 87.

27. Ibid., p. 78.

28. Ibid., p. 79.

29. *Sermons for the Times*, No 4. Quoted in Wilkinson, *The Church of England and the First World War*, p. 253.

30. *The Guardian*, 10 June 1915, quoted in ibid., p. 253.

31. Machin, *Politics and the Churches in Great Britain*, p. 330.

32. See Clements, *Lovers of Discord*, p. 181.

33. Hastings, *A History of English Christianity*, p. 221.

34. *Letters of Virginia Wolf*, III, 1923–1928 (1977), pp.457f. Quoted in Hastings, p. 236.

35. Davies, *Worship and Theology in England: From Newman to Martineau* p. 124.

36. Ibid., p. 350.

37. Williams, 'Religious Belief and Popular Culture', pp. 306, 307.

38. Ibid., p. 307.

39. Ibid., p. 308.

5. The Church of England 1901 to 1945

1. Lockhart, *Gordon Cosmo Lang*, p. 241.

2. For the life and teaching of Randall Davidson see especially Bell, *Randall Davidson*.

3. Knight, *The Nineteenth-Century Church*, p. 17.

4. Reservation is the practice of keeping the bread, and also occasionally the wine, consecrated at the eucharist, in order to use it at another time for

the purpose of holy communion.

5. Reported in 'The Kensit Crusade', *Record*, January 1900, p. 68. See also Editorial., 'The Forces of Neo-Anglicanism', *Record*, 25 May 1900, p. 505, and an advertisement, 'The Church in Danger', Islington Clerical Meeting Report, 1907, p. 6.

6. Elliott-Binns, *The Evangelical Movement*, p. 71.

7. On the Parish and People Movement see Jagger, *A History of the Parish and People Movement*.

8. This summary of pre-war Anglican Modernist beliefs is based on Stephenson, *The Rise and Decline of English Modernism*, pp. 7–9.

9. See Streeter (ed), 'Introduction' in *Foundations*, p.vii.

10. Norman, *Church and Society in England*, pp. 222, 225.

11. Ibid., p. 127.

12. Ibid., p. 127.

13. Ibid., p. 165.

14. Hempton, *The Religion of the People*, p. 65. See also McLeod, *Class and Religion*, pp. 216–23.

15. Hempton, *The Religion of the People*, p. 65.

16. Ibid., p. 52. The present summary of rural religion as depicted by Flora Thompson is based on Hempton's resume.

17. Masterman, *The Condition of England*, p. 220.

18. Ibid., p. 221.

19. Lloyd, *The Church of England*, p. 77.

20. See for instance Editorial, 'A Righteous Cause', *Churchman*, September 1914, p. 641; Editorial, 'The Great War', *Churchman*, October 1914, p. 721; C.J. Proctor, Opening Address, Islington Clerical Meeting Report, 1915, pp. 10, 11; Henry Wace, 'Christianity and War', Islington Clerical Meeting Report, 1915, pp. 21, 22; and W. Edward Chadwick, 'German Christianity (?) and the Great War', *Churchman*, November 1914, pp. 811, 812.

21. Marrin, *The Last Crusade*, p. 83.

22. Ibid., pp. 109, 110.

23. See Bell, *Randall Davidson*, Vol II, pp. 740–44.

24. Marrin, *The Last Crusade*, p. 110.

25. Prestige, *The Life of Charles Gore*, p. 370.

26. Marrin, *The Last Crusade*, p. 142.

27. See for example C.J. Proctor, Opening Address, Islington Clerical Meeting Report, 1915, p.9; and M.W., 'To Conscientious Objectors. An Open Letter', *Record*, 13 July 1916, p. 577.

28. See for examples of these opinions Editorial, 'Exemption of the Clergy', *Churchman*, February 1916, p. 84; Albert Mitchell, Letter to the Editor, *Record*, 11 November 1915; and Leading Article, 'Reprisals', *Record*, 21 October 1915, p. 920.

29. See Wilkinson, *The Church of England and the First World War*, pp. 295, 296.

30. Prestige, *The Life of Charles Gore*, p.389; quoted in ibid., p. 101.

31. Caroline E. Playne, *Britain Holds On, 1917–18*, London 1933, pp.112f.; quoted in ibid., p.101.

32. Quoted in Reckitt, *Maurice to Temple*, p. 161.

33. Wilkinson, *Dissent or Conform?*, p. 187.

34. The Earl of Birkenhead, *Halifax*, London 1965; quoted ibid., p. 188.

35. Hastings, *A History of English Christianity*, p. 348.

36. Quoted in ibid., p. 349.

37. Ibid., p. 349.

38. Iremonger, *William Temple*.

39. See Henson, *Retrospect of an Unimportant Life*, Vol 3, pp. 39, 48, 57, 59 68, 69, 77, 142, 143, 540–42.

40. For the life and teaching of Bishop George Bell see Jasper, *George Bell*.

41. Reckitt, *Maurice to Temple*, p. 166.

42. Ibid., p. 164.

43. Ibid., p. 168.

44. Ibid., p. 169.

45. John Orens, 'Priesthood and Prophecy: the Development of Anglo-Catholic Socialism' in Leech and Williams (eds), *Essays Catholic and Radical*, p. 171.

46. Ibid., p. 172.

47. Hensley Henson, *Quo Tendimus?*, the Primary Charge delivered at his Visitation, London 1924, pp. 84, 86.

48. For this work the revised edition of 1944 is used.

49. Tawney, *Religion and the Rise of Capitalism*, p. 279.

50. Pickering, *Anglo-Catholicism*, p. 56.

51. H.A. Wilson, *Received with Thanks*, London 1940, pp. 88, 89.

52. Clarke, *The Oxford Movement and After*, p. 289.

53. Selwyn (ed), *Essays Catholic and Critical*.

54. Ibid., p.xxvii.

55. Ibid., p.v.

56. Ibid., pp. vi and xvi.

57. Ramsey, *From Gore to Temple*, p. 104.

58. Ramsey, *The Gospel and the Catholic Church*, p.vi.

59. Ibid., p.6.

60. Ibid., p. 36.

61. Ibid., p. 208.

62. For the life, work and teaching of Charles Gore see especially Prestige, *Charles Gore*.

63. For a good account of the Prayer Book revision process and debate see Bell, *Randall Davidson*.

64. For a contemporary expression of this unifying Evangelical concern see H.W. Hinde, President's Introduction, 'The Present Position Concerning Prayer Book Revision', Islington Clerical Meeting Report, 1925, pp. 39, 40.

65. Lockhart, *Cosmo Gordon Lang*, p. 300.

66. The National Church League was founded in 1906 by the amalgamation of the National Protestant Church Union (founded 1893) and the Church of England League (founded 1904, and formerly the Ladies' League, founded 1899). In 1950 the National Church League amalgamated with the Church Association to form the Church Society.

67. See 'The Church Pastoral-Aid Society' in *Churchman*, April 1935, p. 116.

68. Hastings, *A History of English Christianity*, p. 207.

69. Lloyd, *The Church of England*, p. 234.

70. Quoted in Iremonger, *William Temple*, p. 224.

6. *The Free Churches and the Roman Catholics 1901 to 1945*

1. See Hastings, *A History of English Christianity*.

2. For these comments see Munson, *The Nonconformists*, pp. 244, 245.

3. See Brogan, *The English People*, p. 121.

4. Hastings, *A History of English Christianity*, p. 126.

5. Clifford, *Venture in Faith*, p. 29.

6. These examples are taken from Hastings, *A History of English Christianity*, pp. 119–21.

7. Ibid., p. 120.

8. MS letters from Lloyd George to W. Robertson Nicoll, 1902–15, p. 235.

9. Quoted in Munson, *The Nonconformists*, p. 293.

10. For details see Munson, *The Nonconformists*, note 7, p. 348.

11. Ibid., pp. 301f.

12. Ibid., pp. 304, 305.

13. Wilson, *Religion in Secular Society*, p. 56.

14. Ibid., p. 51.

15. *Congregational Year Book*, 1876, p. 493. No great reliance can be placed on the precision of the figures from this source but they give an indication of the situation.

16. Jones, *Congregationalism in England*, p. 319. This section, as with all the sections of the present work on Congregationalism, owes much to Jones, which is the standard work on the subject.

17. *Congregational Year Book*, 1901, p. 628.

18. Jones, *Congregationalism in England*, p. 388.

19. Mudie-Smith (ed), *The Religious Life of London*, pp. 288–89.

20. Underwood, *A History of English Baptists*, p. 248.

21. See Payne, *The Baptist Union*, p. 177.

22. Wilson, *Religion in Secular Society*, p. 202.
23. Payne, *The Baptist Union*, p. 213.
24. Morgan (ed), *They Became Anglicans*, pp. 30–31.
25. See Davies, *Worship and Theology in England. The Ecumenical Century*, p. 377.
26. This section on Quakerism owes much to Jones, *The Later Periods of Quakerism*, Vol II.
27. Ibid., p. 942.
28. Swift, *Lively People*, p. 159.
29. J.M.Turner, 'Methodism in England 1900–1932' in Davies, George and Rupp (eds), *A History of the Methodist Church in Great Britain*, Vol III, pp. 311, 312.
30. Ibid., pp. 313, 314.
31. Lax, *His Book*, p. 192.
32. Moore, *Pit-men, Preachers and Politics*, p. 27.
33. Hempton, *The Religion of the People*, p. 70.
34. Local studies include MacLaren, *Religion and Social Class*; Yeo, *Religion and Voluntary Organisations in Crisis*; Foster, *Class Struggle and the Industrial Revolution*; Joyce, *Work, Society and Politics*; and Cox, *The English Churches*.
35. See Cox, *The English Churches* and Hempton, *The Religion of the People*, especially ch. 3.
36. Hempton, *The Religion of the People*, p. 68.
37. Turner, 'Methodism in England 1900–1932' in Davies, George and Rupp (eds), *A History of the Methodist Church in Great Britain*, Vol III, p. 321.
38. John T. Wilkinson, 'The Non-Wesleyan Traditions from 1849' in ibid., p. 177.
39. Agenda Representative Session 1933, p. 541, quoted in Brake, *Policy and Politics in British Methodism 1932–1982*, p. 314.
40. For the history of English Pentecostalism, especially in the context of the worldwide growth of Pentecostalism, see Hollenweger, *The Pentecostals*.
41. Gilbert, *Religion and Society*, p. 46.
42. Mathew, *Catholicism in England*, p. 238.
43. Ibid., p. 236.
44. For the details cited in this passage see Hastings, *A History of English Christianity*, pp. 134, 135.
45. Mathew, *Catholicism in England*, pp. 256, 257.
46. Davies, *Worship and Theology in England. The Ecumenical Century*, p. 257.

7. *1945 to 1998: Context and General Situation*

1. Wolffe, *God and Greater Britain*, p. 199.
2. Ibid., pp. 199–201.
3. Ibid., p. 211.
4. See Sandhurst, *How Heathen is Britain?*
5. Wilson, *Religion in Secular Society*, pp. 28, 29.
6. Brierley, *'Christian' England*, p. 9.
7. Details of the methods used in the survey are given in ibid.
8. Ibid., p. 30.
9. Ibid., p. 31.
10. Royle, *Modern Britain*, p. 338.
11. See Brierley, *'Christian' England*, pp. 32–47.
12. Religious Research Project, Social Science Research Council grant no. HR 7720.
13. Royle, *Modern Britain*, p. 338.
14. For the life of Tom Rees see Rees, *His Name was Tom*.
15. For the life of Billy Graham see Pollock, *Billy Graham*.
16. Ibid., p. 65.
17. Ibid., p. 175 and n.1.
18. Ibid., p. 178.
19. For an account of the Inter-Varsity Fellowship see especially Johnson, *Contending for the Faith*; and see also Tatlow, *The Story of the Student Christian Movement*.
20. For the Jesus movement and the charismatic movement see Buchanan, *Encountering Charismatic Worship*; Dunn, *Baptism in the Holy Spirit*; England, *The Spirit of Renewal*; Gunstone, *Pentecostal Anglicans*; Harper, *A New Canterbury Tale* and *Bishop's Move*; Hocken, *Streams of Renewal*; Newbigin, *The Household of God*; Urquhart, *When the Spirit Comes*; Watson, *One in the Spirit* and *The Charismatic Movement*.
21. This useful summary of van Buren's theism as depicted in *The Secular Meaning of the Gospel* is to be found in Welsby, *A History of the Church of England*, p. 115.
22. For this helpful resumé of Cox's view of modern technological culture see ibid.
23. Paul Avis, ' "The Church's One Foundation" ', *T*, 89, 1986, p. 259.
24. Badham (ed), *Religion, State, and Society in Modern Britain*, p. 4.

8. *The Church of England 1945 to 1998*

1. For the life and teaching of William Temple see Iremonger, *William Temple*. This is one of the best biographies of any church leader ever published, and among the elite in all biographical literature, which will stand

the test of time and remain a standard work.

2. Welsby, *A History of the Church of England*, pp. 4,5.

3. Ibid., p.5.

4. Quoted in Carpenter, *Cantuar*, p. 487.

5. For the life of Geoffrey Fisher see Purcell, *Fisher of Lambeth*, and more especially Carpenter, *Archbishop Fisher*.

6. For the life, work and teaching of Wand see Peart-Binns, *Wand of London*.

7. Wand, *Recovery Starts Within*, p. 150.

8. Peart-Binns, *Wand of London*, p. 149.

9. Ibid., p. 152.

10. Ibid.

11. J.W.C. Wand, *Our Day of Opportunity*, London 1948, p. 66.

12. Dix, *The Shape of the Liturgy*, p.xi.

13. Ibid., p. 48.

14. See Jagger, *History of the Parish and People Movement*.

15. Lloyd, *The Church of England*, p. 481.

16. *Canterbury Chronicle of Convocation*, October 1947, pp. 187ff.

17. Ibid., pp. 173ff.

18. Hebert, *Fundamentalism and the Church of God*, pp. 10, 13.

19. Lloyd, *The Church of England*, p. 597.

20. Vidler (ed), *Soundings*, pp.6,7.

21. Edwards (ed), *The Honest to God Debate*, p.7.

22. Robinson, *Honest to God*, p.7.

23. Ibid., p.7.

24. See Edwards (ed), *The Honest to God Debate*, p. 91.

25. Packer, *Keep Yourselves from Idols*, p.4.

26. Ibid., p.4.

27. Ibid., p.5.

28. Ibid., pp. 10, 11.

29. Ibid., p. 14.

30. I John 5.21.

31. Packer, *Keep Yourselves from Idols*, pp. 19, 20.

32. Mascall, *The Secularisation of Christianity*, p. 40.

33. Ibid., p.1.

34. Ibid., p. 109.

35. Ibid., p. 189.

36. Ramsey, *Image Old and New*, pp. 3,4.

37. Ibid., p.7.

38. Ibid., p.9.

39. Catherwood, *Five Evangelical Leaders*, p.9.

40. Capon, *Evangelicals Tomorrow*, p. 14.

41. See comments in King, *The Evangelicals*, p. 12.

42. Welsby, *A History of the Church of England*, p. 214.
43. 'Foreword' to *Anglican Evangelicals and their New Assembly*.
44. 'Preface' to *Catholicity*.
45. *Catholicity*, p. 13.
46. Ibid., p. 13.
47. Ibid., p. 15.
48. Dick Ladborough, quoted in Chadwick, *Michael Ramsey*, p.v. This is an outstanding biography and will, most probably, be regarded as the difinitive work on Ramsey.
49. Quoted in ibid., p. 114.
50. Ibid., p. 205.
51. Ibid., p. 322.
52. The scheme will be discussed in detail later.
53. For the life and teaching of Graham Leonard see Peart-Binns, *Graham Leonard*.
54. For an account of this event and comments on it from a conservative Anglican Catholic point of view see Oddie, *The Crockford's File*.
55. For this succinct description of the essence of Robinson's christology see Welsby, *A History of the Church of England*, p. 235.
56. Don Cupitt, 'The Finality of Christ' in *T*, December 1975, p.625.
57. This brief summary of Lampe's christology is to be found in Welsby, *A History of the Church of England 1945–1980*, p.237.
58. John Goldingay, 'James Barr on Fundamentalism', *Churchman*, October 1977, p. 295.
59. Barr, *Fundamentalism*, p.8.
60. Cupitt, *Radicals and the Future of the Church*, p.1.
61. Ibid., p. 14.
62. Ibid., p. 16.
63. Jenkins and Jenkins, *Free to Believe*, pp. 34, 35.
64. Edwards (ed), *The Honest to God Debate*, pp. 20, 21.
65. Quoted in Peart-Binns, *Living with Paradox*, p.xi.
66. Quoted in ibid., p.xii.
67. The present comments on the Paul Report and the Morley Report are indebted to Welsby, *A History of the Church of England*, pp. 131–39.
68. Donald Coggan, *Word and World*, London 1971, p. 75.
69. Welsby, *A History of the Church of England*, p. 160.
70. Leaver, *A Hymn Book Survey*, p.4. The development of Evangelical hymnody during the 1960s and 1970s, and indeed up to the end of the century, was part of a greater evangelical interest in spirituality. This was exemplified by the introduction in 1982 of the Grove booklets on spirituality.

9. *The Free Churches and the Roman Catholics 1945 to 1998*

1. For these figures and their breakdown see Currie, Gilbert and Horsley, *Churches and Churchgoers.*

2. The following figures are taken from Brierley, '*Christian' England*, p. 38.

3. See Wilson, *Religion in Secular Society* and *Contemporary Transformations of Religion.*

4. These and other figures in this paragraph are taken from Jones, *Congregationalism in England*, p. 390.

5. Council Report, 1950, pp. 5,6.

6. *Free Church Federal Council: Annual Report and Directory*, 1961, p. 27.

7. For these comments see Gay, *The Geography of Religion in England*, pp. 132, 133.

8. Ibid., pp. 122, 123.

9. Brierley, '*Christian' England*, p. 38.

10. Ibid., p. 40.

11. For these figures see Davies, 'Since 1932' in Davies, George and Rupp (eds), *A History of the Methodist Church in Great Britain*, Vol III, pp. 363, 364, and Brierley, '*Christian' England*, p. 38.

12. Davies, art.cit., p. 365.

13. Royle, *Modern Britain*, p. 337.

14. Wilson, *Religion in Secular Society*, p. 202.

15. Ibid., p. 202.

16. Ibid., pp. 202, 203.

17. Ibid., p. 203.

18. Quoted in Welsby, *A History of the Church of England*, p. 80.

19. Turner, *Conflict and Reconciliation*, p. 202.

20. *Conversations between the Methodist Church and the Church of England*, p. 62.

21. Peart-Binns, *Graham Leonard*, p. 64.

22. Buchanan et al, *Growing into Union*, p.130.

23. This section is greatly indebted to Hollenweger, *The Pentecostals.*

24. See ibid., p. 187.

25. Iain MacRobert, 'The new black-led Pentecostal churches in Britain' in Badham (ed), *Religion, State, and Society in Modern Britain*, p. 127.

26. Ibid., p. 128.

27. Dunn, *First United Church of Jesus Christ.*

28. The figures in this and the following paragraphs, as indeed in this section as a whole, are taken from Brierley, '*Christian' England.*

29. Hocken, *Streams of Renewal*, p. 112.

30. The comments on the house churches owe much to Walker, *Restoring the Kingdom.*

31. Hornsby-Smith, 'The Roman Catholic Church in Britain', p. 87. This is

an article to which this present section is indebted. See also Hornsby-Smith and Lee, *Roman Catholic Opinion.*

32. See Brierley, *'Christian' England,* p. 71.

33. The following comments are based on Welsby, *A History of the Church of England,* pp. 85, 86.

34. Quoted in ibid., pp. 179, 180.

35. The following brief summary is based on Pawley (ed), *The Second Vatican Council,* pp. 13–27.

36. Pickering, *Anglo-Catholicism,* p. 203.

37. Hornsby-Smith, 'The Roman Catholic Church in Britain', p. 89.

38. Brierley, *'Christian' England,* p. 33.

39. Ibid., p. 33.

40. The Orthodox Church in different parts of the world comes within one of a number of Patriarchates.

10. *Global Mission 1833 to 1998*

1. The present section owes much to Elliott-Binns, *Religion in the Victorian Era;* a book which highlights 1841 as a pivotal year.

2. Stanley, *The Bible and the Flag,* p. 61. This book is an important study of missionary activity in the nineteenth century, and the present work is indebted to it.

3. Stock, *History of the Church Missionary Society,* Vol I, p. 251.

4. Elliott-Binns, *Religion in the Victorian Era,* p. 381.

5. *Wesleyan Methodist Magazine,* 5th ser. II, 1856, p. 894. See also Williams, 'The Recruitment and Training of Overseas Missionaries'.

6. Stanley, *The Bible and the Flag,* p. 65.

7. J.Campbell (ed), *The Farewell Sermons of Robert Moffat in Edinburgh, Manchester, and London,* London 1843, p. 109, quoted in ibid., p. 65.

8. See for example Williams, 'The Recruitment and Training of Overseas Missionaries'.

9. Stanley, *The Bible and the Flag,* pp. 67, 68.

10. Ibid., p. 74.

11. L.Schapera (ed), *Livingstone's Missionary Correspondence 1841–1856,* pp. 301–302, quoted in ibid., p. 73.

12. R.Allier, *La Psychologie de la conversion chez les peuples non-civilises,* 2 vols, Paris 1925.

13. Rowell, *The Vision Glorious,* p. 161.

14. Carpenter, *Church and People,* p. 428.

15. The present account of missionary work in Eastern Africa is based on Wilson, *The History of the Universities' Mission to Central Africa.*

16. The following account rests heavily on Hennell, *Sons of the Prophets,* pp. 68–90, and Yates, *Venn and the Victorian Bishops Abroad.*

17. For example see the *Record*, 13 January 1865, and Bentley, 'The Transformation of the Evangelical Party in the Church of England', p. 436.

18. For the life and work of C.T. Studd see Norman P. Grubb, *C.T. Studd*.

19. Stock, *History of the Church Missionary Society*, Vol III, p. 284.

20. See CMS. Annual Report 1886–87, p.4, and Bentley, 'The Transformation of the Evangelical Party in the Church of England', p. 441.

21. For the early history of the China Inland Mission see Dr and Mrs Howard Taylor, *Hudson Taylor and the China Inland Mission. The Growth of a Work of God*, London 1934.

22. For the early history of the South American Missionary Society see Thompson, *An Unquenchable Flame*.

23. Balleine, *A History of the Evangelical Party in the Church of England*, p. 205.

24. Neill, *A History of Christian Missions*, p. 320.

25. Quoted in ibid., p. 321.

26. See the *Daily News*, 25 April 1885, quoted in ibid., p. 207.

27. See especially Stanley, *The Bible and the Flag*.

28. Neill, *A History of Christian Missions*, p. 450.

29. Bradley, *The Call to Seriousness*, pp. 86, 87.

30. Henry Rowley (ed), *Speeches on Mission*, London 1874, p. 212.

31. Ibid., p. 212.

32. Bradley, *The Call to Seriousness*, pp. 89, 90.

33. Stanley, *The Bible and the Flag*, p. 184.

34. See Porter, '"Commerce and Christianity"'.

35. Pickering, *Anglo-Catholicism*, pp. 86, 87.

36. Quoted in Wilson, *The History of the Universities' Mission to Central Africa*, p.1. This is a work to which the present account of the work of the mission is greatly indebted.

37. Ibid., p.4.

38. Neill, *A History of Christian Missions*, p. 352.

39. This section on Congregational involvement in overseas mission is indebted to Jones, *Congregationalism in England*.

40. *Evangelical Magazine*, 1850, p. 323.

41. Jones, *Congregationalism in England*, p. 385.

42. For a history of the BMS see Stanley, *The History of the Baptist Missionary Society*, especially chs 1 and 2.

43. Underwood, *A History of the English Baptists*, p. 196.

44. Briggs, *The English Baptists in the Nineteenth Century*, p. 294.

45. Stanley, *The History of the Baptist Missionary Society*, p. 141.

46. Ibid., p. 141.

47. Ibid., p. 131.

48. Ibid., p. 68.

49. Quoted in M. Allen Birtwhistle, 'Methodist Missions' in Davies, George and Rupp (eds), *A History of the Methodist Church in Great Britain*, Vol III, p. 38. This is an article to which the present section owes much.
50. Ibid., p. 39.
51. These figures are taken from Neill, *A History of Christian Missions*, p. 457.
52. W.Temple, *The Church Looks Forward*, London 1944, pp. 2–3.
53. See Hastings, *A History of English Christianity*, p. 93.
54. Ibid., p. 93.
55. See ibid., p. 91.
56. Ibid., p. 95.
57. Ibid., pp. 95, 96. For missionary theology and strategy in the years from the 1920s to the 1950s see also G.H. Anderson, 'The Theology of Missions 1928–58'.
58. Barrett (ed), *World Christian Encyclopaedia*, p.4.
59. Yates, *Christian Mission in the Twentieth Century*, p. 130.
60. See Groves, *The Planting of Christianity in Africa*; Vol III, pp. 149, 179 and Vol IV, pp. 63, 128–29.
61. Barrett (ed), *World Christian Encyclopaedia*, p. 529.
62. Murray, *Proclaim the Good News*, p. 269.
63. Yates, *Christian Mission in the Twentieth Century*, p. 200.
64. For an exposition of this approach see Stott, *Christian Mission in the Modern World*.
65. In what follows I am indebted to Yates, *Christian Mission in the Twentieth Century*.
66. Kraemer, *The Christian Message in a Non-Christian World*, pp.vi–vii.
67. Nock, *Conversion*, pp. 60, 97.
68. Warren, *Social History and Christian Mission*, p. 11.
69. Cragg, *The Call of the Minaret*, p. 305. See also C.Lamb, 'The Call to Renewal'
70. Yates, *Christian Mission in the Twentieth Century*, p. 200.
71. *International Review of Missions*, 65, 257, January 1976, pp. 30–33.
72. Newbigin, *The Other Side of 1984*, p. 47. See also Newbigin, *Foolishness to the Greeks*.
73. See especially Goodall, *The Ecumenical Movement*, and Rouse and Neill (eds), *A History of the Ecumenical Movement*.
74. Hastings, *A History of English Christianity*, p. 97.
75. Ibid., p. 97.
76. Ibid., p. 98.
77. Ibid., p. 98.
78. Lloyd, *The Church of England*, p. 470. The quotations are also taken from Lloyd, pp. 469, 470.
79. See for example Packer (ed), *All in Each Place*, and Buchanan, Mascall

and Packer, *Growing Into Union.*

80. This present section is indebted to Welsby, *A History of the Church of England.*

Index of Names

General Index